PSALM CULTURE AND EARLY MODERN ENGLISH LITERATURE

Psalm Culture and Early Modern English Literature examines the powerful influence of the biblical Psalms on sixteenth- and seventeenth-century English literature. It explores the imaginative, beautiful, ingenious and sometimes ludicrous and improbable ways in which the Psalms were "translated" from ancient Israel to Renaissance and Reformation England. No biblical book was more often or more diversely translated than the Psalms during the period. In church psalters, sophisticated metrical paraphrases, poetic adaptations, meditations, sermons, commentaries, and through biblical allusions in secular poems, plays, and prose fiction, English men and women interpreted the Psalms, refashioning them according to their own personal, religious, political, or aesthetic agendas. The book focuses on literature from major writers like Shakespeare and Milton to less prominent ones like George Gascoigne, Mary Sidney Herbert, and George Wither, but it also explores the adaptations of the Psalms in musical settings, emblems, works of theology and political polemic.

HANNIBAL HAMLIN is Assistant Professor of English at The Ohio State University, Mansfield. He has published articles on the Psalms and early modern English literature in *Renaissance Quarterly*, *Spenser Studies*, and *The Yale University Library Gazette.* He has also published an edition of and commentary on the first correspondence between Robert Lowell and Ezra Pound in *The Yale Review* and an article on biblical allusion in Shakespeare's *Coriolanus* in *Never Again Would Birds' Song Be the Same: New Essays on Poetry and Poetics, Renaissance to Modern* edited by Jennifer Lewin (2002).

PSALM CULTURE AND EARLY MODERN ENGLISH LITERATURE

HANNIBAL HAMLIN

PUBLISHED BY THE PRESS SYNDICATE OF THE UNIVERSITY OF CAMBRIDGE
The Pitt Building, Trumpington Street, Cambridge, United Kingdom

CAMBRIDGE UNIVERSITY PRESS
The Edinburgh Building, Cambridge, CB2 2RU, UK
40 West 20th Street, New York, NY 10011–4211, USA
477 Williamstown Road, Port Melbourne, VIC 3207, Australia
Ruiz de Alarcón 13, 28014 Madrid, Spain
Dock House, The Waterfront, Cape Town 8001, South Africa

http://www.cambridge.org

First published 2004

Printed in the United Kingdom at the University Press, Cambridge

Typeface Adobe Garamond 11/12.5 pt. *System* LaTeX 2ε [TB]

A catalogue record for this book is available from the British Library

Library of Congress Cataloguing in Publication data
Hamlin, Hannibal.
Psalm culture and early modern English literature / Hannibal Hamlin.
p. cm.
ISBN 0 521 83270 5
1. English literature – Early modern, 1500–1700 – History and criticism. 2. Christianity and literature – England – History – 16th century. 3. Christianity and literature – England – History – 17th century. 4. Bible. O. T. Psalms – Paraphrases, English – History and criticism. 5. Bible. O. T. Psalms – Criticism, interpretation, etc. – History – 16th century. 6. Bible. O. T. Psalms – Criticism, interpretation, etc. – History – 17th century. 7. Religion and literature – History – 16th century. 8. Religion and literature – History – 17th century. 9. Bible. O.T. Psalms – In literature. I. Title.
PR428.C48H36 2004 820.9′382232 – dc21 2003055172

ISBN 0 521 83270 5 hardback

To Cori

Contents

Figures

Acknowledgments

Portions of this work have appeared in articles in scholarly journals. Part of chapter 1 appeared as "'Very mete to be used of all sortes of people': The Remarkable Popularity of the 'Sternhold and Hopkins' Psalter," in *The Yale University Library Gazette* 75:1–2 (October, 2000). Versions of chapters 5 and 7 appeared as "Another Version of Pastoral: English Renaissance Translations of Psalm 23," in *Spenser Studies* 16 (New York, 2002), 167–96, and "Psalm Culture in the English Renaissance: Readings of Psalm 137 by Shakespeare, Spenser, Milton and Others," in *Renaissance Quarterly* 55:1 (Spring, 2002), 224–57. I am grateful to the editors of these journals for permission to republish this material.

This book is the product of a number of years of work, and my scholarly and personal debts are too many to acknowledge in full. For crucial support and counsel at Yale, I thank my dissertation advisor John Hollander, as well as Lawrence Manley, Annabel Patterson, Thomas Greene, John Rogers, Leslie Brisman, and David Quint. My interest in biblical allusion and English poetry began much earlier at the University of Toronto while I was studying with Eleanor Cook, to whom I shall always be indebted. For helpful comments on various parts of this study, some presented at conferences, I want also to thank Anne Lake Prescott, Margaret Hannay, Paula Loscocco, and Thomas Herron. I am also grateful to my readers at *Renaissance Quarterly*, Diane Kelsey McColley, P. G. Stanwood, and Paul F. Grendler, who offered a number of useful suggestions on my study of Psalm 137. My colleagues at The Ohio State University, especially Barbara McGovern, John King, and Christopher Highley, have been unfailingly supportive. I have benefited from the resources of a number of libraries, and I would like to thank the staffs of the Yale Libraries, especially the Beinecke Rare Book and Manuscript Library (Stephen Parks in particular), the New York Public Library, and the British Library. At Cambridge University Press, my anonymous readers provided some helpful and detailed advice, and Victoria Cooper has been all that one could wish in an editor. I am also indebted to the meticulous and patient labor of my copy-editor, Margaret Deith. Turning to more personal debts, I am grateful for the interest my parents-in-law, Abner and Shirley Martin, have shown in my work on the Psalms. Their enthusiasm has led to what is almost certainly the first reading of the countess of Pembroke's psalms in a Canadian Mennonite church. My own parents, Cyrus Hamlin and Rosamond Greeley Hamlin, have encouraged my work at every stage, and my father has been a shaping influence on my development as a teacher and scholar. My wife, Cori Martin, deserves all the gratitude customarily expressed to a spouse in the sub-genre of "acknowledgments," but she has also been my most influential editor and critic, and the source, direct or indirect, of more of my ideas than I can remember. Only she knows how much of this book is really hers.

Note on the text

Unless otherwise noted, biblical citations are from the King James Version (KJV). Citations from the psalm translations of the English Bibles (Coverdale, the Great Bible, Geneva, Bishops', King James) are from *The Hexaplar Psalter*, ed. William Aldis Wright (Cambridge, 1911). Wherever possible, the original spelling of quoted material has been maintained, even though this results in the occasional risk of confusion ("the" for "thee," for instance). Contractions, however, have been expanded, the archaic use of u/v, i/j, and long s modernized, and elaborate variations in font size and character have been normalized. To avoid adding further complications to an already substantial body of citations, page numbers have been omitted when psalms are quoted from whole psalters, on the principle that psalm numbers provide sufficient reference. Page numbers have been supplied for all selected psalms included in larger volumes.

Introduction

The Renaissance was a cultural movement founded on the enterprise of translation, in which works of classical culture were rediscovered and transformed into scholarly Latin as well as European vernaculars. Yet, the culture of early modern England involved the translation of not one but two ancient cultures, two ancient literatures, the classical and the biblical, though traditionally less critical attention has been paid to the latter than the former. The earl of Surrey and Richard Stanyhurst translated Virgil's *Aeneid*; Arthur Golding and George Sandys translated Ovid's *Metamorphoses*; but all four translated the Psalms, as did John Milton, Sir Philip Sidney, the countess of Pembroke, Sir Thomas Wyatt, Sir Francis Bacon, Henry Vaughan, Phineas Fletcher, and Richard Crashaw. Virtually every author of the period (Shakespeare, Spenser, Bunyan, Donne, Herbert, and Jonson) translated, paraphrased, or alluded to the Psalms in their major works. In fact, the translation, or "Englishing," of the biblical Psalms substantially shaped the culture of sixteenth- and seventeenth-century England, resulting in creative forms as diverse as singing psalters, metrical psalm paraphrases, sophisticated poetic adaptations, meditations, sermons, commentaries, and significant allusions in poems, plays, and literary prose, by English men and women of varied social and intellectual backgrounds, accommodating the biblical texts to their personal agendas, whether religious, political, or aesthetic.

The Protestant Reformation sanctioned and even demanded vernacular translations of the Bible, but no biblical book was translated more often or more widely in the subsequent two centuries than the Psalms. The singing of psalms in meter to catchy tunes, sometimes to popular melodies borrowed from secular songs, was an essential component in the rapid spread of Reformation ideas; many of Martin Luther's own first publications were metrical psalms and hymns.[1] The educational value of the Psalms was

[1] Inka Bach and Helmut Galle, *Deutsche Psalmendichtung vom 16. bis zum 20. Jahrhundert* (Berlin and New York, 1989), 89–99.

affirmed by Richard Hooker (stating a view which had been repeated by Christian writers since Basil originally expressed it in the fourth century), when he asked, "What is there for man to know that the Psalmes are not able to teach?"[2] Like Luther, John Calvin wrote metrical translations of the Psalms for congregational singing in the Genevan Church (continuing the French tradition begun by Clément Marot), designed to instruct while they delighted, and wrote an extensive commentary on the Psalms, praising them in their multiformity as representing an "Anatomy of all the partes of the Soule."[3] This view was shared by John Donne, who described the Psalms as the "Manna of the Church" since, just "as Manna tasted to every man like that that he liked best, so doe the Psalmes minister Instruction, and satisfaction, to every man, in every emergency and occasion."[4]

Many Renaissance poets similarly held the Psalms in high esteem, not only for their religious truths but for their literary quality as well. One of the earliest to express this view was Petrarch, who himself composed a series of Latin "Psalms" – actually original compositions but intended to evoke the style and tone of the Vulgate Psalms. In a letter he thanked Giovanni Boccaccio for sending him Augustine's sermons on the Psalms, stating that he could imagine no "greater work of such tremendous literary merit or wealth of content." With this prized volume, he could "sail David's sea with greater assurance, avoiding the reefs, unafraid of his waves of words or collisions with mysterious meanings."[5] In another letter he elucidates one of his own pastorals in which a shepherd named "Monicus," apparently voicing the author's opinion, praises another shepherd's singing above that of the great poets of classical antiquity: "The shepherd whose singing Monicus prefers to Homer and Vergil is none other than David."[6] Several hundred years later, at the other end of the Renaissance, Milton made the same comparison between the Psalms and "those magnific odes and hymns

[2] Richard Hooker, *Of the Laws of Ecclesiastical Polity*, Book V, in the Folger Library edition of *The Works of Richard Hooker*, vol. 2, ed. W. Speed Hill (Cambridge, MA, and London, 1977), 150 (chap. 37.2).

[3] For Calvin's Psalms 36, 46, 91 (90), 113, and 138, see *Calvin's First Psalter [1539]*, ed. Sir Richard R. Terry (London, 1932). Calvin's versions were later replaced by Marot's in the Genevan Psalter of Marot and Théodore de Bèze. Calvin's epistle to "the godly Readers" is cited from *The Psalmes of David and others. With M. John Calvins Commentaries*, trans. Arthur Golding (London, 1571), sig. *6[v].

[4] John Donne, "The second of my Prebend Sermons upon my five Psalmes," in *Donne's Prebend Sermons*, ed. Janel M. Mueller (Cambridge, MA, 1971), 91.

[5] Petrarch, "To Giovanni Boccaccio, an expression of gratitude for sending Augustine's book on the Psalms of David," *Fam.* XVIII, 3, in *Letters on Familiar Matters, Rerum familiarum libri XVII–XXIV*, trans. Aldo S. Bernardo (Baltimore and London, 1985), 47. Petrarch's "Penitential Psalms" (c.1355) were translated into English by George Chapman in 1612.

[6] Petrarch, *Epistolae de rebus familaris* 10:4, cited in James Kugel, *The Idea of Biblical Poetry* (New Haven and London, 1981), 213.

wherein Pindarus and Callimachus are in most things worthy," writing that the former, "not in their divine argument alone, but in the very critical art of composition may be easily made appear over all other kinds of Lyrick poesy, to be incomparable."[7] Such views were widespread among European literati.

Two general yet essential questions should be addressed here in order to provide a framework for what follows. First, what are the Psalms? The answer to this question may seem self-evident, yet in many ways a "psalm" is difficult to define as a specific literary genre. Indeed, this generic indeterminacy is partly responsible for the rich variety of Renaissance psalm translations. The second question concerns the use of the term "translation." Again, what seems clear at first glance proves more problematic on closer scrutiny. For example, given the necessarily complex relationship between a work and its translation, to what extent can a translation itself be considered an "original" work? Questions of originality and the authority of the "original" were complicated for Renaissance psalms by the fact that most translators did not read Hebrew and therefore relied on previous Latin, English, or other vernacular translations, and by the fact that there was universal ignorance regarding the specific formal workings of Hebrew poetry. To what extent were these questions raised by Renaissance translators themselves?

To begin with, the simplest description of a "psalm" is that it is one of the 150 texts that make up the biblical Book of Psalms.[8] Although more critical readers recognized that these texts might have been written at different times by different authors (various attributions are indeed made in some of the headnotes of the Psalms, as in Psalm 90, "A prayer of Moses," or Psalm 85, "A Psalme of the sonnes of Corah"),[9] still, the popular idea persisted throughout the Renaissance that all of them had been composed by King David. George Wither, for instance, in his *Preparation to the Psalter* (1619), outlined the arguments against Davidic authorship in great detail, yet ultimately preferred to set them aside:

> Neverthelesse; Seeing there are so many probable Evidences, to make it credible, that David was at least composer of farre the greatest part, if not of all the Psalmes: Seeing the holy ghost hath vouchsafed him so great a favour, as to make him his noble Instrument, whereby he conveyeth unto us so many heavenly raptures, for

[7] John Milton, *The Reason of Church Government* (1642), in *John Milton: Complete Poems and Major Prose*, ed. Merritt Y. Hughes (New York, 1957), 669.

[8] This is the title of the book in the Vulgate and most vernacular bibles. The Hebrew title is *Tehillim* ("praises").

[9] Coverdale's translation in the Great Bible (1539).

the comfort of our soules: And forasmuch also as the enemies of Christ thinke to make it an advantage on their parts, to deny him as much as may be of that sacred worke; I would not (even for those respects) that hee should bee robbed of any honour, which I thought might appertaine unto him by those excellent Poems.[10]

Despite widespread agreement among Wither's contemporaries as to who wrote the Psalms, their genre is difficult to define in any way that would have been generally understood in the sixteenth and seventeenth centuries. The Psalms consist mostly of short texts, though they do vary in length from the abrupt two verses of Psalm 117 to the copious 176 verses of Psalm 119. (Psalm 119 actually can be said to consist of a sequence of short sections, but some of the other psalms are also relatively long: Psalm 106, for instance, has 48 verses, and Psalm 78 has 72.) The common understanding was that the Psalms were poems, but, as will be discussed in detail below (see chapter 3), the precise nature of Hebrew poetry was not understood by anyone, not even the learned, so no one could define the genre of "psalm" in any consistent or accurate way. In fact, based on the writings of Jerome and other church fathers, the general view was that the Psalms encompassed a wide variety of genres and forms. Even without reference to Hebrew, one could perceive some of this variety, distinguishing psalms of praise and thanksgiving, lament, invective, and wisdom.[11] Some of the psalms are historical narratives, some seemingly liturgical prayers or responses, some introspective personal meditations. There are psalms about kingship, about the history of Israel, about David, about moral doctrine. These are all distinctions of subject, tone, and purpose, however; no one in the sixteenth and seventeenth centuries could clearly distinguish among these on the basis of formal conventions except by purely speculative analogy to the conventions of such genres in the poetry of other languages, especially Latin and Greek.

Paul's counsel to the Christians of Colossae – "Let the word of Christ dwell in you richly in all wisdom; teaching and admonishing one another in psalms, hymns, and spiritual songs" (Coloss. 3:16) – offers an apparent distinction among these lyric genres, but in practice one cannot clearly distinguish even these three "kinds" on the basis of formal conventions.[12]

[10] George Wither, *A Preparation to the Psalter* (London, 1619), Spenser Society reprint (New York, 1884, rpr. 1967), 34.

[11] There have been many attempts to categorize the Psalms generically. The most important modern work in this area is Hermann Gunkel's *The Psalms: A Form-Critical Introduction*, trans. T. M. Horner (Philadelphia, 1967, orig., 1951). See also Claus Westermann, *Praise and Lament in the Psalms*, trans. Keith R. Crim and Richard N. Soulen (Atlanta, 1981, orig., 1961).

[12] The sorts of careful delineation of generic conventions made, for example, for the hymn and ode by Philip Rollinson and Paul Fry cannot be made for the psalm, which is defined, in the Renaissance at

As Philip Rollinson notes, the Greek *hymnos* "refers to a song, poem, or speech which praises gods and sometimes heroes and abstractions."[13] By this definition, a great many of the Psalms are clearly hymns. The Protestant tradition, however, tended to distinguish between psalms and hymns (as in the separate sections for psalms and canticles in the "Sternhold and Hopkins" psalter; see chapter 1), yet many of the "hymns" in later hymnals are in fact psalm paraphrases. The word "psalm" is even less helpful than "hymn" in establishing generic boundaries, deriving from the Greek *psalmos*, "a song sung to the accompaniment of a plucked instrument." The Hebrew terms for these songs are more general still: *mizmor* ("song") and *tehillah* ("praise"), the latter providing the title of the Hebrew book, *Tehillim*.[14]

Neither can one recognize formal distinctions between the "songs" in the Book of Psalms and those found elsewhere in the Bible. A number of other songs in the Old Testament, such as the Songs of Moses and Deborah (Exodus 15 and Judges 5), were commonly associated with the "Psalms" proper. That there might be "psalms" outside of the Book of Psalms is, in fact, perfectly logical, given that one of them (Psalm 18) also appears in the Second Book of Samuel (2 Samuel 22), where it is sung by David after his victory over Saul. Even with a knowledge of Hebrew, the generic distinction of the "psalm" is difficult. As James Kugel has shown, the very notion of Hebrew "poetry" may be questionable, with the heightened, more formally self-conscious style of Hebrew in which many of the Psalms are framed found elsewhere in biblical passages, some of which are not generally thought of as at all "poetic."[15] This said, it remains true that,

least, by its generic diversity. See Rollinson, "The Renaissance of the Literary Hymn," *Renaissance Papers*, 1968 (Durham, NC, 1969), 11–20; Fry, *The Poet's Calling in the English Ode* (New Haven and London, 1980), esp. 1–14. This is not to say that attempts were not made to categorize biblical songs on the basis of Paul's categories, as in the marginal gloss in the Geneva Bible (1560): "By Psalmes hee meaneth all godly songs which were written upon divers occasions, and by Hymnes, all such as conteine the praise of God, and by spirituall songs, other more peculiar and artificious songs which were also in praise of God, but they were made fuller of Musicke" (cited in Barbara Kiefer Lewalski, *Protestant Poetics and the Seventeenth-Century Religious Lyric* [Princeton, 1979], 38). By this description, hymns are a sub-category of psalms. What the editors mean by "artificious songs" is not clear (perhaps something like a Renaissance anthem or motet).

13 Rollinson, "hymn," in *The New Princeton Encyclopedia of Poetry and Poetics*, ed. Alex Preminger and T. V. F. Brogan (Princeton, 1993), 542.

14 Robert Alter, "psalm," in the *New Princeton Encyclopedia*, 995–96.

15 Kugel, *Idea of Biblical Poetry*, esp. chap. 2. Kugel gives numerous examples of critical dilemmas connected with "parallelism" and the definition of "poetry." Jer. 25:18–26, for instance, which presents a list of Moabite cities, exhibits the characteristics of Hebrew "poetry," leading one scholar to label it as such, despite admitting that it does not seem in any other way "poetic" (ibid., 82–83). There is a circularity to arguments about the "poetic," since in order to identify a passage as "poetic" one requires a definition, which in turn can only truly be tested on the basis of specific examples. Despite

although no one in the Renaissance accurately understood the nature of Hebrew "poetry," they remained convinced that the Psalms were indeed poems, and the concern of this study is with what Renaissance readers and writers thought them to be, rather than with current debates.

The fact that Hebrew was so little known in sixteenth- and seventeenth-century England meant that there was essentially no "original," no accessible, authoritative text with which to compare a translation, and as a result, for the vast majority of their readers, the English Psalms were the *only* Psalms (supplemented for some by "cognate" versions in Latin, German, or French). More importantly, English translations of the Psalms held a different status than English translations of either classical literature or vernacular works in other European languages, in that they were not intended as a crib for those who couldn't get at the original texts, nor as a kind of second-best version for the monoglot. The Psalms were not really conceived of as "texts" in the way that translations of Catullus or Petrarch were. They were holy Scripture and, as such, had a unique function, being *used* by English Christians every day, or at least every week, of their lives: they were sung in the services of the English Church, attendance at which was compelled by law if not by personal belief; they were sung at home as part of personal or family devotions; they were recorded in diaries, interpreted in commentaries and sermons, alluded to in the sacred texts of the liturgy and in the secular plays of the theater alike; they were among the most familiar texts in sixteenth- and seventeenth-century England. Because of the central place of the Psalms in English daily life, and their vital functions within the body of English culture, they were thus, in a powerful if peculiar sense, *English* works.[16]

Translations are a generally problematic category of literature. For instance, one common standard, at least in this century, for measuring the quality of a literary work is its originality. But "originality" is itself a problematic concept.[17] Normally an "original" work is considered to be one that

Kugel's prominence in the field of biblical "poetry," it should be noted that there remain dissenting views. Alter, for instance, makes notable claims for the legitimacy of Hebrew "poetry." See Robert Alter, *The Art of Biblical Poetry* (New York, 1985).

[16] Actually, one could make similar claims for the status of some of the most widely known and widely translated classical literature, like Horace's *Odes* or Ovid's *Metamorphoses*, that also had a formative influence on English culture. But I am concerned with exploring the complex nature of English translations of the Psalms rather than with distinguishing them categorically from other literary works that may well share some of this complexity.

[17] For an extended exploration of the concept, see John Hollander, "Originality," in *The Work of Poetry* (New York, 1997), 13–38. Danielle Clarke offers a useful critique of the general modern attitude toward the "literal" translation: "A judgement that a translation is literal presupposes that it is read exclusively in relation to its source text, rather than in the context to which it is directed; it also

is new, fresh, independent of prior works, the opposite of a work that is derivative, imitative, or commonplace. In the context of translation, however, the "original" work is not at all new; it is in fact the oldest version, the one on which any translation is based. As a result, a translation's lack of "originality" in the second sense makes it difficult for us to perceive it as "original" in the first sense, however imaginative or genuinely inventive it may be. Some of the translations of the English Renaissance are nevertheless considered to be among the period's literary masterpieces. Ezra Pound (whose own translations are among the most "original" in modern English) describes Golding's translation of the *Metamorphoses* as "the most beautiful book in the language."[18] When John Keats sings the praises of the *Iliad*, it is in the translation of George Chapman, on whom Keats bestows an equal share of credit:

> Oft of one wide expanse had I been told
> That deep–brow'd Homer ruled as his demesne;
> Yet did I never breathe its pure serene
> Till I heard Chapman speak out loud and bold.[19]

F. O. Matthiessen goes so far as to suggest that some of the best Elizabethan translations, Thomas North's Plutarch, for instance, are not only the equal of but actually superior to their originals.[20] The reason, Matthiessen explains, is that translators like North, or Philemon Holland (translator of Pliny), aimed not at the "meticulous imitation of the classical style," but at "the production of a book that would strike into the minds of their countrymen," resulting in English versions that naturalized the originals, that "made the foreign classics rich with English associations," taking Plutarch, Pliny, Montaigne, and others "deep into the national consciousness."[21] These Elizabethan literary works were "original" in a sense we do not customarily apply to translations, but it is in this sense that they – and, I would argue, the English Psalms – confirm George Steiner's insight that it is the process of translation and "the continuum of reciprocal transformation and decipherment which it answers, that determine the code of inheritance in

makes an assumption about the stability or presence of the original to be reproduced," in *Isabella Whitney, Mary Sidney, and Aemelia Lanyer: Renaissance Women Poets*, ed. Clarke (Harmondsworth, 2000), xxvi.

18 Ezra Pound, *ABC of Reading* (Norfolk, CT, n.d.), 58. Pound also includes Golding's Ovid, along with Gavin Douglas's translation of Virgil's *Aeneid*, on his list of suggestions for an anthology of the best English poets (79).

19 John Keats, "On First Looking into Chapman's Homer," in *John Keats: Complete Poems*, ed. Jack Stillinger (Cambridge, MA, and London, 1978, 1982), 34.

20 F. O. Matthiessen, *Translation: An Elizabethan Art* (Cambridge, MA, 1931), 5.

21 Ibid., 6–7, 4.

our civilization."[22] The formation of culture has thus been typically and fundamentally an act of translation.

Another problem in coming to terms with works of translation lies in the gap between theory and practice, evident from at least as early as the Renaissance. Since there is little theoretical writing about translation in sixteenth-century England as compared to France and Italy, there is no clear rationale for the rather loose practice of Elizabethan translators.[23] This may also explain their lack of consistent terminology for distinguishing different degrees of freedom in translation such as John Dryden introduced in the preface to his 1680 translation of *Ovid's Epistles*. He distinguished the categories of "metaphrase," "paraphrase," and "imitation," on the basis of an increasing degree of creative license taken with the text of the original.[24] More than a century earlier, Roger Ascham, in *The Scholemaster*, listed six "wayes appointed by the best learned men for the learning of tonges and encrease of eloquence, viz. *translatio linguarum*, *paraphrasis*, *metaphrasis*, *epitome*, *imitatio*, *declamatio*." Imitation (*imitatio*) does seem for Ascham, as for Dryden, a broader approach than metaphrase (*metaphrasis*) or paraphrase (*paraphrasis*), but the only distinction Ascham perceives between the latter two is that metaphrase involves the translation of verse (verse into verse, verse into prose, or prose into verse), whereas paraphrase is confined to prose, with neither practice being more or less "literal" than the other.

As Ascham's divergent usage indicates, Dryden's taxonomy was a belated attempt to organize a fairly haphazard practice in which "metaphrase," "paraphrase," "imitation," and other terms, such as "translation," and, most simply, "Englishing," were used interchangeably to describe acts that we would probably consider degrees of paraphrase. Actually, as Thomas Greene has noted, even Dryden could not maintain his own careful distinctions between the three kinds of translation, since he concluded his preface to Ovid by admitting that he himself had taken "more liberty than a just translation will allow."[25] Part of Dryden's difficulty lies in his attempt to apply what are essentially schoolroom distinctions to the much more sophisticated and flexible practice of translation by mature writers, himself included.

[22] George Steiner, *After Babel: Aspects of Language and Translation* (London, 1975), 461.

[23] *Critical Essays in the Seventeenth Century*, ed. J. E. Spingarn 3 vols. (Bloomington, IN, and London, 1957, rpr. 1968), vol. 1, xlviii–lviii, esp. lii, n. 2.

[24] John Dryden, preface to *Ovid's Epistles, Translated by Several Hands* (1680), in *John Dryden: Of Dramatic Poesy and Other Critical Essays*, 2 vols., ed. George Watson (London and New York, 1912, rpr. 1967), vol. 1, 268.

[25] Thomas M. Greene, *The Light in Troy: Imitation and Discovery in Renaissance Poetry* (New Haven and London, 1982), 52.

Dryden's careful terminology applied no better to Renaissance psalm translations than to translations of classical or European secular literature. The metrical psalters of George Sandys (1636) and Samuel Woodford (1667), for instance, announced themselves as "paraphrases" and were indeed relatively free versions. Sandys confessed the liberal nature of his paraphrase in his dedication to Charles I:

> And since no narrow Verse such Mysteries,
> Deepe Sense, and high Expressions could comprise;
> Her labouring Wings a larger compasse flie,
> And Poesie resolves with Poesie.[26]

In the preface to his *Paraphrase upon the Psalmes*, Woodford compared his versions with Sandys's, admitting that "In mine will appear a greater liberty, both as to the expression and the different sorts of stanzas which I have us'd."[27] He also condemned metrical translators who turn the English prose psalms into "versions so exactly laboured ad verbum, that what by the unlucky transposing of words, what by leaving out some little particles, wherein the grace of the sentence did consist, they lose all their former beauty, and from excellent Prose, though the language continue the same, degenerate into very indifferent, and untuneable Rhyme."[28] Miles Smyth, on the other hand, also called his metrical psalm translations "paraphrases," but he claimed to be striving for the "genuine sense" as well as metrical sophistication.[29] In 1607 Joseph Hall published *Some fewe of Davids Psalms Metaphrased, for a taste of the rest*, explaining in his preface his desire to see "our english Metaphrase bettered," by which he seems to refer to the standard metrical psalter of Sternhold and Hopkins et al.[30] Neither "Sternhold and Hopkins" nor Hall's attempted betterment seem metaphrases of the sort that Dryden had in mind. Henry King adds a further degree of confusion in *The Psalmes of David from the New Translation of the Bible turned into Meter* (1651). The title implies, as King's preface makes clear, that these metrical psalms are not a new translation at all, but simply the Psalms of the King James Bible "turned into Meter."[31]

26 *A Paraphrase upon the Psalmes of David* [London, 1636], rpr. with *A Paraphrase upon the Divine Poems* [London, 1648], sig. F6^r.

27 Samuel Woodford, *A Paraphrase upon the Psalmes* (London, 1667), sig. c^v.

28 Ibid., sigs. a3^r–a3^v.

29 Miles Smyth, *The Psalms of King David, paraphrased and turned into English verse* (1668), cited in *The Psalmists of Britain*, ed. John Holland 2 vols. (London, 1843), vol. 2, 56–57.

30 *The Collected Poems of Joseph Hall*, ed. A. Davenport (Liverpool, 1949), 125, 128.

31 "I have so closely followed the New Translation of the Psalms in our Church Bibles, that He who is able to read the Prose, may perceive the Reason of the text neither lost, nor abused in the Rhime;

King's conception of translation may seem peculiar, but it was not unique. As David Norton has shown, English attitudes to the Bible in translation were generally odd, maintaining what will likely seem to us an untenable distinction between the truth of the Scripture (what St. Paul terms the "spirit," 2 Cor. 3:6) – which was understood to remain unchanged and accessible despite the variety of translations – and the specific words of a particular translation (St. Paul's "letter").[32] Norton cites Archbishop Matthew Parker's preface to the Psalms in the Bishops' Bible (1568):

> Now let the gentle reader have this Christian consideration within himself that, though he findeth the psalms of this translation following not so to sound agreeably to his ears in his wonted words and phrases as he is accustomed with: yet let him not be too much offended with the work, which was wrought for his own commodity and comfort. And if he be learned, let him correct the word or sentence (which may dislike him) with the better, and whether his note riseth either of good will or charity, either of envy and contention not purely, yet his reprehension, if it may turn to the finding out of the truth, shall not be repelled with grief but applauded to in gladness, that Christ may ever have the praise.[33]

As Norton points out, Parker's preface is evidence of what was a widespread sense that "biblical truth did not lie in any particular form of English words."[34] This has various implications, most notably, for Norton, the lack of interest on the part of Parker and his fellow official translators in the Bible in English as a "literary" text. At the same time, such an attitude also allowed those paraphrasing or imitating the Bible (in Dryden's senses of these words) considerable freedom to take a more "literary" approach to the task.[35] Despite his commitment to the new translation of the Bishops' Bible, for instance, Parker had no qualms about writing his own metrical version of the Psalms, anticipating (and perhaps influencing) the psalter of Sir Philip Sidney and his sister the countess of Pembroke by using a different verse form for each psalm. Parker did not share the Sidneys' literary skill,

Both which without much Un-evennesse, or force are brought to an easy and familiar agreement" (preface to *The Psalmes of David from the New Translation of the Bible turned into Meter* [London, 1651], sig. A3[r]).

32 David Norton, *A History of the English Bible as Literature* (Cambridge, 2000), esp. 35–55.

33 Matthew Parker, cited in ibid., 38.

34 Ibid.

35 I use the term "literary" with some reservations, since the Psalms produced by many translators writing for primarily liturgical or devotional purposes are clearly works of "literature" in some senses of the term. Here and elsewhere, the use of the term "literary" (at least no more problematic than the alternatives, "aesthetic" or "poetic") indicates a primary concern with aesthetic criteria, as opposed to those of linguistic or doctrinal accuracy. This is not to say, of course, that poets were uninterested in accuracy, or that otherwise "literary" versions of the Psalms could not sometimes be used in worship or devotional activities, nor that the experience of reading "non-literary" translations could not include an aesthetic dimension. Despite these qualifications, however, the basic distinction between kinds of psalm translation remains tenable and useful.

but he did share their goal: to create a psalter in which the poetry of the Psalms in English equaled the excellence of the Hebrew poems.[36]

Modern theorists of translation are much occupied with formulating taxonomies such as Dryden's and reformulating basic questions about the possibility of accuracy in translation.[37] For the purposes of this study, however, the theoretical debates are largely beside the point. In the first place, few psalm translators in Renaissance England were translating from Hebrew, and, second and more importantly, it is exactly the "latitude" of these "translations" that often makes them compelling, whether theologically, historically, or aesthetically. In fact, the concern of this book is, in a real sense, with *mis*-translation, or at least with "translation" in a more comprehensive sense than is normally intended. Etymologically, "translation," from the Latin *translatio*, is a "carrying across," and what often seems most interesting about the Psalms in this period is the way in which they are transformed – adapted and assimilated – by being "carried across" from one language and culture to another.[38] What is "lost in translation" is richly compensated for by what is gained. And though there is, of course, interest in how the translators and their readers perceived the relationship between their work and the originals, what makes the English Psalms most intriguing is often not their accuracy but the imaginative boldness of their error (what Harold Bloom might term "misprision").[39] As demonstrated in this study, particularly in the final three chapters, the work of the "translators" in adapting the Psalms often involved creative interpretation somewhat akin to the Hebrew tradition of midrash, the rabbinical explication of biblical stories by means of further stories. Whether or not these English poets were aware of the rabbinic tradition – Milton certainly was – they were engaging in a practice with a history going back to the earliest interpretations of the

36 [Matthew Parker], *The whole Psalter turned into English Metre* (London, [1567]). Though not published under Parker's name, the psalter is generally attributed to him, since he writes of having composed a metrical psalter, and since one of the prefatory poems in the psalter is an acrostic on the name "Matthew Parker." See V. J. K. Brook, *A Life of Archbishop Matthew Parker* (Oxford, 1962), 52. For further consideration of Parker's influence on the Sidneys, see Anne Lake Prescott, "King David as a 'Right Poet': Sidney and the Psalmist," *English Literary Renaissance* 19:3 (1989), 131–51.

37 See, for instance, *On Translation*, ed., Reuben Brower (New York, 1966); Steiner, *After Babel*; *Theories of Translation*, ed. Rainer Schulte and John Biguenet (Chicago and London, 1992); and Umberto Eco, *Experiences in Translation*, trans. Alastair McEwen (Toronto, 2001). But of course the bibliography on translation is immense.

38 It is ironic and perhaps telling that the history of the word for "translation" in most European vernaculars, though not in English, is itself based on a mistranslation from the Latin *traducere*, which meant not "translate" but "lead beyond." Leonardo Bruni made this original and originating error in translating the *Noctes* of Aulus Gellius. See Steiner, *After Babel*, 296, and Eco, *Experiences*, 74.

39 Harold Bloom, *The Anxiety of Influence* (London, Oxford, and New York, 1973), 19–48.

Hebrew Bible.[40] Through paraphrase and adaptation, allusion and echo, writers "translated" the Psalms into poems, sermons, prose allegories, plays, musical works, and meditations, in every case interpreting the "original" by transforming it into something new and "original" in a different sense.

Much of the history of biblical translation, paraphrase, commentary, and allusion in this period is a testament to the authors' efforts to make the strange familiar. The peculiar problems of interpreting the Psalms – and every translation involves interpretation – of filling in gaps and lacunae, of smoothing over inconsistencies, solving conundra and textual cruces, led to what might be termed a practical poetics of psalm translation. Psalm 19, for example, is an amalgam of two distinct texts, which accounts for the abrupt shift after verse 6 from creation hymn to celebration of the law. An attentive reader will perceive this break, and the natural impulse is to try to explain it in terms that will bring the two parts of the psalm together into a unified whole. Wither, for instance, appended to his metrical translation of Psalm 19 a prose meditation that interprets Creation and Law as the two complementary "texts" of divine revelation, the second compensating for our inattentiveness to the first:

> No excuse is left, oh mercifull Father, if we be ignorant of thee, or unconformable to thy will: for, by the book of thy Creatures, it was long-since declared unto the whole world, which Text, being corrupted by humane Inventions, thou didst explaine it againe in the volumes of the Prophets; Since then, it was more illustrated by the writings of the Apostles; And the prime scope of all these Bookes thy blessed Spirit daylie preacheth & interpreteth throughout the world, by ordinarie or extraordinarie meanes.[41]

In 1712 (admittedly a few years beyond the scope of this study), Joseph Addison published a paraphrase of Psalm 19 in *The Spectator*, "The Spacious Firmament on High." At first sight, he appears to have solved the problem of unity with less subtlety than Wither, by simply omitting verses 7–14 pertaining to the Law. Closer inspection, however, reveals that Addison

[40] On midrash, see the essays in *Midrash and Literature*, ed. Geoffrey H. Hartman and Sanford Budick (New Haven and London, 1986). Milton's knowledge of midrash is explored in Golda Werman, *Milton and Midrash* (Washington, DC, 1995). The description of midrash as explicating stories by other stories applies to only one aspect of the rabbinic interpretive practice, of course, which also includes minute textual and contextual analysis. Still, the broader sense is legitimate and frequently used to refer to the literary tradition based on or analogous to midrash. See David Curzon's introduction to his *Modern Poems on the Bible: An Anthology* (Philadelphia and Jerusalem, 1994).

[41] George Wither, Psalm 19, *The Psalms of David Translated Into Lyrick-Verse* (1632), Spenser Society reprint (New York, 1881, rpr. 1967).

interwove the two diverse subjects in order to emphasize, as Wither did, that the Law was readable within the text of Creation:

> What though, in solemn Silence, all
> Move round the dark terrestrial Ball?
> What tho' nor real Voice nor Sound
> Amid their radiant Orbs be found?
> In Reason's Ear they all rejoice,
> And utter forth a glorious Voice,
> For ever singing, as they shine,
> "The Hand that made us is Divine."[42]

Translators exercised similar ingenuity in dealing with the shift in metaphors in Psalm 23 (see chapter 5), in the conflicting injunctions on sacrifice in Psalm 51 (see chapter 6), and in what seemed to many Christians an unacceptable thirst for vengeance at the end of Psalm 137 (see chapter 7). Given the divine authority of Scripture, psalm translators had to assume that any apparent inconsistencies and contradictions were due to their own limited understanding of the text; the alterations they made in their translations were thus improved readings *of* the original, not improvements *on* it.

The organization of *Psalm Culture and Early Modern English Literature* is topical and thematic rather than chronological or author-centered in order to allow for the inclusion of a wide range of materials. The first four chapters describe the history of English metrical psalms in the sixteenth and seventeenth centuries, dividing the narrative according to the two principal types: metrical psalms intended for congregational singing in the worship services of the English Church (chapters 1 and 2), and those intended for serious reading as lyric poetry by the literati (chapters 3 and 4). Chapter 1 examines the most popular (yet most denigrated) book of metrical psalms in sixteenth- and seventeenth-century England, the "Sternhold and Hopkins" psalter, asking why a book so persistently criticized should nevertheless have been reprinted in hundreds of editions, owned by both rich and poor, educated and ignorant, high churchmen and low, and sung in English churches and homes for 150 years. Chapter 2 reformulates the key question of chapter 1, asking why the many "singing" psalters produced with the intention of supplanting "Sternhold and Hopkins" failed in their attempts to do so. The chapter surveys a representative sample of seventeenth-century

[42] Joseph Addison, "Ode," lines 17–24, in *Eighteenth-Century Literature*, ed. Geoffrey Tillotson, Paul Fussell, and Marshall Waingrow (New York, 1969), 823. The original was in *The Spectator*, No. 465 (August 23, 1712).

metrical psalters by some of the most colorful writers of the period: the prolific and polemical George Wither, the world-traveler and translator of Ovid George Sandys, the bishop and elegist Henry King, and the "silkman" Henry Dod, as well as the translators of *The Bay Psalm Book*, the first book published in America.

Chapters 3 and 4 turn from church psalters to the "literary" tradition of psalm translation. Matthew Arnold described Hebraism and Hellenism as rival cultural forces, but, by contrast, the Renaissance approach was consistently syncretic, perceiving not opposition but continuity between the two cultures.[43] For Sidney, Donne, Milton, and many others, the Psalms were the preeminent ancient poetry upon which they believed the later Greco-Roman tradition to be modeled. Furthermore, the fact that David, divinely appointed king and prophet, had written poetry provided Renaissance poets with a crucial precedent and justification for their own poetic vocation. The assumption that the Psalms were written in classical meters, a notion derived largely from remarks by Jerome,[44] gave authority to the efforts of those experimenting with English quantitative poetry; the prominent place of the Psalms in the quantitative movement is examined in chapter 3. Chapter 4 surveys the role of the Psalms in the development of English poetry, as exemplified by the metrical psalms of Sir Thomas Wyatt, the earl of Surrey, and George Gascoigne, Sidney and the countess of Pembroke, Henry Vaughan, Milton and others. The widespread assumption, based on patristic writings, that the Hebrew Psalter represented a cornucopia of verse forms, lyric genres and modes, and was perhaps even the source of classical prosody, stimulated poets to experiment with the formal possibilities of English verse. Many of the English psalms produced as a result are lyric poems as sophisticated as the most accomplished "original" verse of the English Renaissance.

The final three chapters are devoted to examining "translations" of three particularly influential psalms into works of literature, art, song, and theology. In chapter 5, translations of Psalm 23 ("The Lord is my shepherd") offer further examples of the syncretic approach to historical cultures in the Renaissance, showing how poets and commentators merged the biblical and classical pastoral traditions, assimilating two ancient cultures that were radically different but which nevertheless converged in the minds of those

[43] Matthew Arnold, *Culture and Anarchy*, IV, "Hebraism and Hellenism," in *Poetry and Criticism of Matthew Arnold*, ed. A. Dwight Culler (Boston, 1961), 465–98. This syncretic approach, though characteristic of the Renaissance, is of course much older, as attested by the lines of the thirteenth-century hymn, *Dies irae*, which align David's prophetic powers with the classical sibyl's: "*Dies irae, dies illa,/ solvet saeclum in favilla,/ teste David cum Sibylla*" (*The Oxford Book of Medieval Latin Verse*, ed. F. J. E. Raby [Oxford, 1959], 392).

[44] See below, chap. 3, 87–88.

who were committed to the rediscovery of both. Psalm 51 ("Have mercy upon me, O God") was a seminal text for Christian, especially Protestant, conceptions of sin and repentance, inspiring Luther's doctrine of "justification by faith" as well as providing the language of prayer for the liturgy of the English Church, and in the penitential poems of Anne Vaughan Lock, Donne, and George Herbert, which were indebted to that liturgy. As chapter 6 will reveal, Psalm 51 also informs critical scenes of penitence and devotion in *Hamlet* and *Paradise Lost*. Finally, chapter 7 focuses on Psalm 137 ("By the waters of Babylon"), which provided consolation for both political and spiritual exiles, and gave William Shakespeare, Edmund Spenser, and Milton specific language with which to express such alienation (language especially meaningful for poets, since the psalm figured alienation in terms of an inability to sing). The psalm's closing cry for vengeance, seen by some as incompatible with Christian doctrine, was used as a call to arms by polemicists on both sides of the English Civil War. These last chapters, in a sense, present "core samples" of sixteenth- and seventeenth-century English culture, which demonstrate how deeply the biblical lyrics permeated the literary, religious, political, and social strata of the period.

A final word must be said about the limitations of this study. Its scope has been kept deliberately broad, in the hope of demonstrating, as much as is feasible, the rich contribution of the Psalms to English culture in this period. The time frame itself is broad, beginning with the psalms of Wyatt and Sternhold in the 1540s and finishing at the close of the seventeenth century with Nahum Tate and Nicholas Brady. The traditional temporal barriers (the turn of the sixteenth century, or the end of Elizabeth's reign, 1603, or the Restoration of 1660) have been deliberately bridged; English "psalm culture" can thus be seen in continuous development from its origins in the first vernacular translations of Scripture during the Reformation to its eighteenth-century transformation in the rise of Protestant hymnody effected by Isaac Watts and John and Charles Wesley. Of course, even these period boundaries are to some extent artificial. The Psalms were certainly vitally important in medieval culture (though in different ways) and there were admittedly a very few scattered English translations in meter and prose before the sixteenth century.[45] Similarly, there continued to be important literary psalm translations after the seventeenth century, by Watts, Christopher Smart, William Cowper, Joseph Addison, and others.[46]

45 See the collection of essays edited by Nancy van Deusen, *The Place of the Psalms in the Intellectual Culture of the Middle Ages* (Albany, 1999), and Michael P. Kuczynski, *Prophetic Song: The Psalms as Moral Discourse in Later Medieval England* (Philadelphia, 1995).

46 On the Psalms in the eighteenth century, see Donald Davie, *The Eighteenth-Century Hymn in England* (Cambridge, 1993), and J. R. Watson, *The English Hymn* (Oxford, 1997), chaps. 7–11.

Yet, even given the wide scope of this study, I have necessarily been selective in determining what to include, and so the coverage is by no means exhaustive. The psalters examined in chapter 2, for instance, are a small selection from among dozens produced in print and manuscript. Similarly, although the three psalms surveyed in chapters 5, 6, and 7 were chosen because they are among the most influential in the Psalter, studies could fruitfully be made of others, such as Psalm 42 ("Like as the hart desireth the waterbrooks"), or Psalm 130 ("Out of the deep have I called unto thee, O Lord") to name only two.

A final limitation is the confinement to the English tradition, a decision necessitated once again by the size of the topic, as well as by competence. Similar accounts could be made of other national psalm cultures in the period, especially those of Germany and France.[47] While limitations are unavoidable, this study is still in many respects a broad examination of early modern psalm culture, and should convey some sense that the study of the Psalms offers an illuminating perspective on English Renaissance literature and culture that is just beginning to be explored.

[47] Two excellent studies of the Psalms in other European vernaculars are Michel Jeanneret, *Poésie et tradition biblique au XVIe siècle* (Paris, 1969), and Bach and Galle, *Deutsche Psalmendichtung*. See also the studies of Psalm 137 in French (DiMauro, Cave) and Portugese (Creel) cited in chap. 7, n. 5.

PART I

English metrical psalmody

CHAPTER I

"Very mete to be used of all sortes of people": the "Sternhold and Hopkins" psalter

In 1699 King David, the original psalmist, was called back from the dead by Thomas Sternhold and John Hopkins to lend his authoritative voice to their complaint against the *New Version of the Psalms* of 1696. Sternhold and Hopkins, dead themselves for a century and a half, had been authors of the popular metrical psalter used in English churches since at least 1562, affectionately known simply as "Sternhold and Hopkins," now, finally, being made redundant by the *New Version*. As reported by an anonymous satirical broadsheet purporting to be "*Old* John Hopkin'*s*, *and* Tho. Sternhold'*s*, Petition to the PARLIAMENT *Against the New Version of the* Psalms," King David complains to them (in the familiar common meter of "Sternhold and Hopkins") about the effrontery of the new translators, Nahum Tate and Nicholas Brady:

> *Full empty* are the Words, God knows,
> Which now they make me speak,
> I'd rather bear *Goliah's* Blows
> Than what I now do take.

The voices of Hopkins and Sternhold conclude the petition on David's behalf, in terms that would hardly have been taken as a serious defence of the Old Version:

> Thus (Senators) the Royal Bard
> Would have his wretched *Ailments* heard;
> And thus before your Wisdoms Sage,
> He lays the Reasons of his Rage.
> We too must join against these Elves,
> And beg for *David*, and our Selves:
> Oh! For those Lines by *Nich*. and *Nahum*,
> Let no one sing or ever say 'em;
> Nor take our Priviledges from us,
> Whilst I am *John*, and I am *Thomas*.

And your Petitioners shall pray
For evermore and Eke for Aye.[1]

The wit of this satire, not terribly subtle, and which mocks Sternhold and Hopkins more than the intended object of their scorn, depends partly on the reader's ability to recognize "for evermore," "eke," and "aye" as meaningless filler phrases typical of the "Sternhold and Hopkins" psalms at their least inspired, and also on the awareness of "our Priviledges" as a reference to that psalter's special status, protected as it was by the monopoly of the Stationers Company.[2]

This obscure satire is only one of a host of derisory voices raised against *The Whole Booke of Psalmes* (the official title of "Sternhold and Hopkins"). Thomas Browne's "On Sternhold and Hopkins, and the New Version of David's Psalms" actually responds to the purported authors of the 1699 broadsheet, defending Tate and Brady against the "Elizabeth Phrase" and "Farthingal-Rhiming" of "a Brace of dull Knaves":

Tho' the *late Version* fails of the *Spirit* and *Force*
Of DAVID's *Rejoycings*, or DAVID's *Remorse*;
Yet I'm not such a Coxcomb, 'sted of *new Psalms*, to learn *Old*,
Or to quit TATE and BRADY, for Hopkins and *Sternhold*.[3]

Nor are Sternhold and Hopkins the only authors to make King David their mouthpiece on the issue of metrical psalms. In 1703, David spoke the prologue to Roger Boyle's play, *King Saul*, forgiving Sternhold and Hopkins now that a more recent translator (not, it seems, Boyle himself) has done him justice:

Sternhold, *be thou forgot with thy Offence,*
And Hopkins, *thou Assassin to my Sense,*
Musick succeeds your Inharmonious Songs,
And Brittain *does atone for* Brittain*'s Wrongs,*
As David*'s Pleasures,* David*'s Pains Requite,*
And makes him Sing a Poem he would write.[4]

[1] *Old John Hopkins's and Thomas Sternhold's Petition to the Parliament* [etc.] (London, 1699).

[2] There may also be a bawdy pun on the names of the two principal translators, although there is no evidence to establish whether "John Thomas" had the same sense for the ballad writer that it did two centuries later for D. H. Lawrence in *Lady Chatterley's Lover*. On the Stationers Company, see chap. 2.

[3] Thomas Browne, "On Sternhold and Hopkins, and the New Version of David's Psalms," in *The Works of Mr. Thomas Browne*, 4th ed. (London, 1715).

[4] Roger Boyle, earl of Orrery, "Prologue" to *King Saul*, in *The Dramatic Works of Roger Boyle, earl of Orrery*, ed. William Clark Smith, 2 vols. (Cambridge, MA, 1937), vol. 2, 706. According to the editor it is not known if this play was ever performed (vol. 2, 820, note).

The prologue to Thomas Duffett's *Psyche Debauch'd* (1678), a burlesque of Thomas Shadwell's *Psyche*, calls Sternhold and Hopkins themselves from the dead to "rise, and claim your style," the point presumably being that Shadwell was as dull a poet as they were.[5] By the end of the seventeenth century Sternhold and Hopkins had indeed come to epitomize the hack poet. "Sternhold" is even turned into a verb by John Gay in his poem on Sir Richard Blackmore, who produced his own metrical psalter in 1721:

> *Sternhold* himself he *out-Sternholded*,
> Made *David* seem so mad and freakish,
> All thought him just what thought king Achiz.[6]

The criticism of "Sternhold and Hopkins" had begun early in the seventeenth century, if not before. Joseph Hall criticized English metrical psalmody as a whole in his 1598 *Virgidemiarum*, to which John Marston responded, sympathetically defending Sternhold, Hopkins, and others "that doe strive to bring/ That stranger language to our vulgar tongue."[7] John Donne, comparing "Sternhold and Hopkins" (by obvious implication if not by name) to the more artful continental psalters (particularly that of Marot and de Bèze), wondered why the English Church should "more hoarse, more harsh than any other, sing."[8] George Wither, frustrated by the opposition of the Stationers Company to the royal patent ordering his 1623 *Hymnes and Songs of the Church* to be appended to all metrical psalters, complained that "Sternhold and Hopkins" troubled people's devotion, since it was "full of absurdityes, scolescismes, improprietyes, non-sence, and impertinent circumlocutions (to more then twice the length of their originalles in some places)."[9] A less serious but more memorable condemnation was offered in lines attributed to the earl of Rochester and addressed to a particular parish clerk, criticizing his singing of the psalms and, moreover, the psalms themselves:

[5] Thomas Duffett, "Prologue" to *Psyche Debauch'd*, in *Three Burlesque Plays of Thomas Duffett*, ed. Ronald Eugene DiLorenzo (Iowa City, 1972), 153.

[6] John Gay, "*Verses To be placed under the Picture of* England's Arch-Poet: *Containing a Compleat Catalogue of his Works*," in *The Poetical Works of John Gay*, ed. G. C. Faber (London, 1926), 652. This poem was attributed to Gay in the eighteenth century but is described by Faber as a doubtful work (xxv). The reference to "Achiz" is to King Achish, from whose punishment David escaped by feigning madness (1 Samuel 21).

[7] Cited in James Doelman, *King James I and the Religious Culture of England* (Cambridge, 2000), 141.

[8] John Donne, "Upon the translation of the Psalmes by Sir Philip Sidney, and the Countesse of Pembroke his Sister," in *The Poems of John Donne*, ed. Herbert J. C. Grierson, 2 vols. (Oxford, 1912), vol. 1, 349. Donne's reference to God having "translated these translators" means that the poem must have been written after Pembroke's death in 1621.

[9] Wither, *The Schollers Purgatory* (London, 1624; facs. ed. Amsterdam, 1977), 37. On Wither, see below, 52–64.

Sternhold and Hopkins had great qualms
When they translated David's psalms
To make the heart full glad;
But had it been poor David's fate
To hear thee sing, and them translate,
By God! 'twould have made him mad.[10]

Why was so much censorious wit directed at this volume of metrical psalms? What was it about "Sternhold and Hopkins" that created such apoplexy among churchmen and poets alike? Why was metrical psalmody in general such a contested field for so long? Much debate focused on this particular psalm version, yet it would not have been so sharply or so persistently criticized had its critics not felt that metrical psalmody was a matter of some consequence.

METRICAL PSALMS AND THE REFORMATION

The leaders of the Protestant Reformation discovered quickly the power of sung metrical psalms as a means of spreading doctrine. Luther's first lectures (1513) were based on the Psalms, and his metrical psalms and hymns were among his first published works.[11] In its foreword, Luther explains the importance of Johann Walther's 1524 *Wittenburg Gesangbuch*, which included some of Luther's own hymns:

> [A]s a good beginning and to encourage those who can do better, I and several others have brought together certain spiritual songs with a view to spreading abroad and setting in motion the holy Gospel which now, by the grace of God, has again emerged, so that we too may pride ourselves, as Moses does in his song, Exodus 15, that Christ is our strength and song and may not know anything to sing or say, save Jesus Christ our Savior, as Paul says, 1 Corinthians 2.[12]

He goes on to emphasize the particular importance of spiritual songs for young people, that they "might have something to rid them of their love ditties and wanton songs and might, instead of these, learn wholesome things and thus yield willingly, as becomes them, to the good."[13] Even

[10] *The Complete Poems of John Wilmot, Earl of Rochester*, ed. David M. Vieth (New Haven, 1968), 22. The poem is listed as having an "uncertain" attribution. The traditional story was "that it was at Bodicot (a chapelry to Adderbury) that Rochester made his extempore lines addressed to the psalm-singing clerk or sexton" (Vieth quoting Alfred Beesky, *The History of Banbury*, 1841).

[11] Richard Marius, *Martin Luther: The Christian between God and Death* (Cambridge, MA, and London, 1999), 88–104.

[12] Translated by Oliver Strunk, in *Source Readings in Music History: The Renaissance*, ed. Gary Tomlinson (New York and London, 1998), 83.

[13] Ibid., 84.

Luther's opponents recognized the rhetorical power of his Psalms and hymns; one Jesuit stated that "the hymns of Luther killed more souls than his sermons."[14]

John Calvin was opposed to the liturgical use of non-scriptural hymns, but he was as enthusiastic about the Psalms as Luther, and, like Luther, wrote metrical psalms himself. Calvin's "Epistle to the Reader" in *The Geneva Psalter* of 1542 (a work in all its parts indebted to the Lutheran precedent), is cautious but urgent:

> And in truth we know by experience that song has great force and vigor to move and inflame the hearts of men to invoke and praise God with a more vehement and ardent zeal. It must always be looked to that the song be not light and frivolous but have weight and majesty, as Saint Augustine says [*Epistola* 55.18.34], and there is likewise a great difference between the music one makes to entertain men at table and in their homes, and the psalms which are sung in the Church in the presence of God and his angels.[15]

The greatest French metrical psalter was principally the work of Clément Marot and Théodore de Bèze, and their Psalms were the most important influence on English practice, especially given the residence in Geneva of Marian exiles, in particular William Whittingham, the principal translator of the Geneva Bible and probable editor of "Sternhold and Hopkins." Metrical psalms were also translated and sung by Dutch Protestants, notably in the "stranger churches" of sixteenth-century London.[16]

Psalm singing had the support of Scripture, in St. Paul's injunction to the Colossians to "let the word of Christ dwell in you richly in all wisdom; teaching and admonishing one another in psalms and hymns and spiritual songs" (Coloss. 3:16). St. Paul had in mind, of course, the same idea as Luther and Calvin, that the Psalms were an effective means of spreading the Word. Words connected to a melody are far easier to remember, especially when translated into a regular meter. Furthermore, though the Psalms had long been considered a précis of the entire Bible, densely packed with crucial doctrine, metrical translators often gave their texts a polemical edge, adding

[14] Cited in Roland Bainton, *Here I Stand: A Life of Martin Luther* (Nashville and New York, 1950), 346.

[15] Translation by Strunk, in *Source Readings*, 87. Calvin's "great difference" was not perceived by many others, even in his own church, as evidenced by Claude Goudimel's foreword to *The Geneva Psalter* of 1565: "To the melody of the psalms we have, in this little volume, adapted three parts, not to induce you to sing them in church, but that you may rejoice in God, particularly in your homes" (*Source Readings*, 90).

[16] On the *Souterliedekens* and the psalms of Jan Utenhove, see Richard Todd, "'So Well Attyr'd Abroad': A Background to the Sidney–Pembroke Psalter and its Implications for the Seventeenth-Century Religious Lyric," *Texas Studies in Literature and Language* 29:1 (1987), 74–93.

reformed doctrine by means of looser or expanded paraphrase. Luther, for instance, often turned the Hebrew Psalms into Christian hymns by inserting references to Christ or the Trinity.

That metrical psalms in England were aimed at a broad audience is indicated by the vast number written in common meter, the simple meter of the popular ballad stanza. The origins of this meter depend upon a "chicken or egg" question. Some assume that Sternhold and others borrowed the ballad meter from secular songs as part of their attempt to supplant "love ditties and wanton songs." Yet relatively few ballad texts predate the sixteenth century, and the ballad meter was also known as "Sternhold's Meter," leading some scholars to suggest that "ballad meter" was first popularized by metrical psalms.[17] Whether the "common meter" was made common by psalms or secular ballads, it is clear that its use for English metrical psalms reflected the desire of Reformers to make them both accessible and memorable.

ENGLISH METRICAL PSALMS AND "STERNHOLD AND HOPKINS"

The history of English metrical psalmody somewhat predates the Reformation, since Thomas Brampton translated the Penitential Psalms into English verse in the early fifteenth century. But the sixteenth century witnessed an undeniable explosion in the production of singing-psalms. Luther's early influence is evident in the publication of Miles Coverdale's *Goostly psalmes and spirituall songes* (1535?), but that small volume was suppressed and had little influence. The same is true of another early metrical psalter by Robert Crowley, published in 1549 by Crowley himself as *The Psalter of David newely translated into Englysh metre*. Like Sternhold, whose first psalms may have been published in the same year – a good year for metrical psalms, marking as well the first appearance of the psalms of Sir Thomas Wyatt and the earl of Surrey – Crowley used the common meter.[18] Crowley is important as an early champion of the value of the Psalms as poetry, following the lead of the Swiss Reformer Leo Jud, the principal translator of the Latin *Biblia Sacrosancta* that was Crowley's source text. Yet his

[17] See Robin Leaver, *Goostly Psalmes and Spiritual Songes: English and Dutch Metrical Psalms from Coverdale to Utenhove 1535–1566* (Oxford, 1991), 119, citing Edmund Doughtie, *Lyrics from the English Airs, 1596–1622* (Cambridge, 1970) and the use of "Master Sternhold's metre" in various publications of versified scripture of the 1550s.

[18] Wyatt's *Certayne psalmes* (the Penitential Psalms) and the *Certayne Chapters of the proverbes of Salomon*, containing Psalms 31, 51, and 88 by Surrey (unattributed), were published in 1549. Probably for marketing reasons, the publisher of the latter volume attributed it to Sternhold, but this attribution has since been rejected. For publication details, see Rivkah Zim, *English Metrical Psalms: Poetry as Praise and Prayer, 1535–1601* (Cambridge, 1987), 225–26.

psalms, like Coverdale's metrical versions, had a negligible impact on later translators.[19]

The real boom in English metrical psalms begins with Thomas Sternhold, about whom little is known save that he was Groom of the Robes to Henry VIII and Edward VI and that he died in 1549.[20] Sometime between 1547 and 1549, Sternhold published a little volume entitled *Certayne psalmes chosen out of the Psalter of David, & drawen into English metre*, containing nineteen psalms and a dedication to Edward VI, which is the only source of information about the composition of these psalms. Some of them may have been written and sung at the court of Henry VIII, but all that is certain from Sternhold himself is that Edward VI took "pleasure to heare them song sumtimes of me," and that they were published for Edward's continued pleasure, whether in reading them to himself or in having them sung to him by courtiers like Sternhold.[21]

The origins of Sternhold's psalms in the court of Edward VI need to be stressed, given the much later tendency to associate "Sternhold and Hopkins" with the simple devotions of the lower classes. John Dryden explained the failure of rival translations (principally George Sandys's) to supplant "Sternhold and Hopkins" on the basis of popular taste: "Do we not see them stick to Hopkins' and Sternhold's psalms, and forsake those of David, I mean Sandys his translation of them? If by the people you understand the multitude, the οι πολλοι [hoi polloi], 'tis no matter what they think; they are sometimes in the right, sometimes in the wrong; their judgement is a mere lottery."[22] Dryden's condemnation of the judgment of the hoi polloi reflects the development, in the Restoration and afterward, of an association of "Sternhold and Hopkins" with "popular" culture. Alexander Pope, for instance, mentions the prototypical metrical psalmists with affectionate condescension in his description of the role of verse in simple country worship:

> Not but there are, who merit other palms;
> Hopkins and Sternhold glad the heart with psalms;
> The Boys and Girls whom Charity maintains,
> Implore your help in these pathetic strains;

[19] The most extensive treatment of Crowley's psalter, and of his career more generally, is John N. King, *English Reformation Literature* (Princeton, 1982), 219–23, 469–72.

[20] Sternhold's biography, such as it is, may be found in Henry Leigh Bennett's article in the *Dictionary of National Biography* (the *DNB*), ed. Sir Leslie Stephen and Sir Sidney Lee, vol. 18, 1110–11 (Oxford, from 1882), Holland, *Psalmists of Britain*, vol. 1, 91–96, Zim, *English Metrical Psalms*, 85–88, 113–24, and Leaver, *Goostly Psalmes*, 117–26.

[21] Thomas Sternhold, *Certayne Psalmes . . .* (London, [c.1549]), sig. Aiii^r.

[22] John Dryden, *Of Dramatic Poesy: An Essay* (1668), in *Of Dramatic Poesy*, ed. George Watson, 86.

> How could Devotion touch the country pews,
> Unless the Gods bestow'd a proper Muse?
> Verse chears their leisure, Verse assists their work,
> Verse prays for Peace, or sings down Pope and Turk.[23]

Yet the "Sternhold and Hopkins" psalter was "popular" in a broader sense than Dryden or Pope would have liked to acknowledge, and its origins in the verses of Sternhold reflect the judgment of the king and his court rather than the hoi polloi.

The comparison of Sternhold's psalms to those of the French poet Clément Marot is hard to resist, though there is little documentary evidence to connect them. Both men were royal courtiers writing under the sway of the newly fashionable Reformation principles (fashionable at least at the courts of Edward VI and Marguerite de Navarre). Both seem to have been offering an alternative to what Sternhold called "fayned rymes of vanitie," secular songs that provided recreation for the French and English courts.[24] The psalm collections of Marot and Sternhold were filled out by other translators and formed the foundations of complete church psalters published in the same year (1562). (This may not be entirely coincidental, given that the French psalter was published in Geneva where many of the "Sternhold and Hopkins" translators lived during the Marian exile.) A good case has been made for the possibility that Sternhold knew Marot's psalms and was attempting an English equivalent of these sacred texts in verse sophisticated enough to satisfy the courtly taste.[25] Of course, from a modern perspective, the poetry of Sternhold's psalms is not as "sophisticated" as Marot's, favoring a plainer style and confining itself almost entirely to a single meter as opposed to the latter's virtuosic metrical variety. This may simply reflect differences in the predominant national literary tastes of mid-century France and England, but it results in sets of metrical psalms that seem poles apart stylistically.[26] Given the importance placed on psalm-singing

[23] Alexander Pope, "The First Epistle of the Second Book of Horace Imitated," lines 230–36, in *The Poems of Alexander Pope*, ed. John Butt (London, 1963, rpr. 1984), 643. The last line refers to the hymn by Robert Wisdom (translating Luther's *Erhalt uns Herr*), which begins "Preserve us, Lorde, by thy deare word,/ from Turk and Pope defend us, Lord," and which was included in "Sternhold and Hopkins." Elsewhere, in a letter to Swift, Pope makes it clear that he holds Sternhold and Hopkins in contempt as poets, just as Dryden and others did: "My name is as bad a one as yours, and hated by all bad poets, from Sternhold and Hopkins to Gildon and Cibber" (Pope to Swift, Oct. 15, 1725, cited in Butt, *Pope*, 644, note).

[24] Sternhold, *Certayne Psalmes*, sig. Aiii^{r}.

[25] See Zim, *English Metrical Psalms*, 122–24, on the possible influence of Marot on Sternhold through the presence at the English court of Nicholas Denisot, former "gentilhomme de la chambre" to Francis I.

[26] On the English "plain style," see King, *English Reformation Literature*, esp. 138–43.

by almost all the Protestant reformers, the English and French practices may simply have arisen independently, perhaps sharing a common inspiration from Lutheran psalms and hymns.

Within a decade of their first publication, Sternhold's psalms were appearing in church as well as chamber. Sternhold died shortly after his nineteen psalms were published, but he left behind further translations that were added to the original group and published in 1549 as *Al such psalmes of David as Thomas Sternehold late grome of the kinges Majesties Robes, didde in his life time draw into english Metre.* The man behind this augmented edition was John Hopkins, a clergyman who had somehow come into possession of eighteen additional psalms by Sternhold and who added seven of his own psalm translations in an appendix.[27] The intended use of this volume for private devotions or godly entertainment does not seem to have been different from that of Sternhold's original, but a major shift in its function occurred with the death of Edward VI and subsequent accession of the Roman Catholic Mary Tudor, when it became the nucleus of the psalter used in services of public worship by English Protestant exiles in Frankfurt, Geneva, and elsewhere on the continent.

During the Marian exile, English Protestants abroad continued to augment their collection of metrical psalms. When in 1558 Elizabeth I became queen, the Protestant exiles were free to return to England. Thus, *The Psalmes of David in Englishe Metre* (1560) was published in London.[28] Apart from the new psalms and tunes that accompanied every publication, the most significant change from earlier editions published on the continent was the addition of two sentences to the full title: "Very mete to be used of all sortes of people privatly for their godly solace and confort, laiyng apart all ungodly songes & ballades, which tende only to the nourishing of vice, and corrupting of youth. Newly set fourth and allowed, according to the order appointed in the Quenes Maiesties Iniunctions."[29] The first new sentence indicates that the editors and publisher were once again thinking, as Sternhold was originally, of the psalms as devout recreation for the godly "of all sorts." The second sentence indicates they were also intended for singing in church, as had been the practice in Geneva and Frankfurt. The

[27] The article on Hopkins by Henry Richard Tedder in the *DNB* (vol. 9, 1228–29) notes one view, expressed in J. Miller, *Singers and Songs of the Church* (1869), that Hopkins and Sternhold were neighbors in Gloucestershire, but questions the grounds for such a claim.

[28] The year 1560 was also, of course, when the same scholars published the Geneva Bible. A differently enlarged edition of the psalter was published in Geneva in 1561 as *Four Score and Seven Psalmes of David in English Mitre* (STC 16563). See Maurice Frost, *English and Scottish Psalm & Hymn Tunes c.1543–1677* (Oxford, 1953), 8–11.

[29] Frost, *Psalm & Hymn Tunes*, 6.

specific injunctions referred to had nothing to do with the Sternhold and Hopkins psalms per se (though such an inference would have helped sales), but they did stress the benefits of singing in church:

And that there be a modest distinct song, so used in all parts of the common prayers in the Church, but that the same may be plainly understood, as if it were read without singing, and yet nevertheless, for the comforting of such that delight in music, it may be permitted that in the beginning, or in the end of common prayers, either at morning or evening, there may be sung an Hymn, or such like song, to the praise of Almighty God, in the best sort of melody and music that may be conveniently devised, having respect that the sentence of the Hymn may be understood and perceived.[30]

The queen's wording was characteristically ambivalent, allowing for all sorts of music, from congregational metrical psalms to complex choral anthems. Elizabeth enjoyed the anthems of her Chapel composer William Byrd (an avowed Catholic throughout his life) but allowed for those with differing musical and liturgical tastes to sing psalms at appropriate points in the service.[31]

The psalter continued to expand in subsequent editions, printed in both London and Geneva, with additional psalms by William Kethe (the Scottish author of the famous "Old 100th"), Thomas Norton (translator of Calvin's *Institutes*, co-author of *Gorboduc*, and author of the "Induction" to *A Mirror for Magistrates*), John Hopkins, and even several more by Sternhold himself, previously unpublished.[32] Finally, in 1562, the very first edition of *The Whole Booke of Psalmes* was published, with the remaining psalms supplied by Hopkins, Norton, and William Marckant (a clergyman about whom little else is known).[33] Tunes were provided for each psalm, or cross-references pointed to suitable tunes elsewhere in the book. Despite its haphazard history, the dozen or so authors involved in its translations, the varied sources of its tunes, and the persistent tinkering by multiple editors, *The Whole*

30 The Elizabethan Injunctions of 1559, cited in Nicholas Temperley, *Music of the English Parish Church* (Cambridge, 1979), vol. 1, 39, and Peter le Huray, *Music and the Reformation in England 1549–1660* (Cambridge, 1967, rpr. 1978), 33.

31 On Elizabeth's fondness for Catholic liturgy and music, see le Huray, *Music and the Reformation*, 31–55, and also Francis Procter and Walter H. Frere, *A New History of the Book of Common Prayer* (London, 1951), 94, on the continuation of the celebration of the Mass in the Chapel Royal after 1559.

32 On matters biographical, see C. H. Garrett, *The Marian Exiles* (Cambridge, 1938), 204–05, Leaver, *Goostly Psalmes*, 235–37, 247–49, Robert Illing, *The English Metrical Psalter of 1562* (Adelaide, 1983), vol. 1, 35–36.

33 The work of several authors appeared for the first time (Thomas Becon, Robert Cox, Robert Wisdom), but as translators of canticles rather than psalms they fall outside the scope of this study. For further information, see the treatments of the canticles in Leaver, *Goostly Psalmes*; Temperley, *Music of Parish Church*; and Illing, *Metrical Psalter*.

Booke of Psalmes was now complete in the form in which it would remain, with minor alterations, for 150 years and more. It was as this integrated entity – a psalter – that the book had its greatest impact.

"STERNHOLD AND HOPKINS" IN PRACTICE

The Whole Booke of Psalmes was clearly designed for and adaptable to multiple purposes. The long-title of the first edition of *The Whole Booke of Psalmes* in 1562 ("*Very mete to be vsed of all sortes of people priuately for their solace & comfort,*" as in the 1560 *Psalmes of David*)[34] emphasized the private uses of psalms that Sternhold had stressed in his dedication to Edward VI. This recommendation does not necessarily imply that such private practice was the only one thought to be appropriate for these psalms, but such a practice is reinforced by the accompanying biblical epigraphs: "If any be afflicted let him praye, and if any be mery let hym sing Psalmes" (James 5:13); "Let the worde of God dwell plentuouslye in all wisedom teachinge & exhorting one another in psalmes, Hymnes & spirituall songs, & sing vnto the lord in your herts" (Coloss. 3:16).[35] The private and personal application of the psalms is further indicated by the inclusion of "A Treatise made by Athanasius," a translation of the fourth-century church father, "wherin is setforth, how, and in what manner ye may use the Psalmes, according to theffect of the minde" (sig. [+ vii^v]). Interestingly, the 1562 edition also included a supplement, "The use of the rest of the Psalmes not comprehended in the former Table of Athanasius" (sig. Aiii^r), which added to the rather haphazard table a set of applications particularly suitable to Englishmen in the 1560s. The first "use" in the supplement reads, "If thou wouldest prayse God, because he hathe geven us a good Prince whiche wyll and doth punish the enemies of Christes relygion, use the 21.Psalme" (sig. Aiii^r).[36] Athanasius's original recommendations were not without their polemical edge, but on the whole they were more general in their application (such as "If thou art escaped from enemies, and delivered from them which persecute the [*sic*], sing the 18. Psalme" [sig. + viii^r]).[37]

In the edition of 1574, the treatise of Athanasius was omitted (though it was occasionally included in subsequent editions such as 1598, 1604

34 *The Whole Booke of Psalmes* (London, 1562), sig. + i^r. All further citations from the *Whole Booke* will be from this (1562) edition, unless otherwise noted.

35 Not surprisingly, these epigraphs are in the translation of the Geneva Bible (1560).

36 Sternhold's "O Lord how joyfull is the king,/ in thy strength and thy power."

37 "O God my strength and fortitude,/ of force I must love thee:/ Thou art my castell and defence/ in mine necessitie," again by Sternhold.

[altered], 1605, and 1619), and the supplement to Athanasius was never reprinted. This does not mean, of course, that individual Christians did not continue to apply the psalms to their own particular conditions, singing, saying, or reading them silently as they chose, but the radical Protestant polemic had become redundant as the century progressed. The deletions may also reflect the establishment of "Sternhold and Hopkins" as the semi-official singing psalter of the Church, a communal resource equivalent to the modern hymnal and a book for the entire Church institution rather than an exclusive confessional group within it.

Despite its long-title and the implications for personal devotion of Athanasius's treatise, *The Whole Booke of Psalmes* of 1562 was also designed for the purpose of public worship. The most obvious evidence of this liturgical intent is the inclusion at the volume's beginning and end of numerous sacred songs, or "canticles," not found in the Book of Psalms. Although the texts were appropriate to private devotion – a domestic setting was, after all, the context of Mary's first singing of the canticle, *Magnificat*, at the Annunciation – they would have been most familiar from being sung in public worship services according to the rites of the Book of Common Prayer. The most familiar were the songs of praise, *Venite exultemus*[38] and *Te Deum laudamus*, which were sung at Morning Prayer (Matins), and the *Magnificat* (Luke 1:46–55) and *Nunc dimittis* (the "Song of Simeon," Luke 2:29–32), sung at Evening Prayer (Evensong). There were other sacred songs from the Bible, like the *Benedictus* (Zacharias's song from Luke 1:68–79) and the *Benedicite* (the apocryphal "Song of the Three Children" added to the Book of Daniel), as well as ancient hymns like *Veni creator spiritus*. There were versifications of the creed (the Apostles Creed, as well as the *Quicunque vult*, the Creed of Athanasius), the Ten Commandments (two versions), and the Lord's Prayer (also two versions). Finally, there were various other canticles, clearly intended for liturgical use (such as "A prayer unto the holy ghost, to be song before the Sermon" and "A thankes geving after the receyving of the Lordes Supper").[39]

[38] Psalm 95, not included as a separate canticle in the 1562 edition; a different version of the psalm was printed with the canticles in subsequent editions.

[39] The intended use of others is ambiguous (Robert Wisdom's "Preserve us, Lorde," for instance, a translation of Luther's hymn *Erhalt uns Herr*, or the generic songs "The lamentation of a Sinner" and "The humble sute of the Sinner"). The "lamentation" ("O Lord turn not away thy face") and the "Humble sute" ("O Lorde of whom I do depend") were both popular texts, being set by numerous composers for domestic use (see le Huray, *Music and the Reformation*), but there is no clear place for them in the public services of the Book of Common Prayer. It should be noted that the Book of Common Prayer was itself similarly designed for multiple purposes, including private devotion. The public purpose is examined by Ramie Targoff in *Common Prayer: The Language of Public Devotion in Early Modern England* (Chicago, 2001).

Like the canticles, some of the prose prayers included in the 1562 *Whole Booke* also indicate a liturgical intent. Though some were for private use (such as "A Prayer to be sayde before a man begin his worke" and "A formst [*sic*] of prayer to be used in private houses, every morning and evening"), many were appropriate to the corporate worship services of the Book of Common Prayer (for instance, those prayers designated "Morning Prayer" and "Evening Prayer"). The inclusion of these prayers and canticles suggests that the intention of the compilers was that *The Whole Booke of Psalmes* should be used in public worship,[40] as does, unequivocally, a later addition to the long-title: "Set forth and allowed to be song in all Churches, of all the people together before and after Morning and Evening prayer: as also before and after Sermons."[41]

If it is clear from internal evidence that the *Whole Booke of Psalmes* was intended to be used for both public worship and private devotion, it is harder to determine from documentary evidence precisely how it was used in actual practice. One reason for this lies in the ambiguous wording of the Elizabethan Injunctions. Taking the *via media* as always, Elizabeth allowed for a broad spectrum of Protestant worship practices, and this is reflected in the Elizabethan Book of Common Prayer.[42] At Matins, for example, after the *Venite exultemus* was sung (that is, Psalm 95, referred to in the 1559 Book of Common Prayer simply as "this Psalme folowyng"), the rubric reads, "Then shal folow certaine Psalms in ordre as they been appointed in a table made for ye purpose, except there be propre Psalmes appointed for that day."[43] At Evensong, psalms were to be sung before the Old Testament lesson.[44] In the 1549 Book of Common Prayer the Communion service begins with a psalm, adapting the earlier Roman Catholic practice of singing an introit at the opening of the Mass ("Then shall the Clerkes syng in Englishe for the office, or Introite, (as they call it,) a Psalme appointed for that daie").[45] The rubric calling for the introit psalm is omitted in the

40 One should note here the so-called "Middleburg psalms," discussed by Temperley (*Music of Parish Church*, vol. 1, 56), a series of editions of "Sternhold and Hopkins" which omitted all the hymns; later editions provided them on optional sheets at the end of the final gathering of psalms. Their omission of the canticles does not indicate a non-liturgical intent, however, but rather a rejection of the specific liturgies of the Book of Common Prayer.

41 The change is present in the 1574 edition (STC 2444), and perhaps earlier.

42 Actually, in terms of the place of psalmody in the services, no substantive changes were made from the first Edwardian Book of Common Prayer of 1549 (nor were there any, for that matter, in the 1604 Prayer Book of James I).

43 *The Book of Common Prayer. Commonly called The First Prayer Book of Queen Elizabeth. Printed by Grafton 1559*, facsimile edited by William Pickering (London, 1844), sig. I.iii.^{r}; *The First and Second Prayer Books of King Edward VI*, Everyman edition (London and Toronto, 1910, rpr. 1977), 22.

44 *First and Second Prayer Books*, 28; *First Prayer Book*, sig. K2^{r}.

45 *First and Second Prayer Books*, 212. See also Procter and Frere, *New History*, 461.

Elizabethan and Jacobean Prayer Books. This doesn't necessarily mean, however, that psalms, in meter or prose, were not sung at certain points in the service. They seem to have fallen into the category of the paraliturgical, as the motet did in the Roman Catholic liturgy.[46] That is, their use was not specified in the rubrics of the Book of Common Prayer, but seems nevertheless to have been traditional at certain points in the service.[47]

The injunctions also do not specify which translation of the Psalms was to be said or sung. The Book of Common Prayer, though not at first published with a psalter, includes a table of proper psalms and even prints the appropriate introit psalms for each Sunday of the year in Coverdale's translation from the Great Bible of 1539 (which eventually became the psalter included in the Book of Common Prayer). Coverdale's translations in prose might have been set to music, as in the post-Restoration psalm tradition of Anglican chant, whose practice continues to the present day.[48] Yet Anglican chant is not congregational music, but is performed by a professional or highly trained choir. Congregational singing, as Luther recognized, requires a more regular meter than was to be found in Coverdale's translation, however powerful its prose rhythms.[49] Along with regular meter in verse, communal singing also depends on singable tunes with easily accessible and memorable melodies, such as those in most of the Protestant metrical psalters. It is likely that at appropriate points in the service, the "Sternhold and Hopkins" psalms were substituted for the Coverdale versions specified or implied by the Book of Common Prayer.[50]

Though it may date from as early as the 1550s, a decade later, after the return of the Marian exiles and the reinstitution of Protestantism under Elizabeth, the practice of singing metrical psalms in church became widespread. While the debate continued through the seventeenth century about whether music was appropriate in public worship, and, if it was, what kind of music it should be, the congregational singing of metrical

46 See Anthony M. Cummings, "Toward an Interpretation of the Sixteenth-Century Motet," *JAMS* 34 (1981), 43–59, a study based on Sistine Chapel practice, but confirmed for English usage by Frank Ll. Harrison, *Music in Medieval Britain* (London, 1958), 228.

47 See Temperley, *Music of Parish Church*, vol. 1, 53–57.

48 See Peter le Huray, "Anglican chant," *New Grove Dictionary of Music and Musicians* (London, 1980), vol. 1, 430–31.

49 On the distinction between meter and rhythm (a distinction problematized further for literary critics by the differing use of these terms in music theory), see John Hollander, "The Metrical Frame," in *Vision and Resonance* (New York, 1975), 135–64.

50 Leaver suggests (*Goostly Psalmes*, 145) that such a substitution may also have occurred at the Gloria, which in the 1552 Book of Common Prayer was placed after the distribution of Communion, the very place for a metrical psalm in many Reformed liturgies, such as that which Pollanus designed for the French Stranger Church at Glastonbury – the Gloria, according to Leaver, may have been perceived as a "general hymn of praise," to be replaced by other such when appropriate or desirable.

psalms became entrenched in parish churches, while in the cathedrals and collegiate chapels the "Anglican" practice of more elaborate music sung by the choir was upheld, if not without exceptions.[51] Nicholas Temperley has documented the singing of metrical psalms even in the cathedrals, though such "low-church" practices were kept distinct from the main emphases of the service – the sermon and the Communion.[52] The records do not specify which metrical psalms were sung, but the only version widely and continuously in print was "Sternhold and Hopkins."

One can learn more about how the book was used and who used it by examining the physical forms in which the "Sternhold and Hopkins" psalter was available.[53] For instance, many of the surviving copies are bound together with editions of the Book of Common Prayer.[54] Many of these volumes also included copies of the Bible, in various translations – the Bishops', the Geneva, the King James Version, or even the 1535 Coverdale Bible, depending on the year and doctrinal leanings of the owner – as well as instructional aids like the *Genealogies* of "J. S." (describing the lineage of biblical characters) and various maps and indices of biblical names and places. One cannot place too much emphasis on the accidents of bookbinding, which may reflect the practice of the booksellers as much as the purchasers, but it does seem that the "Sternhold and Hopkins" psalter was widely available as one of a collection of service books which were often bound together in a single volume. Church records are of limited help in tracking the use of such volumes, but there are a few records of churches having purchased psalters for the use of their congregations. The church

[51] There was a lively and ongoing debate on the propriety and scriptural basis of singing psalms, let alone hymns, in church worship, but the flurry of tracts increased considerably during the 1640s and 1650s. See, for instance, N[athaniel] H[olmes], *Gospel Musick. Or, the Singing of Psalms* (London, 1644); John Cotton, *Singing of Psalms a Gospel-Ordinance* (London, 1647); Cuthbert Sydenham, *A Christian, Sober and Plain Exercitation on the Two Grand Practical Controversies of These Times; Infant-Baptism, and Singing of Psalms* (London, 1657); Isaac Marlow, *The Controversy of Singing Brought to an End* (1696). The controversy had been going on for some time, however. Lewis Bayly, in *The Practice of Pietie* (London, 7th ed., 1616), admonishes his reader to "beware of singing divine Psalmes for an *ordinarie recreation*; as doe men of impure Spirits, who sing holy *Psalmes*, intermingled with profane *Ballads*. They are *Gods Word*, take them not in thy mouth in vaine" (368–69). In 1597, Richard Hooker defends psalm-singing against Thomas Cartwright's charge that "what beginninge so ever it had, there is no possibilitie it should be good" (*Ecclesiastical Polity*, Book V, 157). Such anxiety about the profane delights of music actually goes back at least to Augustine's *Confessions* (Book 10, chap. 33).

[52] Temperley, *Music of Parish Church*, vol. 1, 42–44.

[53] The following section is based largely on my bibliographical research at the Beinecke Library of Rare Books and Manuscripts at Yale University, whose holdings include some sixty-five copies of "Sternhold and Hopkins" in various editions and formats.

[54] 1588 (STC 2475), 1604 (STC 2512a), 1606 (STC 2519), 1609 (STC 2528), 1612 (STC 2539), 1616 (STC 2555) and so forth.

at Ludlow at which the Sidneys worshiped, for example, bought six copies of "Sternhold and Hopkins" in 1559 and listed ten "Psalters" (unspecified) in 1588.[55] A few additional records of churches buying metrical psalms (unspecified, but probably "Sternhold and Hopkins") have been collected by Temperley.[56]

As mentioned above, the 1562 edition stressed the value of the psalms for personal devotions. Athanasius's treatise showed which psalms were best applied to each situation in which a godly Christian might find himself, and it seems evident from the physical evidence that this advice was taken to heart. For example, one copy of "Sternhold and Hopkins" printed in 1606, and bound with a 1605 Book of Common Prayer, has crosses handwritten in ink in the margin beside some dozen of Athanasius's "uses" of the psalms, indicating that one of the book's owners found these applications particularly relevant.[57] This use was in accord with Sternhold's original intentions, as he expressed them in his dedication to Edward VI. One who shared King Edward's (apparent) devotional tastes was the indefatigable diarist Nehemiah Wallington, who quotes "Sternhold and Hopkins" on two occasions. In 1632 he begins writing a volume on "God's wonderful works and fearful judgements," and after noting the commencement of this project Wallington quotes the final verses of Sternhold's Psalm 73:

> And lo, all such as thee forsake,
> thou shalt destroy each one:
> And those that trust in anything
> saving in thee alone.
> Therefore will I draw near to god,
> and ever with him dwell.
> In god alone I put my trust,
> thy wonders will I tell.
> (vv. 27–28)[58]

[55] See Alan Smith, "Elizabethan Church Music at Ludlow," *Music and Letters* 49 (1968): 112–13; cited in Margaret Hannay, *Philip's Phoenix: Mary Sidney, Countess of Pembroke* (New York and Oxford, 1990), 241, n. 12, who argues that the "Sternhold and Hopkins" psalms were an important part of the regular worship of Mary Sidney and her family (85–86). The small number of psalters purchased may reflect the use of the books by a choir, or by singing leaders (see Temperley, *Music of Parish Church*, vol. 1, 89, on the practice of "lining-out"), or simply the limited budgets of a parish church. Clearly many parishioners owned copies of service books, so it was unnecessary for the church to provide them for all, as is the usual practice today.

[56] Temperley, *Music of Parish Church*, vol. 1, 61–62. He comments that "since most parish churches had to buy the prayer book and prose psalter as well as the metrical psalms, these were frequently sold as a single volume."

[57] *The Whole Booke of Psalmes* (1606, STC 2519) in a deluxe binding, with the Book of Common Prayer, at the Beinecke Library (Mzj 145 +A4 1605).

[58] Cited in Paul S. Seaver, *Wallington's World: A Puritan Artisan in Seventeenth-Century London* (Stanford, 1985), 210–11, n. 15.

Five years later, in 1637, Wallington records that he has been chosen constable for his ward, and celebrates the event by transcribing the last verse of Sternhold's Psalm 66:

> All praise to him that hath not put
> nor cast me out of mind,
> Nor yet his mercy from me shut
> which I do ever find.[59]

Though few people kept such voluminous journals as Wallington, the place of the "Sternhold and Hopkins" psalms in his life was shared by many of his countrymen. Lady Margaret Hoby, for instance, wrote in her diary that she played the orpharion, and scarcely ever sang anything other than psalms.[60] (Given the number of times they were set to music, the psalms of "Sternhold and Hopkins" were very likely among those she sang.) These psalms were sung every week at church, which must have lodged at least a few verses in the memory of most parishioners. But they were readily available at home too. Folio and quarto editions of "Sternhold and Hopkins" were often bound with family Bibles, as in the case of Thomas Ruff, who shortly after the Restoration wrote his name in his copy of the Geneva Bible and *The Whole Booke of Psalmes* (both 1599), wherein a manuscript note records the number of people (8,252) who died from plague and other diseases between August 29 and September 5, 1665. John and Thomas (perhaps sons?) both wrote their names in 1697. Another Geneva Bible of 1611–12, bound with a 1611 Book of Common Prayer and a 1609 *Whole Booke of Psalmes*, records in manuscript the history of Mary Murphy and her family from her birth in 1669 through her death in 1704. Such writings are commonly found in the large Bibles surviving from the sixteenth and seventeenth centuries and confirm the use of the Bible as a family resource.[61] Many of them contained the "Sternhold and Hopkins" psalms, accessible to any family member who wanted to read or sing them.

This singing may have been a solitary pastime (people used to read aloud to themselves so it is conceivable that they also sang to themselves,

59 Ibid.

60 *The Diary of Lady Margaret Hoby 1599–1605*, ed. Dorothy Meads (London, 1930), 92, 99, 148, 165, 181. The orpharion was a steel-stringed member of the lute family that experienced a vogue in England at this time.

61 As was the practice, the large family Bible was used to record a variety of information, genealogical and otherwise, such as the following, perhaps plague-related, home remedy: "to stop spitting of blood take stinging nettles and comfry spring them with whjite wine vineger pound it and straine it and let the party take 4 spoonfulls at a time being sweetend with serop of Redwood" (written on the verso of the title page of the New Testament of a Geneva Bible [1599] at the Beinecke Library [Mlm131 599b]).

or, of course, to God), or it might more likely have been an activity that included family or friends. Such use of *The Whole Booke of Psalmes* is indicated, along with those of public worship and private devotion, in the first complete edition of 1562. Preceding the treatise of Athanasius, the reader of "Sternhold and Hopkins" would find "A shorte Introduction into the Science of Musicke, made for such as are desirous to have the knowledge therof, for the singing of these Psalms" (sig. + ii^r). This self-help guide for the musically disadvantaged seems in itself to indicate home use, although it could also have been intended as homework for the congregation, to improve the church music. Reading on, one finds the editors' intentions expressed more clearly, encompassing all three functions:

> For that the rude & ignorant in Song, may with more delight desire, and good wyl: be moved and drawen to the godly exercise of singing of Psalmes, aswell in common place of prayer, where altogether with one voyce render thankes & prayses to God, as privatly by them selves, or at home in their houses: I have set here in the beginning of this boke of psalmes, an easie and moste playne way and rule, of the order of the Notes and Kayes of singing. (sig. + ii^r)

The "Introduction" is a guide to sightsinging, focusing on "Notes and Kayes," according to the system of modes then in use, as well as matters of melodic and rhythmic notation. One application of this knowledge is clearly the improvement of psalm-singing by Christians "at home in their houses." The singing of metrical psalms at home, often on Sundays or after meals, is well documented. Wallington mentions that his family devotions included psalm-singing.[62] Patrick Collinson notes a number of instances of family psalm-singing, as by the Suffolk minister Samuel Fairclough, who, on Sundays after supper, "caused some part of Foxe's 'Book of Martyrs' to be read and, having prayed, concluded the day with the singing of a psalm."[63] Psalm-singing was a part of regular after-dinner activities in the Wirral in Merseyside, as people from across the peninsula met at the homes of the more prosperous members of the community. Indeed, this domestic practice was widespread among English Protestants, especially those of Puritan leanings.[64] Psalms were even sung by families on the way

[62] Seaver, *Wallington's World*, 211, n. 15. Probably because it was the preeminent psalter and therefore essentially equated with singing-psalms, references to "Sternhold and Hopkins" by name are scarce. In any case, it was undoubtedly the most widely available version.

[63] Patrick Collinson, *The Religion of Protestants* (Oxford, 1982), 265, quoting from Samuel Clarke, *The Lives of Sundry Eminent Persons* (1683).

[64] Collinson, *Religion of Protestants*, 264–68; as he sums it up, "cathechizing, prayer, and psalm-singing . . . was part of the daily round of every godly household."

to and from church. At Calk, Derbyshire, people went home singing psalms after hearing the preacher Julines Herring; John Bruen, with family and household, sang psalms regularly on the way to church.[65]

Catering to those who included psalm-singing among their regular household activities was a growing music publishing industry, which, along with the editions of "Sternhold and Hopkins" containing unison melodies, produced many volumes of psalms set to simple or even relatively complex harmonies, providing a sacred analogue to the volumes of secular madrigals and part-songs much in vogue in the late sixteenth and seventeenth centuries.[66] Several of these volumes appeared under the "Sternhold and Hopkins" title: *The Whole Booke of Psalmes.* John Day printed an edition of *The whole psalmes in four partes* in 1563 (STC 2431), with music by William Parsons and others, but it was apparently not successful, since it was never reprinted.[67] A volume of four-part settings of "Sternhold and Hopkins" psalms by William Damon was published in 1579, apparently without his consent, and Thomas East (or Est, or Este) published another *Whole Booke* with four-part music in 1592 (STC 2482). Thomas Ravenscroft's edition published in 1621 (STC 2575) was perhaps the most successful, although it includes some borrowed material from earlier volumes such as Day's and East's. It contained settings by the best composers of the time: Thomas Tallis (his famous "Canon"), John Dowland, Thomas Morley, Thomas Tomkins, John Milton (Sr.), and others, as well as by Ravenscroft himself. Ravenscroft also includes a lengthy introduction discussing the history of the music of the psalms, and begins by stressing that the harmonized tunes he offers "are so Composed, for the most part, that the unskilfull may with little practice, be enabled to sing them in parts, after a plausible manner."[68] Other volumes containing harmonized settings of "Sternhold and Hopkins" were published by John Cosyn (1585), Richard Alison (1599), William Barley (1599), and even William Byrd (1588 and 1589), committed Catholic though he was. The tunes for these harmonized editions, whether found in the treble voice or, fauxbourdon-style, in the tenor, were still for the most part the familiar ones available in the unison volumes but

65 Ibid., 260.

66 On music publishing in England, which began only in the 1550s, see D. W. Krummel, *English Music Printing, 1553–1700* (London, 1975); R. Steele, *The Earliest English Music Printing* (London, 1965); Kyle C. Sessions, "Song Pamphlets: Media Changeover in Sixteenth-Century Publication," in *Print and Culture in the Renaissance*, ed. Gerald P. Tyson and Sylvia S. Wagonheim (Newark, London, and Toronto, 1986), 110–19.

67 Temperley, *Music of Parish Church*, vol. 1, 53–54.

68 *The Whole Booke of Psalmes*, ed. Thomas Ravenscroft (London, 1621) (STC 2575.3).

harmonized in more or less sophisticated ways depending on the composer involved.[69] Whatever the musical aptitude of the performer, it is evident that the "Sternhold and Hopkins" psalms were sung and heard in homes all over England.

In fact, *The Whole Booke of Psalmes* was "popular" in a broader sense than might usually be acknowledged.[70] Between 1562 and 1596, a period of less than 150 years, "Sternhold and Hopkins" was continuously in print in over 700 editions of all shapes and sizes, printed simply or lavishly, with music or without, bound within the same cover as Bibles, prayer books, and sermons, or on its own.[71] It was even available in shorthand.[72] For a century and a half, it was the most widely known volume of verse in English and made its way into the hands of English men and women of all social classes who otherwise had little in common.[73] The singing of psalms by weavers, for instance, and other Protestants of the artisanal class was proverbial, as indicated by Sir John Falstaff's expression of mock-piety in *Henry IV, Part I*: "I would I were a weaver; I could sing psalms or any thing." Similarly mocking is the reference to a sheep-shearer in *A Winter's Tale* who is said

[69] For more information, see le Huray, *Music and the Reformation*, 370–402, and Illing, *Ravenscroft's Revision of Est's Psalter*, 2 vols. (Adelaide, 1985).

[70] The work of Bob Scribner on popular culture in Reformation Germany provides a theoretical frame that also applies, in certain ways, to the use of "Sternhold and Hopkins." Scribner shows the limitations of the traditional bipolar model that distinguishes sharply between the categories of "popular" and "elite." The subject of his study is the relationship between the "liturgy," the property of the elite (especially the clergy), and what he calls "folklorized ritual," paraliturgical practices like the Boy Bishop or the *Palmesel* (the procession of a figure on an ass on Palm Sunday). Scribner argues that these categories overlap considerably, and that there was a broad overlap in cultural experience (for his study, the complicated elements of religious practice) shared by the members of all classes of society. In the same way, the "Sternhold and Hopkins" psalter, the singing of which was another paraliturgical experience, was familiar to men and women across the social (and doctrinal and political) spectrum. See R. W. Scribner, "Ritual and Popular Religion in Catholic Germany at the Time of the Reformation," in *Popular Culture and Popular Movements in Reformation Germany* (London, 1987), 17–47.

[71] According to the Short-Title Catalogues (Pollard and Redgrave and Wing).

[72] A shorthand edition was published in 1660 by Jeremiah Rich, and another around the same time by Thomas Shelton. The purpose of these curious volumes seems to have been instructional.

[73] That "Sternhold and Hopkins" verses were considered to have a literary as well as devotional status is illustrated in John Bale's 1557 *Scriptorum illustrium maioris Brytannie*, in which Sternhold is clearly described as being a poet, though of a different sort than those who write "*amatoriae & obscoenae cantiones*" (see Zim, *English Metrical Psalms*, 143 and 295, n. 128). This is a natural conclusion, given the widespread sense that the original Hebrew Psalms were poetic texts. Thomas Becon, in *Davids Harpe* (1542), urges schoolmasters to teach the "verses of David" rather than those of Virgil, Ovid, Horace, and others (cited in Hallett Smith, "English Metrical Psalms in the Sixteenth Century and their Literary Significance," *Huntington Library Quarterly* 9:3 [1946], 259). Becon ranks these works on the basis of the critical distinction between sacred and profane, but they are all "verses." King cites Crowley's desire that his metrical psalter will inspire his readers "to delyte in the readynge and hearynge" of poetry (*English Reformation Literature*, 210).

to be a Puritan who "sings psalms to hornpipes."[74] Nehemiah Wallington was one such artisan, a turner, and his journals show that he not only sang or read the psalms, but that he used the "Sternhold and Hopkins" version. On the other hand, aristocrats like Lady Margaret Hoby also turned to the psalms in their spare hours, and "Sternhold and Hopkins" was familiar to other members of her class. For instance, Richard Alison dedicated his *The psalmes of David in meter* (1599), artful musical settings of "Sternhold and Hopkins" texts, to Lady Anne, countess of Warwick, a relation of Lady Margaret's by marriage.[75] (Indeed, Alison's book would have appealed to Lady Margaret too, since they could be sung to the accompaniment of the orpharion, her chosen instrument.)

"Sternhold and Hopkins" was available in small, cheap octavos and duodecimos affordable by the poorer folk, as well as in elaborately printed and bound quartos and folios catering to the wealthy. One copy, bound with the Geneva Bible, is printed in two colors of ink and bound so lavishly, in finely tooled leather with the Garter Arms embossed front and back, that for many years it was thought to have been a copy printed for Queen Elizabeth's Chapel Royal.[76] Another copy survives, bound together with the Bible in the King James Version, in an elaborate satin and needlework binding, stitched in silver thread at Little Gidding, where George Herbert's friend Nicholas Ferrar had established a genteel religious community devoted to prayer and useful crafts, including book-binding.[77] The description in Izaak Walton's *Life of Mr. George Herbert* of the devotional practice of Ferrar and his family emphasizes the central role of the Psalms in their daily routine:

> And there [in the church] they sometimes betook themselves to meditate, or to pray privately, or to read a part of the New Testament to themselves, or to continue their praying or reading the Psalms: and, in case the Psalms were not all alwaies read in the day, then Mr. *Farrer* [Ferrar], and others of the Congregation, did at Night, at the ring of a Watch-bell, repair to the Church or Oratory, and there betake themselves to prayers, and lauding God, and reading the Psalms that had not been read in the day; and, when these, or any part of the Congregation grew weary, or faint, the Watch-bell was Rung, sometimes before, and sometimes after Midnight: and then another part of the Family rose, and maintain'd the

74 William Shakespeare, *Henry IV, Part I*, 2.4.133–34 and *A Winter's Tale*, 4.3.44–45, from *The Riverside Shakespeare*, 2nd ed., ed. G. Blakemore Evans, et al. (Boston and New York, 1997).

75 See *Diary*, 278 n. 441. Lady Margaret records visiting the countess on Feb. 28, 1600/01.

76 STC 2502, at the Beinecke Library (Mlm131 601), owned and signed in the eighteenth century by Harriett, dowager countess of Essex. Despite its lavishness (and the Garter Arms) it seems to have been an expensive trade edition rather than a royal commission.

77 Wing B2449, at the Beinecke Library (Mlm143 657), signed in 1683 by a Judith Bourne.

Watch, sometimes by praying, or singing Lauds to God, or reading the Psalms: and when after some hours they also grew weary or faint, then they rung the Watch-bell, and were reliev'd by some of the former, or by a new part of the Society, which continued their devotions (as hath been mentioned) until morning. – And it is to be noted, that in this continued serving of God, the Psalter, or whole Book of Psalms, was in every four and twenty hours, sung or read over, from the first to the last verse: and this was done as constantly, as the Sun runs his Circle every day about the World, and then begins again the same instant that it ended.[78]

"Sternhold and Hopkins" was read by the well-educated, not only by the unschooled. Editions were printed by the university presses at Oxford and Cambridge, and copies survive bound with the Book of Common Prayer in Latin and Greek, and with manuscript copies of learned academic sermons.[79] It should be noted too, lest one follow Falstaff too closely in associating "Sternhold and Hopkins" and psalm-singing exclusively with the Puritans, that these versions were used by Royalists of presumably high-church leanings as well as their lower-church countrymen. One copy, for example, survives bound with a rare Laudian edition of the Book of Common Prayer, which was suppressed because of its Catholic attitude toward the Mass (signaled by the extra-large type font used for the words of consecration with its consequent implications of transubstantiation).[80] Several editions of "Sternhold and Hopkins" also survive bound in manuscript commonplace books that seem to have been designed as blank notebooks intended specifically for the recording of sermons and prayers in church (hence the inclusion of the singing psalter for the convenience of the worshiper). One of these contains, in addition to various sermons, a "List of Condicions requird in a Meritorious work," notes on the proper practice of public confession, and an explanation of the reasons magistrates are "cald Gods."[81] Such subject matter points to the "Arminian" or high-church persuasion of the volume's owner. After the Restoration, copies of "Sternhold and Hopkins" were bound with the Prayer Book of Charles II, complete

[78] Izaak Walton, *The Lives of John Donne, Sir Henry Wotton, Richard Hooker, George Herbert, and Robert Sanderson* (London, New York, and Toronto, 1927, rpr. 1973), 311.

[79] As with the Beinecke Library's copy of Wing B2526 (1998 287), bound with a Latin *Liturgia* (London 1677), and the Beinecke Library copy of STC 2524 (1607) (Mrp23 w638), bound with a 1638 Greek Liturgy and New Testament.

[80] STC 2599 (1627), at the Beinecke Library (1973 +84).

[81] Osborn pb83. Another later volume (Osborn b248) includes manuscript prayers for Charles II, Queen Katherine, and James duke of York, and a 1669 sermon on 1 Sam. 16:7, beginning, "When God created man as the last of his most noble works, that hee might crown him, as the end, and perfection of his workmanship he made him a King at first; he gave him rule and dominion over all the creatures of the earth."

with added services commemorating the martyrdom of Charles I.[82] By contrast, yet another of the commonplace books bound with "Sternhold and Hopkins" includes a manuscript note dated 29 January 1648, regarding an Order of Parliament concerning "Republican style" in the dating and formulation of parliamentary documents.[83] Another edition of "Sternhold and Hopkins," a volume tiny enough (32mo) to fit in a pocket, was obviously printed for the Puritan (or at least staunch Calvinist) reader, since it included a long prose "Confession" dwelling on matters of Judgment, Election, the sufficiency of Scripture, and ecclesiastical discipline.[84] There is even an edition of "Sternhold and Hopkins" (1606) bound with a Book of Common Prayer (1605) that seems designed to appeal to one for whom Christian and classical mythology were not incompatible, printed with enlarged woodcut initials featuring Greek myths (the letter "B" features Hercules battling Cerberus, "I" has Apollo and Daphne, "L" has Perseus rescuing Andromeda, and so forth).[85]

THE LONGEVITY OF "STERNHOLD AND HOPKINS"

The question of why *The Whole Booke of Psalmes* was so popular for so long is ultimately unanswerable, depending on such elusive matters as taste and the aural perception of poetic meter. The versatility of its design, accommodating private reading and devotion, or communal singing in the church liturgy, as well as a variety of recreational uses, was certainly instrumental in establishing "Sternhold and Hopkins" as the standard psalter for a broad audience. Yet there are other possible factors in the persistence and popularity of "Sternhold and Hopkins." It owes as much, for instance, to the nature of the English publishing business as to the intrinsic merits of the book as a liturgical/devotional/recreational resource. *The Whole Booke of Psalmes* of 1562 was printed by John Day, "*Cum gratia et privilegio Regie Maiestatis.*" To him and his son and heir, Richard, and their assigns, was granted the monopoly of printing all psalms in meter (as well as "the ABC with the little catechism").[86] The monopoly of the Day family was eventually purchased by the Stationers Company during the reign of James I

82 As does the copy of Wing B2481B in the Osborn Collection at the Beinecke Library (Osborn pb86), bound with a 1665 Book of Common Prayer.

83 Wing B2425 (1647) in the Osborn Collection (Osborn b312).

84 Wing 2391B (1642). The edition also contains citations from Ecclesiasticus and Augustine's *Confessions* supporting the use of music in worship.

85 STC 2519 in the Beinecke Library (Mzj145 +A4 1605). The woodcuts were probably borrowed by the printer from another, secular, publication.

86 Cyprian Blagden, *The Stationers' Company: A History, 1403–1959* (Cambridge, MA, 1960), 63.

and became one of the components of the English Stock, the royal grant "to the whole Companie of Stacioners for the benefit of the poore of the same that they and none others shall ymprint the Bookes of private prayers, prymers, psalter and psalmes in English or latin, & Almanrackes [*sic*] and Prognosticacions within this Realme."[87]

Such monopolies were common practice in the publishing trade at the time. They assured a great deal of money for those lucky enough to procure monopolies in perennially popular books, but they also made competition virtually impossible, as George Wither found to his great frustration during James I's reign.[88] The Stationers did from time to time license the printing of other psalters (Sir Edwin Sandys's 1615 *Sacred Hymns*, for instance, a selection of fifty psalms). These were always in limited numbers, however, and were seldom reprinted, assuring the continued hegemony of "Sternhold and Hopkins" in church and home. Offenders against the monopoly, like Wither, were vigorously prosecuted. Of course, no printer can control the sales of his books, but the monopoly of the Days and then the Company of Stationers played an undeniably important role in suppressing alternative versions of the metrical psalms, at least until the abolition of the Courts of Star Chamber and High Commission in 1641 weakened the authority behind the royal patent.[89]

Another factor in the adherence to "Sternhold and Hopkins" may have been its perceived authority as an accurate translation of the Hebrew Psalms. After all, the Genevan translators and editors of *The Whole Booke* had stressed on the title page that it was "conferred with the Ebrue."[90] The earlier partial editions had been even more explicit, stating, as in the 1556 *One and Fiftie Psalmes of David* cited above, that the Psalms had been "conferred with the hebrewe, and in certeyn places corrected as the text and sens of the Prophete required."[91] Such a statement might be expected from the scholars who also translated the Geneva Bible, which was to be the predominant English Bible for the better part of a century.[92] Yet the claim that the new, rival versions were closer to the original Hebrew has been questioned[93] – indeed most new psalters, like most new vernacular Bibles, made the same claim. Of those Genevan exiles who provided psalms for "Sternhold and Hopkins," Whittingham was seemingly the only

87 Ibid., 75, 92.

88 See the treatment of Wither and his psalter in the next chapter. On the Stationers and the psalter, see James Doelman, "George Wither, the Stationers Company and the English Psalter," *Studies in Philology* 90:1 (1993, Winter), 74–82.

89 Blagden, *Stationers' Company*, 130.

90 *The Whole Booke of Psalmes* (1562).

91 Title page cited in Frost, *Psalm & Hymn Tunes*, 5.

92 See Norton, *Bible as Literature*, esp. chaps. 2 and 5.

93 Zim, *English Metrical Psalms*, 140–44.

one who was a Hebrew scholar, though even in his case there is scant evidence on which to rely.[94] Of the others – Kethe, Pullain, Norton, and Marckant – even less is known. It is unlikely that either Sternhold or Hopkins knew any Hebrew, since neither of them was a scholar, and few, even of those who were, knew Hebrew at the time. Like Coverdale and most of the other early psalm translators, Sternhold and Hopkins were probably translating from a combination of other English and Latin translations. This is why the Genevans felt the need to "confer with the Ebrue" and amend the translations of the two original authors.

Yet, even if "Sternhold and Hopkins" (in its post-Genevan state) remained the most accurate metrical translation, would that account for its lasting success? The members of English congregations could hardly distinguish one version from another on this basis. It was evidently enough that they were *told* that "Sternhold and Hopkins" was accurate. This is what they were told about many subsequent psalters too, such as Henry Ainsworth's (he actually knew Hebrew), or Wither's version, "translated in Lyrick-Verse, according to the scope of the Original."[95] But "Sternhold and Hopkins" had established itself first, perhaps taking on the presumed authority of age and tradition. In any case, much as it might disappoint Whittingham and the others, the key to the success of the "Sternhold and Hopkins" psalter was likely not its scholarship.

Since they were also songs, especially songs intended in part for congregational singing in church, the "Sternhold and Hopkins" psalms cannot be analyzed or judged on purely literary grounds. Poets and critics have long been puzzled and frustrated by the popularity of the *Whole Booke*, but the explanation of its lasting popularity undoubtedly depends to a great extent on the power of the tunes to which they were commonly sung. A recent scholar of the English hymn describes the complex nature of congregational singing in terms that apply equally well to both hymns and metrical psalms:

> A hymn exists, not just on the page, but in sound; it functions in a private reading, but also in a church. The building is filled with sound, made by musical instruments and human voices, and the text becomes no longer the marks on the page but a series of sounds in the air. It may be revisited later, and reflected upon, but it is no longer just a text, no longer writing, but something else in addition to writing. In

[94] G. Lloyd Jones, *The Discovery of Hebrew in Tudor England: A Third Language* (Manchester, 1983), esp. 127–32.

[95] Ainsworth's *The Booke of Psalmes Englished* (1612) achieved some currency among sectarians, especially in New England. He published his psalter in Amsterdam, where he led a separatist congregation. See Philipp von Rohr-Sauer, *English Metrical Psalms from 1600 to 1660* (Freiburg, 1938), 50–52. For Wither's long-title, see the Spenser Society reprint of his *Psalmes*.

the sense that it exists in a book, and that book may be held in the hand and read, the hymn is there as writing; but it is only there because it is also music, sacred song, congregational praise.[96]

Richard Hooker was also impressed by the experience of "sacred song," but in his account (paraphrasing Basil) the power of music is celebrated for its didactic role in the teaching of religious doctrine:

[W]hereas the holie spirite saw that mankinde is unto virtue hardly drawen, and that righteousnes is the lesse accompted of by reason of the pronenes of oure affections to that which delighteth, it pleased the wisdome of the same spirite to borrowe from melodie that pleasure, which mingled with heavenly mysteries, causeth the smoothnes and softnes of that which toucheth the eare, to conveye as it were by stelth the treasure of good things into mans minde. To this purpose were those harmonious tunes of the psalmes devised for us, that they which are either in yeares but younge, or touchinge perfection of vertue as yeat not growne to ripenes, might when they thinke they singe, learne. O the wise conceipt of that heavenly teacher, which hath by his skill found out a way, that doinge those things wherein we delight, wee may also learne that whereby wee profitt.[97]

As outlined above, this understanding of music's ability to carry meaning, essentially seducing people into righteousness, was a commonplace among sixteenth-century Reformers, lying at the root of the tradition of metrical psalmody. (The sense of music's primacy is confirmed by the expressions of anxiety about its seductive power that often accompanied statements in its praise. As Hooker noted, "there is nothinge more contagious and pestilent then some kindes of harmonie; then some nothinge more stronge and potent unto good.")[98]

In an essay on the "objective factors" which constitute a successful hymn tune, John Wilson helpfully identifies four key attributes: (1) its melodic outline, (2) its rhythm, (3) its harmony, and (4) its overall structure.[99] Of these, the third, "harmony," is not especially relevant to "Sternhold and Hopkins," since the editions published for congregational singing were printed with melodies only. In terms of the other three factors, it is easy to see why people enjoyed singing the "Sternhold and Hopkins" psalms. The tune for Psalm 1 is a good example:[100]

96 Watson, *English Hymn*, 23.

97 Hooker, *Ecclesiastical Polity*, chap. 38.1, "Of musique with psalmes," 153–54.

98 Ibid., 151. Augustine was similarly nervous about music (see n. 51, above).

99 John Wilson, "Looking at Hymn Tunes: The Objective Factors," in *Duty and Delight: Routley Remembered*, ed. Robin A. Leaver and James H. Litton (Norwich, 1985), 124.

100 Transcribed from *The Whole Booke of Psalmes* (1562), notation modernized. No. 15 in Frost, *Psalm & Hymn Tunes*.

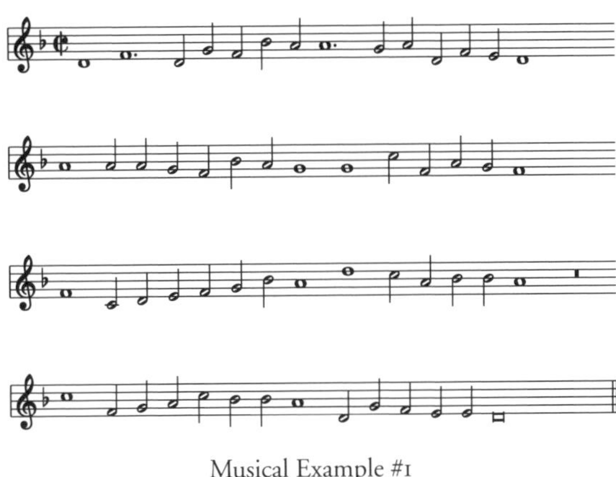

Musical Example #1

The "melodic outline" lies within a single octave, keeping well within the vocal range of the average untrained singer. It also combines stepwise motion with leaps of larger intervals in a way that lends enough variety, yet without too much complexity. Rhythmically, the tune is simple, with only a few slight syncopations caused by the dotted whole notes. Otherwise, it consists of half notes punctuated by longer notes (wholes, dotted wholes, and a final breve) at the middle and end of phrases. The "overall structure" is perhaps the tune's greatest strength. It begins plaintively, with a rising minor third, which falls back and is followed by a sequence of two ascending and overlapping fourths, before falling back from the B-flat to the A (the fifth of this mode, what in modern terms would be called D-minor).[101] The second half of the phrase mirrors the first and returns to the Tonic (D). The second phrase begins on the fifth, but really shifts the mode from D-minor to F-major, closing with an arpeggiated triad C—F—A which then falls stepwise down the major third to finish on F. The first half of the third phrase begins on the same note, descends a fourth to a C, from which it then ascends, but it continues up past the F and repeats the B-flat to A closing figure of the first half-phrase, creating a symmetrical shape. The second half of the third phrase begins by leaping to a D, the highest point in the melody. This, and the neighboring semitone figure, A—B-flat—B-flat—A that ends the phrase, return the tonality to D-minor. The first half

101 For ease of reference and comprehension, modern musical terminology is used to describe these psalm tunes, though the use of "key" and the "major/minor" dichotomy is, of course, anachronistic for mid-sixteenth-century musical practice, as are "half" and "whole" notes.

of the third phrase, built on the triad F—A—C, seems a shift back to the F-major, but the final phrase returns solidly to D-minor, beginning and ending on the Tonic. A number of successful tunes that Wilson cites follow a roughly *aaba* structure. The Psalm 1 tune follows a slightly more complex pattern, but one which also demonstrates the essential combination of "unity" and "variety."[102] The initial and final notes create symmetry and stability: the tune begins and ends on D, as does the first phrase; the second begins on A and ends on F, while the third begins on F and ends on A. Yet the tune is also built around the cadential figure of the B-flat falling to A. The first half-phrase ends with this figure, as do both halves of the third phrase, and the first half of the final phrase. The first half of the second includes the figure but moves through it to a G, marking a shift in tonality. These tonal and thematic repetitions make the tune both satisfying to sing and easy to remember.

Despite its pleasing "structure," however, the tune does not fit the text of Psalm 1 especially closely, and indeed, since the tune is metrically in double common meter (covering two common meter stanzas), some adjustment would have to have been made for verse 6, an odd extra stanza. Verses 1 and 2 of the text (four lines each) take up one complete singing of the tune, as does the double-length, eight-line verse 3, and verses 4 and 5 follow the pattern of the first two. This leaves only the four lines of the final verse, half the length needed to cover the whole tune. Perhaps the last half of the tune would have been repeated. In any case, the plaintive minor mode of the tune does not seem especially suited to Psalm 1's positive focus on the just man who follows the law. It seems no better suited to Psalm 2, the subject of which is warfare among and against the heathen, yet curiously this psalm was intended to be sung to the same tune as the first. Again, there is an extra odd stanza that does not quite fit the tune. Significantly, these factors make the psalm no less enjoyable to sing.

An outstanding feature of the "Sternhold and Hopkins" tunes is their rhythmic energy, generated by a fine tension between a strong regular rhythm and syncopations that, in a curious way, reinforce the regularity by disrupting it. The tune for Psalm 3 has this kind of rhythmic "punch":[103]

102 Wilson, "Looking at Hymn Tunes," 141–45.

103 Transcribed from *The Whole Booke of Psalmes* (1562), notation modernized. No. 17 in Frost, *Psalm & Hymn Tunes*.

Musical Example #2

Yet the plaintive opening of Psalm 3, "O Lord how are my foes increast,/ which vexe me more and more," actually seems better suited to the minor mode of the Psalm 1 melody than this more uplifting major tune (though the tone of the psalm does shift when the psalmist praises the Lord's execution of revenge on his enemies). It is also true that aspects of performance (tempo, volume, style, even vocal timbre) could greatly affect the perception of a tune.[104]

There are many powerful and memorable melodies in the *Whole Booke of Psalmes*, a number of which survive in modern hymnals, which surely testifies to the pleasure congregations derive from singing them. (Hymn 532 in the Episcopal *Hymnal 1982*, for instance, uses the "Old 104th" originally sung to Psalm 104, and the "Old 100th," discussed below, is found in many hymnals.)[105] The literary aspects of these translations are not necessarily an essential component of that pleasure, however. In terms of the experience of singing such psalms, it would make little difference, for instance, that Sternhold's common meter psalms are rhymed *abcb* (as in Psalm 1) whereas Hopkins's are rhymed *abab* (as in Psalm 31). In both cases, the musical phrase creates an irresistible pause after the second line (as in the above example from Psalm 1), at which point the congregation would breathe.

104 The same point is made, in a different context, by Daniel Fischlin, in *In Small Proportions: A Poetics of the English Ayre 1596–1622* (Detroit, 1998), who argues that a performer can make significant differences in how the relationship between music and text is perceived in the English ayre (217–19 and *passim*). The same is true, though in less subtle ways, for the congregational psalm or hymn.

105 *The Hymnal 1982* (New York, 1985), used by the American Episcopal Church. The "Old 100th" is used in this same book for Hymn 377, Kethe's Psalm 100, "All people that on earth do dwell," and Hymn 380, Isaac Watts's "From all that dwell below the skies".

The question of which rhyme scheme might be smoother or create less of a regular "thump" is simply moot, at least in terms of the success of the psalms as songs. So too is the question of irregularity or roughness.

One critic has referred to the "robust crudity" and "surprising energy" that one can find in the "Sternhold and Hopkins" psalm texts.[106] Such praise (however qualified) seems borne out by the nineteenth-century admission of Alice Morse Earle, who goes even further:

> I must acknowledge quite frankly in the face of critics of both this and the past century that I always read Sternhold and Hopkins' Psalms with a delight, a satisfaction that I can hardly give reasons for. Many of the renderings, though unmelodious and uneven, have a rough vigor and a sweeping swing that is to me wonderfully impressive, far more so than many of the elegant and polished methods of modern versifiers.[107]

Though Earle might not have been especially drawn to the sentiments of Psalm 58 (the Psalter's most violent curse), the visceral quality of Sternhold's translation is surely an example of what she calls "rough vigor":

O God breake thou their teeth at once,
  within their mouthe throughoute:
The tuskes that in their great chawbones
  lyke Liones whelpes hange oute.
Let them consume awaye and wast,
  as water renth fourth right:
The shaftes that they do shout in haste,
  let them be broke in flight.
As snailes doo wast within the shell,
  and unto slime do runne:
As one before his time that fell,
  and never saw the sunne.[108]

Yet even some of the more clumsy lines in "Sternhold and Hopkins" could still have been sung with satisfaction to a good tune, which tends to gloss over and regularize any awkwardness.

William Kethe's long meter translation of Psalm 100, for example, "All people that on earth do dwell," is the most famous and long-lived of the "Sternhold and Hopkins" psalm texts. It has survived largely by riding the coat-tails of the "Old 100th" tune. The text itself seems unexceptional, even awkward at points (as in the inverted syntax of "Him serve with fear, his

[106] Coburn Freer, *Music for a King: George Herbert's Style and the Metrical Psalms* (Baltimore and London, 1972), 67 and 70.

[107] Alice Morse Earle, *The Sabbath in Puritan New England* (New York, 1891), 187.

[108] Ps. 58:6–8, *The Whole Booke of Psalmes* (1562).

praise forth tel"). Nor do the words fit the tune especially well, particularly in the last two stanzas:[109]

Musical Example #3

All people that on earth do dwell,
sing to the Lord with chereful voyce:
Him serve with feare, his praise forthe tel:
Come ye before him and rejoyce.

The Lord, ye knowe, is god in dede:
Without our aide, he did us make:
we are his folke: he doeth us fede,
And for his shepe he doeth us take.

Oh, entre then his gates with praise:
Approche with joye his courts unto:
Praise, laude, and blesse his Name always:
For it is semely so to do.

For why? the Lord our God is good:
His mercie is for ever sure:
His trueth at all times firmely stoode,
And shal from age to age indure.[110]

Here is an example of the perennial problem with strophic song settings: even when the music complements the first verse well, it often does so less well with subsequent verses. So, for instance, the strong cadence at the end of the second line of music, with three descending longer notes, is inoffensive and supports the natural word accent in the first verse under the affirmative "chereful voyce." In the third stanza, the musical emphasis given "courtes unto," especially the final syllable, works against the natural word accent. The highest note in the tune, which gives any syllable sung to it an unavoidable emphasis, is the first of the fourth line (C). This seems appropriate for the imperative, "Come," in the first stanza, but in each

[109] Tune for William Kethe's Psalm 100 (the "Old 100th"), transcription based on Frost, *Psalm & Hymn Tunes*, no. 114.

[110] As quoted in Leaver, *Goostly Psalmes*, 237 (Ex. 42).

subsequent stanza, the word given such prominence is, nonsensically, a conjunction ("And, "For," "And"). Finally, one of the few rhetorical nuances in Kethe's translation is the question posed at the beginning of stanza four, "For why?" Yet this interrogative demands a different vocal intonation (rising, with a pause) than is possible with the existing tune, which charges on as if the line were in the same continuous syntax as the first line of the first stanza.

The unavoidable conclusion is that these inadequacies of verse or text-setting have made no difference whatsoever to the lasting success of the psalm as a hymn or to the Church's continuing loyalty to it. English-speaking congregations all over the world have been singing Kethe's words to the "Old 100th" for 450 years, and it is not because Kethe achieved subtleties that surpassed the more modest accomplishments of his colleagues. Kethe's text has survived because, for millions of church singers, it has been inextricably connected to the "Old 100th" tune, partly because of the mnemonic power of music (as the sixteenth-century Reformers well knew, it is much easier to remember words put to a tune, because the tune is easier to remember than the text). The "Old 100th" has survived because it is a satisfying tune. The long history of the popularity of the "Sternhold and Hopkins" psalter can probably be explained in similar terms. The tunes are compelling, congregations enjoyed singing them, the texts were associated with the familiar tunes, and so the whole package resisted change for 150 years. The judgment of the "hoi polloi" was not really the "lottery" that Dryden claimed; it was simply based on non-literary criteria.

CHAPTER 2

"Out-Sternholding Sternhold": some rival psalters

It is a mark of the pervasive seventeenth-century interest in metrical psalms that the project of replacing "Sternhold and Hopkins" attracted a huge diversity of translators, representing a startling range of aesthetic, doctrinal, ecclesiastical, and political positions. Dozens of psalters to rival "Sternhold and Hopkins" were produced in this period, by, among others, the Royalist adventurer George Sandys, the Parliamentarian populist George Wither, the artisan Henry Dod, and Bishop Henry King. The issue of "English" metrical psalmody in fact extended beyond the borders of England. James I himself hoped to produce a new version of the singing-psalms for the British Church. On his death, this psalter was completed by William Alexander, Lord Sterling, and James's son, Charles I, attempted to introduce it to Scotland along with the Book of Common Prayer.[1] The Scots, however, had their own ideas, adopting in 1650 a new psalter, largely the work of Francis Rous, the Puritan provost of Eton College.[2] American independence from the English Church was also marked by the adoption of a new metrical psalter, the famous *Bay Psalm Book* of 1640. Many more psalters were in fact produced than ever saw publication, as attested to by surviving manuscript psalters by Sir John Denham and Thomas, Lord Fairfax, as well as by other less notable authors.[3]

The published psalters fall roughly into two very uneven groups: those (the majority) which tried to beat "Sternhold and Hopkins" at their own game, using the same meters and the (by now) traditional tunes, and those (principally Sandys's) which struck off in a new direction. That none of the many psalters produced in the seventeenth century proved a serious rival

[1] Doelman, *King James I*, 135–157.

[2] Millar Patrick, *Four Centuries of Scottish Psalmody* (London, Glasgow, and New York, 1949), 79–104.

[3] Denham's psalms were published only in 1714, after his death. Fairfax's *A Paraphrase of the Psalms and other Parts of Scripture* survives in the Bliss Collection (see Rohr-Sauer, *Metrical Psalms 1600–1660*, 25–26). John Harington also apparently wrote a psalter, which he tried to publish with the support of James I, but was unsuccessful (see his letter to King James, in *Letters and Epigrams of John Harington*, ed. Norman Egbert McClure [Philadelphia, 1930], 143–44, cited in Doelman, "George Wither," 74).

to "Sternhold and Hopkins" is not really surprising. Sandys was writing for a different audience, or at least for a different style of worship, while the psalters written for popular liturgical use worked against themselves by repeating the existing meters and tunes, leaving little incentive for churches or individuals to invest in the alternative versions when they seemed hardly different from the familiar one they already knew and enjoyed. What follows is a selection of some of the more interesting and important seventeenth-century psalters, with a representative sample of five psalms (1, 22, 84, 100, 148) providing a basis for comparison.[4]

GEORGE WITHER'S BATTLE OF THE (PSALM) BOOKS

One of the most colorful characters among those who produced metrical psalters in the seventeenth century was George Wither. Like so many others', his psalms were written in the same meters as those they were designed to replace, the intention being that congregations would thus not have to give up their favorite tunes. Wither was immensely prolific, beginning his literary career writing satires (sharp enough to put him in prison for a time), then penning several books related to the Psalms and a notable book of emblems, before turning later in life to composing long poems of social and political prophecy (*Britain's Remembrancer* and *Vox Pacifica*, for example). Though his *Hymnes and Songs of the Church* (1623) was approved by James I and his *Preparation to the Psalter* (1619) and *Psalmes of David* (1632) were dedicated, respectively, to James's son and daughter, Prince Charles and Princess Elizabeth, Wither was on the Parliamentary side in the Civil War, fighting as a major in Cromwell's army.[5] A singular moment in the history of the English psalmists came when Wither was taken prisoner during the war. He was in serious danger of execution, but Sir John Denham, himself a poet and translator of psalms, but on the Royalist side in the war, intervened with the king on Wither's behalf, for the stated reason that at least "whilest G. W. lived, he [Denham] should not be the worst Poet in England."[6]

[4] To some extent this is an arbitrary choice of "test" psalms, necessitated by the size and variety of the Psalter, but they are psalms not treated at length elsewhere in this study and represent various genres (a wisdom psalm, a lament, and several hymns of praise).

[5] As further preparation for his psalter, Wither also wrote *Exercises upon the First Psalm* (1620). On Wither's early life, see Charles S. Hensley, *The Later Career of George Wither* (The Hague and Paris, 1969), 14–40, and Joan Grundy, *The Spenserian Poets* (London, 1969), 161–80. On Wither's politics, especially during the Civil War, see Christopher Hill, "George Wither and John Milton," in *English Renaissance Studies Presented to Helen Gardner*, ed. John Carey and Helen Peters (Oxford, 1980).

[6] This story is told in John Aubrey's life of Sir John Denham, in *Aubrey's Brief Lives*, ed. O. L. Dick (Harmondsworth, 1949, rpr. 1982), 183. Not surprisingly, its authenticity has been questioned. See

Wither turned to the Psalms relatively early in his career, publishing first *A Preparation to the Psalter* (1619), in which he expounded on the history and current state of scholarship regarding the nature of Hebrew poetry, his plans to produce a new translation of the Psalter and his reasons for so doing, and the principles he intended to follow in this forthcoming translation (for the elaborately engraved title page, see figure 1). Even if Wither had never produced his *Psalmes*, he would still have an important place in the history of English psalmody, for the *Preparation* was a major contribution to English biblical scholarship, the most extended work on its subject produced before the eighteenth century, and an immensely useful book for the study of the Psalms in this period.

Like so many of his contemporaries, Wither's principal motive in translating the Psalms was dissatisfaction with "Sternhold and Hopkins." He expressed his embarrassment at "Papist" criticism of "*Geneva Jiggs*, and *Beza's Balletts*," and the degraded understanding of the Psalms as poetry that had resulted from the proliferation of inadequate popular versions set to tunes in the Genevan tradition ("Sternhold and Hopkins" the most prominent):

> Because the Elegancies of these sacred *Poems* have in our Language beene over-meanly exprest (or rather for that the prayses of God make teadious Musicke in the eares of most men) they have seemed unto many but barraine and simple *Poesie*; and the greater number take so small heed of their excellencie, that, for ought I can perceive, they sing or read them, with the same devotion, wherewith (as the Proverbe is) Dogges goe to Church. Yea, so far are they from knowing any one degree of their excellency, as I beleeve (but that they will say they talke of God) they can speake as much for the stories of *Guy* of *Warricke*, or *Beavis* of *South-hampton*: which I am sorry for.[7]

In his effort to correct misconceptions about the "Elegancies" of the Psalms, Wither assembled as much as was then known about the nature of Hebrew poetry, drawn from several dozen Latin, Greek, and Hebrew authorities (whom he listed in a catalogue at the beginning of the book, "because I will not presume to deliver anything unto you, meerely upon my owne credit").[8] He got no further than any of his contemporaries toward an

David Norbrook, "Levelling Poetry: George Wither and the English Revolution, 1642–1649," *English Literary Renaissance* 21:2 (Spring, 1991), 217 and n. 2.

[7] Wither, *Preparation*, 68. Page numbers are those of the original text, as reproduced in the Spenser Society edition. *Guy of Warwick* and *Beavis of Southampton* were popular Romances.

[8] Ibid., sig. [A5^r]. The list is impressive, including church fathers like Augustine, Ambrose, Josephus, and Origen as well as more recent scholars, including Cardinal Bellarmine, John Selden, Johannes Reuchlin, and Joseph Scaliger. His Jewish sources include Moses Maimonides and David Kimhi.

Figure 1. Francisco Delaram, title page to George Wither, *A Preparation to the Psalter* (London, 1619).

accurate understanding of the nature of Hebrew poetry, but he was as well versed as any of them in erroneous theories. Wither had a little Hebrew, enough to cast a sprinkling of words and phrases into his book, but not enough to base any of his literary argument on a close-reading of the original text. In his defense, however, none of Wither's more learned contemporaries were any closer to understanding Hebrew poetry than he was.[9]

An interesting feature of Wither's psalm translation is his attitude to the general public, the members of the English Church who for the most part would use his psalter. Despite his show of erudition, he was not aiming his *Psalmes* at the scholarly community, but at the ordinary members of church congregations. Yet he is clear in distinguishing himself from the crowd, especially from those who make spurious claims to interpretive authority on the basis of spiritual inspiration. Wither stresses that "those who know me can tell, that I am no *Weaver*, nor *Shoo-maker*, that would challenge by some extraordinary gifts of the *Spirit* (which he dreames of) the Authority of a Teacher in the Church."[10] (Here again is the psalm-singing weaver mocked by Falstaff in Shakespeare's *Henry IV Part I.*)[11] A few years later, Wither railed against the psalter of Henry Dod, "the silkemans late ridiculous translation of the Psalmes, which was by authority worthily condemned to the fire."[12] Wither's ire seems to have been aroused by a comparison of his own psalms to those of this unworthy artisan (a "silkman" being presumably no better than a "weaver").

Several things are curious about Wither's attitude. First, there is relatively little qualitative difference to the modern ear/eye (or perhaps even seventeenth-century ones) between his psalms and Dod's. Though both Dod and Wither claimed to be responding to a widespread sense of the inadequacies of "Sternhold and Hopkins," they both maintained the meters of the Old Version and intended their psalms to be sung to the customary tunes. Wither may have been the more accomplished metrist of the two, but their psalms are hardly different in kind. Furthermore, Wither was no more translating from the Hebrew than was Dod, as he openly admitted:

> [My] trust is, that I have done nothing but what shall appeare to be decent and allowable; seeing the forme onely of the Worke is new, and little of the matter. For if you have respect to the *Measures*, know that I have not undertaken to present

[9] See Kugel, *Idea of Biblical Poetry*, esp. chap. 6; Israel Baroway, "The Bible as Poetry in the English Renaissance: An Introduction," *Journal of English and Germanic Philology* 32 (1933), 447–80.

[10] *Preparation*, 21.

[11] See chap. 1.

[12] *The Schollers Purgatory* (1624), 33. See Doelman, "George Wither," 76–77, for the argument that the burning of Dod's psalms (for which there is no surviving evidence except Wither's remark) was the result of a violation of the Stationers monopoly.

the world, with any new Translation of my owne, out of the *Hebrew*; but onely turned that which we already have, into *verse* . . .

First, I have endeavoured a *Translation* of the *Psalmes* into verses of severall kinds, keeping (so neere as I could doe) even the very words of our English *Translation*, because I would give the lesse cause of offence to the captious Reader.[13]

These passages indicate some of the strangeness, to a modern reader, of sixteenth- and seventeenth-century notions of translation, especially of the Bible, and raise some interesting questions about the relationship between a translation and its "original."

What, for instance, is one to make of Wither's distinction between "forme" and "matter"? The most obvious aspect of "forme" in metrical psalms is surely meter, yet Wither's meters are identical to the "Sternhold and Hopkins" psalms he intended to replace. He claims it an advantage not to have undertaken any alteration "in respect of the Measures." But what, then, does he mean by "forme"? He doesn't seem to be thinking of words, since he also claims to be following "our English *Translation*." And what of "matter"? This seems to be what a modern reader might think of as "content," and yet how is such "matter" separable from the words in which it is expressed? Wither claims he has stayed close to the existing translation, which is surely a matter of vocabulary. Furthermore, one wonders what Wither has in mind in referring to "our English *Translation*." Since the *Preparation* was published in 1619, he could mean the King James Bible of 1611, the so-called "authorized" version. Yet, as David Norton has pointed out, the King James Version (KJV) was by no means authoritative, or even normative, in the first half of the seventeenth century.[14]

Wither sometimes seems to be following the KJV, but given the number of English Bibles in circulation at this time, let alone separate English psalters (especially Coverdale's Prayer Book version), it is hard to be sure. Wither's Ps. 84:9, for example, begins "Oh God our sheild!," which is closer to the KJV ("Behold, O God our shield") than Coverdale ("Behold, O God our defender"),[15] but the "shield" in the KJV is also found in the earlier translations of the Geneva and Bishops' Bibles. Wither's translation of verse 1, "Oh Lord of Hoasts! how pleasant are/ Thy dwellings," is closer to Coverdale's "O how amiable are thy dwellings" than the KJV's "How amiable are thy tabernacles."[16] Wither's verse 6 – "As, through the vale of tears they goe" – also seems derived from Coverdale, following his semi-allegorical "vale of misery" rather than the KJV's more historical "vale

[13] *Preparation*, 20, 22. [14] Norton, *Bible as Literature*, esp. chaps. 3–11.

[15] Wither, *Psalmes*, original spelling. All citations from Wither's psalms will be from the Spenser Society edition.

[16] Ibid.

of Baca." The truth seems to be that Wither had no single authoritative translation in mind. For Wither, as for many of his non-Hebrew-reading contemporaries, the "original" of the Bible was a kind of notional composite of the prominent existing English versions.[17] For the Psalms, this meant primarily, but not exclusively, the Coverdale Psalter in the Book of Common Prayer, and the Geneva and the King James Bibles. This may well have been the case for most of the history of the Bible in translation. When Sternhold wrote to Edward VI that the King could "judge myne endevoure by youre eare" because "ye have the Psalme it self in youre mynde," he seems to be referring to the same notional original as Wither, though a narrower one, of course, including primarily the Coverdale Bible (1535) and the Great Bible (1539).[18]

To return to Dod the Silkman, he made essentially the same claims as Wither in the preface to *Al the Psalmes of David* (1620) – that he was responding to a general desire to "have the . . . booke of Psalmes reformed in meeter," in the same spirit as King James's "reformation of all the Psalmes in prose."[19] Like Wither, Dod used the same meters as "Sternhold and Hopkins," in fact reducing, for ease of singing, what metrical variety there was in the original *Whole Booke of Psalmes.* (Sternhold and Hopkins had adhered to the common meter, but many of the later translators explored different forms, which gave the psalter an interest not usually acknowledged and one surprisingly similar in its apparent aesthetic motivation to that of the Sidney Psalter, and that of Archbishop Parker.) Dod hoped that his book would "not be found different from the text, by the judgement of the best writers upon the Psalmes that are extant, and approoved by the Church of England namely and principally, the newe translation in the Kings booke, M. Beza afore-said, Tremelius and Junius, Molerus, and Piscator."[20] Dod may not have consulted as many authorities as Wither, but neither was

[17] Norton (*Bible as Literature*, 132) describes this version as "an imagined, not a real one, which [Wither] identified in his own mind with the Hebrew."

[18] Sternhold's dedicatory preface to *Certayne Psalmes*, sig. A.iii.[r]. There were also the so-called Matthew and Taverner Bibles of 1537 and 1539, but these are highly derivative of the Tyndale–Coverdale translations (see Charles Butterworth, *The Literary Lineage of the King James Bible* [Philadelphia, 1941], 110–18, 125–28). It is probably also true, especially in the sixteenth century but also in the seventeenth (for Donne, for instance), that for many people the sense of the "original" Scriptures included, at some level, the Latin of the Vulgate that had been authoritative for so many centuries.

[19] Dod, *Al the Psalmes of David* (n.p., 1620), sig. [*5v]. That Dod followed primarily the KJV is supported by the printing of the King James text in the margins of his psalter.

[20] Ibid. By "M. Beza" he means the Paraphrases on the Psalms of Théodore de Bèze, translated by Anthony Gilby (1580). Immanuel Tremellius and Franciscus Junius produced a Protestant Latin Old Testament (1575–79). Johannes Piscator translated the Bible into German in 1602–03. "Molerus" may be Heinrich Moller, a theologian at Wittenberg and friend of Melanchthon, and author of *Enarrationis Psalmorum Davidis* (Geneva, 1591). For assistance with the identification of Moller, I am indebted to Roger Kuin.

he one of Wither's weavers or shoemakers writing only as the spirit moved him. Even if Dod's psalms were more awkward than Wither's, that does not seem an offence worthy of the public book-burning Wither referred to (see note 12), especially since Dod claimed (like Wither) a royal sanction for his psalms, and wrote that he had been persuaded to publish only because no one more accomplished had done so:

> And whereas I have Waited nowe XVIII yeares for the performance of this worthie worke, by some godly learned, whom I hoped wold have donne it in manner better beseeming the same (as I published in mine epistle, with the said IX Psalmes [his *Certaine psalmes* of 1603]) but sawe it not donne, and my self (the Lords most unworthie) so over-ruled as afore-said, pardon me I praye thee thus to present thee with these my labours, unworthie of thy acceptation.[21]

Wither made the identical claim in his own preface: "I waited long, to see a more exact performance: But, none appearing, answerable to the dignitie of our English-Muses, I have sent forth my Essay, to provoke others, to discover their endeavours, on this subject; that, choice being had, the best might receive the best Approbation."[22]

Wither's condemnation of his fellow translator is certainly ungracious, especially since the burning of Dod's book was likely the result of the same struggle against the monopoly of the Stationers Company that so frustrated Wither, the primary topic of the very book (*The Schollers Purgatory*) in which the lines about Dod appear. The monopoly of the Stationers Company on the printing of English psalters has already been referred to as one of the principal reasons for the longevity of the "Sternhold and Hopkins" psalter (see chapter 1). Wither's difficulties with the Stationers were many and ongoing, as James Doelman has shown (sorting out some confusions from previous studies).[23] The Stationers Company objected first to the unlicensed publication of *Wither's Motto* in 1621. They then refused to honor the patent granted to Wither by James I, instructing that his *Hymnes and Songs of the Church* (1623) be bound with all English psalters. The final conflict was over the publication of the *Psalmes of David*, a project that

[21] Dod's prefatory epistle "To the Christian Reader," sig. [*6^{r-v}]. The modest disclaimer is conventional, but in this case it does have the ring of truth, given the gap between Dod's publications of 1603 and 1620. Doelman (*King James I*) argues convincingly that it was the planned but continually postponed psalter of James I that inhibited the publications of Wither, Dod, and others during his reign.

[22] Wither, *Psalmes*, sig. [A6^{r}]. Perhaps Wither's disclaimer is also genuine, since so many years passed between the publications of the *Preparation* (1619) and the *Psalmes* (1632), but the principal reason for Wither's delay seems to have been his difficulty with the Stationers.

[23] Doelman "George Wither" and *King James I*. The remainder of this paragraph is indebted to Doelman's article on Wither.

occupied Wither over many years. The intended grandeur of the publication is indicated by the folio format of the *Preparation*, with its lavishly engraved title page, which contrasts sadly with the eventual appearance of the *Psalmes* as a plain 16mo published in the Netherlands.

Despite Wither's condemnation of ignorant artisans like Dod and his extensive description of the "Elegancies" of the poetry of the Psalms, his translations were intended for popular use by the unlearned, as he makes clear in his preface:

> I have had more care, to suite the Capacitie of the Vulger, then to observe those Criticisms which arride [delight] the Learned: yet, I hope, with so much discretion, that the best Judgements shall have no cause to despise it. For though the language be plaine, it is significant; and such a Dialect as is likely to continue unchanged when fantasticall expressions will growe as unfashionable as our clothes.[24]

Wither's use of "plaine" style seems to have been intended primarily to encourage churches to use his psalter, overcoming the objections of those who noted that "every man almost, is so well exercised in the Psalmes and tunes allowable in our Church, that he can make one of the Quire: whereas if new notes and Measures, should be brought in their steed, there would be few or none in our assemblies . . . to joyne together in that devotion."[25]

The plainness of Wither's psalms is evident in his translation of Psalm 1, which does not seem radically different from the translations of either Sternhold or Dod:

> The man is blest, who neither straies,
> Where Godles counsellers have gone,
> Nor standeth in the Sinners waies,
> Nor sitteth on the Scorners throne.
> For, in Gods Lawe his pleasures be;
> Theron he day and night bestowes.
> And, therfore shal be like a tree
> Which near unto the river growes.
> His fruites, in season, he doth give,
> Green leaves he shal for ever wear:
> All things he takes in hand shall thrive
> But, thus the Sinner doth not fare.
> (Wither)

> The man is blest that hath not bent,
> to wicked rede his eare:
> nor led his life as sinners do
> nor sat in scorners chair.

[24] Wither, *Psalmes*, sig. [A6r]. [25] *Preparation*, 9.

But in the law of god the lord,
    doth set his whole delight,
and in the law doth exercise,
    him selfe both day and night.

He shall be like the tree that groweth,
    fast by the river side:
Whiche bringeth forth most pleasant fruite
    in her due time and tide.
(Sternhold)[26]

O Blessed man that doth not in
    the wicked counsel walke:
nor stand in sinners waye, nor sit
    in seate of scornefull folke.
But in JEHOVAHS lawe he doth
    repose his wholle delight:
And in his lawe doth meditate
    with comfort daye and night.
And he shalbe lyke planted tree
    by water-rivers aye:
Which duly bringeth foorth his fruit,
    his leafe shall not decaye.
(Dod)[27]

Dod was clearly glued to Sternhold's model, introducing just enough variation to make his psalm recognizably different, though his "by water-rivers aye" introduces a singular awkwardness all his own, of the sort that so irritated Wither. Wither's psalm has few very striking differences from Sternhold's, and, despite the extra syllables of his long meter, it uses just as many lines for these verses as the two common-meter versions. The addition of color to the leaves is pleasant, and his conversion of the "chair" (or "seat," as in KJV) to a "throne" suggests some pointed inclusion of monarchs among the "Scorners." This would be curious, however, in a volume dedicated to the sister of King Charles, and in fact in Wither's earlier *Exercises upon the First Psalme*, he translates the word differently and interprets it without reference to kings: "For, by *Chayre*, or *seate*, is understood; a desperat security, and divelish obstinacy in malicious wickednesse; and hee is properly said to *sit* there, that continues in his perversenesse, without repentance, unto the end of his life."[28] Wither likely chose "throne" because it rhymes (more or less) with "gone." Metrically, apart from the addition of the *ac* rhyme,

[26] Ps. 1:1–4, trans. Thomas Sternhold, in *The Whole Booke of Psalmes* (1562).
[27] Ps. 1:1–4, trans. Henry Dod, *Al the Psalmes.* [28] Wither, *Exercises*, 36 (original pagination).

there is little to distinguish his version from Sternhold's or indeed, apart from the occasional awkwardness, from Dod's.[29]

In other psalms, Wither followed the meter of "Sternhold and Hopkins" even more closely, as in the common meter of Psalm 22:

O God, my God, wherfore doest thou,
 forsake me utterly:
And helpest not when I doo make,
 my greate complaynte and cry.
(Sternhold)

Why hast thou, O my God, my God
 Why hast thou me forgone?
Why, nearer is not thy abode;
 To hear and help my mone?
(Wither)

In this case, Wither has significantly altered the "matter," however much he claimed not to have done so. The English Bibles all complain of God's "far-ness," as in the KJV's "why art thou so far from helping me?" Wither's explicit emphasis on the distance of God's "abode" from humanity, suggesting a God separated from his Creation, is singular and has theological implications (concerning whether God is immanent in or transcendent of the world). Wither also made some subtle changes in vocabulary which emphasize the traditional Christian reading of this psalm as, to quote Wither's description, "a prophecie of Christ his passion."[30] Verse 17, which in the KJV reads "they pierced my hands and feet," was altered by Wither to the more specifically prophetic, "My hands and feet, they nailed fast." He also changed the "congregation" of the Bible versions ("in the midst of the congregation will I praise thee," in the KJV) to the anachronistic but more English "church." But then, this was simply following Sternhold's "And in thy church shall praise thy name."

Unlike Dod, whose principal objection to "Sternhold and Hopkins" was that it was not homogeneous enough, so that "divers of the singing Psalmes [were] much out of use onely because of the difficultie of their tunes,"[31]

[29] The claim of Rohr-Sauer that "Wither's own innovation in the CM [common meter] is a definite caesura at the end of the first *ab*," while accurate as far as Wither's practice is concerned, seems equally true of Sternhold's and Dod's (Rohr-Sauer, *Metrical Psalms 1600–1660*, 17). Rohr-Sauer also states that Wither is closer to the Hebrew than is "Sternhold and Hopkins," which, if true, can only be coincidental, given how derivative of previous English versions his are, along with his limited knowledge of Hebrew.

[30] From Wither's headnote to the psalm. Wither's Christian typological reading of Psalm 22 is hardly original, of course, since Christ himself quotes it on the cross (Matt. 27:46).

[31] Dod's preface to *Certaine Psalms*, 3.

Wither maintained even the meters set to the most idiosyncratic tunes. John Pullain's translation of Psalm 148 (in "Sternhold and Hopkins") uses a stanza consisting of four iambic trimeter lines and four dimeters, rhymed *ababcddc*:

> Geve laud unto the Lord,
> From heaven, that is so hie:
> Praise him in dede and word
> Above the starrie skie.
> And also ye
> His angels all,
> Armies royall
> Prayse him with glee.

Wither uses the same stanza (the sixth and seventh lines are printed as one long tetrameter, but the rhyme pattern suggests that this arrangement is simply typographical):

> The Lord of heav'n confesse;
> On high, his glories raise:
> Him, let all Angels blesse;
> And, all his Armies praise.
> Him, glorifie
> Sunn, moone and starres; yee higher Spheares,
> And, Cloudie skie.

The reason for Wither's adherence to Pullain's metrical model is simple – it fits the old tune, which, though it continued to be printed in some seventeenth-century editions of "Sternhold and Hopkins," is surely one of the "difficult" ones Dod hoped to make obsolete (notably, his Psalm 148 is written in common meter):[32]

Musical Example #4

[32] Transcribed from *The Whole Booke of Psalmes* (1562), notation (except rests) modernized. No. 174 in Frost (*Psalm & Hymn Tunes*), though Frost's transcription must be from an edition later than 1562, since it introduces a B-flat not in the original and has different note values for the final lines. For the history of variations on this tune in the early editions of "Sternhold and Hopkins," see Illing, *English Metrical Psalter*, vol. 2, "Psalm 148."

Unlike many of the tunes in "Sternhold and Hopkins," this one begins with a wide leap, avoids any clear tonal center, and punctuates the short lines of Pullain's psalm stanza with longer note values that interrupt the contour of the musical line. Wither may have been trying to accommodate the traditional tunes, but in this case he seems likely to have been perpetuating one that was traditionally hard to sing.[33]

A few of Wither's psalms are written in more unusual meters, notably a short trimeter line of (apparently) his own devising. Psalm 100 uses this meter, with an added (and, for the "Sternhold and Hopkins" psalms, still more unusual) feminine rhyme:

Rejoyce in God, yee Nations,
    In chearfulnes, adore him;
With joyfull acclamations,
    Present your Selves before him:
For, God the Lord, did make us,
    No hand therein had wee;
He, for his flock doth take us,
    His Pasture-sheep wee be.
His Gates and Courts, possesse yee,
    To thanck him, goe yee thither;
His Name, with gladnes, blesse yee,
    And sing his praise togeither:
For, God is kinde, for ever,
    His grace, he freely daignes;
His Truth, will faile us never,
    For, endles, it remaines.

It is hard to know what Wither intended congregations to make of this psalm and others like it, since it would not fit the tune normally sung for Psalm 100 (common meter in the 1562 *Whole Booke* and long meter in the more famous "Old 100th" sung to the version of the psalm by William Kethe substituted in later editions)[34] and he provided no indication of an alternative tune.[35] Significantly, Wither included a second version of Psalm

[33] It is worth noting that, though Pullain's meter proved quite popular, being used by Tate and Brady for their Psalm 148 and by Richard Baxter for his hymn, "Ye holy angels bright," these two texts were (and still are) sung to other tunes. In *The Book of Common Praise* of the Anglican Church of Canada (Toronto, 1938), for example, the former is sung to "Croft's 136th" (by William Croft, 1709) and the latter to the wonderful "Darwall" (Rev. J. Darwall, 1770). In this same meter (6.6.6.6.4.4.4.4.) is John Ireland's beautiful tune "Love Unknown," usually sung to Samuel Crossman's 1664 hymn, "My song is love unknown."

[34] For the tune of the "Old 100th," see chap. 1, 48–50.

[35] There is some confusion about the musical aspect of Wither's psalter. Rohr-Sauer states (*Metrical Psalms 1600–1660*, 17) that it was published with tunes composed by Orlando Gibbons. In fact,

100, this time in long meter. In any case, despite Wither's efforts and his long battle with the Stationers, and despite, further, the prominent place which he is generally accorded (as here) in the history of English psalmody and hymnody, his psalter was largely ignored by his contemporaries, if indeed they were even aware of it.

GEORGE SANDYS: PSALMS FOR KING AND COURT

George Sandys was another remarkable character of Renaissance psalmody.[36] His father, Edwin Sandys, was archbishop of York. George, the youngest of seven sons, embarked on a life of poetry and adventure. After some years at Oxford, he spent many months traveling in Turkey, Egypt, the Holy Land, and Italy, and published his journals as *A Relation of a Journey begun An: Dom: 1610. Foure Bookes Containing a description of the Turkish Empire, of Ægypt, of the Holy Land, of the Remote parts of italy, and Ilands adjoyning* (London, 1615). His next adventure was in Virginia, where he lived for about ten years as Treasurer of the Virginia Company. During his years in Virginia, in which he also lived through the notorious Jamestown Massacre of 1622, he wrote a translation of Ovid's *Metamorphoses*, published in installments from 1621 to 1626. This celebrated work is often described as one of the first literary productions in America, though at least part of it was finished before Sandys left London. On his return to England in 1625, Sandys was made a Gentleman of the Privy Chamber to Charles I and became attached to Falkland's court at Great Tew, a major cultural center whose visitors included William Chillingworth, Sidney Godolphin, Henry Hammond, Edward Hyde, Edmund Waller, and perhaps Abraham Cowley, Thomas Hobbes, and John Selden.[37] It was during this time that he wrote and published his biblical paraphrases, as well as *Christ's Passion*, a translation of a Latin verse tragedy by Hugo Grotius.

Next to the Sidney Psalter, the *Paraphrase upon the Psalmes* by George Sandys was the most highly praised English translation of the Psalms in

Gibbons wrote tunes for Wither's earlier *Hymnes and Songs of the Church*, while the *Psalmes* was published without music and was explicitly intended to be used with the existing church tunes: "respecting them who cannot attaine to many Tunes, I confined my selfe to such kinds of Verse as I found in the old Psalmebooke; fitting them in such manner, that every Psalme in this Booke, may be sung to some Tune formerly in use" (*Psalmes*, sig. [A6^{v}]).

36 The biographical information on Sandys in this paragraph is based on Richard Beale Davis, *George Sandys, Poet-Adventurer* (London and New York, 1955).

37 Some scholars are rightly skeptical about many of the so-called literary or cultural "circles" of early modern England (see n. 53 on the "Pembroke Circle" in chap. 3). The point is not that there was such a "circle," with a particular membership, but simply that Great Tew was a cultural center visited at one time or another by many eminent figures, and that Sandys was often there.

the Renaissance. The *Paraphrase* was published in 1636 with verse epistles by Sir Dudley Digges and Lucius Cary, Viscount Falkland. When it was reprinted with Sandys's paraphrase of Job and other biblical poems, there were further poems of praise from Henry King, Thomas Carew, Sidney Godolphin, and Edmund Waller. This publication, utterly unlike Wither's, was clearly a literary event.

In the 1636 volume, Digges used a favourite image from Psalm 137 to praise his cousin Sandys. The Jews in exile in Babylon found themselves unable to sing, so they hung their harps on willows; Sandys, in Digges's view, enabled his countrymen to take up their harps again:

> Amphion did a Citie raise,
> By his Layes:
> The Stones did dance into a Wall,
> At his call.
> But your divinely-tuned Aire,
> Doth repaire
> Ev'n Man himselfe, whose stony Heart,
> By this Art,
> Rebuildeth of its owne accord,
> To the Lord,
> A Temple breathing holy Songs,
> In strange Tongues.
> You fit both Davids Lyre, and Notes,
> To our Throats.
> See, the greene Willow now not weares,
> Of their Teares
> The sadly silent Trophyes, wee
> From the Tree,
> Take downe the Hebrew Harps, and teach,
> In our speech,
> What ever wee doe hate, what feare,
> What love deare.[38]

Digges went on to say that he and his countrymen owed it to Sandys that God is "delighted with our Griefe," since "unto You wee owe the Joyes,/ The Sweet Noise/ Of our ravisht Soules."[39]

Falkland was more formally restrained in his verses, but full of praise, especially for Sandys's turning from secular to sacred poetry:

[38] Digges, "An Ode to my worthy Kinsman Master George Sandys upon his Excellent Paraphrase on the Psalmes," in Sandys, *Psalmes*, sig. G[r]. Digges's reversal of the figure of exile in Psalm 137 is notably similar to that used by Edmund Waller in his praise of Davenant's *Gondibert*, which is interesting, given that Waller also contributed a poem to Sandys's volume. See below, chap. 7.

[39] Ibid., sig. G2[r].

yet now thou hast
Diverted to a purer Path thy Quill,
And chang'd Parnassus Mount to Sions Hill:
So that blest-David might almost Desire
To heare his Harp thus echo'd by thy Lyre.[40]

Falkland's praise continues in terms that explain much of the distinction between Sandys's psalms and Wither's:

To them [the envious] thy Excellence would be thy Crime:
For Eloquence with things Prophane they joyne;
Nor count it fit to Mixe with what's Divine;
Like Art and Painting laid upon a Face,
Of it selfe sweet; which more Deforme then Grace.
Yet, as the Church with Ornaments is Fraught,
Why may not That be too, which There is Taught?
. . . .
For since the Way to Heaven is Rugged, who
Would have the Way to that Way be so too?[41]

Much of Wither's *Preparation to the Psalter* had taken pains to demonstrate the very "Eloquence" of the Psalms that Falkland praised Sandys for drawing out. Yet Wither kept his psalter deliberately simple, so that everyone would be able to use it, reading and understanding the Psalms and singing them to the traditional tunes. Sandys was not at all concerned with their popular use, and Falkland's reference to "the Church [that] with Ornaments is Fraught" allies him and Sandys with the kind of church service introduced by Archbishop Laud, which emphasized the aesthetics of worship and minimized congregational singing. In a sense, the aesthetic differences between the psalters of George Wither and George Sandys reflect the widening social, ecclesiastical, and political divide in English society that was soon to lead to the Civil War.

Like the Sidneys, Sandys cast the Psalms into a variety of meters, attempting to dress them in English poetic forms worthy of the (notional) elegance of the Hebrew originals.[42] His Psalm I is a good example of his heroic couplets (defined by their "closure" or confinement of syntax within each pair of lines):

40 Falkland, "To my Noble Friend Mr. George Sandys, upon his excellent Paraphrase on the Psalmes," in Sandys, *Psalmes*, sig. F8^r.

41 Ibid., sig. F8^v.

42 Sandys's psalter is included in this chapter among the "rivals" to "Sternhold and Hopkins," though clearly, unlike Wither and others, Sandys was not trying to produce a "new and improved" version of the old church psalter. Sandys's psalms were accompanied by music, and intended for use in worship (and therefore quite different from the Sidney psalms discussed in chaps. 3–4), but they were psalms for the performance of a trained singer or choir rather than congregational singing psalms.

That man is truely blest, who never strayes
By false advice, nor walks in Sinners wayes;
Nor sits infected with their scornfull pride,
Who God contemne, and Pietie deride.
But wholly fixeth his sincere delight
On heavenly Lawes; those studies day and night.
He shall be like a Tree that spreads his root
By living streames, producing timely fruit:
His leafe shall never fall: the Lord shall blesse
All his indevours with desir'd successe.[43]

Sandys's use of enjambment emphasizes the parallel antitheses in the psalm, between those who stray "By false advice" and those who delight "In heavenly Lawes." Both phrases are pointedly suspended over the first line of their respective utterances, the first negative (he is blest who does not X), the second positive (but he in fact does Y). In the first case, there may even be a sense in which the syntax itself "strayes" over the expected bounds of the pentameter. (Such an effect indicates the distance between Sandys's psalms and the singing-psalms of the "Sternhold and Hopkins" tradition; the unavoidable end-stopping of the psalm tunes' musical lines, necessitated in part by the breathing of the singers, worked against any use of enjambment.) Despite his attention to formal detail, Sandys's paraphrase is quite compact, using 16 lines to Wither's 20.

It is interesting that, like Sandys, both Sidney and Milton translated Psalm 1 into iambic pentameter couplets. The two later poets may each have had Sidney in mind, but they may all have been responding to the psalm's epigrammatic quality. The genre of epigram, most characteristically a simple couplet, was expanded in the Renaissance to include slightly larger forms, while retaining the pith and compression of the classical epigram.[44] The sonnet, for example, showed the influence of the epigrammatic style, as did the short verse paragraph used in Sidney's, Sandys's, and Milton's translations of Psalm 1. In both its concision and its sententiousness, this paragraph also resembles certain Horatian odes, especially as they were translated into English verse,[45] and it is significant that Psalm 1 seems sometimes to have been read as a Christian version of Horace's Ode 1.22,

[43] Sandys, *Psalmes*. All citations from Sandys's psalms will be from the 1648 edition.

[44] On the Renaissance transformations of the epigram, see Rosalie L. Colie, *The Resources of Kind* (Berkeley, 1973), 67–75, and Alastair Fowler, *Kinds of Literature* (Cambridge, MA, 1982), 195–202.

[45] A number of seventeenth-century translations of Horace employ the same form as Sandys's Psalm 1. See the anonymous Ode 2.3 (once attributed to Ben Jonson) and the 1625 translation of the same ode by Sir Thomas Hawkins, in *Horace in English*, ed. D. S. Carne-Ross and Kenneth Haynes (Harmondsworth, 1996), 77–78, 87–88.

"*Integer vitae*" (without Horace's final reversal of his opening moral statement, turning, after all, to his love, "Lalage").[46] Thomas Campion's ayre, for instance, "The man of life upright," usually read as a paraphrase of Horace, actually takes only its opening from Ode 1.22, subsequently blending in non-Horatian elements derived partly from Psalm 1: "scorning all the cares that fortune brings," he "makes the heav'n his booke,/ His wisedome heev'nly things."[47]

The other "sample" psalms demonstrate Sandys's metrical and stanzaic variety. Psalm 22 has stanzas of six iambic tetrameter lines, rhyming *ababba* (one of the few combinations *not* tried out by the Sidneys), and he eschewed the explicitly Christian vocabulary favored by Wither. Sandys's "My hands and feete transfixed are" leaves the typological interpretation to the reader and his "great Assembly" is more general than either Wither's "church" or the KJV's "congregation," though it does hint of a political allusion to the Parliament. Sandys's Psalm 84 returns to couplets, but in short tetrameter lines of seven syllables, that are, unusually, trochaic:[48]

Lord, for thee I daily crie;
In thy absence hourely die.
Sparrowes there their young ones reare;
And the Summers Harbinger
By thy Alter builds her nest,
Where they take their envi'd rest.
O my King! O thou most High!
Arbiter of Victorie!
Happie men! who spend their Dayes;
In thy Courts, there sing thy Praise!

Unlike those of his Psalm 1, the lines of this psalm are consistently end-stopped, yet Sandys still emphasizes a parallelistic rhetoric through

46 Horace, Ode 1.22, *The Odes of Horace*, ed. and trans. David Ferry (New York, 1997), 60–61. The Renaissance treatment of this ode much resembles some Christian responses to Psalm 137. In both cases, the rather troubling final lines of the originals were sometimes tacitly omitted to preserve the desired moral seriousness or propriety. On Psalm 137, see chap. 7.

47 Campion, "The man of life upright," lines 17, 19–20, in *The Works of Thomas Campion*, ed. Walter R. Davis (New York, 1970), 43. Davis notes the "free paraphrase" of Horace. But the man's "scorn" surely comes from the "seate of the scornefull" that is in all the English Bible versions (and Sternhold and Sidney have "Scorners"). Similarly, there is nothing in Horace about studying the heavens, which echoes the psalm's "in his law will he exercise him self daye and night" (Coverdale), or "heavenly lawes; those studies day and night" (Sandys).

48 Actually, these lines are in that meter which is easy enough to describe, but impossible to define satisfactorily in terms of classical metrical terminology. It is either a catalectic or "tailless" trochaic tetrameter (missing the final unstressed syllable) or, alternatively, an acephalous or "headless" iambic (missing the initial syllable). Neither description seems adequate, since it is not clear that a syllable is really "missing" from either end of the line. In any case, whatever the terminology, the effect is identical.

anaphora and rhyme. The short hymn of praise, Psalm 100, uses a stanza that looks like many in the Sidney Psalter, though it is actually identical to that of Psalm 148 in "Sternhold and Hopkins" (and Wither):

All from the Suns uprise,
    Unto his Setting Raies,
Resound in Jubilees
    The great Jehovahs Praise.
        Him serve alone;
        In triumph bring
        Your Gifts, and sing
    Before his Throne.

Avoiding the peculiar "Sternhold and Hopkins" tune, Sandys provided his Psalm 100 with a new, more singable melody by Henry Lawes:[49]

Musical Example #5

This musical example demonstrates another way in which Sandys's *Paraphrase upon the Psalmes* differed radically from Wither's psalter and its other predecessors: it was published with entirely new tunes by Lawes, Gentleman of the Chapel Royal, an eminent composer of songs and masques (including, most notably, the music for Milton's *Comus*).[50] Falkland's laudatory poem stated that the effect of Sandys's psalms on some "Colder Hearts" was

Much like to them to that Disease Inur'd
Which can be no way, but by Musick curd.

[49] Lawes's tune for Psalm 47 (sung also to Psalm 100). Transcribed from Sandys, *Psalmes*, notation modernized and one obvious error corrected (B-flat changed to F, measure 8).

[50] The one earlier psalter similar to Sandys's in this musical respect was that of Archbishop Matthew Parker, published c.1567 with tunes by Thomas Tallis. Still, while Tallis's wonderful melodies later entered the English hymn tradition, Parker's psalter was published obscurely and had no impact on public worship. See Zim, *English Metrical Psalms*, 135–39.

Lest one should miss the reference, the word "Tarantula" was printed in the margin. Apparently, between the fifteenth and seventeenth centuries, there was an epidemic of a disease called "tarantism" (named after the town Taranto in Apulia where it was particularly common) that caused its sufferers to dance hysterically. Through at least two etymological muddles, it was thought that the disease, purportedly caused by a tarantula's bite, could be cured only by the dance called the tarantella.[51] Falkland's allusion to this legendary disease, like Digges's allusion to Amphion, was intended to show the power of music, and music was indeed a vital component of Sandys's psalter. Many seventeenth-century psalters were not published with any music at all. Sometimes this was because, like Wither's, they were to be sung to the tunes everyone already knew. More rarely, as with the Sidney Psalter, it was because they were intended for reading rather than singing. As the title page announced, Sandys's psalms were

Set to new Tunes for private
Devotion: and a thorough
Base, for Voice or
Instrument
By
Henry Lawes, one of the Gentlemen of
His Majesties Chapell-Royall.

This was a singular announcement, with important implications. Sandys's psalms were not intended for public worship, and would indeed not have been suitable for congregational use because his meters did not fit the traditional tunes. This was actually lamented by Richard Baxter – "Oh that he had turned the Psalms into metre fitted to the usual tunes!" – but Baxter missed the point.[52] Sandys explicitly published his psalms for "private devotion," and the fact that the music was arranged for performance with "thorough-base" indicates a style of musical performance suited not to the parish church but to court or chamber, or the private chapels of the aristocracy. Certainly, these tunes do not show the free declamatory style, full of dramatic leaps and expressive chromaticism of Lawes's secular

[51] OED, s.v. "tarantism," "tarantella," "tarantula."

[52] From Baxter's preface to his *Poetical Fragments* (1681), cited in *The Poetical Works of George Sandys*, ed. Richard Hooper, 2 vols. (London, 1872), vol. 1, xii. Baxter also translated the Psalms, in a curious version that could be sung to either common-meter or long-meter tunes, certain words in brackets being omissible without affecting the sense. See Rohr-Sauer, *Metrical Psalms 1600–1660*, 38. Holland describes Baxter as addicted to psalms, and quotes his account of his practice of domestic psalm-singing: "It was not the least comfort that I had in the converse of my late dear wife, that our first in the morning, and last in bed at night, was a Psalm of praise, till the hearing of others interrupted it" (*Psalmists of Britain*, vol. 2, 95–96).

songs.[53] Yet, though Lawes's psalm tunes would have been singable by most amateurs, the thorough-bass notation indicates a performance by one or only a few voices, to keyboard accompaniment (harpsichord or organ), with perhaps a bass viol emphasizing the bass line.[54] The musical antecedents for these psalms are the settings of the "Sternhold and Hopkins" texts by the composer Richard Alison, set for four voices with lute or orpharion and designed for domestic devotional entertainment, or the psalm settings in William Byrd's *Psalmes, songs and sonnets* and Campion's *Ayres*.[55] Baxter didn't seem to notice that Sandys's Psalm 100 actually *is* in a meter "fitted to the usual tunes," but Sandys (or rather Lawes) pointedly provided a different one.

Sandys's Psalm 148, like his Psalm 84, is in tetrameter couplets, and is to be sung to the same tune, printed first with Psalm 29 (all three psalms being of one genre: the hymn of praise). Lawes's tune in this case is not actually very different in its contour from many of the standard church tunes, though once again it is set to a thorough-bass accompaniment:[56]

Musical Example #6

[53] On Lawes's songs, see Ian Spink, *English Song: Dowland to Purcell* (London, 1974), 75–99.

[54] For a brief summary of the technique and history of thorough-bass, see the article in Don Randel, *The New Harvard Dictionary of Music* (Cambridge, MA, and London, 1986), s.v. As is evident in the examples cited from Sandys's psalter, thorough-bass notation consists of a single bass line, essentially like a figured bass but without the figures. The instrumentalist (most likely a keyboardist) who was called upon to fill out the harmonies of the line had to supply his own harmonic figuration as seemed appropriate. Instruments other than, or in addition to, the organ were used in church in the seventeenth century, as in the verse anthems of Orlando Gibbons or Thomas Tomkins, but the essential point remains, that such music was choral rather than congregational, for performance rather than participation. See le Huray, *Music and the Reformation*, chaps. 9–10.

[55] See above, chap. 1, 37–39, and le Huray, *Music and the Reformation*.

[56] Lawes's tune for Psalm 29 (also sung to Psalm 148). Transcribed from Sandys, *Psalmes*, notation modernized.

The translation is especially effective in its verses calling successively on all the elements of Creation to join in the praise:

Let the Earth his Praise resound:
Monstrous Whales, and Seas profound,
Vapours, Lightning, Haile, and Snow,
Stormes which when he bids them blow:
Flowry Hills, and Mountaines high,
Cedars, neighbours to the Skie,
Trees that fruit in season yield,
All the Cattell of the Field,
Salvage beasts, all creeping things,
All that cut the Aire with wings.

Sandys was one of the few English translators of this psalm actually to have seen the cedars it mentions, as well as, no doubt, a number of "Monstrous Whales" (which he substitutes for the KJV's fanciful "dragons") and "Salvage beasts," though his success in these lines has less to do with personal experience than, once again, his ability to preserve or even heighten the parallelism of the original.

Sandys's *Paraphrase upon the Psalmes* had an unusual history during the seventeenth century. The volume was dedicated to the "god-like King" Charles I and his wife, Henrietta Maria, "who like a fruitfull Vine,/ To this our Royall Cedar joyne."[57] Charles apparently enjoyed them, and is even reported to have consoled himself by reading Sandys's psalms while he was imprisoned in Carisbrooke Castle on the Isle of Wight in 1647.[58] Sandys's psalms continued to be associated with King Charles after his execution, partly through the publication in 1655 of *Select Psalmes of a New Translation.* The "Translation" was not, in fact, new. The tiny pamphlet contained five psalms: two previously unpublished translations of Psalms 137 and 104 by Thomas Carew (like Sandys, a Gentleman of Charles's Privy Chamber), along with Psalm 20 and excerpts from Psalms 66 and 111 from the "old" translation of Sandys. Though the title page announced that the psalms were to be sung by a "Chorus of five parts, with Symphonies of Violins, Organ, and other Instruments," to music composed by Henry Lawes, no music was printed. The purpose of the book was clearly political – a Royalist lament and statement of solidarity with the martyr-king (executed on January 30, 1649).

57 "To the King" and "To the Queene" in Sandys, *Psalmes*, sigs. [F6^r] and [F6^v].
58 Reported by Sir Thomas Herbert, *Memoirs of the Last Two Years of Charles* (1702), cited in Davis, *Campion*, 243, n. 61.

It begins with Carew's translation of the Psalm of Exile (137), symbolizing, in this context, the mourning exile of the defeated Royalists, who call for revenge on their enemy, "Cruell *Babel.*"[59] (For an extensive discussion of this and other uses of Psalm 137, see chapter 7.) Next come six innocuous lines of Sandys's Psalm 66, "Happy sonns of Israel,/ Who in pleasant Canaan dwell,"[60] but the attentive reader was surely intended to supply, either from memory or another edition at hand, some of the rest of the psalm:

Lord, Thy pow'r all pow'r exceeds!
Conquest on Thy sword doth sit,
Trembling foes through fear submit.
Let the many-peopled earth,
All of high and humble birth,
Worship our Eternal King,
Hymns unto His honour sing.
. . . .
Endless His dominion,
All beholding from His throne.
Let not those who hate us most,
Let not the *rebellious* boast.
Bless the Lord; His praise be sung
While an ear can hear a tongue.
He our feet establisheth,
He our souls redeems from death.[61]

Carew's Psalm 104 is followed by an obviously pointed selection from Sandys's Psalm 111:

Lord aloft thy triumphs raise,
While we sing thy Power and Praise:
My Soul, the honour of the King,
Shall in the great Assembly sing;
His Praise, while Men have Memory
And pow'r of speech, shall never die.[62]

Sandys's use of "Assembly" in Psalm 22 (see p. 68 above) may or may not be free of political implication; its inclusion in the 1655 publication (after Sandys's death, of course) was certainly not. The book closes with Sandys's Psalm 20, "The Lord in thy Adversity/ Regard thy cry," whose final lines voice the Royalist hope:

59 *Select Psalmes* (1655), 3. 60 Ibid.
61 Sandys, *Psalmes*, italics added. 62 *Select Psalmes* (1655), 6.

O save us Lord! thy suppliants heare,
And in our aide, great King, appeare.
Lord aloft thy Triumphs raise,
While we sing thy power and praise.[63]

It has been suggested that *Select Psalmes* was published for the use of Royalists, perhaps only as a memento of King Charles, perhaps for use in private chapels (though music would have to have been supplied).[64] Sandys obviously had no hand in the publication of the *Select Psalmes* (nor did Carew, both being dead some years), yet its intended use was perfectly in keeping with the author's intentions concerning the *Paraphrase upon the Psalms*. The 1655 publication indicates that Sandys's psalms were indeed used by those for whom he wrote them, and that this use continued long after his death in 1644.[65]

Sandys's psalms also had an influence on subsequent poets, including Carew, whose promise in his verses to Sandys he seems to have kept:

Prompted by thy Example then, no more
In moulds of Clay will I my God adore;
But teare those idols from my heart, and Write
What his blest Sp'rit, not fond Love, shall endite.[66]

Though he never intended them for publication, least of all in a complete psalter, Carew translated a number of psalms in addition to those printed in *Select Psalmes*.[67] Sandys's psalms may also have triggered a response from John Milton. His 1648 translation of Psalms 80–88 into common meter may have been intended as a submission to the committee of the Westminster Assembly engaged in seeking a new metrical psalter to replace "Sternhold and Hopkins."[68] Yet one critic has suggested, alternatively, that Milton first wrote the psalms as a response to Henry Lawes's Royalist *Choice Psalmes*, published earlier in 1648, a volume of propagandistic intent similar to that of the 1655 *Select Psalmes* and also using Sandys's paraphrases.[69] Milton may

63 Ibid., 7.

64 Clifford Bartlett, in notes for the recording *Henry Lawes: Sitting by the Streams*, The Consort of Musicke, dir. Anthony Rooley (Hyperion Records, London, 1984), 4.

65 One mark of Sandys's influence has been noted by C. B. Hardman, who argues that the song sung by the Bermudans in Andrew Marvell's "Bermudas" derives from Sandys's *Paraphrase upon the Psalmes*. See "Marvell's 'Bermudas' and Sandys's *Psalms*," *Review of English Studies* 32:125 (1981), 64–67.

66 "To my worthy friend Master George Sandys," in Sandys, *Psalmes*, sig. [A8^{v}].

67 On his Psalm 51, see chap. 6.

68 See David Masson, *The Life of John Milton*, 5 vols. (London, 1877), vol. 1, 243, cited in John Milton, *Complete Shorter Poems*, ed. John Carey (Harlow, Essex, and New York, 2nd ed. 1977), 309. Some years later, Milton also translated Psalms 1–8 into more sophisticated English meters. See chap. 4, 139–44.

69 Margaret Boddy, "Milton's Translation of Psalms 80–88," *Modern Philology* 64:1 (1966), 1–9.

then have proposed the singing of his Psalms 80–88 (many of them on the subject of kings and warfare) at a prayer meeting of the parliamentary army at Windsor.

There is no conclusive evidence in support of any of these claims, but it is certainly puzzling that Milton should translate this group of psalms into the popular common meter so uncharacteristic of his usual style. It is hard to believe that they were intended for singing-psalms, however, partly since Milton's penchant for enjambment, while it creates poetic interest, works against the structure imposed by the traditional tunes. Milton would undoubtedly have been aware of this, especially since his father, John Milton, had been a respected composer who, as mentioned in chapter 1, contributed to Thomas Ravenscroft's harmonized version of *The Whole Booke of Psalmes* (1621).[70] The younger Milton would thus presumably have understood the metrical requirements of singing psalms. The continuous syntax of lines 2–3 in Psalm 84 demonstrates his "sense variously drawn out":

> How lovely are thy dwellings fair!
> O Lord of Hosts, how dear
> The *pleasant* tabernacles are!
> *Where thou dost dwell so near.*
> My soul doth long and almost die
> Thy courts O Lord to see,
> My heart and flesh aloud do cry,
> O living God, for thee.
> There even the sparrow *freed from wrong*
> Hath found a house of rest,
> The swallow there, to lay her young
> Hath built her *brooding* nest.[71]

The other peculiarity of Milton's psalm translations is their distinctly private and personal tone. Following the traditional practice of Bible translators, Milton italicized his additions to the Hebrew original (which, unlike most of his fellow psalm translators, he could understand). Usually, however, translators added words for clarification, or to suit an English idiom, or, in metrical versions, to fill out a line, but none of these reasons explains Milton's sparrow "*freed from wrong*," or the "*brooding*" swallow (who seems to anticipate Milton's muse in *Paradise Lost* who "Dove-like satst brooding

70 See Ernest Brennecke, Jr., *John Milton the Elder and his Music* (New York, 1938), esp. chap. 6.

71 Milton, Psalm 84, lines 1–12, in *Shorter Poems* (italics as in the original). Lines 5–6, 9–10, and 11–12 are also enjambed, but run-on lines are more common in this position in common-meter stanzas, reflecting their kinship to the fourteener couplet.

on the vast Abyss/ And mad'st it pregnant").[72] This sounds rather too much like Milton talking to himself to be convincing as a public text intended for liturgical song, and indeed the only publication of these psalms was in Milton's 1673 *Poems*.[73]

Another poet who, like Carew, had written admiring verses for Sandys's 1638 *Paraphrase upon the Divine Poems* was Henry King. King stated that Sandys's muse

> rekindled hath the Prophets Fire,
> And Tun'd the Strings of his neglected Lyre;
> Making the Note and Ditty so agree,
> They now become a perfect Harmony.

Curiously, although King goes on to contrast Sandys's psalms with what must be a reference to the "Sternhold and Hopkins" tradition, when King himself came to translate the Psalms, it was just that tradition which he followed:

> I must confess, I have long wisht to see
> The Psalmes reduc'd to this Conformitie [i.e., that of Sandys's *Paraphrase*]:
> Grieving the Songs of Sion should bee sung
> In Phrase not diff'ring from a Barbarous Tongue.
> As if, by Custome warranted, wee may
> Sing that to God, wee would be loth to Say,
> Farre be it from my purpose to upbraid
> Their [Sternhold, Hopkins et al.] honest meaning, who first offer made
> That Booke in Meter to compile, which you
> Have mended in the Forme, and Built anew.
> And It was well, considering the Time
> Which scarcely could distinguish Verse and Rhime.
> But now the Language, like the Church, hath won
> More Luster since the Reformation;
> None can condemne the Wish, or Labour spent
> Good Matter in Good Words to represent.[74]

[72] *Paradise Lost*, 1.21–22, in *Complete Poems*, 212. Of course, birds "brood" outside of Milton, but the word is so charged in his poetry (occurring also in the earlier "On the Morning of Christ's Nativity," l. 68) that it is hard to ignore.

[73] Nevertheless, some of Milton's psalms have been sung as congregational hymns and remain in many hymnals to this day. See no. 389, "Let us with a gladsome mind," set to the tune "Monkland," in *The Hymnal 1982* (New York, 1985), the hymnal of the American Episcopal Church; also, in the same book, no. 462, "The Lord will come and not be slow," set to "York," a tune from a late edition of "Sternhold and Hopkins" (1621). The same text is set to the "Old 107th" (originally composed for the Genevan Psalter by Louis Bourgeois), in *The Book of Common Praise* (Toronto, n.d.), the hymnal of the Anglican Church of Canada. These hymns are included in many other hymnals in the United States, Canada, Great Britain, and elsewhere.

[74] "To my much honoured friend Master George Sandys," in Sandys, *Psalmes*, sig. [A6^{v}].

HENRY KING: "GOOD MATTER IN GOOD WORDS"

In 1651 Henry King, by that time bishop of Chichester, published *The Psalmes of David From the New Translation of the Bible Turned into Meter.* As the title page announced, it was not a psalter like Sandys's, but another intended "To be sung after the Old Tunes used in the Churches." In a letter to James Ussher, archbishop of Armagh (famous for working out the chronology of the Bible), King explained his method as a kind of poetic *via media* between two extremes which he saw as equally unsuccessful:

I was (I confesse) discouraged, knowing that Mr. George Sandys, and lately one of our prætended Reformers, had failed in Two different Extreames; The First too elegant for the vulgar use, changing both the Meter and Tunes wherewith they had been long acquainted; The Other as flat and poor, as lamely worded and unhandsomly rhimed as the Old; which, with much confidence, he undertook to amend. My Lord, I now come forth, an Adventurer in a Middle-way, whose aim was, without affectation of Words, to leave them not disfigured in the Sense.[75]

In the fifteen or so years since Sandys's publication, King apparently came to the conclusion that, admirable as his version was as poetry, it was too "elegant for vulgar use" of the congregation in church singing (for which use, of course, Sandys never intended it). A new translation had to fit the meters and, more importantly, the tunes of the Old Version. Unlike one of the "prætended Reformers," however – and King likely meant either Francis Rous or William Barton, whose Sternholdesque psalters were published in 1643 and 1644 respectively – King wanted to avoid the perennial problem plaguing psalters that attempted to "improve" "Sternhold and Hopkins" while maintaining its meters, namely, that they made no improvement at all. King's compromise seems reasonable, but, despite a positive contemporary response to his psalms – Samuel Woodford, for example, offered mild praise, noting that King's translation "is close, exactly answering the Text, and for that kind of measure, which himself has truly observ'd to be the least graceful of any, very smooth, and roundly express'd" – they had as little practical impact as Wither's.[76]

King was an accomplished poet, as attested by his many elegies (including those for his friends Ben Jonson and John Donne, and the often-anthologized "Exequy" on the death of his wife). In his psalms, however, he used the plain style that the church psalms seemed to demand. Not only

[75] Quoted in *Poems and Psalms by Henry King DD*, ed. J. Hannah (Oxford and London, 1843), 139.
[76] Woodford, *Psalms*, sig. [c^{v}].

did he follow the "Sternhold and Hopkins" meters, which (as Woodford noted) he consciously recognized was "of All others least gracefull,"[77] but he further constrained himself by adapting common meter to the seventeenth-century taste for the rhyming couplet. The 8.6.8.6 stanza rhyming *abab* is perhaps more difficult to make "fall in naturally" than Sternhold's original *abcb* (see chapter 1), but the *aabb* rhyme in common meter is more difficult still, as was recognized even in the seventeenth century:

> Yet [King] pitched upon an unlucky method in his Translation, to make every first and second, every third and fourth line of a Psalm to answer and rhime to one another; whereby, in the short measures especially of eight and six feet [presumably he means syllables], (which is the common one) he was too much hamper'd and confin'd, so that the words could not fall in so naturally as they ought.[78]

This may be overstating the case somewhat, but such "unnaturalness" is not hard to find in King's version, as in the first lines of Psalm 1:

> The man is blest whose feet not tread
> By wicked counsailes led:
> Nor stands in that perverted way,
> In which the Sinners stray;
> Nor joynes himselfe unto the chaire
> Where Scorners seated are;
> But in God's Law both dayes and nights
> To meditate delights.[79]

These metrical constraints are reduced somewhat with the addition of the extra syllables in the second line of long meter, as in Psalm 22 (quoting the second stanza):

> But Thou in Holinesse dost dwell,
> O Thou the praise of Israel!
> Our Fathers plac'd their trust in Thee;
> And Thy deliverance set them free.
> They cry'd to Thee, surpriz'd with feare,
> And from Confusion saved were.
> But I a worme, and no man am;
> Reproach of men, and peoples shame.

77 King's preface to the *Psalmes* (1651), sig. [A3r]. All citations of King's psalms are from this, the first edition.

78 John Patrick, *A Century of Select Psalms* (1679), cited in Ronald Berman, *Henry King and The Seventeenth Century* (London, 1964), 92.

79 King, *Psalmes*.

King's announced intention to improve the "Old Version" naturally calls for a comparison of his new versions with "Sternhold and Hopkins" (in this case, Sternhold's Psalm 22):

Even thou that in thy sanctuary,
  and holy place dost dwell:
Thou art the comfort and the joye,
  and glory of Israell,
And he in whom our fathers olde,
  had all theyr hope for ever:
And when they put their trust in thee,
  So diddest thou them deliver.

They were delyvered for ever, when
  they called on thy name:
And for the fayth they had in thee,
  they were not put to shame.
But I am nowe become a worme,
  more like then any man:
And outcast whom the people scorne,
  with all the spite they can.[80]

King's translation is more compact, taking only one stanza to Sternhold's two. King's diction is also more "modern," according to mid-seventeenth-century usage, and, at least in this example, his syntax is less "unnatural" than Sternhold's. But apart from this it does not seem a marked improvement on its predecessor. King's language rarely shows creativity, but this is not surprising, since he admits that he has deliberately "followed the New Translation of the Psalms in our Church Bibles, that He who is able to read the one, may perceive the Reason of the text neither lost, nor abused in the Rhime."[81] King's sole purpose in producing this psalter was thus to provide a version of the Psalms that matched both the sense of the King James Bible and the tunes of the "Sternhold and Hopkins" psalter. Since most congregations were reasonably happy with these existing books, it seems hardly surprising that King's psalms failed to supplant them in church worship.

THE BAY PSALM BOOK

King's lack of success in ousting "Sternhold and Hopkins" is representative of the many "improved" imitations of the Old Version that were published

[80] *The Whole Booke of Psalmes* (1562). [81] Preface to King, *Psalmes*, sig. [A3r].

and forgotten in the seventeenth century. The only English psalter with any lasting success was that mentioned above, by Francis Rous, perhaps the "prætended Reformer" in King's letter to Ussher, but this success was not in England: Rous's 1643 *Psalmes of David* became the basis for the Scottish Psalter of 1650, authorized by the Scottish General Assembly and still in use in the twentieth century.[82] The other psalter which had considerable success outside of England was *The Bay Psalm Book* (first published with the same title as "Sternhold and Hopkins," *The Whole Booke of Psalmes*). It was written abroad, in a British colony, and was printed in Massachusetts in 1640, the first book published in America, yet its roots were solidly in the "Sternhold and Hopkins" tradition.

The motivation for its publication was different again from any of its predecessors discussed so far. Not all criticisms of "Sternhold and Hopkins" objected to its lack of elegance. Some thought it *too* elegant. The Quaker Henry Clark, for instance – surely one of those who linked, in Falkland's phrase, "Eloquence with things Prophane" – referred contemptuously to Sternhold and Hopkins as "mere poets."[83] The earlier editors of *The Bay Psalm Book* held much the same opinion. On the surface, as its actual title suggests, it appeared to be yet another edition of "Sternhold and Hopkins," including even the usual scriptural epigraphs from Colossians 3 and James 5. It was not. Its editors, the Revs. John Eliot, Richard Mather (father of Increase and grandfather of Cotton), and Thomas Weld, announced in a lengthy preface what was essentially a purposeful anti-aesthetic:

> If therefore the verses are not alwayes so smooth and elegant as some may desire or expect; let them consider that Gods Altar needs not our pollishings: Ex. 20. for wee have respected rather a plaine translation, then to smooth our verses with the sweetnes of any paraphrase, and soe have attended Conscience rather then Elegance, fidelity rather then poetry, in translating the hebrew words into english language, and Davids poetry into english meetre; that soe wee may sing in Sion the Lords songs of prayse according to his owne will; untill hee take us from hence, and wipe away all our teares, and bid us enter into our masters joye to sing eternall Halleluiahs.[84]

The editors seem to have been determined to include their psalm translations among the causes of those earthly tears. A few verses from Psalm 84

[82] See Patrick, *Scottish Psalmody*, 79–230.

[83] In *A Description of the Prophets* (1655), 21, cited in Nigel Smith, *Perfection Proclaimed: Language and Literature in English Radical Religion* (Oxford, 1989), 334, n. 61.

[84] Preface to *The Bay Psalm Book*, facsimile reprint of the original 1640 edition (Chicago, [1956]), sigs. [**3^{v}–**4^{r}].

will demonstrate the translators' indifference to the problem of metrical awkwardness that so concerned Wither and King:

Behould o God our shield: the face
 of thine annoynted see.
For better's in thy courts a day,
 then *elsewhere* thousands bee:
I rather had a doore-keeper
 be i'th house of my God:
then in the tents of wickednes
 to settle mine aboad.
Because the Lord God is a Sun,
 he is a shield also:
Jehovah *on his people* grace
 and glory will bestow.[85]

At their worst, these psalms can be almost unreadable:

They God forgot their saviour; which
 in Egipt did great acts:
Works wondrous in the land of Ham:
 by th'red sea dreadfull facts.
And sayd he would them waste; had not
 Moses stood (whom he chose)
'fore him i'th breach, to turne his wrath,
 lest that hee should waste those.[86]

The opening of *The Bay Psalm Book*'s Psalm 22 is an effective demonstration of how the rhythm of sung common meter, requiring a pause at the end of the short second and fourth lines, disrupts any attempt to run the syntax over the line:

My strength like a potsherd is dryed;
 and my tongue fast cleaveth
unto my jawes, and thou hast brought
 me to the dust of death.
For dogs have compast me about;
 th'assembly me beset
Of the wicked; they pierced through
 my hands, also my feet.[87]

85 Ibid., Ps. 84:9–11. 86 Ibid., Ps. 106:21–23. 87 Ibid., Ps. 22:15–16, italics added.

The awkwardness would be emphasized when this text was sung, since an 8.6.8.6. tune reinforced the inflexible metrical structure.

More surprising than *The Bay Psalm Book*'s doggedly inelegant verse, at a time when psalm translators in England were trying desperately to avoid this, is its rapid and singular success. There were eventually seventy editions, almost thirty in the first few decades after its initial appearance.[88] The explanation for this phenomenon must lie in the peculiarities of its readership. Since it was the first book published in America, it had no rivals, at least in terms of the ease of acquisition. It also appeared in the midst of, and was sanctioned by, the Puritan society of New England, a hot-house environment free of the natural enemies that preyed on new psalters in England (notably the Company of Stationers, but also competing religious denominations and social and political factions). Even in New England, however, the drive to reform the Psalter eventually appeared in *The Psalms, Hymns, and Spiritual Songs of the Old and New Testaments*, an improved version of the *Bay Psalm Book* published in London by (among others) the president of Harvard, Henry Dunster, in whose house the original had first been printed.[89] Like "Sternhold and Hopkins," *The Bay Psalm Book* was a book writers loved to hate, and for many years critics like the Rev. Elias Nason exercised their wit in lambasting this peculiar volume:

> Welde, Eliot, and Mather mounted the restive steed Pegasus, Hebrew psalter in hand, and trotted in warm haste over the rough roads of Shemitic roots and metrical psalmody. Other divines rode behind, and after cutting and slashing, mending and patching, twisting and turning, finally produced what must ever remain the most unique specimen of poetical tinkering in our literature.[90]

The point to be made about *The Bay Psalm Book*, however, is not that its translators were incompetent poets, since they imply that they could have written more smoothly if they had wished to, but that they deliberately chose to produce a psalter that was not aesthetically pleasing but textually accurate and (therefore) theologically correct. The pleasures of reading and singing the Psalms were thus not to be found in their rhymes and meters but in their substance. That the readers of *The Bay Psalm Book* did experience such pleasures is attested to by the diary of Judge Samuel Sewall (1674–1729), which records its author's "Humble acknowledgement" to God of

88 Rohr-Sauer, *Metrical Psalms 1600–1660*, 52–57.

89 Ibid., and Earle, *Sabbath*, 145.

90 Cited in Earle, *Sabbath*, 154. Nason (1811–1887) was himself the author of the *Congregational Hymn Book* (Boston, 1857).

the "great comfort and merciful kindness received through singing of His Psalmes" in this version.[91]

It was not until 1696 that the hegemony of the "Sternhold and Hopkins" psalter was finally overthrown by Tate and Brady's *A New Version of the Psalms of David*, a book that appeared in many respects similar to it. Tate and Brady kept to the traditional meters and tunes, but produced an entirely new translation rather than a revision of "Sternhold and Hopkins," updating the language (by this time a century and a half out of date) and "smoothing out" the verse according to late seventeenth-century tastes. One recent historian of the English hymn has suggested that their success depended partly on riding a contemporary wave of linguistic reform, reflected in the resolution passed in 1664 by the Royal Society's committee on improving the language:

> They [the Royal Society] have therefore been most rigorous in putting in execution, the only remedy, that can be found for this *extravagance*: and that has been, a constant Resolution, to reject all the amplifications, digressions, and swellings of style: to return back to the primitive purity, and shortness, when men deliver'd so many *things*, almost in an equal number of *words*.[92]

In other words, by the end of the century, the more florid style of Sandys, let alone Sidney and Fletcher, was passing out of favor, and the plain and compact common meter of Tate and Brady suited the new tastes.

It probably did not hurt the sale of the *New Version* that it was "Allowed and Permitted to be used in all Churches, Chappels and Congregations" by King William III,[93] just as "Sternhold and Hopkins" had been by Queen Elizabeth. And, of course, the Company of Stationers was also involved, eager as always to promote the sales of the lucrative English Stock. The control of the Stationers Company over the printing trade was reinstituted after the tumultuous years of the Interregnum, first by the Printing Act of 1662 and then by further ordinances in 1678, 1681, and 1683.[94] It is a sign of how much power the Stationers had lost, however, as well as a recognition that the time had come for a replacement to "Sternhold and Hopkins,"

91 Cited in Earle, *Sabbath*, 156–57.

92 Thomas Spratt, *The History of the Royal Society* (1667), in Tillotson et al., *Eighteenth Century Literature*, 27. The passage, slightly abbreviated, is quoted by Watson (*English Hymn*, 98), who makes the claim for the New Version's timeliness.

93 See the announcement opposite the title page to *A New Version of the Psalms of David* (London, 1701).

94 Blagden, *Stationers' Company*, 153–77.

that in 1696 they entered into a partnership with Tate and Brady for the printing of their *New Version of the Psalms*, dividing the profits into three equal shares.[95] However much had changed, and despite its "newness," the *New Version* paid homage to the Old in perpetuating the meters established as normative for English metrical psalms by decades of singing "Sternhold and Hopkins" to its familiar tunes over the previous 150 years.

[95] Holland, *Psalmists of Britain*, vol. 2, 104.

CHAPTER 3

The Psalms and English poetry I: "Greece from us these Arts deriv'd": psalms and the English quantitative movement

Renaissance poets were interested in the Psalms for several obvious reasons: they were the oldest poetry known at the time; they were written under direct inspiration from God, which indicated his approval of writing poetry; and they included poems in an almost exhaustive variety of lyric modes and – so it was supposed – meters. In an often-quoted passage in his *Defence of Poetry*, Sir Philip Sidney describes divine poetry as the earliest and preeminent of the three literary kinds (divine, philosophical, and poetry "strictly speaking"):

> The chief, both in antiquity and excellency, were they that did imitate the unconceivable excellencies of God. Such were David in his Psalms; Solomon in his Song of Songs, in his Ecclesiastes, and Proverbs; Moses and Deborah in their Hymns; and the writer of Job: which, beside other, the learned Emanuel Tremellius and Franciscus Junius do entitle the poetical part of the Scripture. Against these none will speak that hath the Holy Ghost in due holy reverence. (In this kind, though in a full wrong divinity, were Orpheus, Amphion, Homer in his Hymns, and many other, both Greeks and Romans.) And this poesy must be used by whosoever will follow St. James's counsel in singing psalms when they are merry, and I know is used with fruit of comfort by some, when, in sorrowful pangs of their death-bringing sins, they find the consolation of the never-leaving goodness.[1]

As Israel Baroway first pointed out, Sidney's ideas about Hebrew poetry were primarily derived from the two contemporary Hebraists he mentions in this passage, Immanuel Tremellius (1510–1580) and Franciscus Junius (1545–1602), who made a "Protestant" (i.e., supplanting the Vulgate) Latin translation of the Old Testament out of the Hebrew published between 1575 and 1579.[2] The same few ideas of the "antiquity and excellency" of biblical poetry, the Psalms in particular, had wide currency in the late sixteenth and

[1] Sir Philip Sidney, *A Defence of Poetry*, in *Miscellaneous Prose of Sir Philip Sidney*, ed. Katherine Duncan-Jones and Jan van Dorsten (Oxford, 1973), 80.

[2] Israel Baroway, "Tremellius, Sidney, and Biblical Verse," *Modern Language Notes* (March, 1934), 145–49.

seventeenth centuries. Like Sidney, George Puttenham also seems to have been concerned with those who might speak against poetry:

King *David* also and *Salomon* his sonne and many other of the holy Prophets wrate in meeters, and used to sing them to the harpe, although to many of us ignorant of the Hebrue language and phrase, and not observing it, the same seeme but a prose. It can not bee therefore that anie scorne or indignitie should justly be offred to so noble, profitable, ancient and divine a science as Poesie is.[3]

Eventually, in *Paradise Regained*, Milton puts these opinions in the mouth of Jesus himself. Satan offers the temptation of the riches of classical culture – surely a powerful attraction for Milton – but "our Savior sagely thus replied":

Or if I would delight my private hours
With Music or with Poem, where so soon
As in our native Language can I find
That solace? All our Law and Story strew'd
With Hymns, our Psalms with artful terms inscrib'd
Our Hebrew Songs and Harps in Babylon,
That pleas'd so well our Victor's ear, declare
That rather Greece from us these Arts derived;
Ill imitated, while they loudest sing
The vices of thir Deities, and thir own
In Fable, Hymn, or Song, so personating
Thir Gods ridiculous, and themselves past shame.
Remove their swelling Epithets thick laid
As varnish on a Harlot's cheek, the rest,
Thin sown with aught of profit or delight,
Will far be found unworthy to compare
With Sion's songs, to all true tastes excelling,
Where God is prais'd aright, and Godlike men,
The Holiest of Holies, and his Saints.[4]

That these are Milton's views as well as the Savior's is indicated by a similar description of biblical poetry in his earlier pamphlet, *The Reason of Church Government*, quoted previously (see Introduction), in which Milton compares "those magnific odes and hymns" of Pindar and Callimachus to "those frequent songs throughout the law and prophets" which "not in their divine argument alone, but in the very critical art of composition, may be easily made appear over all the kinds of lyric poesy to be incomparable."[5]

[3] George Puttenham, *The Arte of English Poesie* (1589), facsimile edition (Kent, OH, 1970), 25. Other similar passages from Elizabethan and Jacobean critical essays by Barnaby Googe, John Northbrooke, Thomas Lodge, John Harington, George Wither, and Henry Peacham are cited by Baroway, "Bible as Poetry," 473–74, 469.

[4] *Paradise Regained*, 4.331–49, in *Complete Poems*, 523.

[5] *Complete Poems*, 669.

While there was general agreement that the Bible contained much poetry, the nature of Hebrew poetry was completely obscure, even for those who, like Milton, knew Hebrew. (Sidney, who did not know Hebrew, wrote that the Book of Psalms "is fully written in metre, as all learned hebricians agree, although the rules be not yet fully found.")[6] This was an obstacle to biblical criticism, but proved an advantage to poets, since they were thus free to make whatever connections they liked to their own poetic practice. The principal patristic authority on Hebrew poetry was Jerome, who was in turn transmitting "truths" culled from Philo and Josephus. It was Jerome who made the strongest connection between biblical and classical poetry, a connection of obvious appeal to Renaissance humanists:

> What is more musical than the Psalter? which, in the manner of our Flaccus [i.e., Horace] or of the Greek Pindar, now flows in iambs, now rings with Alcaics, swells to a Sapphic measure or moves along with a half-foot? What is fairer than the hymns of Deuteronomy or Isaiah? What is more solemn than Solomon, what more polished than Job? All of which books, as Josephus and Origen write, flow in the original in hexameter and pentameter verses?[7]

No one in the Renaissance could have said precisely where in the Scriptures these iambs, Alcaics, hexameters, and pentameters were to be found, or have shown how they should be scanned, nor indeed could Jerome himself likely have done so, yet Jerome and his patristic sources were accepted as sufficient proof that the Psalms and other biblical passages were constructed in the same way as Greek and Latin poetry. This notion appealed to the syncretic tendencies of readers and writers eager to connect the two ancient streams that flowed together into the turbulent cultural pool of Renaissance and Reformation England.

For translators and poets, Jerome's comments could be interpreted in different ways, according to their sense of how English poetry ought to develop. Those committed to the adaptation of classical quantitative meter to English verse gained encouragement from the notion that Hebrew verse was constructed according to the same principles as Greek and Latin, and among the curious sixteenth-century experiments in writing English quantitative verse are a number of translations of the Psalms. Others, though equally committed to the general transmission of classical culture, were more flexible in their approach to English verse, adapting the "Hebraic"/classical quantities to the exigencies of English accent, producing

[6] Sidney, *Defence*, 77. On the history of ideas about Hebrew poetry, especially parallelism, see Kugel, *Idea of Biblical Poetry*.

[7] "Preface to Eusebius," cited in Kugel, *Idea of Biblical Poetry*, 152.

a species of English hexameter or Sapphic, which was and was not indebted to the ancient originals.

THE PSALMS AND ENGLISH QUANTITATIVE VERSE

Derek Attridge, the foremost authority on the subject, admits that, compared to the great accentual-syllabic poetry of Elizabethan England, the quantitative poetry produced by English classicists has now an academic rather than an aesthetic interest.[8] Most modern readers of such experimental verse will concur, and Attridge's assessment is no less true of the quantitative psalm translations than of the secular poetry, but the place of the Psalms in the quantitative movement needs to be stressed. Apart from the authority that the notion of quantitative biblical poems gave to the movement, there were actual experiments in quantitative psalm translation by Richard Stanyhurst, the countess of Pembroke, and Abraham Fraunce.

Stanyhurst (1547–1618) was an Irish Catholic who spent much of his life on the continent.[9] He wrote a history of Ireland as well as Latin poetry and quantitative translations. His verse was praised by the father of the English quantitative movement, Gabriel Harvey, but his peculiar spelling and diction (his "carterlie varietie as no hodge plowman in a countrie but would have held as the extremitie of clownerie") was condemned by Thomas Nashe, who supported his case by citing a pair of lines from Stanyhurst's translation of part of Book 8 of the *Aeneid*:

> Then did he make heavens vault to rebounde, with rounce robble hobble
> Of ruffe raffe roaring, with thwick thwack thurlery bouncing.[10]

These lines also attracted the scorn of Joseph Hall, who quotes them in the sixth satire of his *Virgidemiarum* (1597), attacking the quantitative poets (and perhaps Stanyhurst specifically):

> Another scorns the homespun thread of rhymes,
> Match'd with the lofty feet of elder times:
> Give me the number'd verse that Virgil sung,
> And Virgil's self shall speak the English tongue:

[8] Derek Attridge, *Well-Weighed Syllables* (Cambridge, 1974), 165.

[9] See Colm Lennon, *Richard Stanihurst the Dubliner 1547–1618* (Blackrock, 1981). I am grateful to Thomas Herron for directing me to this biography.

[10] Thomas Nashe, preface to Greene's *Menaphon* (1589), in *Elizabethan Critical Essays*, ed. G. Gregory Smith (London, 1904), vol. 1, 315. For the passage from one of Harvey's letters to Spenser as well as biographical information on Stanyhurst, see Edward Arbor's introduction to his edition of Richard Stanyhurst. *Translation of the first Four Books of the Aeneis of P. Virgilius Maro . . . 1582*. (London, 1895), vii–xxiv.

"Manhood and garboils shall he chant" with changed feet,
And head-strong dactyls making music meet.
The nimble dactyl striving to outgo,
The drawling spondees pacing it below.
The lingering spondees, labouring to delay,
The breathless dactyls with a sudden stay.
Whoever saw a colt wanton and wild,
Yoked with a slow-foot ox on fallow field,
Can right areed how handsomely besets
Dull spondees with the English dactylets?
If Jove speak English in a thund'ring cloud,
"Thwick thwack, and riff raff," roars he out aloud.
Fie on the forged mint that did create
New coin of words never articulate.[11]

Clearly Stanyhurst's singular approach to poetic language (full of what his nineteenth-century editor calls "agglutinated words," "mimetic words," and "mimetic sentences" like those quoted by Nashe) was not in sympathy with the literary tastes of his late sixteenth-century contemporaries.[12]

Stanyhurst appended translations of Psalms 1–4 in quantitative meters to his *Thee First Foure Bookes of Virgil his Aeneis* (1582). The meters, according to Stanyhurst's own descriptions, are "Iambical verse," "Heroical and Elegiacal verse," "Asclepiad verse," and "Saphick verse," respectively.[13] He explains his experiments as testing some of the other meters of classical poetry:

As thee *Latinists* have diverse kindes of verses besydes the *Heroiacal*: so our *English* wyl easelye admyt theym, althogh in the one language or oother they sowne not al so pleasinglie too the eare (by whose balance thee rowling of thee verse is too bee gaged) as the sole *heroical*, or the *heroical* and thee *elegiacal* enterlaced one with the oother.[14]

He is offering a sampling of the range of meters available, corresponding at least partly to Jerome's description of the Psalms' metrical variety (iambics, heroic hexameters, and Sapphics). Perhaps Stanyhurst also had in mind Horace's *Odes*, the first nine of which are in nine different meters as a show

[11] Joseph Hall, Satire VI, *Virgidemiarum* (1597), in *Satires by Joseph Hall*, ed. Samuel Weller Singer (London, 1824), 16–17.

[12] See Arbor's introduction to Stanyhurst, *Translation*, xxiii–xxiv. Yet there is something marvelous about his wild, highly alliterative, and visceral language. Stanyhurst was also a spelling reformer, though in this too he was rather eccentric, perhaps due to his effort to match pronunciation to his sense of quantity (which, as Attridge shows, has nothing to do with actual speech sound), perhaps partly because of the peculiar accents of his own Irish English.

[13] Ibid., 125, 127, 130. [14] Ibid., 125.

of poetic skill.[15] In any case, there is no apparent reason why each of these meters should have been chosen for these psalms, and, as he admits, some of the meters work better in English than others.

Iambics had a history originating in the invective of Archilochus and the Dionysian dithyramb, and the meter was described by Aristotle as that closest to common speech. None of these associations or characteristics seems especially appropriate for Psalm 1.[16] Heroic hexameters suit Psalm 2, which concerns kings and warfare against the heathen, and Asclepiadics have associations with tragedy appropriate to Psalm 3, subtitled "A Psalme of David when he fledde from the face of Absolom his sonne," but also in this meter are Sidney's "O sweet woods, the delight of solitariness!" from the *Old Arcadia* and Horace's Ode 1.5, translated by Milton as "What slender Youth bedew'd with liquid odours," neither of which seem exactly tragic.[17] Sapphics were used for a variety of lyric subjects and modes, and were among the most popular classical forms among vernacular poets. The reason for this is that in the practice of Horace, the Latin Sapphic developed a fairly regular accentual pattern over top of the graphic quantitative system borrowed from the Greek.[18] This meant that English poets could write quantitative Sapphics that still read well in English, giving the stanza what Stanyhurst termed the "prehemynencye" over all other "base and foot verses."[19] Stanyhurst's Sapphic Psalm 4 demonstrates how easy it is to read the quantitatively accurate lines accentually:

> Theare wheat and vineyards, that ar haplye sprouting,
> And oyle, in plenty toe the store cel hurded,
> With pryde, and glorye to the stars inhaunceth
>   Worldlye men huffing.
>
> Thogh that I see not, with a carnal eysight,
> Thee blis and glory, that in hevn is harbourd:
> Yeet with hoape stand I, toe be theare reposed,
>   And toe be resting.[20]

Yet there is no compelling reason why Stanyhurst should have translated this particular psalm into Sapphics. It is perhaps worth noting that George

15 See the comment by T. E. Page, in his ed. of *Q. Horatii Flacci Carminum Libri IV* (London, 1883, rpr. 1970), xxxvi.

16 See T. V. F. Brogan, "iambic," in *New Princeton Encyclopedia*, 548–50.

17 James W. Halporn and T. V. F. Brogan, "Asclepiad," *New Princeton Encyclopedia*, 102. Sidney, *The Old Arcadia*, ed. Katherine Duncan-Jones (Oxford, 1985), 145–46. Milton, Ode 1.5, in *Horace in English*, 88–89.

18 See Attridge, *Well-Weighed Syllables*, 210–12.

19 Stanyhurst, *Translation*, 131.

20 Ibid., 132.

Buchanan, in his popular version of the Psalms in Latin meters, chose quite different meters for Psalms 1–4 (heroic hexameters, alternating hexameters and iambic trimeters, iambic trimeters and dimeters, and hexameters and Alcmanic dactylic tetrameters, respectively).[21]

The translation of heaven as "Olympus" in Stanyhurst's Psalm 2 indicates one reason for the inclusion of the psalm translations with the four books of Virgil – to emphasize the unity of the two ancient cultures, biblical and classical:

> Wyth franticque madnesse why frets thee multitud heathen?
> And to vayn attemptings what furye sturs the pepil?
>
> Al thee worldlye Regents, in clustred coompanye, crowded,
> For toe tread and trample Christ with his holye godhead.
>
> Breake we there hard fetters, wee that be in Christian houshold,
> Also from oure persons pluck there yrnye yokes.
>
> Hee skornes theire woorcking, that dwels in blessed Olympus:
> And at thiere brainsick trumperye follye flireth.[22]

Of course, the Hebrew psalm is wrenched in two directions in this translation, toward Greek myth with "Olympus," and also toward the Christian New Testament with the anachronistic (or typological) rendering of "his anoynted" (in Coverdale) as "Christ." This is actually etymologizing rather than allegorizing, since "Christ" comes from Greek "Χρίστός," meaning, as the classicist Stanyhurst knew, "annointed" (OED, s.v. "Christ"). Still, the allegorizing is there, however supported by etymology. Stanyhurst is actually anticipated in this move by the translators of the Geneva Bible, who also give the last part of verse 2 as "against his Christ" (although they do not mention Olympus). Described in literary histories primarily as a classicist, Stanyhurst's notes on his translation of this verse show considerable knowledge of biblical languages as well as the history of exegesis:

> And therefor in thee 12. verse, thee *Prophet* layeth downe an exhortation too theese men of state, not onlye not too band agaynst *Christe*, but also too submit theymselves too his loare, as too *God*, who would have his soon honored: which verse I have translated according too thee vulgar edition, *apprehendite disciplinam*, where with thee *Greek* text δραξασθε παιδιαζ, and also the *Chaldye* interpretoure agreeth, as *Petrus Galatinus* hath observed: yeet the *Hebrue Nas ku bar*, or *Nassecu Bar*, may bee too more advantage of us *Christians*, and too thee confusion of

[21] George Buchanan, *Paraphrasis Psalmorum Davidis Poetica* (London, 1583), "Carminum Genera," 305–06.

[22] Stanyhurst, *Translation*, 127.

thee *Iewes* ootherwise translated. *S. Hierom* turneth yt, *adore purely*, or *adore thee soon*, which approoveth thee deitye of *Christ*: *Felix* translateth yt, *kisse thee soon*, or *embrace the soon*: wherein also the prerogative of *Christ* is manifested.[23]

Thomas Herron suggests that Stanyhurst's *Aeneis* had a concealed political purpose, subtly adapting Virgil's original to criticize the Elizabethan colonial rule and promote the establishment in Ireland of a new "Rome," based on the Roman Catholic Church.[24] This would explain Stanyhurst's cryptic reference in the dedication to Lord Dunsany to the "deepe and rare poynctes of hydden secrets" of his translation, and there may be "hidden secrets" in the psalm translations too. The political context adds another level of meaning to references to the "il mens segnorye" in Psalm 1 and the central issue of kingship in Psalm 2 (with a complaint against "wordlye Regents" and God's promise that "eke of the ethnicks heyre wil I make the" as well as God's gift "toe thy seisin" of "wyde places earthlye").[25] Many of the terms Stanyhurst uses do seem politically loaded, though this is perhaps natural enough given the content of these four psalms. In any case, Stanyhurst's translation project, while sharing the syncretic approach and cultural ideals of his English Protestant contemporaries (Stanyhurst was after all a schoolmate of Henry Sidney, father of Philip and Mary), must certainly also be read in terms of the more particular linguistic, political, and religious aspirations of a sixteenth-century Irish Catholic. Here once again, as so often, the practice of translating the Psalms is shared by a diverse group of writers who meet on this common cultural ground, if nowhere else.[26]

The quantitative practice of the countess of Pembroke probably derives from that of her brother, who included quantitative poems in his *Arcadia* (dedicated to Pembroke), if not in his own psalms. Pembroke's psalms in quantitative meters, Psalms 120–27 and two variant versions of Psalms 89 and 122, are usually mentioned in studies of Elizabethan quantitative experiments. In fact, as early as 1621, Alexander Gil praised the Sidney Psalter for containing all the lyric genres of Roman poetry.[27] Attridge has

[23] Ibid., 129.

[24] Thomas Herron, "Richard Stanyhurst's *Aeneis* (1582): Political Poetry?" (unpublished conference paper, Sixteenth Century Studies Conference, Cleveland, OH, November, 2000). I am grateful to Thomas Herron for sharing this paper with me.

[25] Stanyhurst, *Translation*, 125, 127–28.

[26] On some important political implications of seventeenth-century psalm translation, particularly the Royalist appropriation and redefinition of the Psalms, see Paula Loscocco, *Eikonoklastic Song: Milton and Royalist Poetics* (forthcoming).

[27] Alexander Gil, *Logonomia anglica* (1621), cited in Anne Lake Prescott, *French Poets and the English Renaissance* (New Haven and London, 1978), 245, n. 32.

high praise for Pembroke's quantitative psalms, singling out her Psalm 89. He argues that this poem is the best of all Elizabethan efforts at producing a genuinely English hexameter.[28] By making accent and quantity coincide, Pembroke produces a poem which gives the intellectual satisfaction of the graphic quantitative pattern but can also be read, without stumbling, as a poem in native English accentual meter:

> These things in visions to thy prophets plainly revealed
> thus were uttred againe, on a man very mighty reputed:
> one exalted, I have, Devoted, wholly to serve mee
> David I meane, whose head hath streamd by my sacred anointing
> force and strength from me, shall mightily ever uphold him
> no manifest violence no cloaked villany hurt him
> his cruel oppressors prickt on by malicious envie
> prostrat in his presence will I lay past hope of rissing
> never shall hee my kindnes want my fidelity never
> raisd to that haight of rule that from seas watery border
> unto the streames Eufrates rolls, all lands shall obey him.[29]

What distinguishes Pembroke's translation from less successful quantitative poems is not just her handling of accent, but, as in all her psalms, the imaginative power of her language. The last two lines quoted above are an effective elaboration of Coverdale's "I will set hys dominion also in the see, and hys ryght hande in the floudes" (verse 25), with or without quantity, as is her verse 37 (in Coverdale, the strong but straightforward "He shall stande fast for evermore as the moon"): "[David I will not faill] while night in unaltred order/ Hides the repining day with moons pale silver adorned."[30]

As the editors of Pembroke's works note, the group of quantitative psalms from the principal manuscript of the Sidney Psalter, transcribed by John Davies of Hereford (and known to textual scholars as "A"), are the first eight of the "Psalms of Degrees."[31] That Pembroke should choose to render these particular psalms, with their singular history and associations, in quantitative meters is surely significant, especially as they are the only quantitative poems in the Davies manuscript. The title of these psalms comes from the common superscription to Psalms 120–34, "A song of Degrees," as labeled in the Geneva, Bishops', and King James Bibles, or, as in the Great Bible, "A song of the steares [stairs]." In the Revised Standard

[28] Attridge, *Well-Weighed Syllables*, 204–05. See chap. 4, below, for a discussion of the Sidney Psalter in the context of English verse.

[29] *The Collected Works of Mary Sidney Herbert, Countess of Pembroke*, vol. 2, *The Psalmes of David*, ed. Margaret P. Hannay, Noel J. Kinnamon, and Michael G. Brennan (Oxford, 1998), 286.

[30] Ibid. [31] Ibid., 431.

Version, the title is translated as "A Song of Ascents."[32] Whatever translation is used, the meaning of the Hebrew "*Shir hammaloth*" is a puzzle, and has been debated by biblical scholars for centuries. Some have argued, following the translation "stairs," that these psalms were sung by the Levites on the fifteen steps of the temple that separated the women's court from the men's. Others have suggested that the title refers to a particular type of "climactic" parallelism, a poetic structure unique to these psalms. An older view is that the "Ascent" refers to the return of the Babylonian exiles to Jerusalem. The commentators in *The Interpreter's Bible* reject all of these (there is no evidence for the "steps" theory, not all of Psalms 120–34 use "climactic parallelism," and several of them seem much later than the end of the Exile) and argue that these were likely a collection of psalms, "something like a handbook of devotions," used "by pilgrims who came up to Jerusalem to be present at the great feasts."[33]

The commentaries that would have been most familiar in late sixteenth-century England were Calvin's, translated by Arthur Golding in 1571 to accompany Golding's own psalm translations, and de Bèze's, translated in 1580 by Anthony Gilby as *The Psalmes of David, truly opened and explaned by Paraphrasis*. Calvin is characteristically skeptical, rejecting anything speculative:

> This Psalme [120] and the next fowerteene folowinge, are called Psalmes of Greeces, Steppes, Stayers or Degrees: but in what consideration, it is not agreed uppon, even amonge the Hebrewe Doctoures. Some surmyse, that there were fifteene Greeces or Steppes up too that parte of the Temple that was appoynted for the Men: and that the women stayed still beneath: but it is a fonde geasse, and we knowe howe large scope the Jewes take untoo themselves in darke caces, to feyn what they list. Some understand this mounting, or going up, too bee their returne from the captivitie of Babylone: which is utterly constreyned. For it is manifest that the more part of them were made eyther by David, or by Solomon: and it is easie too gather by the conteintes of them, that as many of them as were made by David, were woont to bee sung in the Temple whyle hee was yit alyve.[34]

What Calvin finally allows is the modest notion that the "Degrees" has something to do with the rising pitch of the chant (he is followed by the Geneva Bible editors, who gloss the title with, "That is, of lifting up the

32 *The Interpreter's Bible*, vol. 4 (New York and Nashville, 1955). In their exegetical notes, William R. Taylor and W. Stewart McCullough note that some modern Bibles translate the phrase as "A Pilgrim Song" (638).

33 Ibid., 638–39.

34 Golding, *Calvin's Commentaries*, fols. 191^{v}–192. Given the long history of Christian allegorizing from at least Augustine to Luther, Calvin's association of speculative readings of "darke caces" with the Jews seems rather odd, not to say prejudiced.

tune & rising in singing").[35] De Bèze's interpretation is more interesting. He acknowledges the "Temple steps" theory but prefers the argument that they celebrate the end of the Exile:

> but I expound them to be Psalmes of ascensions, which were peculiarlie consecrated to celebrate the returne of the Israëlites out of Babylon: and that they are called psalmes of ascensions in the plural member, not ascension in the singular, because the people returned, not al together, but some under Zorobabel, and other some after under Ezra, and lastlie other returned with Nehemiah: at the which time at the length, when the worship of god was newlie to be ordeined againe, and civil government to be restored, then is it supposed that both these Psalmes, and the residue were gathered by Ezra into one volume, and that these were appointed as most apt to declare the benefit: the which also it is probable that they were afterward wonted to be sung, chieflie of them that went up to Jerusalem, were said to ascend, both for the situation of the citie, and also for the woorthines of the temple.[36]

Without straying too far into the kind of "fonde geasse" that irritated Calvin, it might be argued that the key to Pembroke's choice of quantitative meters for the first eight of the Songs of Degrees lies in their association with the return from exile, but an exile conceived culturally and spiritually rather than physically and politically.

The proponents of the Renaissance and Reformation movements (often one and the same) sought to reconnect themselves with the greatness of antique culture, whether classical or Hebraic. There was a sense of return or homecoming after the cultural exile of the Middle Ages, however questionable this assessment of medieval culture may now seem. Jacques Lefèvre d'Etaples asked, "Why may we not aspire to see our age restored to the likeness of the primitive Church, when Christ received a purer veneration, and the splendour of His Name shone forth more widely?" Boccaccio wrote, primarily of Dante and Petrarch, that, "In our age, if I observe well, more illustrious men have come up from heaven, generous spirits who wish to raise up again with all their strength the oppressed art of poetry, and to recall it from exile into its former abode."[37] In the translation of the Psalms into classical meters, the two ancient cultures (and literatures)

[35] *The Bible and Holy Scriptures* [Geneva Bible] (Geneva, 1560), Lazarus Ministry Press facsimile (Columbus, OH, 1998), 262.

[36] Anthony Gilby, *The Psalmes of David, truly opened and explaned by Paraphrasis. . . . Set foorth in latine by that excellent learned man Theodore Beza. And faithfully translated into English, by Anthonie Gilbie* (London, 1581; first ed., 1580), 304.

[37] Lefèvre d'Etaples, from *Commentarii initiatori in IV evangeliis praefatio* (1522), and Boccaccio, "To Jacopo Pizzinghe," from *Lettere edite ed inedite di Giovanni Boccaccio* (1877), quoted in *The Portable Renaissance Reader*, ed. James Bruce Ross and Mary Martin McLaughlin (New York, 1961), 85, 123. Translations by McLaughlin.

are brought together and renewed in the present. In an important study of Philip Sidney's experimental verse, Marin Mersenne is quoted on the nature of classical, quantitative meter:

> The art of rhythm encompasses the study of number as it applies to the objects of sight, sound, and touch; for the inquiring mind that considers intellectual numbers in their purity, descends to the matter that accompanies them and renders them perceptible, in order to raise itself, somehow, to an intellectual and rational plain and disengage itself from change, mutability, and corruption.[38]

Mersenne's treatise was published in 1636, but Seth Weiner suggests that Mersenne is a late figure in a long tradition of thinking on "the study of number" and that he is expressing ideas that would have been familiar to Sidney.[39] Weiner goes on to apply this metaphysical-theological approach to "number" to a reading of Sidney's Psalm 6, written in the same accentual Sapphics as poem number 59 in the *Old Arcadia* (and the only two such in Sidney's work). Both poems are lovers' complaints, but the psalm subsumes and transfigures the earlier secular lyric:

> But unlike Basilius' song, the Psalmist's complaint is an antidote to sinful love: the love song becomes a song of reconciliation with God. It is worth noting, in this connection, that Sidney's friend Du Plessis Mornay, in his treatise on *The Trewnesse of the Christian Religion*, had related the separation of love songs from sacred songs to general fragmentation that occurred at the Fall. Sidney, who began a translation of Mornay's work, was likely to know the passage well. In its light, psalm 6 can be seen (in terms of its formal counterpart, OA 59) as an attempt to re-integrate the poet of love with the divine and with the philosopher.[40]

Perhaps Pembroke was simply thinking of "degree" in its musical sense (OED s.v. "degree" 11), as a step in the scale (and "scale" itself derives from

[38] Marin Mersenne, *Harmonie Universelle* (1636), in Seth Weiner, "The Quantitative Poems and the Psalm Translations: The Place of Sidney's Experimental Verse in the Legend," in *Sir Philip Sidney: 1596 and the Creation of a Legend*, ed. Jan van Dorsten et al. (Leiden, 1986), 201.

[39] There is, of course, a long and ancient tradition of numerological readings of the Psalms, in which "number" in the formal (poetic) sense would be aligned in significant ways with "number" arithmetically, proportionally, or cosmically conceived. See, for one good treatment of the subject, Maren-Sofie Røstvig, "Structure as Prophecy: The Influence of Biblical Exegesis upon Theories of Literary Structure," in *Silent Poetry: Essays in Numerological Analysis* ed. Alastair Fowler (London, 1970), 32–72. Røstvig has a section on numerological interpretations of the Songs of Degrees, which includes references to Renaissance commentaries that explain these fifteen psalms in light of the fifteen steps of the temple, the number being the sum of seven and eight, the numbers of "life" and "eternity" (see 43–44). Might Pembroke have had this number lore in mind when she stopped her quantitative experiments after the first eight of the Songs of Degrees (signifying the reaching for eternity that Mersenne and perhaps Sidney had in mind)? But this is perhaps a "fonde geasse."

[40] Weiner, "Quantitative Poems," 212–13.

the Latin, "*scala,*" a flight of steps, just as the etymology of "degree" comes from "*gradus,*" step). The quantitative experiments were, after all, closely connected with musical practice, as in the *musique mesurée* of Jean Antoine de Baïf and the *Académie de Poésie et de Musique* which influenced Sidney as well as Thomas Campion.[41] Because of its apparently "musical" properties (essentially organized temporal duration), as well as its associations with the mythical unity of music and poetry in the Greek *mousikē*, quantitative meter gave poets like Sidney the sense that they could achieve "the perfect union of music and poetry," once again circumventing the Fall.[42]

Yet greater unity is achieved or at least implied in Pembroke's Psalms 120–27, a literary, cultural, and spiritual integration even more complex than her brother's in his Psalm 6 (as described by Weiner). In verse 2 of Psalm 120, the prayer Coverdale renders as "Delyver my soule, O Lorde, from lyenge lippes, and from a disceatfull tonge" is turned to address a more specifically poetic deceit by Pembroke:

> Lord ridd my soule from treasonous eloquence
> of filthy forgers craftily fraudulent:
> and from the tongue where lodg'd resideth
> poisoned abuse, ruine of beleevers.[43]

This is the kind of prayer that appears often in Donne and Herbert, expressing the anxiety natural to the religious poet, eager to achieve in his poetic creation a Creation writ small but concerned not to appear proud of his own conceit. The Psalms offer several ways out of this dilemma for Pembroke: first, she is translating Scripture, not writing a poem of her own invention; second, David's Psalms provide, as discussed above, a more general justification for the writing of poetry; finally, Pembroke's eloquent translation of Psalm 120 is a prayer for deliverance from eloquence of the wrong kind.[44] Yet, moreover, since this version of the psalm is in quantitative Alcaics (recall Jerome's statement that the Psalter "rings with Alcaics"), it recaptures the original eloquence of the Hebrew psalm, and at the same time aligns it with the eloquence of Alcaeus, Horace, and other Greek and Latin poets who used the meter. Later in the psalm, Pembroke writes,

41 See ibid., 196–97 and *passim,* and Attridge, *Well-Weighed Syllables*, 121–26. Baïf also translated the Psalms into meter (not quantitative).

42 Weiner, "Quantitative Poems," 203. On the myth or actuality of the union of music and poetry in classical Greece, see John Hollander, *The Untuning of the Sky* (Princeton, 1961), 20–51; Claude V. Palisca, *Humanism in Italian Renaissance Musical Thought* (New Haven and London, 1985).

43 Pembroke, *Works*, vol. 2, 212.

44 For a complicated expression of this problem of eloquence in Donne's "A Litanie" in connection to Psalm 51, see below, chap. 6.

Ah God! too long heere wander I banished,
to long abiding barbarous injury.[45]

"Barbarous" meant originally "not Greek or Latin," and had specifically linguistic connotations, connected by Roger Ascham, in his *The Scholemaster*, to the sixteenth-century debates about vernacular poetry:

In deede, *Chauser*, *Th. Norton* of Bristow, my L. of Surrey, *M. Wiat*, *Th. Phaer*, and other Jentlemen, in translating *Ovide*, *Palingenius*, and *Seneca*, have gonne as farre to their great praise as the copie they followed could cary them; but, if sich good wittes and forward diligence had bene directed to follow the best examples, and not have bene caryed by tyme and custome to content themselves with that *barbarous* and rude Ryming, emonges their other worthy praises, which they have justly deserved, this had not bene the least, to be counted emonges men of learning and skill more like unto the Grecians than unto the Gothians in handling of their verse.[46]

The barbarous "Gothians," of course, sacked Rome and destroyed the classical culture that Renaissance humanists like Ascham were trying to revive. Gabriel Harvey uses the same term in reference to vernacular, rhyming verse in a letter to Edmund Spenser about the contribution of Sidney and Edward Dyer to "our new famous enterprise for the Exchanging of Barbarous and Balductum Rymes with Artificial Verses," and is followed later by William Webbe (who wrote that rhyme "first began to be followed and maintained among the *Hunnes* and *Gothians* and other barbarous Nations") and Thomas Campion ("In those lack-learning times, and in barbarized Italy, began that vulgar and easie kind of Poesie . . . which we abusively call Rime and Meeter").[47] Pembroke's addition of the barbarian exile to the psalm may be further evidence that she was thinking of the Songs of Degrees in de Bèze's sense, transposed to the context of the (English, Protestant) Renaissance return from cultural exile.

Interestingly, there are also suggestions in this group of psalms that Pembroke had in mind her brother's earlier experiments with quantitative meters, or at least his commitment to the classical revival. There is a possible nod to Sidney in Pembroke's Psalm 123, in which the psalmist looks to heaven for mercy and relief:

45 Pembroke, *Works*, vol. 2, 213.

46 Roger Ascham, *The Scholemaster* (1570), in Smith, *Elizabethan Essays*, vol. 1, 30, italics for "barbarous" added.

47 Harvey, Spenser–Harvey correspondence, in Smith, *Elizabethan Essays*, vol. 1, 101; Webbe, *A Discourse of English Poetrie* (1586), in ibid., vol. 1, 239; Campion, *Observations in the Art of English Poesie* (1602), in ibid., vol. 2, 329. On the history of this cultural attitude to rhyme, see Attridge, *Well-Weighed Syllables*, 100–02.

right as a waiters eye on a gracefull master is holden:
as the look of waitresse fix'd on a lady lieth:
soe with erected face, untill by thy mercy relived,
ô Lord expecting, begg we thy frendly favour.[48]

The first use of "erected" cited in the OED is the famous passage in Sidney's *Defence of Poetry* describing the power of human creation (mirroring the divine Creation of which man himself is the greatest achievement) to surpass mere works of nature: "Our erected wit maketh us know what perfection is."[49] Zim notes several interesting allusions to Sidney's *Astrophil and Stella* sonnets in Pembroke's psalms (Psalm 73, "It is most true that God to Israell," and *AS* 5, "It is most true, that eyes are form'd to serve"; Psalm 51, "My trewand soule in thy hid schoole hath learned," and *AS* 1, "my trewand pen"; and Psalm 73 again, "O what is he will teach me clyme the skyes?" and *AS* 31, "With how sad steps, ô Moone, thou climb'st the skies").[50] Zim interprets these allusions as a mark of admiration on Pembroke's part for the poetic achievement of her brother, and this also seems valid for Psalm 123.[51] Yet, in this particular instance, the invocation of the "erected wit" from Sidney's *Defence* seems especially pointed. Pembroke's quantitative psalms derive from her brother's practice in the quantitative poems of the *Arcadia*, and yet take his practice a step further toward that "perfection" he describes (what Mersenne calls the "intellectual and rational plain" free from "change, mutability, and corruption") by yoking together both classical and biblical poetic models. There is also a poignancy in Pembroke's image of herself (in the posture of the psalmist in Psalm 123), with eyes raised to heaven where her brother now resides, which recalls her poem "To the Angell spirit of the most excellent Sir Phillip Sidney":

Receive theise Hymnes, theise obsequies receive;
if any marke of thy sweet sprite appeare,
well are they borne, no title else shall beare.
I can no more: Deare Soule I take my leave;
Sorrowe still strives, would mount thy highest sphere
presuming so just cause might meet thee there,
Oh happie chaunge! could I so take my leave.[52]

48 Pembroke, *Works*, vol. 2, 215.

49 Sidney, *Defence*, 79. The crucial qualification is that "our infected will keepeth us from reaching unto it."

50 Zim, *English Metrical Psalms*, 199–201.

51 Ibid., 201.

52 In *The Psalms of Sir Philip Sidney and the Countess of Pembroke*, ed. J. C. A. Rathmell (Garden City, NY, 1963), xxxviii.

Abraham Fraunce was patronized by the countess of Pembroke, and though the existence of a wide "Pembroke Circle" has been seriously called into question, he at least was certainly writing under her influence.[53] The volume in which his psalms appeared, *The Countess of Pembrokes Emanuell* (1591), was dedicated to her, following the precedent of Sidney's own *Countess of Pembrokes Arcadia*, and Fraunce even includes her as the character "Pembrokiana" in his *The Countess of Pembrokes Ivychurch* (1591), a translation of Tasso's *Aminta*. Like Pembroke (and her brother), Fraunce avoids the characteristic problem of English quantitative verse – that its disdain of English accent makes it unreadable – by making the verse work accentually as well as quantitatively.[54]

Like Stanyhurst, Fraunce also included the occasional classical allusion in his psalms. The opening of his Psalm 1 praises him who does not sit "downe with a scorner/ In the maligning chayre, that makes but a mock of Olympus," which converts the wickedness of the biblical sinner into a kind of hubris.[55] Jehovah and Zeus are amalgamated in Fraunce's Psalm 73:

> Tis but a vaine conceipt of fooles, to be fondly referring
> Every jesting trick, and trifling toy to the Thunderer.[56]

For the most part, however, Fraunce's psalm translations do not draw attention to their classicism, either allusively or metrically. Interestingly, certain of his rhetorical schemes actually imitate (consciously or not) Hebrew parallelism. As James Kugel demonstrates, "parallelism" does not involve stating the same thing twice, but a kind of "A + B" structure, where "B" may repeat certain elements of "A" with variations or additions, include contrasting or parallel terms, be in apposition to "A," or follow or complete a sequence begun in "A," among other possibilities.[57] The repetitions and inversions in Fraunce's translation of Ps. 1:2–3, for example, might easily be described in terms of Kugel's "A + B" variations (though he also uses the favorite rhetorical scheme of his patron, chiasmus):

[53] For the critique of the Pembroke Circle, see Mary Ellen Lamb, "The Myth of the Countess of Pembroke," *Yearbook of English Studies* 11 (1981), 194–202; "The Countess of Pembroke's Patronage," *English Literary Renaissance* 12 (1982), 162–79. On Fraunce and Pembroke, especially his *countess of Pembrokes Ivychurch*, see Lamb, *Gender and Authorship in the Sidney Circle* (Madison, WI, 1990), 32–47.

[54] Attridge, *Well-Weighed Syllables*, 193.

[55] Fraunce, *The Countesse of Pembroke's Emanuell together with Certaine Psalmes*, in *Miscellanies of the Fuller Worthies Library*, ed. A. B. Grosart (London, 1871), 117. The page references are to the numbers of Grosart's volume (printed at bottom), not those of Fraunce's book (top right).

[56] Ibid., 135.

[57] Kugel, *Idea of Biblical Poetry*, 4–7 and *passim*. Parallelism is not exactly a "form," as Kugel demonstrates, since the two hemistichs may have no semantic relationship whatsoever.

Night and day by the same his footsteps duly directing,
Day and night by the same, hart, mynde, soule, purely preparing.
This man's like to a tree, to a tree most happily planted
Hard by a brooke, by a brooke whose streames of silver abounding
Make this tree her fruite, her pleasant fruite to be yeelding,
Yeelding fruite in tyme to the planters dayly rejoycing.[58]

The pattern of the last four lines depends upon a series of clauses, each of which begins with the last element (a noun phrase) of the preceding one, creating a kind of incremental repetition. Each "B" clause, then, repeats part of but further develops the preceding "A" (as in "Makes this free her fruite" followed by "her pleasant fruite to be yeelding"). Coverdale, in his verse 2, uses a similar if simpler structure, which corresponds closely to the Hebrew in linking the two verse halves by the repetition of the phrase "in the/his law":

But hys delight is in the law of the lorde, & in his law wil he exercise himself day & night.

Very little is known of Fraunce, including whether he might have known Hebrew. It has been suggested that Pembroke may have, through the Herbert family chaplain, Gervase Babington, so perhaps Fraunce learned something of the language through her (or from Babington himself).[59]

Whatever his sense of Hebrew, Fraunce's psalms can be quite effective. Donald Davie goes so far as to suggest that his Psalm 73 may be the most successful English version of this psalm.[60] Fraunce's verses 18–20 bear this out:

Then did I see how they did stand in their slippery places,
Lifted aloft, that their downefalling might be the greater.
Lyving Lord, how soone is this theyr glory triumphant
Dasht, confounded, gone, drownd in destruction endles?
Their fame's soone outworne, theyr name's extinct in a moment,
Lyke to a dreame, that lyves by a sleepe, and dyes with a slumber.[61]

Despite Thomas Nashe's jibe that English hexameter verse "goes twitching and hopping like a man running upon quagmires, up the hill in one syllable and down the dale in another, retaining no part of the smooth gait which he vaunts himself with among the Greeks and Latins," Fraunce uses the

58 Fraunce, *Emanuell*, 117–18.
59 See Jones, *Discovery of Hebrew*, 240–41, as well as, on Babington, Hannay, *Philip's Phoenix*, 132–35.
60 *The Psalms in English*, ed. Donald Davie (Harmondsworth, 1996), 87.
61 Fraunce, *Emanuell*, 136.

length of his hexameters to significant effect.[62] The enjambment at the end of the third line is brought to a dramatic stop with "Dasht," beginning the next line with an abrupt caesura, and the length of this line almost mocks itself in drawing out to the final position the word "endles."

The problem with Fraunce's quantitative verse, like that of Sidney, Campion, and its more accomplished practitioners, is that in solving the problem of awkwardness by aligning quantity and accent, they raised the question of whether the intellectually conceived (as opposed to audibly perceived) quantity was not simply redundant.[63] In fact, Sidney, Spenser, and Campion turned away from the quantitative experiments to write accentual-syllabic verse in the native tradition, and the movement quickly died out.

CLASSICAL METERS IN ENGLISH ACCENTS

The history of the adaptation of classical quantitative meters to English accentual-syllabic verse actually begins before the experiments in English quantity. As his recent biographer W. A. Sessions argues, the last of the earl of Surrey's psalm translations, Psalm 55, is the earliest example of unrhymed English hexameters. The poem is usually regarded as incomplete, work on it having been ended by its author's execution on January 19, 1547, and its metrical experiment was not imitated by psalm writers before the 1580s.[64] It is significant, however, that the psalms were part of Surrey's broader effort to graft English poetry onto the stocks of classical and biblical antiquity, and Surrey's hexametric Psalm 55 may have been in the mind of later classicists, including Stanyhurst, and especially Fraunce and Pembroke. Surrey may also have been one of those "in sorrowful pangs of their death-bringing sins" that Sidney was thinking of in the passage from the *Defence* cited above, those who found in the Psalms the "fruit of comfort" and "the consolation of the never-leaving goodness."[65] Certainly, Surrey's psalm provided a model for the personal application of the Psalms by English translators.

Psalm 55 suited Surrey's situation perfectly, a petition for favor and revenge by one who has been betrayed not by an enemy but by, in Surrey's

[62] Quoted in Davie, *Psalms in English*, 87. [63] Attridge, *Well-Weighed Syllables*, 228–36.

[64] Although Surrey's experiment in transplanting classical meter seems not to have caught on immediately, his Psalm 55 does seem to have initiated a practice of translating this particular psalm – so suitable with its cry of betrayal and call for vengeance – in the Tower. Sir Thomas Smith and John Dudley, earl of Warwick, each wrote a metrical version of Psalm 55 when they were in the Tower. That Dudley's version, at least, was modeled on Surrey's is suggested by the inclusion of both in the Arundel Harington Manuscript, the commonplace book of John Harington, who was himself in the Tower with the Dudleys in 1554. See *The Arundel Harington Manuscript of Tudor Poetry*, ed. Ruth Hughey, 2 vols. (Columbus, OH, 1960).

[65] See above, 85.

words, "Myne old fere and dere frende, my guyde," just as Surrey himself had been charged with treason by his old friend, Sir Richard Southwell.[66] Sessions shows that Surrey's curse, "Rayne those unbrydled tungs! breake that conjured league!" which extrapolates on the first half of verse 9 (in Coverdale, "Destroye their tonges (O Lorde) & devyde them"), is another autobiographical reference, to the conspiracy which had destroyed him. The existence of such a conspiracy has been questioned by some modern historians, but such at least was the contemporary interpretation of Surrey's downfall.[67] Surrey's psalm becomes increasingly personal, to the point where it departs entirely from the original, breaking down into cryptic allusions and closing with an untranslated Latin verse:

> Friowr, whose harme and tounge presents the wicked sort
> Of those false wolves, with cootes which doo their ravin hyde,
> That sweare to me by heaven, the fotestole of the Lord,
> Who though force had hurt my fame, they did not touche my lyfe:
> Such patching care I lothe as feeds the welth with lyes.
> But in th'other Psalme of David fynd I ease:
> Iacta curam tuam super dominum et ipse te enutriet.[68]

The "Friowr" [friar] remains unidentified and obscure, though the following description of wolves in sheep's clothing (the false prophets of Matt. 7:15) is clear enough. Emrys Jones reads the "other Psalme" in the penultimate line as a reference to what follows (in Latin), the last line of this psalm. Sessions suggests that the Latin is crucial to the sense of the poem's close, that Surrey finds consolation ("ease") not just in the promised vengeance of Ps. 55:23 but in the language of the Roman culture he was trying to transplant into England. As Sessions puts it, Surrey puts his trust "as much in Latin as in God."[69] Yet powerful as this reading may be, Surrey's cultural project was, of course, one of translation, and its ultimate goal lay not in the Latin language but in the creation of an English poetry and culture to match those of ancient Rome.

Whether or not Philip or Mary Sidney had Surrey's precedent consciously before them, the Sidney Psalter contains a number of psalms in English adaptations of classical meters, especially hexameters, but also elegiacs and

66 See W. A. Sessions, *Henry Howard the Poet Earl of Surrey* (Oxford, 1999), 361, 366–68. For the text of the poem, see *Henry Howard, Earl of Surrey, Poems*, ed. Emrys Jones (Oxford, 1964), 101–02.

67 Sessions, *Henry Howard*, 361–66.

68 Surrey, *Poems*, 102. The last verse in the Vulgate continues, "*non dabit in aeternum fluctuationem justo*"; in Coverdale's English, the whole verse (23) is "And as for them, thou (O God) shalt bringe them into the pytte of destruecion. The blood thrustye and disceatfull men shall not lyve out half their dayes. Nevertheless, my trust shalbe in thee, (O Lord)."

69 Sessions, *Henry Howard*, 26.

Sapphics. Philip Sidney used a hexameter line in three of his translations, though none of them employs the strict blank verse of Surrey's Psalm 55. Sidney's Psalm 2 is written in rhyming couplets of alternating hexameters and trimeters. As noted above in connection with Stanyhurst's translation of this psalm into quantitative hexameters, the subject of warfare, kings, and right rule may have suggested the use of this heroic meter:

> What ayles this heathenish rage? What do theis people meane
> To mutter murmures vaine?
> Why do these earthly kings and lords such meetings make,
> And counsel jointly take,
> Against the lord of lords, the lord of every thing,
> And his anoynted King?[70]

Sidney's Psalms 15 and 18 are similarly adaptations of the hexameter, the first using a single rhyme through all of its 13 lines, and the second amalgamating the classical heroic line with the English "heroic" stanza associated with kingship, rhyme royal.[71] There is no obvious reason for using a hexameter line for Psalm 15, but Psalm 18, like Psalm 2, is about the battle against the ungodly and it closes with a celebration of God's deliverance of Israel's king (and psalmist):

> He nobly saves his King, and kindness keeps in store.
> For David his Anoynt, and his seed ever more.[72]

The headnote to the psalm emphasizes its connection with the life of King David: "To him that excelleth. A Psalme of David the servant of the Lord, which spake unto the Lord the wordes of this song (in the day that the Lord delivered him from the hand of all his enemies, & from the hand of Saul)."[73] Even without the headnote, this association would have been obvious, since a poem virtually identical to Psalm 18 appears near the end of the David story in 2 Samuel 22.

The two hexameter psalms of the countess of Pembroke, 76 and 141, follow her brother's practice of using the meter for heroic or royal subjects. Psalm 76, according to the Geneva Bible editors, "setteth forthe the power of God & care for the defence of his people in Jerusalem, in the destruction of

[70] *The Poems of Sir Philip Sidney*, ed. William A. Ringler (Oxford, 1962), 271.

[71] The *ababbcc* stanza, normally decasyllabic, was first used by Chaucer in *Troilus and Criseyde*, but is associated with royalty through its use by James I of Scotland in his *Kingis Quair*. The term "royal" (originally "balades ryale") appears first in reference to Chaucer's use of the stanza for an elevated, serious subject. See Martin Stevens and T. V. F. Brogan, "rhyme royal" in *New Princeton Encyclopedia*, 1065–66.

[72] Ibid., 293.

[73] From the Geneva Bible (1560).

the armie of Saneherib."[74] Pembroke translates the psalm into five stanzas rhymed *ababcc*, and points to the literary-historical associations of the hexameter line in an addition to verse 5, concerning God's punishment of the proud:

> Above proud princes, proudest in their theevery,
> thou art exalted high, and highly glorified:
> their weake attempt, thy valiant delivery,
> theire spoile, thie conquest *meete to be historified.*[75]

The reference, in hexameter verse, to the "historification" of God's (and Israel's) victory over the enemy, whether Sennacherib or some other heathen power, suggests very strongly the use of the hexameter for the "historification" of the conquests of Achilles and Aeneas in the classical epics of Homer and Virgil. Since the psalm itself is the actual history deemed "meete" in Pembroke's additional half-line, this implies that the psalm is a kind of epic in miniature, which accords with the traditional understanding of the heroical poetry of the Old Testament. The critic and translator Thomas Lodge, in his *The Famous and Memorable Works of Josephus* (1609), translated Josephus's description of the meter of the Song of Moses (Exodus 15): "Moses likewise composed an Ode in Hexameter verse, containing the prayses of god, and a thanksgiving for the favour he had done unto them. All these things have I particularly declared, according as I have found them in holy Scriptures."[76] As Israel Baroway has demonstrated, it was a critical commonplace in the Renaissance that the Song of Moses and other biblical poems (Moses' song in Deuteronomy 33, for instance, or parts of the Prophets) were in hexameters, and these were understood to be the precursors and even models for the verse of the Homeric epics.[77] In this context, Pembroke's choice of accentual hexameters for Psalm 76 and for Psalm 141 (like Psalm 18, according to the Geneva Bible editors, another psalm concerning David's struggle against Saul) makes perfect sense.

Pembroke may have gotten the idea for her genuinely Sapphic psalm (125) from Stanyhurst's Psalm 4, or indeed from the general popularity of the verse form, but she may also have been influenced by Philip Sidney's translation of two psalms into accentual Sapphics, or English adaptations of the classical Sapphic. Such an anglicization of the Sapphic was inevitable, given the

[74] Ibid., 251. [75] Pembroke, *Works*, vol. 2, 101, italics added.

[76] Cited in Israel Baroway, "The Hebrew Hexameter: A Study in Renaissance Sources and Interpretation," *ELH* 2 (1935), 73.

[77] Ibid., 72–78. The poet and translator Barnabe Googe went so far as to argue that the Psalms themselves were "written . . . in perfect and pleasant hexameter verse" (ibid., 79).

regular accentual pattern already present in the Latin Sapphics of Horace (mentioned above). Sidney's Psalm 6 is in four-line stanzas consisting of three lines of iambic pentameter and a concluding dimeter:

> Lord, let not me a worme by thee be shent,
> While Thou art in the heat of thy displeasure:
> Ne let thy rage, of my due punishment
> Become the measure.[78]

True to the model of the original Sapphic, Sidney enjambs every third line, so that the last two lines are effectively a broken fourteener (though short a syllable and broken differently from the usual English 8 and 6). Sidney's Psalm 9 is a looser adaptation of the Sapphic stanza, adding an extra pentameter line and not following the enjambment of the final lines:

> With all my heart O lord I will prayse Thee,
> My speeches all Thy marvailes shall descry:
> In Thee my joyes and comforts ever be,
> Yea even my songs thy name shall magnify,
> O Lord most high.[79]

As Weiner has argued (see n. 38), Sidney's Psalm 6 is a lover's complaint, like his Sapphic in the *Old Arcadia* (no. 59), "Get hence foul grief, the canker of the mind." Sidney's reason for using a modified Sapphic in Psalm 9 seems less clear. Of course, neither of his Sapphics has quite the topicality of his sister's, given the powerful association of the form with the original female poet. Pembroke makes effective use of the pointed abruptness of the Sapphic's short fourth line to give metrical emphasis to the unshakable solidity of both the walls of Jerusalem and the protection of Jehovah:

> As Sion standeth very firmly stedfast,
> never once shaking: soe on high Jehova
> who his hope buildeth, very firmly stedfast
> ever abideth.
>
> As Salem braveth with hir hilly bulwarkes
> roundly enforted: soe the greate jehova
> closeth his servantes, as a hilly bullwark
> ever abiding.[80]

Of the other classical meters and stanzas adapted for English translations of the psalms, the most important is the Pindaric ode, which was used by several seventeenth-century poets in translating Psalm 137, "By the waters

[78] Sidney, *Poems*, 276. [79] Ibid., 279. [80] Pembroke, *Works*, vol. 2, 216.

of Babylon, I sat down and wept" (see the discussion of the versions by Davison, Fletcher, Crashaw, and Oldham below, chapter 7). The conception of some of the psalms as odes derives, once again, from Jerome. The passage from his "Preface to Eusebius" cited above (p. 87) compares the psalms to the poems of Horace, Pindar, and Sappho, all authors of odes, though conceived and fashioned rather differently.[81] Apart from the several renderings of Psalm 137, there are a number of translations of other psalms that use long, irregular stanzas that may derive from the Pindaric ode, Fletcher's Psalms 62 and 130, for instance, or Crashaw's Psalm 23 (formally much the same as his other psalm, 137).

Samuel Woodford's *Paraphrase upon the Psalms of David* (1667) translated the entire psalter into Pindaric odes. Woodford was strongly influenced by the Sidney Psalter, having seen it in manuscript through the graces of John Wilkins, the dean of Rippon (some years later he himself transcribed what is now known as the "B" manuscript of the Sidney Psalter from an original his brother had been using to hold coffee grounds).[82] The form of the ode, however, he based loosely on Abraham Cowley's translation of Psalm 114 in his incomplete epic, *Davideis*, though Cowley's stanza is longer and metrically more varied:

When *Isra'el* was from bondage led,
Led by th'*Almighties* hand
From out a foreign land,
The great *Sea* beheld, and fled.
As men pursu'ed, when that fear past they find,
Stop on some higher ground to look behind,
So whilst through wondrous ways
The sacred *Army* went,
The *waves* afar stood up to gaze,
And their own *Rocks* did represent,
Solid as *Waters* are above the *Firmament*.[83]

Woodford had no intention of providing a psalter for use in church. It was printed without music or any indications for the singing of the psalms. Although in his dedication to the bishop of Winchester Woodford claimed

[81] See Stephen F. Fogle and Paul H. Fry, "ode," in *New Princeton Encyclopedia*, 855–57.

[82] Pembroke, *Works*, vol. 2, 308–10.

[83] Cowley, *Davideis*, book 1, lines 483–93, *A Critical Edition of Abraham Cowley's* Davideis, ed. Gayle Shadduck (New York and London, 1987). In Cowley's poem, Psalm 114 is sung by David to calm the enraged Saul. Woodford explains in his preface that "reading over with a little more than ordinary intention the CXIV. Psalm of Mr. Cowleys, I was again warm'd, and in imitation of him I was resolved once more to try how well or ill I could write after so excellent a Copy." *Paraphrase*, sig. b3[r].

to have "design'd" his psalter "to the *Service of the Altar,*" it seems entirely unsuited for any liturgical use. His purpose seems to have been primarily the provision of a reading translation of the Psalms that gave some sense of their quality as poems and demonstrated that "Theology and Poesy have in all ages of the World gone hand and hand, nor is there really such disparity between their Natures, as is generally, though without any reason, imagined."[84] Woodford's stanzas vary somewhat from psalm to psalm in length and rhyme scheme, but he used the loose form of the English Pindaric throughout, and the opening of his Psalm 84 is representative:

I.
Triumphant General of the Sacred Host,
Whom all the strength of Heav'n and earth obey,
Who hast a Thund'ring Legion in each Coast,
And Mighty Armies lifted, and in pay;
How fearfull art Thou in their head above,
Yet in Thy Temple, Lord; how full of Love?

II.
So lovely is Thy Temple, and so fair,
So like Thy self, that with desire I faint;
My heart and flesh cry out to see Thee there,
And could bear any thing but this restraint:
My Soul do's on its old Remembrance feed,
And new desires by my long absence breed.[85]

The only other meter derived from classical verse employed in the Sidney Psalter is an adaptation of elegiacs (what Susanne Woods calls "pseudo-elegiac couplets"),[86] which Pembroke used for Psalm 114. The normal elegiac consists of alternating hexameter and pentameter lines. Pembroke further reduces the short line, alternating hexameters and tetrameters, but the effect is very similar. Her reasons for using this meter are unclear, since it was traditionally associated either with rather racy love poems (such as Ovid's elegies, famously translated by Marlowe) or with poems of mourning and lament (hence the familiar modern sense of "elegiac"). Psalm 114 has nothing to do with love, and, since it celebrates the Exodus out of Egypt, is anything but mournful.

The most famous literary use of Psalm 114 prior to the late sixteenth century was at the beginning of Dante's *Purgatorio*, where Dante and Virgil hear the first verse ("*In exitu Israel de Aegypto*") sung by the souls arriving

84 Woodford, *Paraphrase*, sig. a2[r]. 85 Ibid.

86 Susanne Woods, *Natural Emphasis: English Versification from Chaucer to Dryden* (San Marino, 1984), 296.

on the shores of Mount Purgatory.[87] Perhaps the associations of the elegiac couplet with mourning derived from this passage, or from Dante's famous anagogical reading of Psalm 114 in his letter to Can Grande as "the passing of the sanctified soul from the bondage of the corruption of this world to the liberty of everlasting glory."[88] By this reading, the psalm would celebrate death as a transfiguration, so that the form of the classical lament would be appropriate but would itself be transfigured by the Christian conception of death as rebirth into new life (the psalm was part of the Catholic Easter liturgy, as Dante was aware, celebrating the Resurrection of Christ).[89]

Philip Sidney had certainly read Dante (he mentions him several times in the *Defence*), so it is likely that Pembroke had done so too. That she knew Italian is clear from her translation of Petrarch's *Trionfo della Morte*. Yet whether she had Dante in mind or not, his anagogical reading of the psalm is much the same as that of other biblical exegetes. Luther, for example, in his *First Lectures on the Psalms* (admittedly unpublished), begins his commentary on Psalm 114 by asserting that "this exodus is spiritual and takes place with the feet of the soul."[90] Augustine understands the Exodus as the Christian's renunciation of the world through the Grace of God.[91] Pembroke's use of a classically derived meter in this psalm may, like her use of quantitative meters in the first group of the Songs of Degrees, signal the end of cultural as well as spiritual exile. As in her Psalm 120, her Psalm 114 introduces the notion of barbarism, which had such powerful linguistic, literary, and cultural overtones in the sixteenth century:

> At what tyme Jacobs race did leave of Aegypt take,
> And Aegypts barbrous folk forsake.[92]

Once again, Pembroke may be celebrating more than the Exodus or even the return from exile of the earthbound soul; the quasi-elegiac stanzas, like her hexameters, Sapphics, and Alcaics, celebrate the return of English culture to its "true" classical and Hebraic roots, here conceived of as not only mutually compatible but as inextricable links in a continuous cultural chain.

87 Dante, *The Divine Comedy 2: Purgatorio*, canto 2, lines 46–51, ed. and trans. John D. Sinclair (New York, 1939, rpr. 1980), 34–35.

88 *Letters of Dante*, trans. Paget Toynbee (2nd ed., Oxford, 1967), 199. See also Sinclair's note to *Purgatorio*, canto 2, 41–42.

89 See Sinclair's note to *Purgatorio*, canto 2, 41–42.

90 *Luther's Works*, vol. 11, *First Lectures on the Psalms* II, ed. Hilton C. Oswald (Saint Louis, 1976), 393.

91 "But Egypt, since it is said to mean affliction, or one who afflicteth, or one who oppresseth, is often used for an emblem of this world; from which we must spiritually withdraw, that we may not be bearing the yoke with unbelievers." Augustine, *Expositions on the Book of Psalms*, trans. H. M. Wilkins (Oxford, 1853), vol. 5, 276.

92 Pembroke, *Works*, vol. 2, 183.

Milton was later to translate Psalm 114 into Greek hexameters with much the same polemical purpose, converting the psalm into a hymn to English Protestantism, looking forward to the final delivery of the true Reformed Church.[93] That he chose to write in Greek once again demonstrates the widespread sense that the origin of classical prosody lay in the Hebrew Psalms, and that the Hebraic and the Hellenic were simply stages in the continuous cultural history that reached its pinnacle (so many hoped) in the achievements of poets in sixteenth- and seventeenth-century England.

[93] See Stella P. Revard, *Milton and the Tangles of Neaera's Hair: The Making of the 1645 Poems* (Columbia and London, 1997), 84–86. As Revard points out, the sense of urgency in Milton's hymn to the Protestant cause would have been even greater at the publication of his Greek psalm in 1645 than at the time of its composition in 1634.

CHAPTER 4

The Psalms and English poetry II: "The highest matter in the noblest forme": psalms and the development of English verse

Important though it was for English poets to have the authoritative precedent of David as a poet and the Psalms as poetic models, the influence of the Psalms on English poetry was complicated by the lack of any accurate and demonstrable knowledge of the nature of Hebrew poetry. Despite this ignorance, poets nevertheless worked under the assumption that the Psalms were a storehouse of all modes, forms, and meters a poet might wish to use. In his poem praising the Sidney psalms, Donne describes David's divinely inspired poems as "The highest matter in the noblest forme," and, given his lament that the Psalms are "So well attired abroad, so ill at home" (probably contrasting Sternhold and Hopkins with Marot and de Bèze), the "forme" was obviously of real importance to him.[1] As a result of this sense of the richness of Hebrew verse, the Psalms became a testing-ground for the development of English versification in the sixteenth and seventeenth centuries, as poets translated psalms into virtually all the available lyric forms, and invented many more besides. The Sidney Psalter was the preeminent and most influential example of such inventiveness.[2] Yet the history of psalms as a site of poetic experimentation begins earlier, with the paraphrases of Sir Thomas Wyatt and George Gascoigne (as well as Anne Vaughan Lock's Psalm 51, treated in chapter 6).[3]

Wyatt's psalms are among the few that have received substantial critical attention, and the insights of his many critics do not need to be repeated

[1] "Upon the translation of the psalmes by Sir Philip Sidney, and the Countesse of Pembroke his Sister" (lines 11, 38), in Donne, *Poems*, vol. 1, 348–48.

[2] Called by Hallett Smith, "a School of English Versification." See "English Metrical Psalms," 269.

[3] Lock's "Meditation of a Penitent Sinner: Written in Maner of a Paraphrase upon the 51. Psalme of David," perhaps the first sonnet sequence in English, certainly deserves to stand with the formally experimental psalms of Wyatt, Gascoigne, and the Sidneys. See Roland Greene, "Anne Lock's *Meditation*: Invention Versus Dilation and the Founding of Puritan Poetics," in *Form and Reform in Renaissance England*, ed. Amy Boesky and Mary Thomas Crane (Newark and London, 2000), 153–70. The other great early Tudor innovator in English literary history, the earl of Surrey, was metrically quite conservative in most of his psalm translations (except for Psalm 55 – see chap. 3), which he wrote in poulter's measure.

here.[4] Wyatt's *Penitential Psalms* seem not to have had a substantial influence on subsequent psalm translation, but his innovative meter may have influenced Sidney's choice of *terza rima* for his Psalm 7, "O Lord my God, Thou art my trustfull stay," and even John Milton's in his paraphrase of Psalm 2, "Why do the Gentiles tumult." The choice of *terza rima*, as Robert G. Twombly suggests, was probably based on the paraphrases of the Penitential Psalms by Luigi Alamanni.[5] Apart from a brief experiment in Chaucer's "Complaint to his Lady," Wyatt's is the first significant use of *terza rima* in English, though the form had a long history in Italian, from its invention by Dante in the *Commedia* to its use in the Renaissance by Boccaccio and Petrarch (in the *Trionfi*, for instance, one of which the countess of Pembroke translated into English *terza rima*).[6] In fact, Wyatt was an inveterate experimenter and is credited with introducing the Italian (Petrarchan) sonnet into English as well as the Petrarchan canzone. The most important Italian model for his *Penitential Psalms* was Pietro Aretino's (prose) *I Sette Salmi de la Penitentia di David* (1534), from which Wyatt derived the basic structure linking the seven psalms, with interpolations between them, to form a continuous narrative about David's penitence for his adultery with Bathsheba. Wyatt's *Penitential Psalms* are thus an excellent example of the complexity of Renaissance psalm translation, since they import the Hebrew texts through the intermediary of Italian versions in prose and meter (and, conversely, the techniques of Italian prosody through the medium of the biblical Psalms). They are also the first free paraphrase of the Psalms in English by a major poet, in which the original is adapted to the poet's personal situation and concerns in accordance with Renaissance notions of *imitatio*.[7] Wyatt can thus be said to initiate the subsequent practice of poetic psalm paraphrase from Surrey to Milton.

More immediately, Wyatt's creation of a continuous narrative by adding connecting verses to link the psalms into a larger poetic structure, based on Aretino's precedent, may have influenced George Gascoigne in his

[4] See, for instance, H. A. Mason, *Humanism and Poetry in the Early Tudor Period* (London, 1959), 206–21; Robert G. Twombly, "Thomas Wyatt's Paraphrase of the Penitential Psalms of David," *Texas Studies in Literature and Language* 13:3 (Fall, 1970), 349; Stephen Greenblatt, "Power, Sexuality, and Inwardness in Wyatt's Poetry," in *Renaissance Self-Fashioning* (Chicago and London, 1980), 115–56; Zim, *English Metrical Psalms*, 43–74; and, most recently, Elizabeth Heale, "Lute and Harp in Wyatt's Poetry," in *Sacred and Profane*, ed. Helen Wilcox et al. (Amsterdam, 1996), 3–16. Wyatt's Psalm 51 is treated in chap. 6.

[5] *Opere Toscane* (1532). See Twombly, "Wyatt's Paraphrase," 349.

[6] See Lawrence J. Zillman and Clive Scott, "*terza rima*," *New Princeton Encyclopedia*, 1271. Pembroke's translation of Petrarch, *The Triumph of Death*, is in Pembroke, *Works*, vol. 1, 273–82.

[7] On *imitatio* in the Renaissance, with reference to psalm translation, see Zim, *English Metrical Psalms*, chap. 1, and, more broadly, Thomas Greene, *Light in Troy*.

paraphrase of Psalm 130.[8] Gascoigne's only psalm translation appears in his anthology *Posies* (1575), within a narrative of the author's own experience, a frame sometimes omitted when the psalm is anthologized, but which greatly affects the perception of the poem by the reader. In the earlier, purportedly unauthorized, publication of Gascoigne's poems, *A Hundreth Sundrie Flowres* (1573),[9] the editor did not include the text of the psalm paraphrase itself, but he did include the poetic introduction to the psalm (a sonnet), as well as a prose description of the supposed situation in which the psalm was composed:

The occasion of the wrighting hereof (as I have herde Master Gascoigne say) was this, riding alone betwene Chelmisforde and London, his minde mused uppon the dayes past, and therewithall he gan accuse his owne conscience of muche time misspent, when a great shoure of rayne did overtake him, and he beeing unprepared for the same, as in a Jerken without a cloake, the wether beeing very faire and unlikely to have changed so: he began to accuse himselfe of his carelesnesse, and thereuppon in his good disposition compiled firste this sonet, and afterwardes, the translated Psalme of Deprofundis *as her followeth.*

The Skies gan scowle, orecast with mistie clowdes,
When (as I rode alone by London way,
Clokelesse, unclad) thus did I sing and say:
Behold quoth I, bright *Titan* how he shroudes
His hed abacke, and yelds the raine his reach,
Till in his wrath, *Dan Jove* have soust the soile,
And washt me wretch which in his travaile toile,
But holla (here) doth rudenesse me apeach,
Since *Jove* is Lord and king of mightie power,
Which can commande the sunne to shew his face,
And (when him list) to give the raine his place.
Why do not I my wery muses frame,
(Although I be well soused in this shoure,)
To wrighte some verse in honor of his name?[10]

In *Posies*, Gascoigne's corrected edition of the earlier "unauthorized" volume, the prose introduction was omitted and the psalm followed the

8 A similar use by Francis Quarles of original verses to connect a group of metrical psalms (1–8) has recently been discovered and published by Karl Josef Höltgen, "New Verse by Francis Quarles: The Portland Manuscripts, Metrical Psalms, and the *Bay Psalm Book* (with text)," *English Literary Renaissance* 28:1 (Winter, 1998), 118–41.

9 As Felicity A. Hughes notes, the current critical consensus is that, despite the "editor's" claims to the contrary, the 1573 volume was published by Gascoigne himself as a bid for patronage. See "Gascoigne's Poses," *Studies in English Literature* 37 (1997), 1–19.

10 George Gascoigne, *A Hundreth Sundrie Flowres*, ed. G. W. Pigman (Oxford, 2000), 290.

sonnet. The "prologue" (prose and verse) is as interesting as the paraphrase itself, however, and not only because it may indicate a debt to Wyatt. The context transforms the psalm into a personal expression of Gascoigne's own "conscience of muche time misspent," conditioned at least in part by his long rainy journey. By inserting the *De profundis* into an autobiographical narrative, Gascoigne provides his psalm with the kind of specific personal, even social occasion that was an essential component of the Renaissance lyric.[11] This transforms the psalm from a straightforward translation of Psalm 130 into an "original" literary work, as is implied by the title in both *A Hundreth Sundrie Flowres* and *Posies*, "Gascoigne's *Deprofundis*."[12]

The psalm was actually one that was traditionally read as an occasional and deeply personal poem. Gascoigne's readers would no doubt have remembered that Psalm 130 was one of the seven Penitential Psalms – the group Wyatt translated – supposedly composed by the repentant King David out of remorse and guilt for his affair with Bathsheba. Encouraging its application to similar situations, the headnote to the psalm in "Sternhold and Hopkins" describes it as "an effectuous prayer of hym that for his sinnes had susteyned great afflictions, and not withstanding, he fully trusteth, and assureth himselfe to obteyne mercy and forgevenes of his synnes, and at length delivereth from all evilles."[13] This perfectly suits Gascoigne's stance in *Posies* as the repentant libertine, apologizing to unnamed "reverend Divines" for "sundrie wanton speeches and lascivious phrases" that they had censured in his earlier volume.[14] *Posies* is presented as a fully expurgated and morally improved edition of the *Hundreth Sundrie Flowres*, but as Felicity A. Hughes argues, and as many of Gascoigne's readers would now agree, this is simply another of the author's many poses.[15] Gascoigne plays the part of the repentant sinner, but mocks his critics from behind his mask. David was the perfect model for such penitence: his sin had been sexual, he had been censured by the prophet Nathan ("grey-heared" like Gascoigne's censors),[16] and he had the sanction of Scripture, the Church (at least in retrospect), and God himself. He was also, like Gascoigne, a poet and a

[11] See Arthur F. Marotti, *Manuscript, Print, and the Renaissance Lyric* (Ithaca and London, 1995), 2–10. In fact, much of the verse in Gascoigne's *Sundrie Flowres*, including riddles, verse epistles, and courtly games, was pointedly occasional, emphasized by the inclusion of descriptions of the original social contexts of its composition.

[12] The author's name is also included in the titles of the "original" poems (i.e., not translations), "Gascoignes good morrow," "Gascoygnes good night," and "Gasoignes woodmanship," which suggests that the psalm is "Gascoignes" no less than the secular lyrics (see *The Complete Works of George Gascoigne*, ed. John W. Cunliffe [Cambridge, 1907, rpr. 1969], vol. 1, 58, 55, 348).

[13] *The Whole Booke of Psalmes*, 338.

[14] Gascoigne, *Works*, vol. 1, 3.

[15] Hughes, "Gascoigne's Poses," 16.

[16] Gascoigne, *Works*, vol. 1, 4.

soldier.[17] It may also have been in Gascoigne's mind that, despite his penitence, David kept the spoils of his sin, Bathsheba.

That "Gascoigne's *Deprofundis*" is part of this complex and ironic role-playing is suggested further by the inclusion of the psalm in the first section of the book, "Flowers," so termed "bycause being indeed invented upon a verie light occasion, they have yet in them (in my judgement) some rare invention and Methode before not commonly used."[18] The reader is being alerted to the true nature of Gascoigne's penitence by his inclusion of a penitential psalm in the midst of poems "more pleasant than profitable." Later in *Posies*, in the "Weedes" section, Gascoigne includes a poem which further calls attention to the ambiguities involved in playing the role of King David:

Davids salutacions to Berzabe wherein are three sonnets in sequence, written uppon this occasion. The deviser hereof amongst other friendes had named a gentlewoman his Berzabe, and she was content to call him her David. The man presented his Lady with a booke of the Golden Asse, written by Lucius Apuleius, and in the beginning of the booke wrote this sequence. You must conferre it with the Historye of Apuleius, for else it wyll have small grace.[19]

The roles of David and Bathsheba are here part of the amorous game of courtly lovers, to be read in that context as well as that of "the History of Apuleius," itself another narrative of love, moral lapse, and repentance. Gascoigne has so many poses that it is impossible to tell whether his contrition is genuine, satirical, or some combination of the two, but if we "conferre" his psalm with this later poem and its accompanying "key," we might well interpret it in the context of the full history of King David, both the adulterous lover and the contrite penitent, as well as in the context of courtly games like that of the "deviser" and his "gentlewoman."[20]

17 Gascoigne's multiple roles are summarized in the title of C. T. Prouty's *George Gascoigne, Elizabethan Courtier, Soldier, and Poet* (New York, 1942, rpr. 1946).

18 Gascoigne, *Works*, vol. 1, 13. The tripartite division of *Posies* into "Flowers," "Weedes," and "Herbes" is not present in the *Hundreth Sundrie Flowres* and seems part of Gascoigne's apologetic strategy.

19 Ibid., 463.

20 An ironic reading of Gascoigne's Davidic pose is further borne out by two other references to David and Bathsheba, in *The Adventures of Master F. J.* (*Works*, vol. 1, 385) and in "The lover encouraged by former examples, determineth to make vertue of necessitie" (*Works*, vol. 1, 94–95). In both cases, David provides an attractive model for the courtly lover. At the very least, this suggests that Richard Helgerson's argument for Gascoigne as a "prodigal poet," whose career begins with scandalous love poetry and ends with sober moral treatises like *The Droomme of Doomes Day*, requires some qualification. The moral works are separated from the prodigal ones by only a year or less, and, according to a note in Gascoigne's *The Complaynt of Phylomene* (1576), "Gascoigne's *Deprofundis*" was written as early as April of 1562 (*Works*, vol. 1, 3). Even if Gascoigne's penitence is genuine, then, it comes and goes over much of his career. See Helgerson, *The Elizabethan Prodigals* (Berkeley, Los Angeles, and London, 1976).

"Gascoigne's *Deprofundis*" is also a remarkable psalm translation in its allusion to older English poetry. Gascoigne's journey, with its drenching "shoure," the sun in "shroudes," and with "Dan Jove" sousing the "soile," seems a deliberate evocation of earlier English poets, especially Chaucer in the general prologue to *The Canterbury Tales*, also dominated by "the shoures of Aprill." It is with Chaucer, after all, that the archaic title "Dan" (or "daun") is particularly associated. Spenser's reference to "Dan Chaucer" in *The Faerie Queene* (4.2.32) depends on Chaucer's own frequent use of the word:

> Wher shal I calle yow my lord daun John,
> or daun Thomas, or elles daun Albon?
> . . . .
> I neyther am Ennok ne Elye,
> Ne Romulus, ne Ganymede,
> That was ybore up, as men rede,
> To hevene with daun Jupiter,
> And made the goddys botiller.[21]

These echoes of Chaucer may also point to the *Canterbury Tales* as the general model for Gascoigne's travel poem.

Gascoigne's paraphrase is also stylistically allusive, its self-conscious use of archaic style and diction anticipating Spenser's half-antique, half-invented English in *The Shepheardes Calender* and *The Faerie Queene*. Furthermore, by the standards of sixteenth-century English psalm translation, "Gascoigne's *Deprofundis*" is unusually preoccupied with an older form of literary artifice, based largely on the devices of alliteration and assonance. Gascoigne relishes the sounds of the English language, but in his *Certayne Notes of Instruction*, he is critical of reckless sound effects of the sort favored by Richard Stanyhurst, and, intriguingly, he refers to Chaucer as his authority on this: "For it is not enough to roll in pleasant woordes, nor yet to thunder in *Rym*, *Ram*, *Ruff* by letter (quoth my master *Chaucer*), nor yet to abounde in apt vocables or epythetes, unlesse the Invention have in it also *aliquid salis*."[22] Gascoigne goes on to explain that "by this *aliquid salis* I mean some good and fine devise, shewing the quicke capacitie of a writer."[23] The "*aliquid salis*" in the case of "*Deprofundis*" seems to be partly the self-conscious nod to Chaucer and earlier English poets. Significantly,

[21] Geoffrey Chaucer, prologue to "The Monk's Tale," *Canterbury Tales*, 1929–30, and *House of Fame*, 588–92, in *The Complete Poetry and Prose of Geoffrey Chaucer*, ed. John H. Fisher (New York, 1977).

[22] Gascoigne, *Certayne Notes of Instruction*, in Smith, *Elizabethan Essays*, vol. 1, 47. For a discussion of Stanyhurst, see chap. 3, above.

[23] Ibid.

the alliteration in this poem is actually structural, harking back to the meter of another of England's "classic" poets, William Langland. *Piers Plowman*, reprinted several times in the sixteenth century, was written in a four-stress line consisting of two alliteratively linked hemistichs:[24]

In a somer seson * whan soft was the sonne,
I shope me in shroudes * as I a shepe were,
In habite as an heremite * unholy of workes,
Went wyde in þis world * wondres to here.
Ac on a May mornynge * on Malverne hulles,
Me byfel a ferl * of fairy, me thoughte;
I was wery forwandred * and went me to reste
Under a brode banke * bi a bornes side.[25]

Although Gascoigne's psalm is written largely in iambic pentameter, its persistent use of alliteration gives it the superficial appearance of an accentual meter notably similar to Langland's (and not present in Gascoigne's other poems). His line has a consistent caesura after the fourth syllable, and the second half-line is generally linked to the first by structural alliteration on stressed syllables:

From depth of doole wherein my soule doth dwell,
From heavy heart which harbours in my brest,
From troubled sprite which sildome taketh rest,
From hope of heaven, from dreade of darkesome hell.
O gracious God, to thee I crye and yell.
My God, my Lorde, my lovely Lord aloane,
To thee I call, to thee I make my moane.
And thou (good God) vouchsafe in gree to take,
This woeful plaint,
Wherein I faint.
Oh heare me then for thy great mercy's sake.[26]

The Anglo-Saxon style and diction of the psalm also correspond to the solidly English poetics Gascoigne favored in *Certayne Notes*, rejecting foreign borrowings and "inkhorne" terms, because he had "rather regarde to make our language commendable in it self, than gay with the feathers of straunge birds."[27]

It will be apparent from the stanza quoted above that Gascoigne uses another rhetorical scheme – anaphora – to knit together his lines. Anaphora

[24] See W. W. Skeat's introduction to his edition of *Piers the Plowman* (Oxford, 1924), xii. Incidentally, one of the publishers was Robert Crowley, who published his own metrical translation of the Psalms in 1549 (see Zim, *English Metrical Psalms*, 134–35).

[25] *Piers the Plowman* (lines 1–8).

[26] Gascoigne, *Works*, vol. 1, 60.

[27] Gascoigne's *Certayne Notes*, cited in Ronald C. Johnson, *George Gascoigne* (New York, 1972), 75.

is not a device particularly associated with Chaucer or Langland, but it is regularly found in the Psalms, as in the Geneva Bible translation of Psalm 29:

> Give unto the Lord, ye sonnes of the mightie: give unto the Lord glorie and strength.
> Give unto the Lord glorie due unto his Name: worship the Lord in his glorious Sanctuarie.
> The voice of the Lord is upon the waters: the God of glorie maketh it to thunder: the Lord is upon the great waters.
> The voice of the Lord is mightie: the voice of the Lord is glorious.
> The voice of the Lord breaketh the cedres: yea, the Lord breaketh the cedres of Lebanon.[28]

The first four lines of Gascoigne's opening stanza to Psalm 130 begin with "From," and the anaphora intensifies through each succeeding stanza, culminating in the final stanza, in which the repetition of "He wyll" at the beginning of eight lines creates an almost incantatory, ritual effect to close the poem:

> Hee wyll redeeme our deadly drowping state,
> He wyll bring home the sheepe that goe astraye,
> He wyll helpe them that hope in him alwaye:
> He wyll appease our discorde and debate,
> He wyll soone save, though we repent us late.
> He wyll be ours if we continewe his,
> He wyll bring bale to joye and perfect blisse.
> He wyll redeeme the flocke of his electe,
> From all that is,
> Or was amisse.
> Since Abrahams heyres dyd first his Lawes reject.[29]

The litany of restitution suits perfectly Gascoigne's attempt to cast himself as the prodigal son returned, whether from honest motives or not – he certainly looked forward to tasting the fatted calf at court, though not, perhaps, to leading a life of moral reformation. In any case, "Gascoigne's *Deprofundis*" is the psalm translation most preoccupied with literary artifice between those of Wyatt and the Sidneys.

The greatest achievement in literary psalm translation in the English Renaissance is the Sidney Psalter. In *The Arte of English Poesie*, George Puttenham discusses the "Arte" of what would now be called English accentual-syllabic verse in terms of five types of proportion: the number of

[28] Geneva Bible (1560). [29] Gascoigne, *Works*, vol. 1, 62.

lines in a stanza, the number of syllables in the line, the choice of rhymes, the spacing and patterning of rhymes, and the use of lines of different lengths to make visual shapes.[30] The full potential of all of these proportions was explored by Philip and Mary Sidney, countess of Pembroke, in the Sidney Psalter, making it in essence a source-book for English poetic form. Philip Sidney began translating the Psalms late in his short life, likely in the 1580s, and completed the first 43 before his untimely death in the Dutch wars in 1586. Pembroke finished the project, translating the remaining 107 psalms and revising some of her brother's.[31] Though it was not printed until the nineteenth century, it circulated widely in manuscript and had a considerable influence on seventeenth-century poets. That the Sidney Psalter is a tour de force of the fashioning of English verse forms does not by any means suggest that it was an exercise in pedantry or "mere" artifice. Many of the Sidney psalms can stand, as poems, alongside the greatest lyric accomplishments of the period, and it is this, as much as their celebrated formal variety, which explains their profound influence on the poetic practice of Donne, Herbert, Vaughan, Milton, and many others.

The metrical and formal variety of the Sidney Psalter has been acknowledged by a number of critics, notably Susanne Woods, in her study of the development of English prosody, and the editors of the recent *Collected Works of Mary Sidney Herbert*.[32] There is no volume of lyrics of a similar quality, variety, and coherence in English verse before Herbert's *The Temple*, for which the Sidney Psalter was clearly the model (and which then itself inspired works like Vaughan's *Silex Scintillans* and Christopher Harvey's *The Synagogue*). The quantitative meters, and the English meters derived from them, have been discussed in the previous chapter. In addition to these psalms in classical forms, there are two sonnets (Psalms 100 and 150, the former Spenserian, the latter a variation on the Petrarchan), poems in *terza rima* (Psalms 7 and 30) and *ottava rima* (Psalm 78), rhyme royal (Psalms 51 and 63), as well as variations on the popular common meter of

30 See Puttenham, *Arte*, 78–114. Puttenham discusses these proportions at some length; I take the précis of his five basic proportions from Attridge, *Well-Weighed Syllables*, 90.

31 For the history of the Sidney Psalter, see, among other works, Pembroke, *Works*, esp. vol. 1, 1–80, and vol. 2, 3–32; and Hannay, *Philip's Phoenix*, 84–105. The fact that Pembroke translated over two-thirds of the final psalter, including many of the most thematically and formally interesting of the psalms, is reflected in the relatively greater emphasis on her translations over her brother's in this chapter. At the same time, the project was the genuinely collaborative achievement of, as Donne put it, "Two, by their bloods, and by thy spirit one," so that what is said of the psalter as a whole generally applies to both of its authors. It was also as a whole, as a complete lyric collection, that the Sidney Psalter had its influence on subsequent poets, who do not seem to have distinguished between its two authors.

32 See Woods, *Natural Emphasis*, App. B, which lists and describes the forms of the Sidney psalms; see also the "Table of Verse Forms," in Pembroke, *Works*, vol. 2, 469–84.

"Sternhold and Hopkins" (Psalm 19, in lines of eight and seven syllables, and Psalm 112, in nine and seven). There are also acrostics (Psalm 117, the first letters of the twelve lines spelling out "PRAISTHELORD," as well as Psalm 111, whose first letters, mimicking the Hebrew original, run through the alphabet from "A" to "U"). There are psalms in hexameters, pentameters, tetrameters, trimeters, and various combinations of these, in meters iambic, trochaic, and mixtures of both (as in Psalm 90), in short stanzas and long ones, in as many rhyme schemes as could be accommodated in the 150 psalms. The huge Psalm 119, another acrostic in which each section begins with a letter of the alphabet, is cornucopian in itself, each section composed in a distinct and original stanza form. The Sidney Psalter was both a practical argument for the literary value of the Psalms, and an argument for the poetic potential of the English language.

That the Sidney psalms were "original" in founding a broader tradition of devotional poetry has been appreciated for some time, though they also built on the work of previous metrical psalmists, including Gascoigne.[33] Their importance in originating a new, more "literary" approach to psalm translation has received less attention, however, and their psalms' "originality" as literary works still needs further urging. (It is telling that the only complete edition of the Sidney Psalter has been out of print for decades.)[34] Note, for example, the sophisticated balance of internal and end rhyme and the use of varied line lengths in Pembroke's Psalm 92:

> O lovly *thing*,
> to *sing* and praises frame,
> to thee, ô lord, and thy high name
> with early *spring*
> thy bounty to display,
> thy truth when night hath vanquisht day
> yea so to *sing*,
> that ten *string*'d instrument
> with lute, and harp, and voice consent.
> (lines 1–9)[35]

33 Pembroke's Psalm 130 shows the influence of Gascoigne's in certain phrases and rhyme words. See Roy T. Ericksen's persuasive if somewhat overstated article, "George Gascoigne's and Mary Sidney's Versions of Psalm 130," *Cahier-élisabéthains* 36 (1989), 1–9.

34 Rathmell's of 1963. The separate editions of the psalms by Ringler (Sidney) and Hannay, Kinnamon, and Brennan (Pembroke) are excellent, but they impose a division on the Sidney Psalter that would likely have pleased neither of its authors.

35 Pembroke, *Works*, vol. 2, 139, italics added. All subsequent citations from the countess of Pembroke's psalms will be from this edition in the *Collected Works* with line numbers incorporated into the text.

Even more complex is her Psalm 140, written in six-line stanzas in the first four lines of which the last syllable of one line rhymes with the fourth syllable of the next. The final lines are an end-rhymed couplet:

> Protect me lord, preserve me sett me *free*
> from men that *be*: soe vile, soe viol*ent*:
> in whose ent*ent* both force and fraud doth l*urk*
> my bane to w*ork*: whose tongues are sharper th*ings*
> then Adders st*ings*: whose rusty lipps enclose
> a poisons hurd, such in the Aspick growes.
>
> (lines 1–6, italics added)

The evilness of the slanderers is reinforced by Pembroke's imaginative diction, especially her ingenious pun on "vile" and "violent," repeated in the psalm's second stanza, which suggests an etymological relationship between these terms (false, of course, since "vile" derives from L. *vilem*, "low" or "base," and "violent" from L. *vis*, "strength" or "force").

As mentioned above, the Sidney Psalter contains, as is in fact announced on the title page of one of the manuscripts, "divers & sundry kindes of verse, more rare, & excellent, for the method & varietie then ever yet hath bene don in English."[36] One might ask, though, to what extent there is any logic to the choice of any particular form, whether it is related to something in the psalm itself. This does seem to be the case with a number of psalms. The alphabetical poems are simply translating into English the forms of the Hebrew originals. The acrostic in Psalm 117, however – Pembroke's invention – is an exclamation of praise perfectly appropriate to the subject of the psalm. The long acrostic in Psalm 119 is of a different sort than 117, since the inclusion of the entire alphabet signified, as Maren-Sophie Røstvig points out, that the psalm encompassed all of creation (it is mainly about God's universal Law). Røstvig cites Baptista Spagnuola Mantuanus (1448–1516), known as "Mantuan," who calls Psalm 119's acrostic a "*lusum poeticum . . . sed admirabile obtectum mysterio, ut fere omnia sunt prophetica*" [a poetical game . . . but admirably concealed by means of a mystery, so that

[36] Reprinted in Rathmell, *Psalms of Sidney and Pembroke*, xxxiii. In Rathmell's introduction, he states that among all the 171 psalms (considering Psalm 119 as twenty-two different poems), there are only four repeated forms: 8 and 118, 32 and 71, 60 and 119s, and 70 and 144 (xvii). Even these few exceptions contain small variations, however. Psalm 8, unlike Psalm 118, closes with a stanza with an extra couplet. Psalms 32 and 71 do have the same 8.8.7.8.8.7. stanza, but the pattern of accents is different, the latter being strictly trochaic or headless iambic, the former mixing iambic and trochaic lines. Psalms 70 and 144 are not identical at all, their rhyme schemes being *ababcddc* and *ababcdcd*, respectively.

it supports all prophecies].[37] According to this reading, Psalm 119 uses a manifold poetic form to express the comprehensive significance and scope of its prophecy. Pembroke's use of a different form for each of the twenty-two sections is thus simply an intensification of this formal expression of totality or universality.

The rhyme royal for Psalm 51 may have been chosen for its association with kings, this being the psalm most powerfully associated with King David (see chapter 6). *Ottava rima* was associated with Italian narrative verse, most notably Ariosto's *Orlando Furioso*, and Pembroke's psalm in this meter (Psalm 78) is one of the most extended narratives in the psalter, recounting the history of God's covenant with Israel. Psalm 93 consists of two stanzas rhymed *ababbaba*. Might this mirrored structure reflect the psalm's subject of the oneness and stability of God?

> he who endles one remaines
> one, the same, in changlesse plight.
> (lines 7–8)

The complex internal rhymes of Psalm 140 seem a kind of hidden verbal net, a schematic equivalent of the snares of the wicked from which the psalmist prays for deliverance:

> Save I say Lord, protect me, sett me fr*ee*
> from those that b*e* so vile, so viol*ent*:
> whose thoughts are sp*ent* in thincking how they m*ay*
> my stepps betr*ay*: how nett of fowle missh*ape*
> may me entr*app*: how hid in traitor grasse
> their conning cord may catch me as I passe.
> (lines 7–12, italics added)

As noted in the previous chapter, many of the psalms written in hexameters have serious subjects, often concerning empire and kingship. Many of the songs of praise are written in short lines, as are Psalms 99, 108, and 117. Another of the short-line psalms, in alternating trimeters and dimeters, is Psalm 52, one of Pembroke's most powerful poems, but it is hardly a song. In this case, the formal choice seems to have to do with the rhetorical effect of the short lines, creating a tone of abrupt and even angry declamation appropriate to the psalm's criticism of wicked rulers:

[37] Røstvig, "Structure as Prophecy," 50–52. Mantuan's *In omnes Davidicos Psalmos . . . commentaria* was published in Rome in 1585. Interestingly, he is better known as a poet, whose pastoral eclogues were read in sixteenth-century English schools and would surely have been known to the Sidneys (see Paul Alpers, *What Is Pastoral?* [Chicago, 1996], 175–77).

Tyrant whie swel'st thou thus,
    of mischief vanting?
since help from god to us,
    is never wanting?

Lewd lies thy tongue contrives,
    lowd lies it soundeth:
sharper then sharpest knives
    with lies it woundeth.
        (lines 1–8)

The verse form helps to create a persona for the speaker here, a sharp and impatient political critic, something like an angry Jeremiah. Despite all these psalms in which there is some significant relationship between form and content, however, there are many more in which there seems to be none. The Sidneys' editors have pointed out, for instance, that a number of the stanza forms are borrowed, without any apparent rationale (and not necessarily for the same psalms), from the French metrical psalter of Marot and de Bèze.[38] The choice of most of the formal and metrical patterns is inexplicable, as one would largely expect, since most meters, rhyme schemes, and stanza forms do not have a specific meaning or traditional associations.

A notable feature of some "literary" psalm translations, as discussed above in connection with Wyatt, Surrey (chapter 3), and Gascoigne, is the focus on inwardness and the exploration of the self. A number of their psalms were expressions of powerful emotions or explorations of inner states, but later Renaissance authors intensified and dramatized these qualities. Even more than Pembroke's Psalm 52, her Psalm 73 is a powerful instance of the creation of a persona, of a psychological state, through the development of a particular poetic voice. The psalm is a theodicy, a deliberate thinking through of the problem of evil in the world and the burning question framed by Jeremiah, which Calvin quotes in his commentary on this psalm: "Wherefore doth the way of the wicked prosper?"[39] Pembroke's emphasis on the psalmist's psychological struggle with this question is implicit in the psalm itself, of course, but she probably found the idea for the more explicit representation of a torturous process of thought in Calvin's commentary.

[38] See Ringler's commentary in his edition of Sidney's *Poems*. There is a discussion of some of Sidney's uses of the French psalter in Zim, *English Metrical Psalms*, 71–78. For reasons of space, Mary Sidney's editors are less exhaustive in their annotation of sources than Ringler, but see the commentary in the *Works*, vol. 2, as well as the essay on "Literary Context," vol. 2, 12–14.

[39] Jer. 12:1 (KJV).

Calvin is concerned to point out how serious a stumbling block the question of the prosperity of the wicked is to a faith in God's providence:

Now then, how slenderly we have tasted of Gods providence, experience itself sheweth. All of us confesse, that the world is ruled by Gods hand: but if it were fastened in our hartes in deede, our faith would be far constanter to overcome adversities. But now, seeing that every slyght occasion shakes us out of this knowledge, it appeereth that wee were not so persuaded in good earnest and in very deede. Besydes this, Satan overcasteth us with darknes by innumerable slyghtes: and there is so much mistynes in the confused affaires of the world, that it is a hard matter to beleeve that God regardeth the earth. For the most part, the ungodly are in their ruffe: and forasmuch as they provoke Gods vengeance wilfully, it seemeth that they shall not be punished for their mockage, bycause he forbeareth them. The good and playne sort, being pinched with povertie, oppressed with many displeasures, vexed with many wrongs, and covered with shame and reproche, are fain to sygh and grone: and the more that they endever too doo good to all men, so much with the greater licentiousnes dare the wicked sort abuse their patience: whom wool not such things move to bee so wicked as to think, that the world is tumbled by Fortune?[40]

Calvin goes on, in his remarks on verse 1, to note that the opening adverb ("*Yit* is God good too Israell," in the Geneva Bible, italics added) indicates that "wheras David maketh a broken beginning: it is woorth notinge, that before hee brake foorth into this manner of speeche, he floted amonge his doutfull and stryving conceytes."[41] We have plunged into David's troubled thoughts *in medias res*, as it were, and his rhetoric is appropriately rushed and informal:

Now then we perceyve how vehement Davids exclamation is. For he getteth him not up into the pulpit, to dispute like a philosopher, and to frame a tale of trime fyled speech: but with ful breth to boast himself of the victorie that he had gotten, as though, hee had bin scaped out of hell. For to thentent he may by his own example shew how hard an incounter it was: he doth as it were power out hys bowels in the sight of all men, and will have somewhat more to bee understood, than he expresseth in words.[42]

In response to Calvin's reading of David's turbulent outpourings Pembroke translates Psalm 73 into a subtle and sophisticated expression and exploration of psychological uncertainty and spiritual doubt, almost in the manner of Shakespeare's soliloquies or Donne's lyrics.[43] Before describing

40 Golding, *Calvin's Commentaries*, fol. [273^{v}]. 41 Ibid., fol. 274[^{r}]. 42 Ibid.

43 Pembroke certainly knew Calvin's *Commentaries*, in Golding's translation, which is one of the most commonly cited sources for the Sidney psalms. See Rathmell, *Psalms of Sidney and Pembroke*, xix–xx; Hannay, *Philip's Phoenix*, 86.

the development of her thought, leading to its dangerous questioning of providence, the poet takes the precaution of stating the conclusion she has reached:

> It is most true that god to Israell,
> I meane to men of undefiled hartes,
> is only good, and nought but good impartes.
> (lines 1–3)

With the next line, though, the poet turns back to the doubts that so disturbed her:

> Most true, I see, albe, almost I fell
> from right conceit into a crooked mynd;
> and from this truth with straying stepps declin'd
> for loe my boiling brest did chafe and swell
> when first I saw the wicked proudly stand,
> prevailing still in all they tooke in hand.
> and sure no sicknes dwelleth where they dwell:
> nay so they guarded are with health and might,
> it seemes of them death dares not claime his right.
> (lines 4–12)

The spiritual-psychological allegorization of the "straying steps" (quite literal in the Bible versions, as in the Geneva's "my steps had welnere slipped") is emphasized by the "crookedness" of the mental path down which the psalmist almost errs. In the next stanza, following the original psalm, Pembroke shifts from the past to the present, in effect turning from the report of a past action to one working itself out in the present, line by line:

> They seeme as privileg'd from others paine:
> the scourging plagues, which on their neighbours fall,
> torment not them, nay touch them not at all.
> (lines 13–15)

The tone of Pembroke's translation is unusually colloquial, deliberately aiming at the style of direct, informal speech, following Calvin's rhetorical interpretation of the psalm as not at all a "trime fyled speech." Her speaker interrupts and corrects herself, with phrases beginning with "nay," "Most true," and "it seemes," as she works the problem out in her mind. A kind of parallel rhetoric emphasizes this improvisatory quality to the speech, where the psalmist makes a statement, then repeats a phrase with an added qualification or intensification:

. . . and if they thinke on ought,
their thought they have, yea have beyond their thought.
they wanton grow, and in malicious vaine
talking of wrong, pronounce as from the skies!
soe high a pitch their proud presumption flyes.

Nay heav'n itself, high heav'n, escapes not free
from their base mouths; and in their common talk
their tongues noe less then all the earth do walk.
(lines 20–27)[44]

The psalmist – David in Calvin's view – goes on to paraphrase the questions of the doubters, "how can it bee/ that god doth understand?" (lines 31–32), and then admits doubt himself:

Nay ev'n within my self, my self did say:
in vain my hart I purge, my hands in vain
in cleanes washt I keepe from filthy stayn,
since thus afflictions scurge me ev'ry day.
(lines 37–40)

The concentration of this inner turmoil is created by another intensifying negative ("Nay") and even more by the division of the self into two, identifying the speaker as the self "within my self." Pembroke has in this psalm translation achieved a striking representation of complex thought in progress, similar to some of the soliloquies Shakespeare was writing for Richard III at roughly the same time.

One of Pembroke's certain sources for the poetic exploration of the self, in all its contradictions, is Philip Sidney's sonnet sequence *Astrophil and Stella*. As others have noted, Pembroke's Psalm 73 begins with a direct allusion to Sidney's sonnet 5:[45]

It is most true, that eyes are form'd to serve
The inward light: and that the heavenly part
Ought to be king, from whose rules who do swerve,
Rebels to Nature, strive for their owne smart.[46]

Mary Sidney's psalm has been called a sacred parody of her brother's sonnet, though the verbal parallels are not extensive. What is striking is the similarity of subject matter: the power and proper exercise of human reason. Yet, while Sidney's sonnet ends with a neat rejection of the entire logical process it

44 Pembroke's subtle but distinct allusion to Satan's "going to and fro in the earth, and from walking up and down in it" (Job 1:7) intensifies the sense of wickedness here.
45 The allusion is noted in Pembroke's *Works*, vol. 1, 68–69, and Zim, *English Metrical Psalms*, 199–200.
46 Sidney, *Astrophil and Stella*, 5, lines 1–4, in *Poems*, 167.

has gone through, resting in the one undeniable truth "that I must Stella love," the psalm, in Pembroke's translation, actually affirms the axiom with which it begins, that God is good "to men of undefiled hearts." This is an important distinction, for while it has often been argued that Pembroke's work was dependent upon her brother's, which she was simply continuing and completing, she here not only acknowledges her brother's model but asserts its supercession by her own more serious psalm.

There may be further connections between the *Astrophil and Stella* sonnet and Pembroke's psalm. Both condemn idolatry, for instance, the sonnet acknowledging that

It is most true, what we call Cupid's dart,
An image is, which for ourselves we carve;
And, fooles, adore in temple of our hart,
Till that good God make Church and Churchman starve.[47]

This is itself a secular parody of religious imagery and language, familiar enough in the Petrarchan tradition. Pembroke turns the parody back to its sacred origins in her translation (whereas the original makes no mention of idols):

the faithlesse fugitives who thee despise,
shall perrish all, they all shalbe undone,
who leaving thee to whoorish Idolls runn.
(lines 79–81)

That these lines may derive from Sidney's description of the false worship of Cupid is indicated by the previous line, which describes God as the "fortresse of my hart" (line 78). God as a fortress is a metaphor familiar from Luther's hymn paraphrase of Psalm 91, "Ein feste burg ist unser Gott," but the addition of the heart points in a different direction, to the convention of Petrarchan poetry, where the beloved is a fortress assaulted by the lover (Sidney's sonnet 12 employs it, and Donne's "Batter my heart, three-personed God" is a sacred parody of it, with God as attacker rather than defender). It seems Pembroke is recalling her brother's admission that Cupid is an idol, but whereas Sidney's Astrophil cannot help persisting in his idolatry, Pembroke's psalmist rejects all forms of false worship, appropriating even the metaphors of idolatrous love poetry for righteous ends. Even the last three lines of Pembroke's psalm look back to the *Astrophil and Stella* sonnet, to its affirmation that the "eyes are form'd to serve/ The inward light." This is another of the axioms overturned in the sonnet's final

47 Ibid., lines 5–8.

line ("and yet true that I must Stella love"). The final lines of Pembroke's translation can be read as a paraphrase of the opening lines of Sidney's sonnet. They are entirely her own addition to the original psalm, and they affirm what her brother's poem denies:

> but as for me, nought better in my eyes
> than cleave to god, my hopes in hym to place,
> to sing his workes while breath shall give me space.
> (lines 82–84)

If Psalm 73 shows Pembroke anticipating or matching the kind of representation of complex thought more familiar in Shakespearean soliloquy, another of her psalms demonstrates her fondness for the metaphysical conceit, which may partly explain why Donne found the Sidney psalms so exciting. Like Psalm 73, Psalm 139 is a Wisdom psalm, one of a group of what Gerhard von Rad terms "theological problem poems."[48] However, while Psalm 73 wrestles with the question of evil in the world and the doubt raised by the prosperity of the wicked, Psalm 139 is an extended meditation on God's omniscience and the mysteries of creation, especially the creation of man. The stanza Pembroke invents for this psalm is one of those irregular forms that so appealed to Herbert:[49]

> O lord in me there lieth nought,
> but to thy search revealed lies:
> for when I sitt
> thou markest it:
> no lesse thou notest when I rise:
> yea closest clossett of my thought
> hath open windows to thine eyes.
> (lines 1–7)

This opening stanza announces the subject that will be explored for most of the psalm, the universal reach of God's "eyes." Pembroke's "closest clossett" (an almost anagrammatic pair and a figure she returned to in her translation of Psalm 143, "My cave, clossett where I wont to hide," line 41) conveys deep interiority and is an imaginative domestication of what the Geneva Bible had translated merely as "thought." In fact, the nearly identical spelling of this adjective and its noun suggest a succession of inwardly receding closets within closets like the "self within my self" of Pembroke's Psalm 73. Another interesting modification of the original Psalm 139 is in Pembroke's rendering

48 See Gerhard von Rad, *Wisdom in Israel*, trans. James D. Martin (London, 1972), 40, 49, 108–10.

49 Compare, for instance, the similar mixture of tetrameters and dimeters, in a roughly hourglass shape, in Herbert's "Affliction."

of verse 9's "uttermost partes of the sea" (Geneva Bible) as something suggestive of Renaissance explorations of the Americas:

> ev'n ledd to West he would me catch,
> nor should I lurk with western things.
> (lines 34–35)

The emphasis on the West may be a reference to the "uttermost parts" recently arrived at by Elizabethan navigators, partly financed by the Pembrokes.[50]

What really captures Pembroke's imagination in this psalm, however, is the meditation on human creation, the fashioning of the embryo in the womb.[51] A comparison of her expansion of verses 13–18 with Coverdale's version (rich in itself) shows the powerful originality of which her paraphrase is capable, both in terms of form and metaphor:

> For my reynes are thyne, thou hast covered me in my mothers wombe.
> I wil geve thankes unto the, for I am wonderously mad: marvelous are thy workes, and that my soule knoweth right well.
> My bones are not hyd from the, though I be made secretely, and fashyoned beneth in the earth.
> Thyne eyes se myne unparfectnesse, they stande all written in thy boke: my dayes were fashyoned, when as yet there was not one of them. (Coverdale)[52]

> Each inmost peece in me is thine:
> while yet I in my mother dwelt,
> all that me cladd
> from thee I hadd.
> thou in my frame hast strangly delt;
> needes in my praise thy workes must shine
> so inly them my thoughts have felt.
>
> Thou, how my back was beam-wise laid,
> and raftring of my ribs dost know:
> know'st ev'ry point
> of bone and joynt,

[50] See Hannay, *Philip's Phoenix*, 42. The editors of Pembroke's *Works* (vol. 2, 440–41), Hannay among them, note this allusion, the idea for which Pembroke seems to have found in de Bèze's paraphrase ("whereby I might flee even into the farthest part of the west," de Bèze, *Psalmes of David*, 335).

[51] The subject was obviously of interest to Pembroke. Another of her memorably "metaphysical" passages in the psalms is concerned with embryology: "so make them melt as the dishowsed snaile/ or as the Embrio, whose vitall band/ breakes er it holdes, and formlesse eyes do faile/ to see the sunn, though brought to lightfull land" (Psalm 58, lines 21–24).

[52] Coverdale (Great Bible, 1539), verse numbers omitted.

how to this whole these partes did grow,
in brave embrodry faire araid,
though wrought in shopp both dark and low.

Nay fashonles, ere forme I toke,
thy all and more beholding ey
my shaplesse shape
could not escape:
all these, with tymes appointed by
ere one had beeing, in the booke
of thy foresight, enrol'd did ly.
(Pembroke, lines 43–63)

What makes these stanzas "metaphysical" is what Samuel Johnson, in his famous remarks in the *Life of Cowley*, called "*discordia concors*" or the "most heterogeneous ideas . . . yoked by violence together."[53]

The description of man as "in brave embrodry faire araid," deriving probably from Calvin's commentary on the Hebrew verb "*Rakam*," which, he writes, "signifyeth *to weave toogither*," comes from the women's world of domestic craft.[54] Yet in the next line this "embrod'ry" is described as being "wrought in shopp both dark and low," which seems to suggest needle-work being hammered out by the village blacksmith or the Nibelungs. The combination is a powerful disjunction, dependent on Pembroke's ability to "wreath iron pokers into true-love knots" (to borrow Coleridge's description of Donne).[55] The "beam-wise" laying of the back and "raftring" of the ribs gives the human body a massive solidity supported by the strong alliteration, structural like Gascoigne's but perhaps even more appropriately so, given Psalm 139's thematic concern with mysterious internal structures. Pembroke's psalm continues, "My god, how I these *studies* prize,/ that doe thy hidden workings show!" (lines 64–65, italics added), a significant alteration of Coverdale's more neutral "How deare are thy *councels* unto me O God?" ("*thoughts*" or "*cogitations*" in the other English

[53] Samuel Johnson, *Life of Cowley*, in Tillotson et al., *Eighteenth Century Literature*, 1077. It is one of the ironies of literary criticism, of course, that what Johnson intended as a disparaging comment should have become accepted as a description of merit and strength.

[54] Golding, *Calvin's Commentaries*, fol. [231^{v}]. Chanita Goodblatt has pointed out that this interpretation seems to derive from Hebrew exegesis (David Kimhi specifically), but how it made its way into the Genevan commentaries is uncertain. Goodblatt and Mayer I. Gruber, "Dialogue and David's Voice: Jewish Exegesis and Christian Hebraism in the Sidneian Psalms," essay in preparation, read at David in Medieval and Renaissance Culture, The Eighteenth Barnard Medieval and Renaissance Conference, December 7, 2002.

[55] Samuel Taylor Coleridge, *Poetical Works*, ed. Ernest Hartley Coleridge (Oxford, 1969), 433.

Bibles).[56] Not only does she introduce the "studies" dear to Renaissance humanists – suggesting some form of natural science or theology or, in "the booke/ of thy foresight," biblical scholarship – but the agent of the study is shifted from God to man, the creature's learned "searching out" imitating that of his Creator ("Search me, my god," line 85).[57]

Psalms 73 and 139 are only two of Pembroke's 107 psalms, but they suffice to demonstrate an essential point about the Sidney Psalter – that whatever else it may be, it is an essentially literary work. It was as a book of poems, rather than as a psalter with any sort of liturgical or devotional purpose (it had a negligible influence on seventeenth-century church psalms), that the Sidney Psalter had its greatest impact. Many sixteenth- and seventeenth-century English poets translated psalms in the literary mode practiced by the Sidneys, including the satirist Joseph Hall, Thomas Carew, Sir Henry Wotton, Henry King, Sir Francis Bacon, and Sir John Davies.[58] Some of these have been discussed in other contexts in other chapters, but the Sidney psalms also influenced the literary psalms written by Francis Davison, Phineas Fletcher, Henry Vaughan, and John Milton that will be the subject of the remainder of this chapter.

Though his anthology *A Poetical Rhapsody* (1602) was an important contribution to English poetry, Francis Davison (?1575–?1619) is a figure given little space in literary histories. He is mentioned twice, for example, in C. S. Lewis's *English Literature in the Sixteenth Century*, and only in brief references to the *Rhapsody*.[59] Yet he was a poet as well as an editor, contributing a number of poems to the *Rhapsody* (dedicated to Pembroke's son, William Herbert, third earl of Pembroke), alongside its more famous authors, including Spenser, Sidney, Donne, and the countess of Pembroke. In the preface to the *Rhapsody*, Davison announces his plan to publish "some graver work," which likely refers to the translation of the Psalms by Davison, his brother Christopher and others, selections of which survive in several manuscripts in the British Library (Harl. MSS 3357, 6930 and Rawlinson Poet. MS 61), one of which bears the title, *Divers Selected Psalms of David, in verse, of a different composure from those used in the*

56 Coverdale, Ps. 139:17, italics added.

57 A similar idea is expressed by Sir Francis Bacon in *The Advancement of Learning* (1605) when, quoting Prov. 25:2, he writes that "the glory of God is to conceal a thing, but the glory of the king is to find it out." *Francis Bacon: A Critical Edition of the Major Works*, ed. Brian Vickers (Oxford and New York, 1996), 151.

58 King's alternative version of Psalm 130 "paraphrased for an Antheme" as opposed to his complete psalter, which was designed for use in church (see chap. 2).

59 C. S. Lewis, *English Literature in the Sixteenth Century* (Oxford, 1954), 523, 601.

Church.[60] It is perhaps a mark of Davison's accomplishment as a poet that the translation of Psalm 137 now attributed to him was published as Donne's in the seventeenth century.[61] It is intriguing that Davison's verse introduction to his psalm translations includes lines that sound strikingly like Donne's "Upon the Translation of the Psalms by Sir Philip Sidney, and the countess of Pembroke his Sister." For example, Davison begins with an invocation, "Come, Urania, heavenly Muse," and then plays on the relationship between earthly and heavenly singing:

> Oh! my soul, bear thou a part;
>   And my heart,
> With glad leaps, beat thou the measure!
> Powers of soul and body meet,
>   To make sweet,
> Sweet and full this music's pleasure!
> . . . .
> Sacred triple Majesty,
>   One in Three!
> Grant, oh grant me this desire.
> When my soul, of body frail
>   Leaves the gaol,
> Let it sing in this blest quire![62]

Donne's poem adds two other choirs to the heavenly (one on earth and one in the cosmic spheres), but, like Davison, he looks forward to joining the celestial singing on his death:

> We thy Sidneian Psalms shall celebrate,
> And, till we come th'extemporal song to sing,
> (Learned the first hour, that we see the King,
> Who hath translated these translators) may
> These their sweet learned labours, all the way
> Be as our tuning, that, when hence we part
> We may fall in with them, and sing our part.[63]

[60] On Davison, see the introduction by A. H. Bullen to his edition of *Davison's Poetical Rhapsody*, 2 vols. (London, 1890). The manuscript title is given in Davie, *Psalms in English*, 92.

[61] Psalm 137, in Donne, *Poems*, vol. 1, 424–26 (and see Grierson's notes, vol. 2, cxxvi). This psalm appears in Donne's *Poems* of 1633 and subsequent editions, but it is printed in Davison's Harleian manuscript collections. It is printed – and celebrated – as Donne's in Holland, *Psalmists of Britain*, vol. 2, 287–88.

[62] Printed in Francis Davison, *The Poetical Rhapsody*, ed. Sir Harris Nicolas, 2 vols. (London, 1826), vol. 2, 321–23. All further citations from Davison's psalms will be from this edition, with page references incorporated into the text.

[63] Donne, *Poems*, vol. I, 349–50.

It is difficult to know if there is any borrowing from one of these poems to another, since neither was immediately published (Donne's appears first in the 1635 edition of his *Poems*). Perhaps the most that can be said is that it is not surprising that one of Davison's poems was published as Donne's, since there was apparently, on some level, an affinity between them.

Davison's translations of Psalms 137 and 23 (in three versions), which are among his most accomplished and interesting, are discussed below in chapters 7 and 5, respectively. His Psalm 30 will serve here to show both the literary interest of his psalms and his debt to the Sidney Psalter. Davison's stanza is an irregular combination of long and short lines, like many of Philip and Mary Sidney's:

> Lord, to thee, while I am living,
> Will I sing hymns of thanksgiving;
> For thou hast drawn me from a gulph of woes,
> So that my foes
> Do not deride me. (336)

The rhythmic effect is similar to that of one of Sidney's Sapphic variations, Psalm 27:

> The shining Lord he is my light,
> The strong God my salvation is.
> Who shall be able me to fright?
> This lord with strength my life doth blisse;
> And shall I then
> Feare might of men?[64]

A more specific debt to Sidney may lie in Davison's introduction of "tears" to the psalm, interpreting the psalmist's "cries" ("Then cried I unto the, O Lorde," in Coverdale's verse 8) in a rather baroque fashion:

> Then thus I pour'd forth prayers and doleful cries,
> With weeping eyes,
> Like wat'ry fountains. (338)

The affect here anticipates its culminating expression in Richard Crashaw's "blubbering Mountain" that "Weeping melts into a Fountain" (Psalm 23 – see chapter 5), but the tears may derive from Sidney's translation of Psalm 30, verse 5:

[64] Sidney, *Poems*, 306.

Well may the Evening loath the eyes
In clouds of teares, but soon as sun
Doth rise again, new joyes shall rise.[65]

Davison extends the figure of tears, contrasting it with blood. He pours out copious quantities of the one, in hopes that he will not have to shed the other:

IX.
In my blood there is no profit;
If I die, what good comes of it?
Shall rotten bones, or senseless dust express
Thy thankfulness,
And works of wonder?

X.
Oh, then, hear me, prayers forth pouring,
Drown'd in tears, from moist eyes show'ring;
Have mercy, Lord, on me; my burthen ease,
If thee it please,
Which I groan under. (338)

Davison takes the blood from the original psalm verse ("What profyt is there in my bloude, whan I go down to the pytte?" in Coverdale), as does Sidney before him.[66] The tears, however, are found only in Sidney and Davison.

Phineas Fletcher (1582–1650), one of the large literary family of Fletchers, is most noted as a follower of Spenser and the author of *Piscatorie Eclogues* and *The Purple Island* (both 1633).[67] In *Poeticall Miscellanies* (1633), he included "Certain of the royal Prophets Psalmes metaphrased," translations of Psalms 42, 63, 127, 137, 1, and 130. His psalms are written in a variety of stanza forms, two of them (127 and 130) corresponding to the meters of the church psalms of "Sternhold and Hopkins." The rest adopt stanzas derived from secular lyric. One of Fletcher's favourite forms is that adapted from the Pindaric ode, which he uses for Psalms 63 and 130, as well as Psalm 137, discussed below in chapter 7. Psalm 42 ("Like as the hert desireth the water brookes" in Coverdale) is composed in a stanza Spenser uses in the January

65 Ibid., 311. As Marjory E. Lange points out, however, there was a considerable interest in various instances of David's weeping in this period, so perhaps Davison came up with the idea independently. See *Telling Tears in the English Renaissance* (Leiden, 1996), 129–36. Lange also includes an extensive discussion of weeping in Crashaw, though without mention of his psalms (222–44).

66 Sidney, *Poems*, 311.

67 On Fletcher, see Frank S. Kastor, *Giles and Phineas Fletcher* (Boston, 1978), 77–136.

and December eclogues of *The Shepheardes Calendar* and *The Teares of the Muses*. Fletcher also recommends tunes to which his psalms might be sung, as, for example, Psalm 42, "which agrees with the tune of *Like the Hermite poore*," a popular lyric printed, among other places, in the miscellany *The Phoenix Nest* (1593), and now attributed to Sir Walter Raleigh.[68]

Fletcher derives some of his metaphors from Sidney's psalms. Like Coverdale and the other English Bibles, Fletcher translates the deer in verse 1 ("*cervus*" in the Vulgate) as "hart," enabling him to make the common English pun on "hart" and "heart" in the first and second of his stanzas:

> Look as an hart with sweat and bloud embrued,
> Chas'd and embost, thirsts in the soil to be;
> So my poore soul with eager foes pursued,
> Looks, longs, O Lord, pines, pants, and faints for thee:
> When, O my God, when shall I come in place
> To see thy light, and view thy glorious face?
>
> I dine and sup with sighs, with grones and teares,
> While all thy foes mine eares with taunting load;
> Who now thy cries, who now thy prayer heares?
> Where is, say they, where is thy boasted God?
> My molten heart deep plung'd in sad despairs
> Runnes forth to thee in stream of teares and prayers.[69]

Fletcher's "molten heart" is borrowed from Sidney (though they may also be thinking of Ps. 22:15, "my hert also in the middest of my body is even lyke melting waxe," in Coverdale), and he similarly matches the weeping eyes and weeping heart, linking together the copious bodily fluids Davison contrasts in his Psalm 30. The second stanza of Sidney's Psalm 42 obviously appealed to Fletcher's predilection for physical and metaphorical fluids:

[68] Giles and Phineas Fletcher, *Poetical Works*, ed. Frederick S. Boas, 2 vols. (Cambridge, 1909), vol. 2, 249. For "Like to a Hermite," see *The Phoenix Nest (1593)*, ed. Hyder E. Rollins (Cambridge, MA, 1931, rpr. 1969), 77–78. As Rollins notes, this song was printed many times. In *To day a man, To morrow none: Or, Sir Walter Rawleighs Farewell to his Lady* (1644) it is attributed to Raleigh, and is accepted as such in *The Poems of Sir Walter Raleigh*, ed. J. Hannah (London, 1875, 1892). It was common practice, in both singing psalters and secular ballads, to recommend tunes as Fletcher does. Interestingly, however, some of the ancient headnotes to the psalms seem to have served the same function. Calvin interprets the biblical note for Psalm 22, "upon the hynd of the morning," as "the beginning of some common ballet," though he dismisses any further speculation on such a question as seeking "a deepe misterie in a smal matter" (Golding, *Calvin's Commentaries*, fols. [77^{v}]–78^{r}).

[69] Fletcher, *Poetical Works*, vol. 2, 249.

Day and night my teares outflowing
Have been my ill feeding food,
With their dayly questions throwing:
Where is now Thy God so good?
    My heart melts remembring so,
    How in troops I wont to go,
    Leading them his prayses singing,
    Holy daunce to God's house bringing.[70]

Sidney intensifies the flooding imagery expressed in Coverdale, and Fletcher's version adds floods on floods, repeating the word four times in two lines:

One depe calleth another because of the noyse of thy water pipes all thy waves & stormes are gone over me. (Coverdale)

All Thy floods on me abounded,
Over me all thy waves went.
(Sidney)[71]

Flouds of thy wrath breed flouds of grief and fears;
And flouds of grief breed flouds of plaints and teares.
(Fletcher)[72]

Fletcher's psalm belongs to the same tradition of literary tears and weeping as Davison's Psalm 30, a tradition which, as Marjorie E. Lange observes, includes the weeping of Petrarchan lovers as well as the penitential tears of David. Sacred and secular weeping come together in the poem whose tune Fletcher suggested for his Psalm 42. "Like to a hermit poor" is a secular love lyric using the language of religious devotion. The poet's statements that "My food shall be of care and sorrow made" and "My drink nought else but tears fall'n from mine eyes" are a parodic allusion to Ps. 42:3, "My teares have been my meate daye & night" (Coverdale).[73] But Fletcher turns the parody back on itself by using the secular tune for his non-parodic translation of the psalm.

Henry Vaughan wrote under the shadow – a comforting rather than a menacing one – of George Herbert, "whose holy *life* and *verse*," Vaughan wrote, "gained many pious *converts* (of whom I am the least)."[74] Like Herbert, Vaughan included psalm translations (65, 104, 121) among his lyrics in *Silex Scintillans* (1650 and 1655). Vaughan has been described as a

[70] Sidney, *Poems*, 334. [71] Ibid.
[72] Fletcher, *Poetical Works*, vol, 2, 249. [73] "Like to a hermit" in *The Phoenix Nest*, 77.
[74] Introduction to *Silex Scintillans* (1650), in *Henry Vaughan: The Complete Poems*, ed. Alan Rudrum (Harmondsworth, 1976, rev. 1983), 142.

mystical nature poet, the natural world being for him a "system of divine hieroglyphs," in which all creatures revealed the glory of their Creator.[75] His choice of psalms reflects his love of natural creation, as in Psalm 104, which has been called a "glorification of Yahweh for his creative work, and the continued existence of the earth, and all that is in it, by his will."[76] (This psalm was also translated by Carew, Wotton, and much later, appropriately enough, by the author of *The Seasons,* James Thomson.) Vaughan's stanza consists of three pentameters and a final trimeter, another variation on the Sapphic pattern used by the Sidneys. Vaughan's imagination was particularly drawn to verses 10–24, describing God's provision of sustenance for all creatures:

> These [the earthly waters] to the beasts of every field give drink;
> There the wild asses swallow the cool spring:
> And birds amongst the branches on their brink
> Their dwellings have and sing.
>
> Thou from thy upper springs above, from those
> Chambers of rain, where Heaven's large bottles lie,
> Dost water the parched hills, whose breaches close
> Healed by the showers from high.
>
> Grass for the cattle, and herbs for man's use
> Thou mak'st to grow; these (blessed by thee) the earth
> Brings forth, with wine, oil, bread: all which infuse
> To man's heart strength and mirth.
>
> Thou giv'st the trees their greenness, even to those
> Cedars in *Lebanon*, in whose thick boughs
> The birds their nests build; though the stork doth choose
> The fir-trees for her house.
>
> To the wild goats the high hills serve for folds,
> The rocks give conies a retiring place:
> Above them the cool moon her known course holds,
> And the sun runs his race.
>
> Thou makest darkness, and then comes the night;
> In whose thick shades and silence each wild beast
> Creeps forth, and pinched for food, with scent and sight
> Hunts in an eager quest.

[75] J. B. Leishman, cited in R. A. Durr, *On the Mystical Poetry of Henry Vaughan* (Cambridge, 1962), 19. On "Vaughan and Nature," see 17–19.

[76] W. O. E. Oesterly, *The Psalms*, 2 vols. (New York, 1939), vol. 2, 440.

The lion's whelps impatient of delay
  Roar in the covert of the woods, and seek
Their meat from thee, who dost appoint the prey
    And feed'st them all the week.

This past, the sun shines on the earth, and they
  Retire into their dens; Man goes abroad
Unto his work, and at the close of day
    Returns home with his load.

O Lord my God, how many and how rare
  Are thy great works! In wisdom hast thou made
Them all, and this the earth, and every blade
    Of grass, we tread, declare.[77]

Vaughan's "large bottles" are a striking addition to the psalm. As Donald Davie notes, there are bottles in Job: "Who can number the clouds in wisdom? or who can stay the bottles of heaven?" (38:37, KJV).[78] Vaughan certainly knew his Bible, but he may have found his bottles in an intermediate source. Herbert's "Praise III" combines an allusion to another biblical bottle (Ps. 56:8, "Thou tellest my wanderings, put thou my teares into thy bottle") with the bottles in Job:

I have not lost one single tear:
        But when mine eyes
Did weep to heav'n, they found a bottle there
    (As we have boxes for the poore)
Readie to take them in; yet of a size
        That would contain much more.[79]

As in Psalm 56, God takes the weeper's tears in a bottle; as in Job, the bottle is in heaven. Vaughan may well have been aware of the whole cluster of texts.

Vaughan's psalm is formally as well as allusively interesting. Jonathan F. S. Post has pointed out that the twenty-four stanzas into which Vaughan divides the thirty-five verses of the psalm mirror the twenty-four hours in a day, suggesting that the poem runs through a complete round of hourly devotions to the totality of Creation.[80] Stylistically, the most notable feature of the psalm is Vaughan's consistent use of enjambment, a technique which emphasizes the already obvious distance between this literary paraphrase

77 Vaughan, *Complete Poems*, 258–59. 78 Davie, *Psalms in English*, 159.
79 Herbert, *English Poems*, 165. For a discussion of Herbert's bottle of tears, see Lange, *Telling Tears*, 213–14.
80 Jonathan F. S. Post, *Henry Vaughan: The Unfolding Vision* (Princeton, 1982), 90.

and the generally end-stopped psalms, intended for church singing, in the "Sternhold and Hopkins" tradition (including Herbert's self-consciously plain Psalm 23, which alludes to the church psalms). The first two lines of the stanza immediately following those just quoted are strongly enjambed, and are then, especially in the second case, brought up short by sharp caesuras early in the following lines:

So doth the deep and wide sea, wherein are
 Innumerable, creeping things both small
And great: there ships go, and the shipmen's fear
  The comely spacious whale.[81]

Vaughan's syntax is in constant tension with the organization of his lines into stanzas, which gives considerable rhythmic interest to his poem.

This is also a feature of a number of the Sidney psalms, as in the second stanza of Pembroke's Psalm 84 ("How lovely is thy dwelling"):

 Alas? the Sparow knoweth
the house, where free, and fearelesse she resideth:
 directly to the neast the Swallow goeth,
where with hir sonnes she safe abideth.
  ô Alters thine, most mighty
  in warre, yea most allmighty:
 thy Alters lord: ah? why should I
 from Alters thine excluded ly?

(lines 9–16)

It has been pointed out that Pembroke's Psalms 51 and 130 survive in musical settings in BL Additional MS 15117, but the evidence of stanzas like this one surely establishes that even if her psalms were sung, they were not written primarily for singing, since except in the most through-composed of settings (a style uncharacteristic of Elizabethan and Jacobean secular song) it would be impossible to retain any sense of Pembroke's complex working against the pattern of her irregular stanzas.[82]

The most noted practitioner of enjambment in the period is Milton, whose *Paradise Lost* famously excels in "the sense variously drawn out from one Verse to another."[83] Milton translated psalms throughout his life. His earliest efforts (Psalms 114 and 136) were, as the 1645 *Poems* announces, "done by the Author at fifteen years old."[84] A year later, in 1634, Milton

81 Vaughan, *Complete Poems*, 259.

82 On these settings, see Pembroke, *Works*, vol. 2, 368. For another argument for the "essentially literary nature" of the Sidney psalms (which applies also to the countess of Pembroke's), see Coburn Freer, "The Style of Sidney's Psalms," *Language and Style* 2:1 (1969), 68–69.

83 See the preface to *Paradise Lost* on "The Verse" in *Complete Poems*, 210.

84 Quoted in *Shorter Poems*, 6.

translated Psalm 114 again, into "Greek heroic verse" (see chapter 3).[85] As mentioned in chapter 2, Milton translated Psalms 80–88 into common meter in 1648. Finally, in 1653, Milton translated Psalms 1–8, following the practice of the Sidney Psalter in taking a distinctly literary approach, and using a different meter for each psalm – iambic pentameter couplets, *terza rima*, and a number of regular and irregular stanzas. That Milton should translate so many psalms, at so many points in his life, should come as no surprise, since one of his earliest biographers notes that "David's Psalms were in esteem with him above all poetry,"[86] an opinion which reiterates Milton's own statements in *The Reason of Church Government* (see Introduction). Milton's estimation of the Psalms is also evident from their importance in his poetry, and several scholarly works have demonstrated their centrality to *Paradise Lost*, *Paradise Regained*, and *Samson Agonistes*.[87]

A striking feature of Milton's Psalms 1–8 is his careful dating of each one, between August 8 and 14, 1653. (Psalm 1 may have been done earlier, as it is dated only by the year.) Thus far, the significance of such precise dating and whether there is a particular reason for the translation of each of these psalms on the days in question has remained elusive. Christopher Hill has summed up as much as can be said about the occasion of their composition and its meaning for Milton:

> This too was a crucial moment in the history of the Revolution. The Rump of the Long Parliament had been dissolved and replaced by the nominated Barebones assembly. That had meant a breach with the republican Independents, and inevitably led to a revival of royalist hopes. On 10 August the Council of State proposed to set up a High Court of Justice to try royalist plotters *without a jury*. The new assembly divided into radical and conservative wings, of which the latter ultimately proved the stronger. On 15 July a motion to abolish tithes – whose abolition Milton had held to be essential to religious freedom – was only just defeated. The Leveller John Lilburne, returned from the exile to which the Long Parliament had condemned him, was at once arrested, and his trial was ordered. Petitioners supporting him were also arrested. The dissolution of the Rump did not seem likely to forward

[85] Milton's own description, in a letter to his former schoolmaster, Alexander Gill (Dec. 4, 1634), cited in *Shorter Poems*, 234.

[86] The anonymous late seventeenth-century *Life of Milton*, in *Complete Poems*, 1044.

[87] Mary Ann Radzinowicz, *Toward "Samson Agonistes": The Growth of Milton's Mind* (Princeton, 1978), and *Milton's Epics and the Book of Psalms* (Princeton, 1989). Radzinowicz's approach to the question of Milton's use of the Psalms is at times rather broad – tracing his indebtedness on the basis of ideas, themes, or genres, for instance – but her studies do confirm the preeminent importance of this one book of the Bible for Milton's poetry. For other useful studies, see Barbara Kiefer Lewalski, Paradise Lost *and the Rhetoric of Literary Forms* (Princeton, 1985), esp. 35, 193–94, 250–53; Regina M. Schwartz, *Remembering and Repeating: Biblical Creation in* Paradise Lost (Cambridge, 1988), 60–90.

the radical causes in which Milton believed. He had recently become completely blind.[88]

This was, in short, a time of depression for Milton, when his political hopes seemed threatened and his personal situation had become handicapped by his loss of sight. His Psalms 2 and 6 reflect both of these concerns.

The subject of Psalm 2 is presumptuous kings, a subject of obvious topical interest in mid-seventeenth-century England, and certainly one can read the opening lines of Milton's *terza rima* translation in the context of the workings of the Barebones assembly, which must have been a great disappointment to the republican poet:

> Why do the Gentiles tumult, and the nations
> Muse a vain thing, the kings of the earth upstand
> With power, and princes in their congregations
> Lay deep their plots together through each land,
> Against the Lord and his Messiah dear.[89]

Interestingly, this psalm is central to Milton's greater poetic project, *Paradise Lost.* It has been argued that, stylistically, Milton's Psalms 1–8 are the first example of his mature prosody, with an extensive use of enjambment, caesuras occurring early in the line, and frequent metrical subsitutions (reversed feet for rhetorical emphasis).[90] John T. Shawcross has suggested that this may indicate that Milton had returned to work on *Paradise Lost* (the original ideas for which date back to his "studious retirement" between 1632 and 1638) sometime in 1653.[91] That this was so seems to be strongly suggested as well by the close thematic relationship between Psalm 2 and the epic.

In book 5, the Father, much to the surprise of the angels (and chagrin of some), introduces his Son, essentially quoting Psalm 2:

> Hear all ye Angels, Progeny of Light,
> Thrones, Dominations, Princedoms, Virtues, Powers,
> Hear my Decree, which unrevok't shall stand.

[88] Christopher Hill, *The English Bible and the Seventeenth-Century Revolution* (Harmondsworth, 1993), 382–83.

[89] Milton, *Shorter Poems*, 334. All further citations from Milton's psalms will be from this edition, with line numbers incorporated into the text.

[90] W. B. Hunter, Jr., "The Sources of Milton's Prosody," *Philological Quarterly* 28 (1949), 125–44. Many aspects of this article have been sharply criticized (see, for instance, Edward R. Weismiller, "Studies of Verse Form in the Minor Poems," in *A Variorum Commentary on the Poems of John Milton*, vol. 2, *The Minor English Poems*, ed. A. S. P. Woodhouse and Douglas Bush [New York, 1972], 1081–82), but the basic observation on the metrical similarity of Psalms 1–8 and *Paradise Lost* remains valid.

[91] John T. Shawcross, "The Life of Milton," in *The Cambridge Companion to Milton*, ed. Dennis Danielson (Cambridge, 1989), 16–17.

This day I have begot whom I declare
My only Son, and on this holy Hill
Him have annointed, whom ye now behold
At my right hand; your Head I him appoint;
And by my Self have sworn to him shall bow
All knees in Heav'n, and shall to him confess him Lord:
Under his great Vice-gerent Reign abide
United as one individual Soul
For ever happy: him who disobeys
Mee disobeys, breaks union, and that day
Cast out from God and blessed vision, falls
Into utter darkness, deep ingulft, his place
Ordain'd without redemption, without end.[92]

Of course, the scenario described is exactly what happens, Satan being profoundly affronted by the Father's preferment of the Son, so that Ps. 2:6–7 is here made the verbal act that initiates the entire sequence of events in *Paradise Lost.*[93] Milton's quotation of Psalm 2 also incorporates its reiteration in the New Testament, when the lines are uttered by a "voice from heaven" announcing Jesus's divinity at his baptism (Matt. 3:17). Milton's gesture is typical of his urge to creative originality. Just as he strives to "prevent" (i.e., "come before") the wise men in the Nativity Ode, and to write the pre-history of the Bible in *Paradise Lost*, so his allusion to these lines from Psalm 2 presents itself as their fictive first statement, implicitly turning their "restatement" in the Psalms and the Gospels into allusions to *Paradise Lost.*

Milton's translation of Psalm 2 takes few liberties with the original, but it does add one phrase:

he who in heaven doth dwell
Shall laugh, the Lord shall scoff them, then severe
Speak to them in his wrath, and in his fell
And fierce ire trouble them; but I saith he
Annointed have my king (*though ye rebel*)
On Sion my holy hill. A firm decree
I will declare; the Lord to me hath said
Thou art my Son I have begotten thee
This day. (lines 8–16, italics added)

Milton's insertion of "though ye rebel," a clause which can be read either as conditional ("even should you rebel") or simply as a qualifying indicative ("although you do/will rebel"), seems charged with the meaning that this

[92] *Paradise Lost* 5.600–15, in *Complete Poems*, 316–17.

[93] Georgia Christopher calls this emphasis on a "verbal sacrament" a "notably Protestant gesture" (see "Milton and the Reforming Spirit," in Danielson, *Companion to Milton*, 200).

announcement has in *Paradise Lost.* It is only in Milton's epic, after all, that the Father's preferment of the Son is the immediate trigger for the *rebellion* of Satan, which has such consequences for the subsequent history of humanity.[94]

Few poets have ever written their lives into their work so thoroughly or consistently as Milton. By 1653, the rebellion in which he had placed his hopes had failed and he was completely blind, and his subsequent poetry resonates with these facts. The Father's warning of the punishment of the rebel angels, that they will fall "into utter darkness," was surely a particularly fearful threat to Milton, who two books earlier had lamented that "ever-during dark/ Surrounds me, from the cheerful ways of men/ Cut off."[95] Whether on some level he identified with the defeated yet defiant Satan is a more complicated question than can be answered here, but the connection between the defeat of his political dreams and the loss of his sight is certainly implied in his 1653 psalms. Milton's Psalm 6, which is, significantly, the first of the Penitential Psalms, contains another notable insertion, long recognized as an allusion to his blindness:

> Wearied I am with sighing out my days,
> Nightly my couch I make a kind of sea;
> My bed I water with my tears; mine eye
> Through grief consumes, is waxen old *and dark*
> I' the midst of all mine enemies that mark.
> (lines 11–15, italics added)

Verse 7 reads "Mine eie is consumed because of griefe; it waxeth olde because of all mine enemies" (KJV). Milton emphasizes the "eye," in characteristic fashion, by leaving the word suspended at the end of the line, and his is the only version of the psalm in which the eye becomes completely "dark." That this is an echo of his own blindness, especially as represented in *Paradise Lost,* seems confirmed by his rendering of the curse at the end of the psalm, "Let all mine enemies be sore vexed" (KJV):

> Mine enemies shall all be blank and dashed
> With much confusion. (lines 21–22)

The word "blank" (or "blanc") notably occurs in Milton's most famous reference to his blindness in *Paradise Lost* (to repeat and continue the passage quoted above):

[94] One can only speculate, but the sharp enjambment of lines 15 and 16 in Milton's psalm places such emphasis on "This day" that it is hard not to think he means to point to the day announced at the beginning of the psalm, "August 8, 1653."

[95] *Paradise Lost,* 3.45–47, in *Complete Poems,* 259.

> But cloud instead, and ever-during dark
> Surrounds me, from the cheerful ways of men
> Cut off, and for the Book of knowledge fair
> Presented with a Universal blanc
> Of Nature's works to me expung'd and ras'd,
> And wisdom at one entrance quite shut out.[96]

In Psalm 6, he not only laments his blindness, but calls for a mimetic revenge against his enemies, wishing on them the "blank" that afflicts him.

At least in Psalms 1–8, if not in some of his other psalm translations, Milton, like the Sidneys and the other poets considered in this chapter, translated the psalms from primarily literary and personal motives. Such "literary" psalms were different in kind from those written for use in the church. Their authors were preoccupied with verbal artifice, exploring varieties of meter, rhyme, and stanza structure, sophisticated schemes and tropes, and poetic and autobiographical allusions. Psalms of this kind are also marked as "literary" by their self-conscious preoccupation with the exploration and expression of inner psychological states, just as in contemporary secular lyrics, many of them by the same authors. These translations of the Psalms can be distinguished from the translations designed primarily for liturgical or devotional use, which either eschewed aesthetic considerations entirely or else clearly subordinated them to the transmission of the literal sense of the Scripture.[97] The psalms of Wyatt and Gascoigne, of Davison, Fletcher, Vaughan, and Milton, and especially those of the Sidney Psalter, ought to be considered, as indeed they were in their own day, as creative and powerful poems in their own right, not merely as shadows of the biblical "originals."

[96] Ibid., 3.45–50.

[97] See the discussion of these psalms in chaps. 1 and 2. The distinction I am arguing is impossible to maintain perfectly, since, especially in the seventeenth century, aesthetic considerations begin to creep into some of the "church" psalms, and there are somewhat anomalous psalters, like George Sandys's, which, while in the tradition of the singing psalters, nevertheless employs poetic artifice to an unusual degree. With these exceptions, the distinction is, I think, still worth making.

PART II

Case studies in psalm translation

CHAPTER 5

"Happy me! O happy sheep!": Renaissance pastoral and Psalm 23

Among the 150 Psalms, few were translated, paraphrased, explicated, or alluded to as often as Psalm 23. Its popularity was partly due to its being the seminal lyric in the Christian pastoral tradition. Like the quantitative experiments in psalm translation explored in chapter 3, Renaissance versions of Psalm 23 show the commitment of Renaissance poets to a conception of literary history that not only included but amalgamated the classical and biblical traditions. These versions also exemplify a theory of translation that takes the word back to its etymological origins in the Latin *translatio*, the "carrying across" of a text from one language and culture to another. Such "translations" (defined both broadly and specifically) reveal the complexities of the Renaissance conception of pastoral, of the workings of literary genre in general, and of the labors of readers and writers in sixteenth- and seventeenth-century England to make sense of disparate and sometimes incompatible literary and cultural traditions.

The mainstream of English Renaissance pastoral derived most obviously from the literature of classical Greece and Rome, mediated in part by the earlier Renaissance pastorals of continental poets. The principal figures in this tradition are well known: Theocritus and Virgil among the ancients and Sannazaro, Mantuan, Tasso, and Guarini among the moderns. However, the history of pastoral, like that of most genres, is one of increasing complication. In sixteenth- and seventeenth-century England, the long tradition of ancient literature was widely understood to include both the poetry of Greece and Rome and the poetry of the Hebrew Bible, and Renaissance pastoral was profoundly affected by this syncretic approach to literary history. Most obviously, Spenser's *Shepheardes Calendar* and Milton's *Lycidas* joined the classical tradition of pastoral poetry descending from Theocritus and Virgil to the Judeo-Christian tradition of shepherd–sheep allegory exemplified by Psalm 23 and the

Gospels.[1] What is not often recognized is that the syncretic currents flowed in both directions. Poets incorporated biblical pastoral into the classical tradition, but the example of Psalm 23 shows the complementary practice of reading and translating a biblical poem in terms of the literary conventions of classical pastoral. The psalm's sixteenth- and seventeenth-century readers recognized the basic congruence of subject matter between this poem of shepherd and sheep and those of Theocritus and Virgil. In their efforts to assimilate the two ancient strains of pastoral poetry, however, Renaissance poets and commentators encountered difficulties that to the modern critic seem obvious, given the genuine and even fundamental differences between Hebraic and Greco-Roman culture and literature. Yet as different as Psalm 23 is from the *Idylls* and *Eclogues* of Theocritus and Virgil, it was perceived by Renaissance readers as a legitimate, and in the Christian context perhaps *the* legitimate, version of pastoral.[2] This interpretation is pervasive in metrical paraphrases of Psalm 23 and in numerous Renaissance commentaries and sermons that attempted to explain the psalm's pastoral imagery in peculiar and ingenious ways.

The definitions of pastoral that modern critics have been debating for most of the past century are similarly peculiar and ingenious. The existence of a "Christian" pastoral has generally been acknowledged, though occasionally somewhat grudgingly. Even Renato Poggioli, though quite adamant that pastoral and Christianity are incompatible, included a chapter on "The Christian Pastoral" in the book published posthumously as *The Oaten Flute*.[3] The narrowness of his definition is evident in his argument that pastoral was unclassical as well as unchristian. This rather unhelpfully turns most of the history of pastoral literature into a study of aberrations and misappropriations. If Poggioli's essays represent the extreme of the exclusive definition of pastoral, William Empson's *Some Versions of Pastoral* represents the extreme of the inclusive. Since he includes chapters on "proletarian literature," dramatic double-plots, *The Beggar's Opera*, and *Alice in Wonderland*, his notion of pastoral is obviously a broad one. His

[1] There is a huge body of criticism on these poems, but on their blending of classical and Christian, see especially John N. King, *Spenser's Poetry and the Reformation Tradition* (Princeton, 1990), chap. 1, "*The Shepheardes Calender* and Protestant Pastoral Satire," and Revard, chap. 6, "Sporting with Amaryllis: 'Lycidas' – Classical Ode and Renaissance Pastoral."

[2] In this respect, I follow Annabel Patterson's urging that the "central question" concerning pastoral be restated (*contra* Empson and others – see below) to ask "how writers, artists, and intellectuals of all persuasions have *used* pastoral for a range of functions and intentions that the *Eclogues* first articulated." See *Pastoral and Ideology: Virgil to Valéry* (Berkeley and Los Angeles, 1987), 7.

[3] Renato Poggioli, *The Oaten Flute* (Cambridge, MA, 1975), chap. 5. In the title essay of his volume, he writes, "The bucolic ideal stands at the opposite pole from the Christian one." In Poggioli's view, the emphasis in pastoral on retreat was fundamentally unchristian.

insightful description of pastoral as a "process of putting the complex into the simple" certainly allows for other "versions of pastoral" even than he includes, but as a definition of genre it is as problematic as Poggioli's.[4] A useful *via media* is provided by Paul Alpers in *What is Pastoral?* He defines pastoral in terms of its "representative anecdote," which he identifies as the literary representation of shepherds and their shepherding life who are themselves representative of "some or all other men and/or women."[5] This approach is flexible enough to allow for the diversity of pastoral kinds in the Renaissance, a time which famously delighted in generic mixtures, but it is not so broad as to lose sight altogether of the etymological roots of "pastoral" in writing about "pastors" or shepherds.

This chapter surveys the great variety of ways in which sixteenth- and seventeenth-century writers adapted their treatments of Psalm 23 to the conventions of classical pastoral (or to their perceptions of those conventions). The verse-by-verse organization used here (and in the following chapters), though perhaps more familiar from biblical commentary than literary criticism, nevertheless allows for the inclusion of this broad range of material in a concise manner. By way of clarification, the organization of this chapter is not intended to imply that each psalm verse was interpreted by all writers in the same way; neither should it suggest that each individual psalm translation necessarily observed every pastoral convention simultaneously. Rather, it attempts to illustrate the dominant Renaissance perception that Psalm 23 was inherently a pastoral poem that could be read as homologous with those of the classical tradition, and to demonstrate that the interest in these Renaissance versions lies not in their unified approach to this perception but rather in their diversity, resulting from their authors' varied and imaginative solutions to the interpretive problems which inevitably arose in their attempts to mesh the two, possibly incompatible, strains of Hebrew and classical tradition.

DAVID IN ARCADIA

He maketh me to lie downe in greene pastures: he leadeth mee beside the still waters. (v. 2)[6]

One way in which Renaissance translators of Psalm 23 assimilated the psalm with the classical literary tradition of pastoral poetry was by adapting the country setting described in verse 2 to the traditional language of English

[4] William Empson, *Some Versions of Pastoral* (London, 1986; first ed., 1935), 22.

[5] Alpers, *What Is Pastoral?*, 26. See below, 156–57.

[6] KJV (1611).

pastoral in the English translations and imitations of Theocritus, Virgil, and later pastoral poets. The two basic elements of the landscape are what the King James Version renders as "greene pastures" and "still waters." In the prose translations of other English Bibles these natural features remain relatively constant. The Coverdale Bible (1535), Great Bible (1539), and Geneva Bible (1560) all have the "green pasture," and the Bishops' Bible (1568) has "pasture full of grass," a more concrete rendering, leaving the "greenness" implicit. The Catholic translators of the Douai Old Testament (1609–10), following as always the Vulgate ("*in loco pascuai*"), leave both the color and the grass implicit: "in place of pasture there he hath placed me."[7] The descriptions of the water in the English Bibles are more varied, though the basic sense remains constant. In Coverdale's initial translation of 1535 the psalmist was led to "a fresh water," but he changed it in the Great Bible version to the more affecting, but textually unjustified, "waters of comfort." The waters of the Geneva Bible, like those in the KJV, are "still," while in the Bishops' Bible they are "calme." Ever eccentric, the Douai translators substitute "the water of refection" (from the Vulgate's "*aquam refectionis*").[8]

None of this language is particularly reminiscent of secular pastoral literature, but a different practice developed in the metrical translations. The two versions of Psalm 23 in the "Sternhold and Hopkins" psalter remain close to the straightforward prose Bible translations. Sternhold has "pastors fayre" and "waters calme," and Whittingham, "pastures green" and the slightly elaborated "streams which run most pleasantly."[9] Given the relative freedom of metrical paraphrase (as compared to the more literal prose versions of the English Bibles), it was natural for translators to begin to elaborate the spare landscape of the psalm, as Whittingham did. In Archbishop Matthew Parker's psalter, the pastures are not only "greene" but "fat," and the waters are "delicate."[10] Sidney retains the simple "green pasture" but has waters "still and sweet."[11] By the beginning of the seventeenth century, poets were elaborating the pastures and waters in the specific direction of secular pastoral poetry. Francis Davison, the editor of *A Poetical Rhapsody* (1602), one of the most important English anthologies of pastoral poetry, translated Psalm 23 three times, using language similar to that of the secular pastoral poems by Sidney, Spenser, Sir John Davies, and Davison himself,

7 Psalm 22 (23) in the Douai Bible version (1609–10), in *Psalm 23: An Anthology*, ed. K. H. Strange and R. G. E. Sandbach (Edinburgh, 1970), 34. The Vulgate is cited from *Quincuplex Psalterium*, ed. Jacques Lefèvre d'Etaples (1513, facs. rpr. Geneva, 1979).

8 The Vulgate is probably also the source of Coverdale's less obviously Latinate "waters of comfort."

9 *Whole Booke of Psalmes* (1562).

10 [Parker], *Psalter.*

11 Sidney, *Poems*, 301.

among others, collected in the *Rhapsody*. In one of Davison's versions, the fields are "Fresh and green,/ Mottled with spring's flowry painting" and the waters have become "Crystal brooks."[12] In another, "silly sheep" (another conventional phrase from English secular pastoral) feed

through flow'ry meads,
Where a silver spring,
Gently murmuring,
Doth refresh mine anguish,
When with thirst I languish.[13]

The third has rather simple "fields," but through them "a silver brook slideth with lenity."[14]

Davison's translations are more elaborate than most in their borrowings from the self-consciously artificial vocabulary of Renaissance pastoral poetry, but they are not at all unique. Sir John Davies's version of Psalm 23 published in 1624, for example, has a "silver brooke," and a few years later George Sandys's includes "fragrant meads" and "softly sliding waters."[15] George Herbert's is deliberately simple, with only "tender grass" and "streams that gently pass," but the "*Imitatio Herberti*" published in William Barton's 1644 psalter substitutes "flowry" for "tender."[16] Henry King has "fruitfull meads," Miles Smyth (perhaps taking Barton a further step beyond Herbert) "Luxuriant flowry meads," and Sir John Denham "rich luxuriant Fields."[17] In Richard Crashaw's Psalm 23, as one might expect, the fields and streams become positively baroque:

On whose pastures cheerful Spring
All the year doth sit and sing,
And rejoicing smiles to see
Their green backs wear his livery.

. . . .

At my feet the blubb'ring Mountain
Weeping melts into a Fountain,

[12] Davison, Psalm 23, version 1, in Nicholas, *Poetical Rhapsody*, vol. 2, 331.

[13] Davison, version 2, in ibid., 333. [14] Davison, version 3, in ibid., 335.

[15] Sir John Davies, in *The Complete Poems of Sir John Davies*, ed. A. B. Grosart, 2 vols. (London, 1876), vol. 2, 157. Sandys, *Psalmes*.

[16] Herbert, in *The Works of George Herbert*, ed. F. E. Hutchinson (Oxford, 1941), 172. William Barton, *The Book of Psalms in Meter* (London, 1644, rpr. 167?). For a critical assessment of Barton's revision of Herbert, see Eric R. Smith, "Herbert's 'The 23d Psalme' and William Barton's *The Book of Psalms in Metre*," *The George Herbert Journal* 8:2 (Spring, 1985), 33–43.

[17] King, *Psalmes*. Smith, *Psalms of King David paraphrased*. Denham, *A Version of the Psalms of David* (London, 1714). Denham died in 1669, so his psalms obviously date from much earlier than their first printing.

Whose soft silver-sweating streams
Make high noon forget his beams.[18]

With Crashaw as their guide, the psalmist's sheep and shepherd have left the biblical landscape behind altogether and entered Arcadia.

The secular pastoral poetry collected in Davison's *A Poetical Rhapsody* contains enough examples of these "flowery" landscapes to demonstrate the conventionality of such language. The "crystal brooks" of Davison's psalm are from the same artificial landscape as the "crystal waves" in Charles Best's "A Sonnet of the Moon" and the "silver brooks" in Davison's own "Eclogue."[19] One might also compare Davison's and Smyth's "flowry meads" to the "flow'ry banks" where Daphne walks in "Ignoto's" "Eclogue" and the countess of Pembroke's description of Astrea as a "field in flowery robe arrayed."[20] The other early anthology of English pastoral poetry, *England's Helicon* (1600, enlarged 1614), provides further examples of such language. Bartholomew Young, for example, uses "Christaline streames" in his "Cinthia the Nimph," "Christall streames" appear in a poem by "I. M.," and Michael Drayton's "Rowlands song in praise of the fairest Beta" has a "christall flood."[21] Drayton's poem also includes "flowrie meddowes" and Edmond Bolton's "A Canzon Pastoral in honour of her Maiestie" has a "flowrie-adorned field."[22] This language will be familiar to all readers of English pastoral. The silver streams, for instance, were such a commonplace by the time of Robert Herrick's *Hesperides* (1648) that he could take them for granted in his anti-pastoral to the Dean-bourn, a "rude River in Devon," so full of rocks that he could never look on it with content even "Were thy streames silver, or thy rocks all gold."[23] George Herbert uses "Crystal" as a noun in "Ephes.4.30.," the adjective having become so common that it can stand on its own for the river itself.[24] Analogues to Davison's "painted fields" are less common, but descriptions of nature expressed similarly in terms of man-made artifice are found in *England's Helicon*, where, in "Wodenfrides *Song in praise of* Amargana" by "W. H.," Flora spreads the paths on which

[18] Richard Crashaw, *The Poems English Latin and Greek of Richard Crashaw*, ed. L. C. Martin (Oxford, 1927), 102–03.

[19] Bullen, *Davison's Poetical Rhapsody*, vol. 2, 30 and vol. 1, 48.

[20] Ibid., vol. 1, 72 and 40.

[21] *England's Helicon*, reprinted from the edition of 1600 with additional poems from the edition of 1614 (London, 1925), 143, 39, and 31.

[22] Ibid., 32, 24.

[23] Robert Herrick, "*To* Dean-bourn, *a rude River in* Devon, *by which sometimes he lived*," in *The Poems of Robert Herrick*, ed. L. C. Martin (London, 1965), 29.

[24] "If a cleare spring for me no time forbears,/ But runnes, although I be not drie;/ I am no Crystall, what shall I?" "Ephes.4.30.," lines 28–30, in Herbert, *Works*, 136.

Amargana walks with "flowrie tap'stries," and in Milton's *Arcades*, where a singer calls for dancing on "the smooth enamell'd green."[25]

The shift from a natural landscape to an artificial one akin to those in secular pastoral poems is emphasized in versions of Psalm 23 by Davison and Sandys in their inclusion of one of the most artificial features of Renaissance gardens: the maze or labyrinth.[26] The third section of Davison's third translation begins with the ovine narrator "Through bushy labyrinths roaming audaciously."[27] Such labyrinths do not occur naturally, but were designed as a rural entertainment for the well-to-do. Thomas Coryate, for instance, remarked in 1611 seeing "a fine Labyrinth made of boxe," and Pepys records seeing several in 1666.[28] The word even has an explicit connection to the pastoral tradition in its use in Theocritus's *Idyll* XXI, referred to by Sir Thomas Browne as "the rushey labyrinths of *Theocritus*."[29] Like Davison's "labyrinth," Sandys's use of "maze" also converts the psalm's simple setting into an intricate English garden:

The Lord my shepherd, me His sheep
Will from consuming famine keep.
He fosters me in fragrant meads,
By softly-sliding waters leads;

My soul refresh'd with pleasant juice,
And lest they should His name traduce,
Then when I wander in the maze
Of tempting sin, informs my ways.[30]

The enjambment in these lines is clever, since the final line-break suspends the reader between a literal sense of the maze as a garden feature (as in

[25] *England's Helicon*, 67; for *Arcades*, see *Complete Poems*, 79, line 84.

[26] See John Steane, "Renaissance Gardens and Parks," in *The Cambridge Cultural History of Britain*, vol. 3, *Sixteenth-Century Britain* (New York, 1992), 208–21, esp. 214; also, W. H. Matthews, *Mazes and Labyrinths: A General Account of their History and Development* (London, 1922), chaps. 12–15. As Thomas M. Greene has demonstrated, the labyrinth had a broader cultural significance in the Renaissance, in a tradition of dance deriving from classical epic and medieval Christian ritual. See "Labyrinth Dances in the French and English Renaissance," *Renaissance Quarterly* 54 (Winter 2001): 1403–66. The labyrinth is also exploited as a schematic and psychological figure in Lady Mary Wroth's corona, "A Crowne of Sonnetts dedicated to Love," which begins and ends, "In this strang labourinth how shall I turne?" See *The Poems of Lady Mary Wroth*, ed. Josephine A. Roberts (Baton Rouge and London, 1983), 127–34.

[27] Davison, version 3, in Nicholas, *Poetical Rhapsody*, vol. 2, 335.

[28] OED, s.v. "labyrinth" 1b, citations from *Coryat's Crudities* (1611) and Pepys's *Diary* for June 25, 1666.

[29] Sir Thomas Browne, *The Garden of Cyrus*, in *The Major Works*, ed. C. A. Patrides (Harmondsworth, 1977), 336. Theocritus uses "*labyrinthoi*" in *Idyll* XXI, line 11. See *The Greek Bucolic Poets*, ed. J. M. Edmonds, Loeb Classics (Cambridge, MA and London, 1912, rpr. 1996), 246. Theocritus actually uses the word to describe lobsterpots rather than gardens, but it is nevertheless part of his literary vocabulary.

[30] Sandys, *Psalmes*.

Titania's "quaint mazes in the wanton green" in *A Midsummer Night's Dream*),[31] and the allegorical "maze/ Of tempting sin," which becomes clear only in the next line. Thus the psalmist's wandering seems at first a pleasant stroll through the "fragrant meads" but turns out to be a "wandering" in the sense of "erring," straying from the figurative "pathes of righteousness" (verse 3 of most of the Bible translations of Psalm 23, implied if not actually present in Sandys's own).

Many of the more paraphrastic or adaptive translators extended the pastoral language throughout the psalm, even though the original shifts to a different controlling metaphor by verse 5, or even verse 4, depending on how it is read. The English Bibles, for instance, favor "rod and staff" for the protective implements in verse 4, but a number of other versions (including George Joye's 1534 psalter, the Coverdale Bible of 1535, as well as two of Davison's translations) rendered the "staff" as the more obviously pastoral "sheep-hook."[32] The overflowing cup was also transformed into the more rustic "bowls of wine" (Davison), and, most interestingly, a "mazer" which "flows with pleasant wine" (Sandys).[33] Not only is "mazer" a more rustic term, but it is one which, according to the OED, appears only rarely in English literature, most notably in Spenser's *Shepheardes Calender*. In the "August" eclogue one of the prizes in the singing contest between Willye and Perigot is a "mazer ywrought of the Maple warre."[34]

The gloss in the Yale edition notes that a "mazer" is a "wooden drinking bowl (common in fourteenth- and fifteenth-century England; there was a famous one at Sp[enser]'s college, Pembroke Hall)."[35] The gloss of "E. K." originally published with the *Calender* is actually more helpful, since it focuses on the literary rather than the actual history of the cup, noting the models for Spenser's prize cup in Theocritus and Virgil.[36] There are several cups in Theocritus: the "ivy-wood cup" offered to Thyrsis by the admiring goatherd in *Idyll* I, and the "goblet/ carved by Praxiteles"

[31] William Shakespeare, *A Midsummer Night's Dream*, 2.1.99, cited in the OED, s.v. "maze" 4.

[32] George Joye, *Davids Psalter* ([Antwerp], 1534) in Butterworth, *Literary Lineage*, 286. Davison, versions 2 and 3, in Nicholas, *Poetical Rhapsody*, vol. 2, 334, 336. In the commentary of Victorinus Strigelius, translated by Richard Robinson, *A Proceeding in the Harmonie of King Davids Harpe* (London, 1591), the terms are explained: "It is well knowne what are the weapons which Sheepeheards use. For as the silly sheepe are driven or ruled wyth the rod, least they should stray from the fields, so by the staffe they are defended against the violent assault of the Wolves." Then he allegorizes: "The rod therefore signifieth government, and the staffe defence from God: also the staffe may be taken for the word of God, whereupon, we (being wearied with daungers and temptations,) resting and staying ourselves, are then in good securitie and safety" (40).

[33] Davison, version 1, in Nicholas, *Poetical Rhapsody*, vol. 2, 332. Sandys, *Psalmes*.

[34] Edmund Spenser, *The Shepheardes Calender*, "August," line 26, in *The Yale Edition of the Shorter Poems of Edmund Spenser*, ed. William Oram et al. (New Haven and London, 1989), 139.

[35] Ibid., 139. [36] Ibid., 146.

that Comatas plans to give his lover in *Idyll* V.[37] The cups that the rival singers Menalcas and Damoetas offer each other as prizes in Virgil's third *Eclogue* are modeled on Theocritus and establish the place of such cups as essential elements in one of the most familiar of pastoral conventions – the singing-contest:

> I'll stake what you'll admit is greater far
> (Since you're so mad to compete) two beechwood cups;
> The carving's Alcimede's inspired work.
>
> . . . .
>
> For me too Alcimede made a pair of cups.
> The handles he entwined with soft acanthus,
> In the midst set Orpheus and obedient trees.[38]

In both Theocritus and Virgil the cup is associated with the power of art through their makers (the "inspired" Alcimede, the equivalent of Theocritus's Praxiteles) as well as by the elaborate scenes carved on them.

As Paul Alpers points out, the elaborate series of representations on the goatherd's cup in *Idyll* I is Theocritus's adaptation of Homer's more elaborate ekphrasis of the Shield of Achilles in Book 18 of the *Iliad*, reduced to the more limited scope of the pastoral genre.[39] Virgil also emphasized the status of the cup as a symbol of art by including Orpheus, the prototypical singer, on the cup of Damoetas – it is, after all, the prototype of the modern literary prize, awarded to the most skillful singer (poet). The pastoral connotations of the English word "mazer" are confirmed by Dryden's use of it in his translation of Virgil: "One of his Shepherds describes a Bowl, or Mazer, curiously carved."[40] Dryden's use of this archaic word in this context shows his awareness of its place in the (Virgilian) pastoral singing-contest, established by Spenser. Sandys's use of the word, while it has nothing to do with a singing-contest, points back to Spenser, as Dryden's does later, and serves to emphasize both the literariness of Sandys's psalm translation as a self-conscious work of art, and the place of Psalm 23, at least in his view, in the tradition of pastoral running from Theocritus and Virgil to Spenser and other Renaissance imitators.

[37] Theocritus, *Idyll* V, trans. Daryl Hine, *Theocritus Idylls and Epigrams* (New York, 1982), 3 and 23.

[38] Virgil, *Eclogue* III, lines 44–46, trans. Paul Alpers, in *The Singer of the Eclogues: A Study of Virgilian Pastoral* (Berkeley, 1979), 23.

[39] Alpers, *What Is Pastoral?*, 139–40.

[40] John Dryden, "Dedication of the Pastorals to Hugh Lord Clifford, Baron of Chudleigh," *The Works of Virgil in English* (1697), in *The Works of John Dryden* (Berkeley, Los Angeles, and London, 1987), vol. 5, 5. As confirmation of Spenser's influence on the English translations of classical pastoral, one might note also the use of "mazer" in J. M. Edmonds's translation of Theocritus, *Idyll* I, *Greek Bucolic Poets*, 11.

SHEPHERDS AND SHEEP

The Lorde is my shepherde, therefore can I lack nothing. (v. 1)[41]

The "argument" preceding Psalm 23 in the Bishops' Bible of 1568 neatly sums up the psalm's central metaphor: "David resemblyng God to a sheephearde and hym selfe to a sheepe, declareth that all commodities, plentie, quietnesse and prosperitie, ensueth them that be fully perswaded of Gods providence: for God feedeth, norisheth, defendeth, and governeth those that put their wholl trust in hym after a more ample sort then any sheephearde doth his sheepe."[42] While the predominant figure of the shepherd and his sheep might seem to provide evidence in favor of reading Psalm 23 as pastoral, it actually makes the discussion of literary genre more complex. As the etymology of the word suggests, "pastorals" are traditionally about shepherds.[43] Shepherds sing, they debate, they lament, they love, and to some extent (though not nearly so much as in the related but separate genre of georgic) they go about their shepherding chores. The problem with Psalm 23 is that it is primarily about sheep rather than shepherds. The "Lord" is the shepherd, but the speaker of the psalm (whether taken to be David or the later Christian reader/singer) is represented as a sheep. In classical pastoral the reader is not usually encouraged to identify with the flock. Even in the main tradition of "Christian pastoral" the focus is on the shepherds, as in the many neo-Latin poems on the Nativity.[44]

The transformation of shepherd into sheep is one of those modal shifts which Paul Alpers identifies as a regular occurrence in the history of pastoral, the most important of which he sees occurring with Virgil's transformation of the Theocritan model.[45] As mentioned above, Alpers introduces to the discussion of pastoral the useful notion, borrowed from Kenneth Burke, of the "representative anecdote." This anecdote provides a means of identifying the essential characteristics of a mode and its transformations by individual authors, in the way in which the mode *reflects*, *selects* from, and *deflects* from reality:

41 Coverdale's translation from the Great Bible (1539).

42 "The argument of the .xxiij. Psalme," *The holie Bible* [Bishops' Bible] (London, 1568).

43 There are also goatherds in pastoral, and the alternative title to Virgil's poems, *Bucolics*, derives from "cowherd." Yet, despite the separation of sheep and goats which Jesus announces will occur at the Second Coming (Matt. 25:32), as a general rule, pastoral poets, Christian or otherwise, make no significant distinction between the various types of herdsmen.

44 For instance, Peter de Fransz (1645–1704), *Pastores Bethlehemitici*, and a similar Christmas poem by Francesco Patrizi. See W. Leonard Grant, *Neo-Latin Literature and the Pastoral* (Chapel Hill, 1965), 258–89 and 104.

45 See Alpers, *What Is Pastoral?*, 26–28, and chap. 4.

> [W]hat connects pastoral works to each other, what makes them a literary "kind," is the way each deals, in its circumstances and for its reasons, with the representative anecdote of herdsmen and their lives.
>
> To say that this is the representative anecdote of pastoral means that pastoral works are representations of shepherds (and, in post-classical literature, shepherdesses) who are felt to be representative of some other or of all other men and/or women.[46]

The usefulness of this approach lies in its ability to allow for changes in the ways in which the representations work, while preserving a sense of a coherent generic history by emphasizing the continuity of the underlying "anecdote." As Alpers emphasizes, "the representative anecdote is conceived not as a fixed formula but as a generative fiction, which can be elaborated or transformed in accordance with the needs of representation or the claims of representation."[47] Even so strange a transformation as that of Psalm 23 can be accommodated; it simply requires an explanation of the way in which it deals with the "representative anecdote of herdsmen and their lives," allowing, of course, that their herds are an essential part of those lives.

Pastoral literature works, as Empson expresses it, by "putting the complex into the simple," or, in Alpers's more specific formulation, by representing "some other or all other men and/or women" as simple shepherds.[48] The process of representing the relatively more sophisticated by the relatively humble is simply taken to a further degree in Psalm 23. In the usual formulation, the sophisticated men and women who read pastoral poems are represented in those poems by humble shepherds; in the psalm, the "humbling" process continues downward, and the "ordinary" people, the readers, are represented by sheep. This extension of the anecdote is natural enough in a poem which is describing the relationship between God and man, emphasizing the utter dependency of the latter on the care of the former. If God is a shepherd, then all men are sheep. It is telling, though, that the focus of most sixteenth- and seventeenth-century commentaries on Psalm 23 is on the explication of the relationship between a shepherd and his sheep. Such an emphasis by the exegetes seems to acknowledge the distance that had developed between most contemporary readers of the psalm and the literally "pastoral" world in which the psalm was first written, a distance which actually makes the psalm more compatible with Empson's social definition of pastoral.[49]

46 Ibid., 26. (The terms "reflections," "selections," and "deflections" are from Burke's *Grammar of Motives*, cited in ibid., 13).

47 Ibid., 174.

48 Empson, *Some Versions*, 22; Alpers, *What Is Pastoral?*, 26.

49 Obviously, the gap between ancient Israel and Renaissance England is immense and resists any generalized comparison. There was nevertheless a considerable migration from rural to urban areas

Luther's commentary on Psalm 23, translated by Coverdale in 1537 as *An Exposition upon the Twenty-Second Psalm* (Vulgate numbering), explains the pastoral metaphor in order to emphasize human dependency on God:

A sheep must live only by the help, defence, and diligence of his shepherd. As soon as it leaveth him, it is compassed about with all manner of peril, and must needs perish; for it cannot help itself. For why? it is a poor, weak, and innocent beast, that can neither feed nor guide itself, nor find the right way, nor keep itself against any unhappiness or misfortune; seeing this, that of nature it is fearful, flieth and goeth astray. And if it go but a little out of the way, and come from his shepherd, it is not possible for itself to find him again, but runneth ever farther and farther from him. And though it come to other shepherds and sheep, yet it is nothing helped therewith: for it knoweth not the voice of strange shepherds; therefore flieth it from them, and runneth so long astray, till the wolf ravish it, or till it perish some other ways.[50]

Calvin's commentary also takes pains to explain the essential relationship between shepherd and sheep. His focus on the loving care of the shepherd as well as the dependence of the sheep probably derives from the recurrence of the pastoral metaphor in the Gospels of Luke and John, where Jesus calls himself "the good shepherd" (John 10:11) and tells the parable of the lost sheep (Luke 15:4–6):

Now in that God oftentimes in the scripture usurpeth the name, and putteth upon himself the persona of a shepherd: it is no slight token of his tender love towards us. For seeing it is a lowly and homely manner of speech: it must needs be that he is singularly welminded towardes us, that disdeyneth not to embace himself so much for our sake.[51]

Calvin goes on to elaborate the needs of a sheep – good grass, "waters of rest" ("for swift brooks are unhaudsome, yea and for the most part noysome for sheepe to drink of"),[52] and sheepcotes for shelter from the sun – in a detailed description of "herdsmen and their lives."

Like Luther and Calvin, Obadiah Sedgwick, an English "minister of the Gospel," in his posthumous *The Shepherd of Israel* (1658), describes for his

in the sixteenth and seventeenth centuries, resulting in a population with less and less first-hand experience of a literally "pastoral" life, and this may be one explanation for the exegetes' concern to explain the practical realities of shepherding. See Keith Wrightson, *English Society 1580–1680* (New Brunswick, NJ, 1982, rpr. 1992), 127–29.

50 Martin Luther, *An Exposition upon the Twenty-Second Psalm,* trans. Miles Coverdale, in *Remains of Myles Coverdale* (Cambridge, 1846), 288–89. Though the focus of this study is on sixteenth- and seventeenth-century England, some of the most important and influential biblical commentaries were those of continental reformers, especially Luther and Calvin, published in English translations that were widely available.

51 Golding, *Calvin's Commentaries*, fol. [85v]. 52 Ibid., fols. [85v]–86r.

readers the lives of shepherds and sheep. He notes the importance of the pastoral metaphor in the Bible, such that "there is scarce any one Metaphor in all the Scriptures through which God doth seem more delightfully to express himself then this of a shepherd."[53] Interestingly, Sedgwick's commentary may show the influence of the anti-clerical strain in Christian pastoral poetry, exemplified by the "May" eclogue from Spenser's *Shepheardes Calender*, in that his description of shepherds includes both the good and the bad. Jesus is, of course, the quintessential "good shepherd" (John 10:11); the bad shepherds are those clerics ("pastors") who fail to follow his example.[54]

A particularly interesting commentary on Psalm 23 published in England in this period is found in Richard Robinson's translation of the German Lutheran Victorinus Strigelius, *A Proceeding in the Harmonie of King Davids Harpe* (1591). Like the others, Strigelius is primarily concerned with explaining sheep and shepherds, and he draws in John's good shepherd and other passages of biblical pastoral imagery. Unlike any of the other commentators, his explanation of the psalm's representative anecdote quotes extensively from Virgil's *Georgics*, albeit in slightly bastardized excerpts. As evidence for the dependence of sheep on the shepherd, Strigelius cites *Georgics* III, 295–99 and 322–38 (in Latin, to which Robinson adds his own translation using the common meter associated with metrical psalms and popular ballads):

> He suffers in warme Cottages,
> his sheepe to take their meat;
> Till Summer season fresh & greene,
> returned be with heat.
> And store of straw and ferne he layes,
> by handfuls on harde ground.
> Least tender beast by cold or scurffe,
> or gowte doe get deaths wounde.[55]

(Though the georgic mode, in contrast to pastoral, is usually identified with labor and hardship, the passage in *Georgics* III, 322–38, which has the shepherd bringing his sheep to "running water of the brookes," is

[53] Obadiah Sedgwick (1600?–1658), *The Shepherd of Israel, or God's pastoral care over his people. Delivered in divers sermons on the whole twenty-third psalm* (London, 1658), 3.

[54] This convention of anti-clerical satire in Christian pastoral is rooted in Christ's injunction in the sermon on the mount to "beware false prophets, which come to you in sheep's clothing, but inwardly they are ravening wolves" (Matt. 7:15). Of course, Sedgwick may have found the anti-clerical pun in Matthew independently, without the intermediary of pastoral poetry.

[55] Strigelius, *Proceeding in the Harmonie*, 28. The Latin quotations from the *Georgics* are altered in word order and lineation from the standard edition of Virgil (see the Loeb Classics *Virgil*, vol. 1 [Cambridge, MA, and London, 1965], 174–78, 182–86).

uncharacteristic, described by L. P. Wilkinson as an "idyll of summer" in the midst of the harsher georgic world.)[56] To show that "the harmless sheepe needeth not onely good feeding, but also defence," Strigelius cites *Georgics* III, 405–07 and 440–45, describing how the shepherd protects the flock from wolves and disease, carrying them, once again, to "pleasant springs, to quench their thirst."[57] Strigelius (and Robinson) clearly saw Psalm 23 as part of the pastoral tradition which, in its Greco-Roman, as opposed to Hebrew, branch, did include Virgil's *Georgics*.[58] Robinson's translations of Strigelius seem to have been popular enough for him to be able to publish five volumes of them between 1582 and 1598 (Psalm 23 is in the second), the first two volumes being dedicated, respectively, to Ambrose Dudley, earl of Warwick, and Sir Christopher Hatton, then Lord Chancellor of England. Appropriately enough, for a commentary on a pastoral psalm citing Virgil, Robinson addresses Hatton as "Right Honourable and most worthy Mecenas," placing himself in the position of the pastoral poet.[59]

Strigelius's quotations from the *Georgics* point to another peculiarity of Psalm 23's version of pastoral. Traditionally, following the medieval *rota virgilium* which categorized literature in terms of the genres successively employed by Virgil, pastoral and georgic are often considered distinct genres.[60] Pastoral has to do with leisure, as the English connotations of "idyll," the term used by Theocritus for his pastorals, suggest.[61] Georgic has to do with work, as summed up in Virgil's phrase, "*labor omnia vicit*," which complements the parallel phrase in the *Eclogues*, "*omnia vincit Amor*."[62] The problem with a Christian pastoral, as Poggioli argues, is that to the Christian, especially the Protestant, idleness is sinful.[63] Strigelius stresses that Jesus "sitteth not idle in heaven, roioycing onely in his owne power

[56] Virgil, *The Georgics*, ed. and trans. L. P. Wilkinson (Harmondsworth, 1982), 97.

[57] Strigelius, *Proceeding in the Harmonie*, 30.

[58] I address the traditional generic distinction between pastoral and georgic below, but, broadly speaking, they may still be understood as two inflections of the same literary genre or mode, emphasizing, respectively, the leisure and labor of the herdsman's life.

[59] Ibid., sig. A2r.

[60] For a brief description of the *rota virgilium*, see E. R. Curtius, *European Literature and the Latin Middle Ages*, trans. Willard R. Trask (Princeton, 1973; first ed., 1948), 231–32. On the political implications of the pastoral–georgic distinction in seventeenth-century England, see Annabel Patterson, "Pastoral versus Georgic: The Politics of Virgilian Quotation," in *Renaissance Genres*, ed. Barbara Kiefer Lewalski (Cambridge, MA, and London, 1986), 241–67.

[61] As Alpers notes, however, the meaning of the original Greek term is unclear, and does not include the English "idyllic" (*What Is Pastoral?*, 139, n. 2).

[62] Virgil, *Georgics* I, 145 (Loeb Classics). Wilkinson translates this as "Toil mastered everything" (61). The phrase from Eclogue X, line 69, is rendered by Alpers in his edition, "Love conquers all" (*Singer of the Eclogues*, 62–63).

[63] See Poggioli, *Oaten Flute*, 16–21, 105–134. He writes, "[A] Christian georgic is far more natural and possible than a Christian bucolic" (16).

& wisdome."[64] Jesus himself describes his ministry on earth as a labor: "I must work the works of him that sent me, while it is day" (John 9:4). Work is also the necessary human lot following the sin of Adam and Eve and their expulsion from Eden (the original Judeo-Christian pastoral world).

This generic obstacle is, in fact, more apparent than real, looming larger in retrospect to literary critics than it did to Renaissance pastoral poets. First, as is clear from Wilkinson's description of *Georgics* III, 323–38 as an "idyll," the distinction between pastoral and georgic cannot be perfectly maintained even in Virgil. For later writers, such a distinction became both more difficult and beside the point. As Rosalie Colie has demonstrated, literary kinds in the Renaissance were more often mixed than not, and this was not a problem but a source of strength and interest.[65] In fact, as Alpers points out, Christian pastoral almost necessitates a mix of pastoral and georgic, because "in Christian thought ideas of humility are connected with the curse of labor."[66] Furthermore, despite Poggioli's objections, the idyllic (in the modern sense) does have an important place in Christianity, though it is deferred until after death. Jesus does indeed say that he must work, but it is because "the night cometh when no man can work" (John 9:4). In Revelation it is promised to those "which die in the Lord" that "they may rest from their labours, and their works do follow them" (Rev. 14:13). As will be seen below in the section on verses 5–6, this sense of life after death as a kind of pastoral, or at least post-georgic, idyll is part of Psalm 23's rather complex transformation of the representative pastoral anecdote.

This recasting of the idyllic retreat also corresponds rather strikingly to the "modern," as opposed to nostalgic, idyll that Schiller called for in *On Naïve and Sentimental Poetry*:

> Let him [the writer] undertake the task of idyll so as to display that pastoral innocence even in creatures of civilisation and under all the conditions of the most active and vigorous life, of expansive thought, of the subtlest art, the highest social refinement, which, in a word, leads man who cannot now go back to Arcady forward to Elysium.[67]

Unbeknown to Schiller, the Christian pastoral of Psalm 23 (at least as Renaissance readers understood it) had already answered his call. Of course, the heroism of the representative pastoral figure is to some extent belied by

[64] Strigelius, *Proceeding in the Harmonie*, 31.

[65] See Colie, *Resources of Kind*, 76–102, and Fowler, *Kinds of Literature*, 107–08, 181–83.

[66] Alpers, *What Is Pastoral?*, 28.

[67] Friedrich Schiller, *On Naïve and Sentimental Poetry* (1795–96), trans. Julius A. Elias, modified by H. B. Nisbet, cited in Alpers, *What Is Pastoral?*, 36.

the fact that it is the shepherd who works, while the sheep simply lie about grazing and drinking. It is the sheep, after all, who are representative of men, not the shepherd, who is God (or Christ). Whether the idyll of verses 1–3 is, in Schiller's terms, naïve or sentimental, its tranquillity is sharply disrupted by the walk through the valley of the shadow of death in verse 4. This abrupt shift requires explanation on two counts: it introduces an element of danger which seems out of keeping with the pastoral mood (once again modulating to a tone that might be thought more georgic than pastoral), and it clearly implies a journey, a purposeful movement from one place to another which normally has no place in the conventionally static genre of pastoral.[68]

THE VALLEY OF THE SHADOW OF DEATH

Yea though I walke through the valley of the shadowe of death, I wyll feare no evyll: for thou art with me, thy rodde and thy staffe be the thynges that do comfort me. (v. 4)[69]

One of the most memorable geographical features in the Psalter is actually based on a mistranslation, albeit an ancient one. The Hebrew *salmawet*, meaning simply "dark shadows" or perhaps "total darkness,"[70] was re-pointed by scribal copyists in the rabbinic period to mean instead, "shadow of death." The "valley" was a feature of the original Hebrew in both pointings, but Jerome left it out of the Vulgate, which has "*in medio umbrae mortis*." He restored the "valley" in his translation from the Hebrew, "*in valle mortis*."[71] Most English versions combine all these elements, as in the Bishops' Bible verse quoted above. These variations have more than stylistic implications: the inclusion of the valley and, even more so, of "death" (especially when idealized or personified with an initial capital letter) have generated a considerable body of interpretation.

It is possible to read Ps. 23:4 as a continuation of the pastoral metaphor begun in verses 1 to 3, and this is in fact how some Renaissance Christian

68 See Poggioli, *Oaten Flute*, for instance, 4–7. On the primarily static quality of Theocritus's *Idylls*, see Alpers, *What Is Pastoral?*, 140.

69 Bishops' Bible (1568).

70 The first rendering is from *The Interpreter's Bible*, vol. 4, 127, and the second from Mitchell Dahood's translation in the Anchor Bible, *Psalms I*, 145. "*Salmawet*" occurs in several other places in the OT (Job 3:5, Ps. 107:10, Jer. 2:6, etc.), but the same translation/pointing problem applies.

71 Both versions are cited from Lefèvre d'Etaples, *Quincuplex*. Dahood omits the valley entirely in his English translation of verse 4, preferring the simple rendering, "in the midst of total darkness." His reading is based on the Septuagint but differs from that of most modern scholars.

interpreters read it, as, for example, the Geneva Bible editors in the paraphrase for their marginal gloss: "Thogh he were in danger of death, as the shepe that wandreth in the darke valley without his shepherd."[72] Calvin likewise reads the verse in the context of wandering sheep, attempting to explain more of the details of the shepherd's life:

For like as if a sheepe stray up and down in a dark dale, the only presence of the shepherd preserveth hir safe from the ronning in of wyld beasts, and from other annoyances: so now David protesteth that as oft as he shal fal into any daunger, he thinketh himself to have defence ynough in the shepeherdly care of god.[73]

Calvin also seems aware to some extent of the limitations of the Hebrew *salmawet* in its original pointing:

For among the Hebrew grammarians, [Tselimoth] seemeth to be a compounded woord, as if a man should say, [deadly shade]. And David alludeth to the dark swales or the dens of wyld beastes: wherinto if a man come: by and by at the first enterance he meeteth with the feare of death.[74]

Most other commentators and translators, less concerned than Calvin with the original context of the Hebrew Psalms, interpreted the "valley of the shadow of death" as quite a different place than the "green pastures" and "still waters," and one which was part of an allegorical rather than a physical geography. Luther, for example, always keen to allegorize, saw Ps. 23: 4 as a reference to the persecution of the word of God by "the devil and all his angels."[75]

The metrical translators encouraged the allegorizing of the valley with elaborate and fantastical imagery. Sternhold's simple "vale of death" is expanded in the Parker psalter to "death hys wo, his vaale and shadow wyde." Davison's "vale" is even more elaborate:

Yea, through Death's sad vale,
Full of shadows pale,
If my walk should lie;
So my guide were by,
Horror should not fray me,
Death should not dismay me.[76]

From a straightforward figuration of the danger of the shadowy valley, "Death" becomes in these versions fully personified as an active persecuting agent. Crashaw, as so often, represents the baroque extreme:

72 *The Bible and Holy Scriptures* [Geneva Bible].

73 Golding, *Calvin's Commentaries*, fol. 86^{r}.

74 Ibid., fol. [86^{v}], brackets original. "Tselimoth" is simply a different transliteration of the Hebrew for *salmawet*.

75 Coverdale, *Remains*, 304.

76 Davison, version 2, in Nicholas, *Poetical Rhapsody*, vol. 2, 334.

Come now, all ye terrors, sally,
Muster forth into the valley
Where triumphant darkness hovers
With a sable wing that covers
Brooding horror. Come thou, Death,
Let the damps of thy dull Breath
Overshadow even the shade
And make darkness self-afraid.[77]

In terms of modal conventions, the introduction of death into the pastoral world is perfectly appropriate. As Paul Alpers argues, there is a pronounced elegiac strain introduced into pastoral as early as Virgil, and developed in subsequent laments for Daphnis and other dead shepherds.[78] It is this darker side of pastoral which eventually leads to the "*Et in Arcadia ego*" topos, painted so strikingly by Poussin and others.[79] As the pastoral elegies of Theocritus and especially Virgil demonstrate, poets recognized the extension of Death's dominion even into Arcadia long before the Latin epigram was coined in the early seventeenth century, and the presence of "Death" in his dark valley in Ps. 23:4 is therefore not seen as incompatible with pastoral. Some of the metrical translations hint at another explanation of "death valley," however, one which has to do with the admixture of epic in the pastoral mode. Sir John Davies writes, "Therefore although my soule detruded were,/ Even to Hell's gates, yet I not ill should feare."[80] This extends beyond an allegory of danger or persecution to an encounter with Hell itself, which, in addition to reminding the Christian reader of the reach of Christ's power in the apocryphal "Harrowing of Hell," suggests the journey to the underworld which was conventional in Homeric-Virgilian epic. Denham implies this epic descent even more strongly:

To walk in Shades among the Dead,
  My Hopes, not Fears, increase.[81]

One cannot perhaps take this hint of epic very far. The psalmist is not visiting Hades in the way that Odysseus or Aeneas do; it is simply a nod in the direction of the epic by psalm translators steeped in classical literature. (Davies's *Orchestra* is full of classical allusions, for example, and Denham also wrote *The Destruction of Troy*.) What is significant, however, is the

77 Crashaw, *Poems*, 103. 78 Alpers, *What Is Pastoral?*, 34–36.
79 See Erwin Panofsky, "*Et in Arcadia Ego*: Poussin and the Elegiac Tradition," in *Meaning and the Visual Arts* (Garden City, 1955), 295–320.
80 Davies, *Complete Poems*, 157.
81 Denham, *Psalms*. Davison's valley "Full of shadows pale" (quoted above) may also point to the underworld. If Davison's "vale" is read as a shade-haunted Hades/Hell, then his description of the shepherd as a "guide" comes to seem rather Dantesque.

sense of journeying that these versions imply. This is no longer just the aimless wandering of sheep, but a deliberate and purposeful movement from one place to another. As noted above, pastoral is generally held to be static, describing the activities of shepherds in particular places at particular moments.[82] Even the conventional pastoral intrusions into epic are usually moments out of time, set in a "*locus amoenus*" apart from the path of the journeying hero.[83] Psalm 23 is thus, in this respect as in others, an unusual version of pastoral, one that allows for a journey. However, despite the generally static nature of "pure" pastoral (so far as any actual example might be so described), journeying of some sort is almost necessitated in the mixed genres of pastoral drama or narrative (consider, for example, the conventional trips to and from the "green world" in Shakespeare's plays, or the traveling to, from, and around the pastoral world in Sidney's *Arcadia*).

The journey implicit in Psalm 23 is made explicit and expanded in the pilgrimage of Christian in John Bunyan's *Pilgrim's Progress* (1678).[84] Both Christian, and then his wife and children (the latter episode appearing in Part Two, published in 1684), must pass through the Valley of the Shadow of Death on their way to the Celestial City. Bunyan conflates the reference to the valley in Ps. 23:4 with other biblical references to *salmawet* such as Jer. 2:6, "A wilderness, a land of deserts, and of pits, a land of drought, and of the shadow of death, a land that no man passeth through, and where no man dwelt."[85] In the middle of his journey through it, however, Christian hears a man's voice (Faithful's) singing Psalm 23, a broad hint to the reader that the psalm is the principal source for Bunyan's valley: "Though I walk through the Valley of the Shadow of Death, I will fear none ill, for thou art with me."[86] The text Faithful quotes seems to be derived from one of the popular metrical psalters, probably Sternhold's from *The Whole Booke of Psalmes*, which was the first to use the phrase, "Yet will I feare none ill." It subsequently appeared in Henry Ainsworth's *Booke of Psalmes* (1612) and the Scottish Psalter of 1650, though Sternhold's was by far the most popular version.[87] Despite this, Bunyan's description of the valley, full as it is of

[82] See n. 68. [83] See Poggioli, *Oaten Flute*, 9–12.

[84] The use of Psalm 23 in *Pilgrim's Progress* is briefly discussed in David Jasper, "The Twenty-Third Psalm in English Literature," *Religion & Literature* 30:1 (Spring, 1998), 1–11. Jasper's focus, however, is primarily on more recent literature.

[85] As cited (in the KJV) in John Bunyan, *Pilgrim's Progress*, ed. Roger Sharrock (Harmondsworth, 1965, rpr. 1986), 55.

[86] Ibid., 58.

[87] Sharrock (ibid., 284) cites the source as "Sternhold and Hopkins," but there were other versions that were similarly phrased. For Ainsworth and the Scottish Psalter, see Strange and Sandbach, *Psalm 23*, 36, 40. *The Scottish Metrical Psalter of 1635* has "yet would I fear none ill" (see Glasgow rpr., ed. Neil Livingston, 1864).

"hobgoblins, satyrs, and dragons of the pit," owes as much, seemingly, to the macabre elaborations of Davison, Davies, and Crashaw as to Sternhold's simpler common-meter version. The "spies" Christian meets on his way into the valley tell him that "death also doth always spread his wings over it" (recall Crashaw's "sable wing"), and the narrator himself describes his vision of "the mouth of Hell" (like Davies's "Hell's gates") in the middle of the valley.

What is most interesting about Bunyan's narrative is not so much the description of the valley, which is just as one expects the "Valley of the Shadow of Death" to be, but, first, the fact that this borrowing from a biblical lyric appears in an extended narrative at all, and, second, the place of the valley relative to the "green pastures" and "still waters," which Christian also encounters. Bunyan essentially solves a problem inherent in the implied narrative in Psalm 23: if the meadow and stream are a kind of "*locus amoenus*," a place of rest, and the valley of death a necessary obstacle to pass through on the way to some better place, why does the psalm *begin* with the resting-place and only then move to the place of trial? Bunyan seems to have felt that the stops in the implied journey in Psalm 23 were out of order, since the "*locus amoenus*" in *Pilgrim's Progress* (only a temporary stop, of course, on the way to the ultimate goal) is reached only *after* passing through the Valley of the Shadow of Death (and Vanity Fair). Eventually, Christian and Hopeful (his new traveling companion following the martyrdom of Faithful) reach "a pleasant river, which David the King called the River of God."[88] As well as the river which quenches the pilgrims' thirst, they see a "meadow green," green trees, flowers (lilies presumably, since in good pastoral fashion they "toil not, neither do they spin" [Matt. 6:28]), and other pastoral delights. There is even a reference, in the pilgrims' song, to the "crystal streams" discussed above.

Actually, the pilgrims arrive twice at pastoral landscapes reminiscent of Ps. 23:2 in Bunyan's narrative, the second time at the Delectable Mountains, inhabited by shepherds "feeding their flocks," reminiscent of the shepherds in Luke 2:8 ("And there were in the same country shepherds abiding in the field, keeping watch over their flocks by night"). Moreover, Bunyan retains some sense of the original psalmic sequence of pastures-to-valley by showing the Mountains to Christian as a far-off goal before he enters

[88] This "River of God" probably derives from other scriptural rivers as well, such as the "river of thy [God's] pleasures" in Ps. 36:8, but such typological references are by no means mutually exclusive. This river is many biblical rivers at once, including, especially after the "Valley of the Shadow of Death," the "still waters" of Psalm 23. One might add a further typological dimension to the psalm's river by noting John's renaming of it, "the River of the Water of Life" (Rev. 22:1).

the valley.[89] The resemblance of the Delectable Mountains to the "green pastures" of Psalm 23 is made explicit in their second appearance, when Christiana and the children arrive there in Part Two. There is a peaceful river as well as meadows "green all the year long . . . where they might lie down safely." (Compare "He maketh me to lie down in greene pastures," in the KJV.) This is said to be a place where "they will never want meat and drink and clothing, and here they will be kept from thieves and robbers, for this man will die before one of those committed to his trust shall be lost." The echo of Ps. 23:1, "I shall not want," is supported by Bunyan's reference to the care of "this man," who, as the narrator reports, "could gather these lambs with his arm" (Isaiah 40:11). This "man" is another manifestation of Christ, the "good shepherd" of John 10:11, who "giveth his life for his sheep" and who is traditionally conflated with the shepherd of Psalm 23, most importantly by Jesus himself.[90]

Bunyan's interpretation of the valley of Ps. 23:4 was a natural expansion of a narrative already implicit in the juxtaposition of pastures and valley in the psalm, and his vivid description of the dangers of the valley influenced those, like William Cowper, who turned to the psalm in the next century. Cowper's Olney Hymn XL, "The Valley of the Shadow of Death," includes an appearance by one of Bunyan's most memorable villains:

> My soul is sad and much dismay'd;
> See, LORD, what legions of my foes,
> With fierce Apollyon at their head,
> My heav'nly pilgrimage oppose![91]

Bunyan's (and Cowper's) emphasis on the valley as an allegory of trial and the resistance of oppression through the reliance on God's grace also suits the traditional use of Psalm 23 as a psalm of consolation. Augustine recommended the psalm to those facing martyrdom, and it was to Psalm 23, among others, that the Marian martyr John Hooper turned when he was in prison awaiting execution.[92] In *On Christian Doctrine*, Milton cites Psalm 23 as one of those proving the value of fortitude.[93] For many translators, then,

89 Bunyan, *Pilgrim's Progress*, 50.

90 Ibid., 249–50. The reference to the Good Shepherd in John 10 is Jesus's deliberate invoking of the pastoral topos of Psalm 23 in application to himself as son of David and Messiah.

91 *The Complete Poetical Works of William Cowper*, ed. H. S. Milford (Oxford, 1913), 458.

92 See Rowland E. Prothero, *The Psalms in Human Life* (London, 1907), 12, 138.

93 Cited in Radzinowicz, *Milton's Epics*, 10–11. Radzinowicz argues that Adam's "hymn" in *Paradise Lost* 12.561–73 is indebted to Ps. 23:4 ("though I walk through the valley of the shadow of death"), but specific verbal echoes are faint. Still, there may be a general indebtedness to the psalm, in the faithful walking in God's presence, their sole dependence on him, his mercy and goodness, and the suffering and death of the "simply meek."

the journey into peril became an essential part of their understanding of Psalm 23. The psalm text proper provides in itself the necessary consolation to the one undertaking the journey, as in the marvelously self-referential example of Bunyan's Faithful singing about the Lord protecting him in the "Valley of the Shadow of Death" as he actually, or rather allegorically, walks through it.

DINING IN THE LORD'S HOUSE

Thou preparest a table before me . . . and I will dwell in the house of the Lord for ever. (vv. 5–6)[94]

One of the psalm's strangest transformations of the conventional "pastoral anecdote" comes at the meal in verse 5 and involves the inevitable association of the sheep with the paschal lamb, literally the main course of the Passover supper (Exod. 12:1–10), but also, typologically, Christ himself (Matt. 26:20–29), which requires another reversal of the roles of sheep and shepherd. Strictly speaking, the preparation of the table and the subsequent meal are distinct from the perpetual dwelling in the house of the Lord. For many readers of the psalm, however, the dining described in verse 5 is assumed to occur in the location described in verse 6, the house of the Lord. In any case, the setting seems separate from the pastoral scenario introduced at the beginning of the psalm and which perhaps continues through the shadowy valley. In terms of the journey or quest implied by the shift from pastures to valley, the house of the Lord is the ultimate goal toward which the psalmist travels. A shift is thus required at some point from one metaphor to another, since the psalmist begins the journey as a sheep but ends it dining at a table and living in a house, activities inappropriate for even the most pampered flock. Similarly, the Lord begins as a shepherd and ends as a host, providing food and shelter for his guests, as noted in Strigelius/Robinson: "The second part of the Psalme, followeth with a figure or resemblance of an Hoste and hys guest, which also most sweetly describeth the fatherly loving kindnesse of God towardes us."[95]

Strigelius sees Psalm 23 as having two parts, each dominated by a prevailing metaphor, and this accords with Luther's commentary, on which (in this respect) it is probably based.[96] However, just as numerous translators

[94] In the KJV (1611), abridged. [95] Strigelius, *Proceeding in the Harmonie*, 40.

[96] See Coverdale, *Remains*, 282, in which Luther writes that "First, he [David] likeneth himself to a sheep, whom God himself, as a faithful diligent shepherd, doth wondrous well take heed unto" and "After this doth he make himself a guest, whom God prepareth a table." Strigelius cites Luther elsewhere in his commentary.

continued the pastoral metaphor through verse 4's valley of the shadow of death, so also did they assimilate verses 5 and 6 to the pastoral mode, despite the awkward disappearance of shepherd and sheep. Clearly, interpreters were willing to go to considerable lengths to sustain and justify their reading of the psalm in terms of pastoral literature. Strigelius himself tries to smooth over the metaphorical break with a rather complex typological analogy culminating in a striking allegory borrowed from Ignatius:

> [T]hat [verse 6] may be more easily understoode, by considering the representation of the silly Sheepe: for as the sheepe is therfore fedde, that within a while after, shee beeing well filled and fatted, is brought unto her Masters house, and that she may bee made meate, yeeldes her wooll, & serves to other uses for her Maister requisite: so are we in thys life fedde with the worde, and Sacraments, and are after a sort prepared, that we may be fitte meate unto GOD in the life everlasting. That notable saying of *Ignatius* is well knowne: *Let mee be grounde wyth the teeth of beastes, so I may be made fitte bread for* GOD.[97]

This is a bizarre twist on the meal in verse 5, with the guest providing and indeed becoming the food (being "had for dinner" in an unexpected sense), and, even with the help of Ignatius's figuring of himself as "bread for GOD," it doesn't quite fit the movement of the psalm itself.

An interpretation that works better, and that a number of the translators of Psalm 23 seem to have in mind, involves the transformation of the host, rather than the guest, into the more comfortable figure of the Lamb of God in the eucharistic feast. To interpret the meal in sacramental terms as the body and blood of Christ, the Eucharist, requires some finessing of the psalm text, but not as much as does Strigelius's reading of the meal as the Christian's offering of himself as a meal for God. Strigelius is actually aware of the alternative interpretation, acknowledging that a man "of godly zeale" may "applie the Table and Cuppe, unto the ministery of the Gospell and Sacraments" according to the "Analogie of Faith."[98] This is, after all, the reading favored by Luther:

> Besides this [the rod and staff], the Lord hath prepared for her [the "congregation of Christ"] also a table and Easter lamb. When her enemies are very wrothful, gnash their teeth together over her, are mad, unreasonable, in a rage, and out of their wits, and take all their subtilty, power, and might to help them for to destroy her utterly; then doth the beloved Bride of Christ set her down at her Lord's table, eateth the Easter lamb, drinketh of the fresh water, is merry, and singeth: "The Lord is my shepherd, I shall lack nothing."[99]

[97] Strigelius, *Proceeding in the Harmonie*, 42. [98] Ibid., 41.
[99] Coverdale, *Remains*, 313.

In verse 5, according to Luther's reading, the Lord becomes a sheep, the paschal Lamb, sacrificed for the sins of man. This reading of host-as-meal-for-guest can at least be accommodated to the behavior required of a good host. Indeed, this is exactly the metaphor used by Herbert in "Love (III)," in which Love/the Lord as tavern-keeper and host/Host bids the poet enter, sit down, and "taste my meat."[100]

Obviously the gap between the two governing metaphors of Psalm 23 required somewhat tortured refashioning by Renaissance readers and writers in order to accommodate the text to their conception of it as an integrated pastoral lyric. This required a radical reinterpretation of the feast but also of its setting, the final resting-place of the psalmist in the house of the Lord. Especially significant in terms of Psalm 23's particular inflection of the pastoral genre are those readings of the "house" of God that favor grander and more aristocratic architectural terms. In Davison's first paraphrase, for example, the psalmist ends his journey in God's "courts with heav'nly pleasure."[101] The choice of "courts" may be a borrowing from other psalms which use the word (Ps. 84:10, for instance, where "one daye in thy courtes is better than a thousande," in Coverdale's Great Bible version). But it is a particularly appropriate choice for the end of a pastoral psalm, since one of the familiar conventions of pastoral is the lowly shepherd whose "noble" bearing and behavior is finally confirmed by the revelation of his actual nobility, a convention lending support to Empson's claim that the genre is a kind of humble holiday for sophisticated readers. The "salvage man" who rescues Sir Calepine and helps Serena is one of a number of such characters in Spenser's *Faerie Queene*. Other examples from the period include Urania in Sidney's *Arcadia*, "thought a shepherd's daughter, but indeed of far greater birth," the character of the same name in Lady Mary Wroth's *The Countess of Montgomery's Urania*, who – following the model set by Wroth's uncle – seems a shepherdess but is actually the daughter of the king of Naples, and Perdita in Shakespeare's *A Winter's Tale*.[102] In a similar fashion, Psalm 23 has characters appearing to be humble (in this case, sheep) who turn out

[100] C. A. Patrides's gloss on this poem is that it "celebrates not the sacrament in the visible Church but the final communion in Heaven when God 'shall gird himself, and make them to sit down to meat, and will come forth and serve them' (Luke 12.37)." See *The English Poems of George Herbert*, ed. Patrides (London, 1974), 192. There is no evidence for this assertion, and it seems unnecessarily restrictive. Both Herbert's poem and the seventeenth-century reading of Psalm 23 from which it may partly be derived combine the earthly "sacrament" and the "final communion." Indeed, it might be argued that the suggestion or prefiguration of the "final communion" is always part of the power of the eucharistic feast.

[101] Davison, version 1, in Nicholson, *Poetical Rhapsody*, vol. 2, 332.

[102] Sidney, *Old Arcadia*, 284–85.

to be of far higher birth.[103] Their true inheritance turns out to be not just an earthly kingdom, like Perdita's, but the kingdom of heaven. This reading of the psalm, which further accommodates it to the norms of pastoral literature, is emphasized by the transformation of "house" to "courts" or "mansions," as found in the prose glosses to Parker's and Wither's versions:

Leade us, O Lorde by the rules of thy comfortable preceptes, that when we have optaynd the habitation of thy everlasting mansion, we may be fully satisfied with the cup of joyful eternitie. (Parker)[104]

Guide us by thy example [etc.] . . . that we may walke without repininge, through the afflictions of this life; & without fear through the shaddowes of Death, to those mansions, which thou hast appointed for thy chosen flock; in the kingdome of heaven. (Wither)[105]

An especially interesting example of this interpretation was written by that paragon of nobility, and author of the *Arcadia*, Sir Philip Sidney:

Thus thus shall all my dayes be fede,
This mercy is so sure
It shall endure,
And long yea long abide I shall,
There where the Lord of all
Doth hold his hall.[106]

In this context, the "hall" which is "held" by the Lord signifies a chamber of royal or aristocratic audience, or as the OED puts it, "A formal assembly held by the sovereign, or by the mayor or principal municipal officer of a town." It cites the idioms "to keep hall" or "call a hall," to which may be added Sidney's "hold his hall." A citation from Grafton's *Chronicle* (1568) gives the sense of Sidney's phrase, if not the identical wording: "[Christmas] kept at Greenwiche with open hous-hold, and frank resorte to the Court (which is called keping of the Hall)."[107] The association of the phrase with festivity, as at Christmas, is especially apt for Sidney's verse, which celebrates the drinking of what Parker calls "the cup of joyful eternitie." Furthermore, the hall is "open" so even the relatively humble can enter the lordly dwelling

[103] For Christians, the reversal of high and low, mighty and meek, is promised in the Gospels, as in the sermon on the mount ("Blessed are the poor in spirit: for theirs is the kingdom of heaven," Matt. 5:3) or the parable of Dives and Lazarus (Luke 16:19–31).

[104] [Parker], *Psalter*.

[105] Wither, *Psalmes*.

[106] Sidney, *Poems*, 301. A variant of the final lines, based on different manuscripts, is printed in Rathmell, *Psalms of Sidney and Pembroke*, 49: "To thee, I say, ascended up,/ Where thou, the Lord of all,/ Dost hold thy hall." The explicit ascension in this version suggests even more strongly the conventional pastoral apotheosis, discussed below.

[107] OED, s.v. "hall" 7c.

with "frank resorte." It is important to note that "hall" could also be used to refer to a hall of audience or court of justice, as in Westminster Hall (commonly, in sixteenth- and seventeenth-century usage, "the Hall").[108] The "hall" of the Lord is thus, appropriately, a place of judgment as well as festivity, and Sidney suggests neither exclusively one nor the other, though the overflowing cup tips the balance in favor of something like the heroic banqueting hall. This corresponds to the gloss on the psalm's cup and oil in the Geneva Bible, which Sidney would have known: "As was the maner of great feastes."[109]

The journey of the sheep in Psalm 23 ends, then, at a royal feast in the kingdom of heaven, a feast likened to the Eucharist, in which the extreme graciousness (in all senses) of the host/Host is shown by his offering himself as the meat and drink, recalling, once again, the description of the Good Shepherd in Luke who "giveth his life for the sheep." The journey from valley to heavenly hall may also be likened, to draw on yet another pastoral convention, to the apotheosis of the dead shepherd at the end of the pastoral elegy. The elegiac tone has already been introduced by the presence of Death in the valley of the shadow. But the final movement of the representative "sheep" through the valley of death to the idyllic house, hall, courts, or temple of the Lord – by which most interpreters understood "heaven" – suggests the psalmist's ascent to immortality as, in the manner of Daphnis or Lycidas, a kind of pastoral apotheosis.

[108] Ibid., 7b. [109] Geneva Bible (1560).

CHAPTER 6

Psalm 51: sin, sacrifice, and the "Sobbes of a Sorrowfull Soule"

Psalm 51, called the *Miserere* after its Latin incipit, *Miserere mei Deus*, is the preeminent psalm of penitence. It is the middle psalm, and the most important, of the seven Penitential Psalms (6, 32, 38, 51, 102, 130, 143), which before the Reformation had been central to traditional Catholic devotions. These psalms were included in many fifteenth- and sixteenth-century primers for use during private meditations, focusing particularly on the last words of Christ on the cross, which were also traditionally divided into seven (as were the Deadly Sins, the Cardinal Virtues, and other devotional subjects). The seven Penitential Psalms were also used at Catholic funerals as intercessions for the souls of the dead.[1] The earliest surviving metrical psalms in English are in an early fifteenth-century macaronic paraphrase of the Penitential Psalms by Thomas Brampton.[2] Far better known are Sir Thomas Wyatt's *Penitential Psalms* (see chapter 4), translated and adapted from the Italian of Pietro Aretino.[3] Richard Verstegan and John Davies of Hereford also produced metrical versions of the Penitential Psalms, and during a serious illness Sir Francis Bacon translated a set of seven psalms which, while not the traditional "penitential" seven, were evidently written with that set in mind (Bacon chose Psalms 1, 12, 90, 104, 136, 137, and 149). Before Aretino, Petrarch had written a set of "Penitential Psalms" in Latin verse, which, though clearly modeled on the actual psalms, were poems of his own invention. George Chapman translated Petrarch's psalms, rather loosely, into English verse in 1612.[4]

The Penitential Psalms, and Psalm 51 in particular, played a vital role in the liturgy of the English Church as well as in the private prayers and

1 See Eamon Duffy, *The Stripping of the Altars* (New Haven, 1992), 248ff. and 369–71.

2 See Holland, *Psalmists of Britain*, vol. 1, 73–79, where Brampton's Psalm 142 (143) is reprinted. The manuscript, dated 1414, is *Sloan. Num.* 1853. 4. D. in the Cottonian Collection of the British Museum.

3 See Wyatt, *Complete Poems*, 195–216. Wyatt's psalms were published in 1549; Aretino's *I Sette Salmi de la Penitentia di David* in 1534.

4 *The Poems of George Chapman*, ed. Phyllis Brooks Bartlett (New York, 1962), 202–217. Chapman's translation was published in 1612; Petrarch's original was composed c.1355.

devotions of individual Christians. Psalm 51 also had an impact on literature, especially the seventeenth-century religious poetry of John Donne, George Herbert, and others, who, as practicing Christians – Donne and Herbert as priests – were therefore deeply interested in the religious debates of the age. The language of this psalm, its singular metaphors and vocabulary, proved irresistible for Christian writers, who, during these decades of religious turmoil, struggled with the problematic nature of sin and repentance. Psalm 51 was also a text in which sixteenth- and seventeenth-century reformers, Protestant and Catholic alike, found the seeds of ideas that ultimately affected what they believed and how they worshiped, as exhibited in theological writing such as sermons, biblical commentaries, and liturgical forms, genres until recently considered marginal to the history of literature.

MISERERE MEI, DEUS

Have mercy upon me (o God) after thy goodnes, & acordinge unto thy greate mercies, do awaye myne offences. (v. 1)[5]

The subject and purpose of Psalm 51 are stated outright in the first verse: the sinner, conscious of his sin but also of God's goodness, begs for mercy. This verse was one of the most widely known in sixteenth-century England because of its peculiar involvement in the legal loophole known as "benefit of clergy." A vestige of the medieval system of separate civil and ecclesiastical courts, benefit of clergy allowed for those in holy orders to be tried by the bishop rather than the secular magistrate. To prove oneself a clergyman, it was necessary to demonstrate a knowledge of Latin by reciting the "neck-verse," the first verse of Psalm 51. Peculiar as it seems today, this was held to prove the accused a clergyman. The accused "cleric" was thus turned over to the bishop for trial, almost always resulting in lighter sentencing or none at all. After the Reformation, and for some years before it, this law was subject to intense criticism. The number of offenses to which benefit of clergy could be applied was thus gradually reduced, excluding, first, treason and then, in 1576, felonies such as rape, burglary, and "unlawful carnal knowledge of a female under ten years of age."[6] In any case, it was obviously in the interest of anyone engaged in unlawful trade to know this

[5] In the Coverdale Bible version (1535).
[6] G. R. Elton's paraphrase of part four of the 1576 Act, 18 Eliz. I c. 7, in *The Parliament of England 1559–1581* (Cambridge, 1986), 63.

verse.[7] By this period, it was widely known anyway from its use in the liturgy – as Luther wrote, "among them all [the psalms], it is the most widely used in church and daily prayers" – so it must have been a sorry rogue indeed who failed to "construe" the neck-verse.[8]

Luther goes on, in his 1532 lectures, to discuss the importance of the terms set out in the first verse of Psalm 51. The essential opposition, what Luther calls "the conjunction of two things that are incompatible," consists of man's utter depravity on the one hand and God's infinite mercy on the other:

> Look at David here. With his mouth open he breaks out in the words "Have mercy upon me, O God." Thus he combines things that by nature are dissimilar, God and himself the sinner, the Righteous and the unrighteous. That gigantic mountain of divine wrath that so separates God and David, he crosses by trust in mercy and joins himself to God.[9]

Luther goes on to locate the tension in the incommensurability of the principal substantives, "God" and "me." It appears that, at least in this respect, and despite Luther's own claim that "the theology of this psalm is unknown to the schools of the papists," the significance of Psalm 51 cut across denominational boundaries.[10] A century and a half after Luther wrote his lectures, the English Franciscan, Nicholas Cross, interpreted the first verse in the same terms:

> Again, when he reflects on the distance of these Terms *Deus & mei, God and me,* methinks it should startle the greatest Assurance, to consider the *sublimity* of him that is offended, and the *despicability* of the offendour; the *one* is immense and fills all places, the *other* is contracted into the dimensions of a small Body; the one is immutable, and still the same, the *other* is corruptible, and mouldering away every Moment towards that nothing from whence it came; the *one* is eternal, the *other* subject to time; the *one* is the object of Beatitude, the *other* of Misery.[11]

Catholic thinking may have changed after the Counter-Reformation, but the contrast between man's sin and God's righteousness was one which all Christians, in times of penitence, could easily understand.

Some translators of Ps. 51:1 took pains to emphasize the disparity between God and man, grace and sin. Alexander Scott, for instance, writing in

7 On benefit of clergy, see A. G. Dickens, *The English Reformation*, 2nd ed. (University Park, PA, 1991), 111; John Guy, *Tudor England* (Oxford and New York, 1988), 328; and especially Elton, *Parliament*, 63–66, 97–98, 203–04, 301–02.

8 Martin Luther, "Psalm 51, The Psalm Miserere," in *Luther's Works*, ed. Jaroslav Pelikan, vol. 12 (Saint Louis, 1955), 303–410, 304.

9 Ibid., 314, 317.

10 Ibid., 317.

11 Nicholas Cross, *The Cynosura, or, a Saving Star that leads to Eternity. Discovered amidst the Celestial Orbs of Davids Psalms by way of Paraphrase upon the Miserere* (London, 1670), 7.

Scotland sometime in the second half of the sixteenth century, makes the psalmist's groveling ("gruffling") more literal than in the standard versions:

> Lord God deliver me, allace!
> For thy grit mercy, rewth, and grace,
> Sore mornyng, gruffling on my face,
>   Rew on my miserie:
> Als for the multitud and space
> Off thy heich clemenss, heir my cace,
> And my trespass expell and chace,
>   Lord God deliver me.[12]

William Hunnis's extended paraphrase of Psalm 51 in his alliteratively named paraphrase of the penitential psalms, *Seven Sobbes of a Sorrowfull Soule for Sinne*, is exceptional in its extreme contrast between God and man. Before confessing his sin, the penitent recapitulates the Creation and the main events of the Bible as evidence of God's great power and love:

> O thou that mad'st the world of nought,
>   whom God thy creatures call,
> Which formedst man like to thy selfe,
>   yet sufferdst him to fall:
> Thou God, which by thy heavenlie word,
>   didst flesh of virgine take,
> And so becam'st both God & man,
>   for sinfull fleshes sake:
> O thou that sawst when man by sin
>   to hel was overthrowne,
> Didst meekely suffer death on crosse,
>   to have thy mercie knowne.[13]

Subsequent verses mention Noah, Abraham, Lot and Sodom, Daniel in the lion's den, the Exodus, and the children in the fiery furnace, before Hunnis finally arrives at his own deeds, which are as degraded as God's are great and good:

> I do confesse my faults be more
>   than thousand else beside,
> More noisome and more odious,
>   more fouler to be tride,
> Than ever was the loathsome swine,
>   or menstruall cloth beraid:

[12] Cited in Holland, *Psalmists of Britain*, vol. 1, 176. Scott's Psalm 51, "Ane new zeir gift, to the Quene Mary, quhen scho come first hame" was published in 1562.

[13] Hunnis, *Seven Sobbes of a Sorrowfull Soule for Sinne* (London, 1583, rpr. 1597), 35–36.

To thinke thereon my woful soule,
(alas) is yet afraid.[14]

Hunnis chooses his comparisons for more than shock-effect, though they are certainly strikingly "noisome." As will become clear, Christians usually interpreted Psalm 51, especially its final verses, as a prophecy of the substitution of the Gospel for the Law, replacing the ancient Jewish sacrificial practice with the sacrifice of Christ and the "sacrifice" of the "contrite heart" of the penitent. Hunnis has this in mind, since both the "swine" and the "menstruall cloth" point to Jewish law: the dietary code prohibiting certain animals (Leviticus 11) and the purification of women required after menstruation (Leviticus 15), analogous to the pre-Reformation English rite known as "the churching of women" after childbirth. The concern in Leviticus is with the sacrifices necessary to cleanse those who have touched unclean flesh or had unclean issue. Hunnis implicitly emphasizes the obsolescence of the Old Testament sacrificial system; his uncleanness surpasses those of "swine" and "menstruall cloth" and thus requires a greater sacrifice than the Jewish sin-offerings and also a greater mercy from God, both of which are united in the sacrifice of Christ.

JUSTIFYING GOD

Agaynst the only, agaynst the have I synned, and done evell in thy sight: that thou mightest be justified in thy saynges, and shuldest over come when thou art judged. (v. 4)[15]

Verse 4 of Psalm 51 was pivotal in the early development of Reformation theology, since it was the focus for Luther's thinking on the matter of sin and justification by faith. In fact, as Luther notes, he was drawn to the verse because of Paul's quotation of it in his writing on sin and justification in the Letter to Romans. Paul is considering the relative status of Jews and Gentiles in the eyes of God and the question of what is essential for salvation, when he writes,

What advantage then hath the Jew? or what profit is there of circumcision? Much every way: chiefly, because that unto them were committed the oracles of God. For what if some did not believe? shall their unbelief make the faith of God without effect? God forbid: yea, let God be true, but every man a liar; as it is written, That thou mightest be justified in thy sayings, and mightest overcome when thou art judged.[16]

[14] Ibid., 37–38. [15] In the version of the Coverdale Bible (1535).
[16] Rom. 3:1–4 (KJV).

The place where "it is written" is of course Ps. 51:4, which, as Luther notes in his first lecture on Psalm 51, was "very difficult" and a passage "on which almost as many interpretations have been offered as there were interpreters."[17] That Paul himself was drawn to the verse merely emphasized its importance to the young Luther, as he later recounted:

> I greatly longed to understand Paul's Epistle to the Romans and nothing stood in the way but that one expression, "the justice of God" [Rom. 3:4; see Bainton below], because I took it to mean that justice whereby God is just and deals justly in punishing the unjust. My situation was that, although an impeccable monk, I stood before God as a sinner troubled in conscience, and I had no confidence that my merit would assuage him. Therefore I did not love a just and angry God, but rather hated and murmured against him. Yet I clung to the dear Paul and had a great yearning to know what he meant.
>
> Night and day I pondered until I saw the connection between the justice of God and the statement that "the just shall live by his faith" [Rom. 1:17]. Then I grasped that the justice of God is that righteousness by which through grace and sheer mercy God justifies us through faith. Thereupon I felt myself to be reborn and to have gone through open doors into paradise. The whole of Scripture took on a new meaning, and whereas before the "justice of God" had filled me with hate, now it became to me inexpressibly sweet in greater love. This passage of Paul became to me a gate to heaven.[18]

Roland Bainton, who cites the passage above, explains Luther's epiphany in philological terms:

> Light broke at last through the examination of exact shades of meaning in the Greek language. One understands why Luther could never join those who discarded the humanist tools of scholarship. In the Greek of the Pauline epistles the word "justice" has a double sense, rendered in English by "justice" and "justification." The former is a strict enforcement of the law, as when a judge pronounces the appropriate sentence. Justification is a process of the sort which sometimes takes place if the judge suspends the sentence, places the prisoner on parole, expresses confidence and personal interest in him, and thereby instills such resolve that the man is reclaimed and justice itself ultimately better conserved than by the exaction of a pound of flesh.[19]

Interpreting (or translating) "justice" as "justification" in both Paul and Psalm 51 thus gives Luther hope in God's mercy, despite his own sinfulness –

[17] Luther, "Psalm Fifty-One," in *First Lectures on the Psalms I, Luther's Works*, vol. 10, ed. Hilton C. Oswald (Saint Louis, 1974), 235. In his later and much longer lecture on Psalm 51, Luther writes that "because Paul quoted it in the Epistle to the Romans (3:4), it came to be listed among the more difficult passages in all Scripture" (*Luther's Works*, vol. 12, 336).

[18] Cited in Bainton, *Here I Stand*, 65. [19] Ibid., 64.

exactly the implication of the first verse of Psalm 51, as recognized by Luther in his later lectures, quoted above.

Another difficulty for interpreters lay in the precise relationship between human sin and the justification of God. As Luther observed, the phrase "that thou mightest be justified" can be misinterpreted, "as if He could not be justified unless we sinned." One must understand, he continues,

First. All men are in sins before God and commit sin, that is, they are sinners in fact.
Second. To this God Himself bore witness through the prophets and established the same at last by the suffering of Christ, for it is on account of the sins of men that He made Him suffer and die.
Third. God is not justified in Himself, but in His words and in us.
Fourth. We become sinners then when we acknowledge ourselves to be such, for such we are before God.[20]

Luther seems to be arguing here, among other things, that the "justification" of God referred to in the psalm (and by Paul) is not a "judgement" of any kind by men, but rather a fulfillment of prophecy ("in His words"). In the later lectures on Psalm 51, after he had further developed his ideas on justification,[21] Luther returned to this interpretive crux, offering a more confident clarification of the verse in light of Paul's use of it in Romans:

He does not mean that God's righteousness is increased by our sins, as slanderous people charged Paul with saying (Rom. 3:8). He simply says, "I sin only in Thy sight, I do evil only in Thy sight, so that it stands as true that Thou alone art righteous and the Justifier of sinners, that Thou alone dost free from sin in that Thou does not impute it to those who trust in Thy mercy."

Paul clearly shows that this is the meaning in what immediately precedes the quotation from this passage. So the word "that" does not mean our work as a cause. It only means our confession, that we confess two things – that all men are liars or sinners, so that it is established that only God is righteous and the Justifier of the wicked man who has faith in Christ Jesus.[22]

That this interpretation became canonical among reformers is evident in Calvin's obvious reliance on it in his own commentary on Psalm 51. He

[20] *Luther's Works*, vol. 10, 235.

[21] As Richard Marius notes, there has been considerable debate among scholars as to whether Luther's theology of justification by faith was fully developed by the time of his first lectures on the Psalms in 1512. See Marius, *Martin Luther*, 88–89. See also the review of Marius by Patrick Collinson, *London Review of Books*, vol. 21, no. 15 (July 29, 1999), 12–13: "The problem for Luther scholarship, insofar as it lays out the story chronologically, is where to insert the evangelical breakthrough, the discovery of justification by faith."

[22] *Luther's Works*, vol. 12, 338.

buttresses Luther's argument with citations from the Hebrew text, but the interpretation is unchanged:[23]

Moreover the Adverb [that] or the Hebrew word [*Lemognan*] importeth not so much the rendring of a cause in this place, as a consequencie. For Davids falling was not properly the cause that Gods glorye appeered in his judgementes: but forasmuche as by sinning, men darken Gods rightuousnesse: hee sayeth that it avaunceth it self at length by the owne power, so as it appeereth more brightsome: bicause it is the peculiar office of God too bring light out of darknes.[24]

With a boldness born of sixteenth-century advances in biblical philology, Calvin challenges Paul's reading of Ps. 51:4 by reaching back to the original Hebrew text. The last phrase of the verse, which in the KJV reads "and founde pure when thou art judged," and in its citation in Romans (also KJV), "and mightest overcome when thou art judged," is mistranslated: "Paul digresseth from the words of the Prophet in this behalf onely, that by folowing the Greek translation, hee tooke the woord [judge] passively, and in stead of [to be pure] putteth [to overcome.]"[25] Arthur Golding's translation of the second half of the psalm verse, which accompanies the English version of Calvin's commentary (also by Golding), is "that thou mayst bee justified in thy sayinges, and pure in judging."[26] Thus, whether the word is rendered "judge" or "justify," it is God who is the subject and man the object of both clauses.[27] This linguistic insight resolves logically the problem of God's justification by men with which Luther and others struggled. One of the central theological cruxes of the Reformation hinges on a question of translation.

It is always difficult to know how much commentary on the Psalms was familiar to translators, but it is clear that, at least with respect to this verse, translators were wrestling with these same interpretive problems

[23] Luther was aware of the Hebrew only indirectly, through the Latin translation of the Hebrew text of the Penitential Psalms by Johannes Reuchlin, *Septem Psalmi penitentiales*. See *Luther's Works*, vol. 10, 237, n. 1.

[24] Golding, *Calvin's Commentaries*, fol. [202^{v}], brackets original.

[25] Ibid., brackets original. The "Greek translation" is the Septuagint.

[26] Ibid., fol. [201^{v}].

[27] This translation accords with Dahood's in the Anchor Bible: "And so you are just when you sentence,/ and blameless when you judge" (*Psalms II*, 1). Interestingly, although the Geneva Bible follows Calvin in its translation of Ps. 51:4b ("that thou maiest be just when thou speakest, and pure when thou judgest"), the translators of the Bishops' and King James Bibles return to the passive, perhaps in an effort to avoid conflict with Paul. Though it doesn't mention Psalm 51, on the generally problematic nature of New Testament (mis-)quotation of the Old, and its impact on Reformation exegesis, see R. Gerald Hobbs, "Hebraica Veritas *and* Traditio Apostolica: Saint Paul and the Interpretation of the Psalms in the Sixteenth Century," in *The Bible in the Sixteenth Century*, ed. David C. Steinmetz (Durham, NC, and London, 1990), 83–99.

that concerned Luther and Calvin, seeming to follow either the Lutheran–Pauline (passive) or the Calvinist (active) reading of Ps. 51:4. For example, Coverdale's metrical version, in Lutheran fashion, states the final clause passively:

> In thy worde stondest thou stedfastly,
> Thoughe thou be judged wrongfully.[28]

George Wither and Thomas Carew also favor the passive reading, with God being judged for his treatment of the sinner. Wither's God seems almost in danger of being beleaguered by litigation:

> here I do confesse, oh Lord,
> That, when to censure thou art brought,
> Men, true may finde they Truthfull word,
> And, judge thy Judgements as they ought.[29]

One suspects that neither Luther nor Calvin would have approved of the implications of this translation. Carew would probably also not have gained their approval, his sinner repenting so "That all Men might thy Justice see/ When thou art Judg'd for Judging mee."[30] Hunnis's paraphrase in *Seven Sobbes* makes the verse sound like extortion, the sinner bargaining on God's concern for his reputation:

> But sure my hope is firmely fixt,
> that thou wilt me forgive;
> For with thine honor shal it stand,
> to suffer me to live:
> *That al the world may witnesse thee*
> *a judge most just to be,*
> For that thou wilt thy promise keepe,
> to al that trust in thee.[31]

Pembroke, on the other hand, leans toward the Calvinist reading, which she likely knew (see chapter 4), the sinner in her version confessing to God as "Just, judge, true wittnes" in order that "for righteousnes/ thie doome maie passe against my guilt awarded,/ thie evidence for truth maie be regarded."[32] The trial metaphor is made more explicit in another Calvinist rendering by Henry King, in which it is quite clear who is being judged by whom:

[28] Coverdale, *Ghostly Psalms*, in *Remains*, 574. [29] Wither, *Psalmes*.
[30] Carew, *Poems*, 137. [31] Hunnis, *Seven Sobbes*, 40 (italics original).
[32] Pembroke, *Works*, vol. 2, 50.

Against Thee have I sinn'd alone,
Who art my Judge for what is donne:
I cannot hide the blood I spilt,
Nor will excuse my secret guilt;
That at Thy bar when I am try'd,
Thy sentence might be justify'd.[33]

Of course, King's use of "justify'd" here simply returns to the crux with which Luther, Calvin, and others struggled: the true relationship between man's confession and the justification of God's judgment. At least it is clear here that God is in no way being "judged." The version of Thomas Parnell, from the end of the seventeenth century, recasts the verse, leaves out justification, and has God doing the judging, though only in a conditional clause:

So great, my god, my ills have been
'Gainst thee and only thee,
Thy Justice, though I were condemned,
Would good and righteous be.[34]

Other translations are more ambiguous. In one of the earliest sixteenth-century English translations, for instance, the difficulties are avoided altogether by simply expanding the verse and altering it to avoid any causal relationship between the first half and the second: "Agenst the onely to have so sinned it beruweth me and it repenteth me to have had done this grevouse sinne in thy sight: wherfore justifie me acordinge to thy promise and make me clene accordinge to thy equite."[35] Wyatt, on the other hand, covers both interpretive possibilities, or comes down somewhere between them:

Pardon thou then,
Whereby thou shalt keep still thy word stable,
Thy justice pure and clean; because that when
I pardoned am, then forthwith justly able,
Just I am judged by justice of thy grace.[36]

33 King, *Psalmes.*

34 Thomas Parnell (1679–1718), in Davie, *Psalms in English*, 185. According to Davie, Parnell was an Irishman and friend to Swift and Pope.

35 George Joye, *Davids Psalter*, trans. from Zwingli. Joye's use of "equite" (equity) is especially interesting, since it accords well with Luther's sense of justification. As the OED notes, the original sense of "equity" referred to "general principles of justice (the *naturalis aequitas* of Roman jurists) to correct or supplement the provisions of the law" ("equity 3"). By the law, man is doomed, and he therefore appeals (in Psalm 51) to God's Court of Equity to supersede the law and render a merciful judgment, or a "justification" in the sense Bainton describes above.

36 Wyatt, *Complete Poems*, 207.

By showing mercy, God will in some sense be justified; that his word will be kept "stable" and his justice "pure and clean" implies, though it doesn't explicitly mention, an outside opinion like the judgment of men. On the other hand, it is the penitent sinner who is actually judged by God, or at least the "justice of thy grace."

GUILTY MOTHERS AND ORIGINAL SIN

Behold, I was shapen in iniquitie: and in sinne my mother conceived me. (v. 5)[37]

The theology of original sin was first formulated by Augustine, but there are biblical passages which suggest the general notion that, as Mitchell Dahood puts it, "all men have a congenital tendency toward evil."[38] In Gen. 21:8, for instance, God says, "the imagination of man's heart is evil from his youth" (KJV). In the Epistle to the Romans, which was so influential in Luther's thinking about sin, Paul quotes Ps. 14:3, "There is none righteous, no not one."[39] Ps. 51:7 is another verse which has traditionally been read as confirmation of the doctrine of original sin, one especially appealing to Protestants convinced of man's utter depravity, his inability to do anything to effect his own salvation, and his justification by faith alone through the grace of God. As one might expect, Luther responds vigorously to this verse, offering a colloquial paraphrase of it in his later lectures on the psalm:

> The human seed, this mass from which I was formed, is totally corrupt with faults and sins. The material itself is faulty. The clay, so to speak, out of which this vessel began to be formed is damnable. What more do you want? This is how I am; this is how all men are. Our very conception, the very growth of the foetus in the womb, is sin, even before we are born and begin to be human beings.[40]

The verse focuses on the mother as the source of sin. Some psalm translators accept this idea, even emphasize it; others, perhaps sensing this as moral evasiveness, attempt to shift the focus back to the repentant sinner. Calvin was obviously sensitive to this problem, for he writes in his commentary that "David accuseth not his parents, ne putteth over the fault unto them: but cyteth himself to the judgement seate of God, avouching himself too

[37] In the KJV (1611).

[38] See "original sin," in *A Dictionary of Biblical Tradition in English Literature*, ed. David Lyle Jeffrey (Grand Rapids, 1992), 577–79; Dahood, *Psalms II*, 4. For a detailed study, see Alister E. McGrath, *Iustitia Dei: A History of the Christian Doctrine of Justification*, 2 vols. (Cambridge, 1986).

[39] Rom. 3:10 (KJV). The psalm verse in the KJV actually reads, "*there is* none that doeth good, no not one."

[40] *Luther's Works*, vol. 12, 348.

bee a sinful creature, so as he was already a sinner before he was borne intoo the world."[41]

Among those feminizing human sin, however, Alexander Scott writes, "By sin maternall I am send ["sent"?]."[42] George Sandys and Carew emphasize maternal guilt, both employing the image of breast-feeding, with mother's milk as the medium through which sin is transmitted:

> In sin conceiv'd, brought forth in sin,
> Sin sucked I from my mother's breast.
> (Sandys)[43]

> Even from my birth I did begin
> With mothers milk to Suck in Sinn.
> (Carew)[44]

Francis Seagar, actually plagiarizing and revising the earl of Surrey, is blunt in attributing his "fall" to his mother, but allows that she too was subject to "synne":

> subject, my mother was
> Also to it made thrall:
> and when that I, conceyved was
> By her I had my fall.[45]

One might expect a different emphasis from Pembroke, since she was one of the few translators actually to have experienced motherhood. Yet, somewhat like Seagar/Surrey, she subtly shares the burden of guilt, implying that, although the child derives its sin from the mother, the mother's sin, too, is "conceived" in conception and childbirth:

> My mother, loe! when I began to be,
> conceaving me, with me did sinne conceave:
> and as with living heate shee cherisht me
> corruption did like cherishing receave.[46]

Other translators suggest that, though the sinner is born in sin, he compounds his guilt by failing to improve himself or even by furthering his sinfulness. Whittingham, for example, writes that "Yea, [I] of my mother so born was,/ and yet vile wretch remain therein."[47] John Davies of Hereford is even harder on "himself":

[41] Golding, *Calvin's Commentaries*, fol. 203r. [42] In Holland, *Psalmists of Britain*, vol. 1, 176.
[43] G. Sandys, *Psalmes*. [44] Carew, *Poems*, 137.
[45] Francis Seagar, *Certayne Psalmes select out of the Psalter of David* (London, 1553), sig. B.iiii.r. On the relationship between Seagar and Surrey, see Zim, *English Metrical Psalms*, Appendix, no. 31, 228.
[46] Pembroke, *Works*, vol. 2, 50. [47] *Whole Booke of Psalmes* (1562).

For, nought but wickednesse prepar'd the way
to my conception; which to worse did passe;
Then, ere I was, I stood at sinfull stay;
and, when I fell to Being, worser was.[48]

In a similar fashion, King writes that, though he was "In sin conceiv'd" he has "emprov'd, by act and thought,/ Those spots which to the world I brought."[49] Matthew Parker is less revisionist, but he offers the mother a way out by deferring the guilt back to its male originator:

My mother me: conceyvd alas,
in sinne of Adams sect.[50]

Of course, Parker's reader might remember that Eve ate the apple first, but she isn't mentioned, and Adam, in what is perhaps a rather peculiar form of male chauvinism, is here credited with the original sin.

Hunnis also introduces Adam, from whom "first this sinne was drawn," to his extended paraphrase of this verse, but, as in his treatment of verse 4, the effect is one of avoidance of responsibility (heightened in this case by echoes of the Book of Common Prayer's General Confession):

Yea, many a time I am so drawne
to doo I would not do,
And that I would I leave undone,
for want of might thereto.[51]

Anne Vaughan Lock, in her sonnet on this verse (part of a sonnet sequence paraphrasing Psalm 51), treats original sin more complexly. She doesn't mention either Adam or Eve, but emphasizes the corruption of human nature, and the fact that she takes her sin from both the male "sede" and the female "shape" subtly revises the traditional account of the Fall that blames women for the transmission of that corruption:

For lo, in sinne, Lord, I begotten was,
With sede and shape my sinne I toke also,
Sinne is my nature and my kinde alas,

48 Davies of Hereford, *The Dolefull Dove: or, Davids 7. Pentitentiall Psalmes* (1612), in *The Complete Works of John Davies of Hereford*, ed. Alexander B. Grosart, 2 vols. (Edinburgh, 1878), vol. 1, 57.

49 King, *Psalmes.* 50 [Parker], *Psalter.*

51 Hunnis, *Seven Sobbes*, 41. Alternatively, the allusion to the liturgy may support the petition of Hunnis's penitent, if one interprets the allusion as deference to an authoritative text rather than evasion. The words of the General Confession, from the Second (1552) Prayer-Book of Edward VI, are "We have left undone those things whiche we oughte to have done, and we have done those thinges which we ought not to have done, and there is no health in us." See *First and Second Prayer Books*, 348.

In sinne my mother me conceived: Lo
I am but sinne, and sinfull ought to dye.[52]

The Genesis story of the Fall is drawn in only implicitly in Lock's use of an organic metaphor:

Such bloome and frute loe sinne doth multiplie,
Such was my roote, such is my juyse within.[53]

Despite the following claim that "I plead not this as to excuse my blame,/ On kynde or parentes myne owne gilt to lay," the metaphor pleads exactly such an excuse, especially in its suggestion that man is more vegetable than human, subject to his "roote" and "juyse." Or perhaps this emphasizes the extent of his degradation and, therefore, as Lock argues, the greatness of God's mercy.

Another strategy for minimizing the guilt of the mother is the substitution of an abstraction for the actual parent, as in Coverdale's "chylde of wrathe by nature borne."[54] The degradation of abstract human "nature" is developed further in the first emblem in Francis Quarles's *Hieroglyphikes of the Life of Man*, whose epigraph or motto is Ps. 51:5 (KJV). The *Hieroglyphikes*, a more focused work than his *Emblemes*, describes and meditates upon the stages in the life of man with fifteen emblems. The picture in each case is a candle, which burns shorter as the book progresses, and which is occasionally modified by figures added to it. This first emblem begins appropriately with the metaphor of a child's primer:

Man is mans ABC: There is none that can
Reade God aright, unlesse he first spell Man.[55]

Quarles turns eventually to the guiding image of the candle, contrasting the lights of nature and of God:

The Lamp of nature lends
But a false Light; and lights to her owne ends:
These be the wayes to Heav'n; These paths require
A Light that springs from that diviner fire
Whose humane soule-enlightening sunbeames dart
Through the bright Crannies of th'immortal part.[56]

[52] Anne Vaughan Lock, "A Meditation of a Penitent Sinner: Written in Maner of a Paraphrase upon the 51. Psalme of David," in *The Collected Works of Anne Vaughan Lock*, ed. Susan M. Felch (Tempe, AZ, 1999), 66. See also *A Meditation of a Penitent Sinner: Anne Locke's Sonnet Sequence*, ed. Kel Morin (Waterloo, 1997). Lock's "Meditation" was appended to her 1560 translation of Calvin's sermons. It is apparently the first sonnet sequence in English.

[53] Lock, "Meditation." [54] Coverdale, *Ghostly Psalms*, in *Remains*, 575.

[55] Quarles, *Hieroglyphikes of the Life of Man* (London, 1639), printed with *Emblemes* (London, 1639), 323.

[56] Ibid.

Man is himself "a meere Child of night" (another abstract parent figure), "by nature, borne to burne."[57] The burning here plays on the candle image, which burns down as man's life progresses; it also recalls the fires to which the sinful heretic is sentenced and those that await the damned in hell. While this imagery seems at some remove from the psalm, the reader is encouraged to see it in the context of Ps. 51:5, as evidenced by Quarles's repetition of the psalm verse before and after his poetic text. The opening motto is Ps. 51:5 (KJV), and the poem is followed by a quotation from Augustine on original sin, which is essentially a paraphrase of the same verse: "Consider o man what thou wert before thy Birth, and what thou art from thy birth to thy death, and what thou shalt be after death: Thou wert made of an impure substance, cloathed and nourished in thy Mothers blood."[58] Framed in this way by Ps. 51:5, the verse meditation on the false "light of nature" becomes an extended examination of the human "iniquitie" that is the subject of the psalm verse. Quarles's interpretation emphasizes, like those of Davies and King, that, though born corrupt, man is not thereby exempt from responsibility for his condition. He must turn from the "Lamp of nature" to the "great Originall of Light" (alluding to Gen. 1:3) if he is to follow the true path to salvation.[59]

HYSSOP AND PURIFICATION

Purge me with hyssope, and I shal be cleane: wash me, & I shalbe whiter then snowe. (v. 7)[60]

The treatment of "hyssop" in Psalm 51 shows the imaginative lengths to which Christian readers would go in order to interpret the Hebrew psalms in Christian terms. The meaning of the word in the psalm is puzzling, even if one knows that "hyssop" is a kind of herb, strictly speaking native to the Mediterranean, but used also in reference to certain English plants, such as the "Hedge Hyssope" John Gerrarde mentions in his *Herball* (1597).[61] Hyssop was used in Jewish rites of purification, as in the cleansing of the leper in Leviticus 14, and also in the protection of the Israelites from the angel of death visited on the firstborn of Egypt in Exodus 12. Anthony Cope, chamberlain to Catherine Parr, explained the symbolic importance of hyssop in his meditation on Psalm 51: "This herb groweth low, and betokeneth humility: it is also hot, and is a figure of charity. This herb was bound together, and dipped in the blood of a sparrow, or of some other clean bird, upon running water, and herewith the leper was besprinkled, in

[57] Ibid., 324. [58] Ibid., 343. [59] Ibid., 323.
[60] In the Geneva Bible version (1560). [61] Cited in the OED, s.v. "hyssop" 1b.

the old law, when he was clean."[62] John Donne, relying on patristic sources in his sermon on Ps. 51:7, goes into more detail on the herb:

> All the sacrifices of Expiation of sin, in the old Law, were done by blood, and that blood was sprinckled upon the people, by an instrument made of a certain plant, which because the word in Hebrew is *Ezob*, for the nearnesse of the sound, and for the indifferency of the matter, (for it imports us nothing to know, of what plant that *Aspergillum*, that Blood-sprinckler was made) the Interpreters have ever used in all languages to call this word Hyssop . . . But be the plant what it will, the forme and the use of that Blood-sprinckler is manifest. In the institution of the Passeover, *Take a bunch of Hyssop, and dip it in blood.* In the cleansing of the Leper, there was to be the blood of a sparrow, and then Cedar wood, and scarlet lace, and Hyssop: And about that Cedar stick, they bound this Hyssop with this lace, and so made this instrument to sprinkle blood.[63]

The typological relationship between the blood sprinkled from the hyssop and the blood of Christ is first expressed in the New Testament. A sponge, dipped in vinegar, is placed on the end of a hyssop stem for Christ to drink on the cross (John 19:29). Thus the plant is definitively associated with the sacrifice of Christ, which now supplants the ancient Jewish sacrifice in which the plant was originally used (as Donne goes on to note). Paul explains the theology in the Epistle to the Hebrews, showing that the old sacrifice of "the blood of calves and of goats, with water, and scarlet wool, and hyssop" (Heb. 9:19) is no longer sufficient for salvation: "For if the blood of bulls and of goats, and if the ashes of an heifer sprinkling the unclean, sanctifieth to the purifying of the flesh: How much more shall the blood of Christ, who through the eternal Spirit offered himself without spot to God, purge your conscience from dead works to serve the living God?"[64]

The language of sacrifice will be explored further in connection with the final verses of this psalm; the essential point here, however, is that the typological association of hyssop in Psalm 51 with the New Testament sacrifice of Christ allowed Christian interpreters to read verse 7 in terms of their understanding of man's salvation. Cope, for instance, continues his meditation in this typological vein: "in token that our iniquities cannot be purged but by the virtue of Thy SON CHRIST'S PASSION, whom of Thy

[62] Anthony Cope, *Meditations on Twenty Select Psalms*, reprinted from the edition of 1547 by William Cope (London, 1848), 110. The meditation on this verse may derive from Girolamo Savonarola's *A Pithie Exposition upon the .51. Psalme* (according to Abraham Fleming's English title), to which it is very similar, and which was available in an English translation from 1534 (by William Marshall; Fleming's translation, quoted below, dates from 1578).

[63] See *The Sermons of John Donne*, ed. George R. Potter and Evelyn M. Simpson, vol. 5, no. 15, 309.

[64] Heb. 9:13–14 (KJV), chapter and verse division omitted.

hot and fervent charity, Thou didst send down to suffer bitter death for our redemption. Wherefore, being purged with this hyssop, and washed with Thy grace, I shall become more white than is the snow."[65]

Donne also explains the hyssop in terms of Christ's blood:

> This then was *Davids* petition here; first, That hee might have the blood of Christ Jesus applied and sprinkled upon him; *David* thought of no election, hee looked for no sanctification, but in the blood of Christ Jesus. And then he desired this blood to be applied to him, by that Hyssope, by that Blood-sprinkler, which was ordained by God, for the use of the Church.[66]

The introduction of the Church here is not surprising, coming as it does from the dean of St. Paul's, but it also follows naturally from the importance of hyssop in the Jewish temple rites described in Leviticus.

Nicholas Cross, a missionary committed to the restoration of the English Catholic Church, emphasizes the Church even more than Donne does. His meditation on verse 7 in *The Cynosura* interprets "hyssop" somewhat differently, however – as a symbol, not for the sacrifice of Christ's blood distributed in the Mass but rather for the martyrdom of faithful Christians (i.e., Catholics) and the shedding of their blood. For Cross, the sprinkling with hyssop is symbolically appropriate, since, like the Christian, the plant thrives in the midst of adversity. He explains, "*Thou wilt sprinkle me* (sayes he) *with Hysop*, that is, pressures will fall upon me from all sides, for it is proper to *Hysop* to be of a *small growth*, to take root in *Stony* and *Rocky places*, and its *vertue* is *Soveraign* against *tumours*, and *swellings*." He goes on to describe the early history of Christian martyrdom in the days of Diocletian, explaining that these persecutions are the "*flinty soyls*" which promote the growth of the Church:

> Thus we see the *sprinklings of Hysop*, that is, the *Seeds of Humility*, *Patience* and *Constancy* in the *profession* of Christ, have *furnished* the *Church* Universal with *Champions*, and every her *particular Souldier* in all encounters with rules, which exactly observed cannot but end in Glory: So that our *Penitent* hopes, if once *bathed* in these *purifying streams*, he shall be cleansed, and become an object pleasing to the *all-pure Eye* of his Creatour: Wherefore with Reason he inserts this clause, *sprinkle me with Hysop and I shall be cleansed.*[67]

However poignant it may have been for late seventeenth-century English Catholics, Cross's association of hyssop with martyrdom is not evident in any of the English translations of Psalm 51. (The only prominent Catholic

[65] Cope, *Meditations*, 110. [66] Donne, *Sermons*, vol. 5, no. 15, 310.
[67] Cross, *Cynosura*, 138, 141, 146–47.

paraphrase, by Richard Verstegan, has the vaguely sacramental but otherwise straightforward "Whose heav'nly hysope, sacred droppes/ Shal me besprinckle so.")[68] It is true, however, that Psalm 51 was considered the preeminent martyr's psalm by Protestants as well as Catholics. The *Miserere* is featured prominently in John Foxe's *Actes and Monuments* as the psalm most often recited on the scaffold by those facing death, including (across the social spectrum) John Rogers, Lord Henry Gray, Dr. Rowland Taylor, and the apprentice William Hunter.[69] Lady Jane Grey is another notable example, having recited the psalm "in Englysh, in moste devoute manour through out to thende."[70] Her pointed use of an "Englysh" translation had obvious implications in February of 1553/54 when the execution took place, since Mary Tudor had just assumed the throne, and England was once again officially Catholic. It is not recorded which English version Jane Grey recited, but it was more than likely one of Coverdale's (from either the Coverdale Bible or the Great Bible).

BLOOD-GUILTINESS AND HOMICIDE

Delyver me from bloude-gyltynesse o God. (v. 14)[71]

Coverdale's "bloude-gyltynesse" is one of his most powerful additions to the vocabulary of the English Bible. The translators of the Geneva and Bishops' Bibles replaced the word by the more straightforward "blood," but it was reinstated in the KJV and survives even in the Revised Standard Version of 1946/51. There is something almost primal in Coverdale's diction here, yet, according to the OED, he seems to have coined the word. "Bloude-gyltynesse" has a curious ambivalence appropriate to the history of interpretation of Psalm 51. Does it imply guilt *for* shedding someone else's blood or the guilt *of* blood, the curse of original sin running through man's veins? The few later uses of the word cited in the OED favor the former sense, denoting murder,[72] but Psalm 51 includes both senses: while it is used as a penitential text by all Christians confessing the essential sinfulness of human nature, it is also by tradition David's prayer of repentance for his

[68] Richard Verstegan, *Odes in Imitation of the Seaven Penitential Psalmes* ([Antwerp], 1601), 10.

[69] See King, *English Reformation Literature*, 117, and Lydia Whitehead, "*A Poena et Culpa*: Penitence, Confidence and the *Miserere* in Foxe's *Actes and Monuments*," *Renaissance Studies* 4 (1990), 287–99. Though Whitehead's argument for a radical break between pre- and post-Reformation modes of penitence (what she terms a shift "from penance to repentance") seems somewhat overstated, her article is nevertheless an excellent source of information on the place of Psalm 51 in Foxe.

[70] John Foxe, *Actes and Monuments* (London, 1563), 919.

[71] In the Coverdale Bible version (1535).

[72] See the citations of Michael Drayton, Milton, Horace Walpole, and Robert Southey, in the OED, s.v. "blood-guilty."

adultery with Bathsheba and the effective murder of her husband, Uriah the Hittite.

This association of Psalm 51 with the personal history of King David derives from the headnote to the psalm (incorporated in the Hebrew text as verses 1 and 2): "*To the chiefe musition, a psalme of David when the prophete Nathan came unto hym after he was gone in to Bethsabe. ii. Samuel. xi*" (KJV). Yet the psalm's connection to David's biography did not prevent readers from applying it to their own lives. The proper method for applying David's situation to one's own is described by Samuel Smith, in his rather long-winded commentary on Psalm 51, *Davids Repentance*. David, "a renowmed and glorious King of Israel, a holy Prophet of God," Smith writes, is "a famous and most worthy example of Repentance":

> for if David fell, whether shall we fall, if God do but a litle leave us to ourselves? And howsoever by the speciall mercy of God towardes David, this sin of his prevailed not to his eternall condemnation; yet wee see what terrour of conscience, and griefe of heart hee sustayned before hee could bee assured of his former comfort. And this shall all flesh finde, that the pleasures of sinne for a season heere, will bring with them sorrow in the end.[73]

As noted earlier, Psalm 51 was also the central psalm of the seven Penitential Psalms, which played a vital part in Christian private devotion, whether Catholic or Protestant, as well as in the liturgy of the Church, at funerals and in penitential seasons especially. The notion that David's repentance was a model for all Christians hardly needed to be stressed.

Despite the widespread understanding that Psalm 51 applied to and could provide consolation for all sinners, translators tended toward the particular and autobiographical in their treatment of the word Coverdale rendered as "bloud-gyltynesse." George Joye's "Delyver me from that blody synne" points clearly to the particular sin of David's murder of Uriah. The Seagar/Surrey version's "from murder make me fre" is even more specific. Whittingham has "bloody vice." Scott's penitent prays for deliverance "ffrom schedding blude, and homycyd," while Pembroke's prays, "O doe away/ my bloodie crime." In King's version, the sinner confesses, "I cannot hide the blood I spilt." Denham has "Lord, me of Murder don't impeach."[74] It is curious that the metrical translators should so overwhelmingly opt for

[73] Samuel Smith, *Davids Repentance. Or, A Plaine and Familiar Exposition of the Li. Psalme, first Preached, and now Published for the Benefit of Gods Church*, 7th ed. (London, 1625), 3–4. Amusingly, Smith refers to his 550-page volume, surely the longest on the psalm in English, as "this short Comment upon the 51. psalme."

[74] Joye, *Davids Psalter*. Seagar, *Certayne Psalmes*, sig. B.v.^{r}. Whittingham, in *The Whole Booke of Psalmes* (1562). Scott, in Holland, *Psalmists of Britain*, vol. 1, 177. Pembroke, *Works*, vol. 2, 51. King, *Psalmes*. Denham, *Psalms*.

translations of verse 14 that resist the reader's attempt to apply the situation of the psalmist universally, especially when this is just the interpretive or devotional practice urged by the commentators. Perhaps the general application was so familiar that many translators felt it necessary to emphasize its local origins. Perhaps they felt that the psalm would be more meaningful for readers if they understood the situation out of which it was (purportedly) written. By focusing on the sin of murder, they emphasize the psalm's Davidic authorship, drawing attention to the human voice of the psalmist, which may, perhaps, make identification with him easier. At least for the more literarily inclined, the more specific and visceral description of an actual murder rather than the abstract expression of general sinfulness may simply have made for stronger poetry. In any case, as the widespread use and influence of Psalm 51 attests, such specificity does not seem to have hindered penitent Christians from applying the psalm to sins other than murder.

One such application is worth examining, since its putative author was one of the few Englishmen who could actually identify with David on the level of kingship. The *Eikon basilike*, supposedly authored by King Charles I, though now thought to be largely the work of John Gauden, contains dozens of allusions to the Psalms.[75] In his attack on the *Eikon*, which he described as "modelled into the form of a psalter," Milton recognized the book's strategy of identifying Charles with David, both kings by divine right, who, though sinful, were fully penitent for their sins.[76] However, the sins to which Charles confessed were hardly those of which he was accused by Milton and other Parliamentarians. Furthermore, Charles was dead by the time the *Eikon basilike* was published, so the primary aim of the book was to redeem his reputation as a Christian martyr, and to further the cause of his son, the future Charles II.[77] Nevertheless, the use of the psalms was part of the attempt to present Charles as a holy king, and the analogy with David was deliberate.

The sin for which Charles is apparently most remorseful in the *Eikon* is his abandonment of the earl of Strafford, one of his strongest supporters, who was impeached and executed in May of 1641, an action Milton called "the most seasonable and solemn piece of justice that had been

[75] On the authorship of the *Eikon basilike*, see the introduction by Philip A. Knachel to his edition for the Folger Library (Ithaca, 1966).

[76] *Eikonoklastes*, in *Complete Poems*, 192.

[77] On the history of publication of the *Eikon basilike*, advance copies of which appeared on the day of Charles's execution, January 30, 1649, see Knachel, *Eikon basilike*, 1–2.

done of many years."[78] Charles (or Gauden for him)[79] concludes his confession:

This tenderness and regret I find in my soul for having had any hand (and that very unwillingly, God knows) in shedding one man's blood unjustly, though under the color and formalities of justice and pretenses of avoiding public mischiefs; which may, I hope, be some evidence before God and man to all posterity that I am far from bearing justly the vast load and guilt of all that blood which hath been shed in this unhappy war, which some men will needs charge on me to ease their own souls, who am, and ever shall be, more afraid, to take away any man's life unjustly than to lose my own.[80]

Repeating the format used throughout the book, the chapter is followed by a prayer in the tone and diction of the King James Bible, which it also paraphrases at crucial moments:

But thou, O God of infinite mercies, forgive me that act of sinful compliance, which hath greater aggravations upon me than any man, since I had not the least temptation of envy or malice against him and by my place should at least so far have been a preserver of him as to have denied my consent to his destruction.

O Lord, I acknowledge my transgression, and my sin is ever before me.

Deliver me from bloodguiltiness, O God, Thou God of my salvation, and my tongue shall sing of Thy righteousness.

Against Thee have I sinned and done this evil in Thy sight, for Thou sawest the contradiction between my heart and my hand.

Yet cast me not away from thy presence; purge me with the blood of my Redeemer and I shall be clean; wash me with that precious effusion and I shall be whiter than snow.[81]

The near quotation of verses 3, 14, 4, and 7 of Psalm 51 aligns Charles with David as a divinely appointed and favored king, sinful but repentant, to be left to the judgment of God rather than men. Or at least, since he had already been judged and executed by men, to be mourned as a martyr to godless regicides. There is some deviousness in this strategy, visible first in the clause added to Ps. 51:4, "for Thou sawest the contradiction between my heart and my hand." This evasion of responsibility is entirely in contradiction to the pervasive emphasis in Psalm 51 on the *corruption* of the heart and everything else human.

Charles's confession was also an attempt to evade the charge of a major crime by the confession of a misdemeanor. Certainly, causing the death of

[78] *Eikonoklastes*, chap. 2, cited by Hughes in Milton, *Complete Poems*, 791, n. 29.

[79] For ease of reference, I will continue to refer to "Charles" as the author of *Eikon basilike*, recognizing that the attribution is problematic and perhaps fictitious.

[80] Knachel, *Eikon basilike*, 9. [81] Ibid., 9–10.

any man is criminal, but much of England joined Milton in celebrating Strafford's execution. Popular criticism of Charles was hardly based on his abandonment of Strafford, and Charles's attempt to shift the focus in this direction is an interesting case of what one might call a battle of typologies. As Christopher Hill has argued, biblical citation was an important weapon in the conflicts leading up to and through the English Civil War. Criticism of Charles I was supported with reference to Numbers 35 and other Old Testament passages concerning "blood":[82] "Blood defileth the land, and the land cannot be cleansed but by the death of him who caused it to be shed" (Num. 35:33, KJV). "The bread of the needy is their life: he that defraudeth them thereof is a Man of Blood" (Ecclus. 34:22, KJV). Charles was labeled the "Man of Blood," whose punishment was necessary to the health of the country, and the biblical allusions lent such charges moral weight. By confessing "blood-guiltiness" in the case of Strafford, Charles may have been attempting to appropriate the rhetoric of the "Man of Blood" and turn it to his own purpose, deflecting the principal charge by confessing a negligible one, and casting himself in the role of David, who was guilty of a more personal sin and who, when God was punishing the kingdom, prayed that the whole punishment might be laid instead on himself alone.

Indeed, the posture of the penitent King Charles famously portrayed in the *Eikon*'s frontispiece (see figure 2) may also have been intended as a visual allusion to the penitent David, as depicted, for instance, in the woodcut from Hunnis's *Seven Sobbes* (figure 3). One clear precedent for the *Eikon* frontispiece was the title page by the same engraver, William Marshall, for Lewis Bayly's popular devotional handbook, *The Practice of Pietie* (7th ed., 1616),[83] featuring a kneeling penitent in a posture similar to Charles's (figure 4). He is not identified as David, but the props surrounding him point to the David of the Penitential Psalms as the primary iconographic source. In front of Marshall's penitent, for instance, is a classical altar on which is a flaming heart, a strong visual allusion to Ps. 51:16–17 (as in George Wither's emblem, see figure 5). Behind him is an open book on a pedestal, identical to the image of the open Bible in the woodcut of David in Hunnis.[84] The popularity of Bayly's book suggests that not only was the image on its title page the model for Marshall's later image of Charles, but

[82] Christopher Hill, "The Man of Blood," chap. 15 in *Bible and Revolution*. Hill notes his own debt to Patricia Crawford, "'Charles Stuart, That Man of Blood,'" *Journal of British Studies* (Spring, 1997).

[83] No first edition is listed in the STC (the second was published in 1612), which notes that more work needs to be done on the bibliography of this book. *The Practice of Pietie* was reprinted many times over the course of the century and was translated into many languages, including Welsh (Bayly was bishop of Bangor), Italian, and Algonkian.

[84] On Marshall's engravings, see A. M. Hind, *Engraving in England*, vol. 3 (Cambridge, 1952), 102–92.

Figure 2. William Marshall, frontispiece, *Eikon basilike* (London, 1648).

that the later image was intended to recall the former, reinforcing for the reader the general resemblance of Charles to David with a specific visual allusion. Further evidence of the effort to recast Charles as a type of King David is found in the volume of odes by Thomas Stanley, based on the *Eikon basilike*, and published in 1657 as the *Psalterium Carolinum*. Not content with putting David's psalms into Charles's mouth, his supporters wrote Charles an entirely new psalter.

PRAYER, PRAISE, AND POETRY

O Lord open thou my lippes: and my mouth shall set foorth thy praise. (v. 15)[85]

Given the emphasis of so many commentators on the applicability of Psalm 51 to all Christians – as in the long-title of Samuel Smith's *Davids Repentance*,

[85] In the Bishops' Bible version (1568).

Figure 3. Unknown engraver, frontispiece to William Hunnis, *Seven Sobbes of a Sorrowfull Soule for Sinne* (London, 1597).

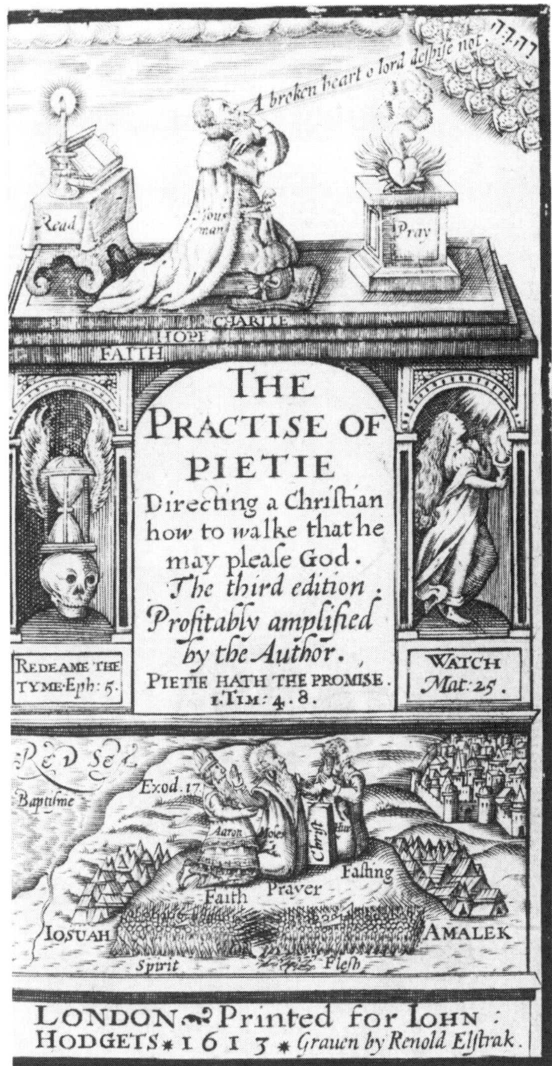

Figure 4. William Marshall, engraved title page to Lewis Bayly, *The Practice of Pietie*, 7th ed. (London, 1616).

Figure 5. Crispin de Passe, engraving from Rollenhagius, *Emblemata Sacra* (1611–1613), reproduced in George Wither, *A collection of Emblemes, Ancient and Modern* (London, 1635), book 2, no. 15.

"Wherein every Faithfull Christian may see before his eyes the Patterne of unfeigned Repentance" – it is not surprising that the psalm should have been absorbed into the liturgy of the English Church. Every service of Morning Prayer and Evening Prayer began with the priest saying or singing the versicle, "O Lorde, open thou my lippes," to which the choir or congregation would respond, "And my mouthe shall shewe forth thy prayse." (This is Coverdale's wording from the 1549 Book of Common Prayer, but by 1552, the pronouns had become plural, "O Lord, open thou our lippes," a natural adjustment if the psalm was to be used as common prayer.)[86] Many verses of Psalm 51 appear throughout the Book of Common Prayer, but "O Lord open thou our lips" may be the most important, since without it, so its use suggests, no prayer would be possible at all: without God's grace, man's lips would remain closed, no prayer would issue forth, and thus no mercy would be forthcoming.

Psalm 51 was similarly important for English religious poetry in the seventeenth century. The prayer, "O Lord open thou my lips," was widely adapted by religious poets as an invocation of the heavenly muse, as indicated in Sandys's translation of the verse:

> Give thou my verse an argument,
> And they Thy goodness shall resound.[87]

A similar interpretation is evident in William Habington's *Castara*. Its third section, "A Holy Man," begins with a poem based on Ps. 51:15, "*Domine labia mea aperies*," whose subject is the rejection of "writing wanton and profane" in favor of devout religious verse:[88]

> Ye glorious wonders of the skies,
> Shine still bright starres,
> Th'Almighties mystick Characters!
> Ile not your beautious lights surprize
> T'illiminate a womans eyes.
>
> . . . .
>
> Open my lippes, great god! and then
> ile soare above
> The humble flight of carnall love.
> Upward to thee Ile force my pen,
> And trace no path of vulgar men.[89]

Ps. 51:15 served as a lyric invocation for many religious poets, nervous about the potential for presumption inherent in their acts of literary creation. In his poem, "A Litanie," Donne probes the matter more deeply: how does the religious poet escape the charge of pride, given that, despite his faith and his sacred purpose, he is still an artificer, a maker of fictions? "A sinner," he writes, "is more musique, when he prayes,/ Then spheares, or

86 *The First and Second Prayer Books*, 21, 28, 349, 356. On the significance of the use of plural pronouns in the Book of Common Prayer, see Ramie Targoff, *Common Prayer*, 28–35.

87 G. Sandys, *Psalmes*.

88 *The Poems of William Habington*, ed. Kenneth Allott (London, 1948), 117.

89 Ibid.

Angels praises be."[90] But he also recognizes the danger of being too devoted to the pleasures of the "musique" rather than its proper subject, God:

> Those heavenly Poets which did see
> Thy will, and it expresse
> In rythmique feet, in common pray for mee,
> That I by them excuse not my excesse
> In seeking secrets, or Poetiquenesse.[91]

Donne closes two stanzas of this poem with variations on the "O Lord open thou our lips" prayer from Psalm 51: "That we may locke our eares, Lord open thine," and "That we may open our eares, Lord lock thine." The close of Donne's next stanza adds a typically metaphysical paradox to the petition: "Heare us, weake ecchoes, O thou eare, and cry."[92] Donne has added a theological twist that is actually implied in the prayer from Psalm 51 that he would have heard so often in the English liturgy, "O Lord, open thou my lips, and my mouth shall show forth thy praise." The psalmist prays to God, but what he prays for is that God will open his lips, in other words that God will not only hear his prayer but give him the ability to pray. What Donne is praying for, then, is really his own prayer (in this case, the poem itself). Human petitioners, poets included, are but "weake ecchoes" of the divine voice, dependent not just on God's hearing us, but on his actually speaking through us. He is both "eare and cry."

Herbert works out essentially the same problem in his poem "Deniall," which, like Donne's "A Litanie," expresses the inability to pray without divine grace. Like Donne, Herbert equates prayer and poetry:

> When my devotions could not pierce
> Thy silent eares;
> Then was my heart broken, as was my verse:
> My breast was full of fears
> And disorder.[93]

Typically of Herbert, there is a unity of form and content in this poem. The "disorder" of the poet's heart – the "broken heart" from Ps. 51:17 – is indeed matched by the "disorder" of the verse, since the final word of the stanza, in this case "disorder" itself, is pointedly unrhymed. The tension produced

[90] Donne, *Poems*, vol. I, 347. Though Donne's poem is quoted from Grierson's edition, the title "A Litanie" (used in the more recent editions of Helen Gardner and A. J. M. Smith, on the basis of many of the extant manuscripts) is preferred to Grierson's "The Litanie" (based on the early printed editions). The indirect article seems more appropriate to the personal, rather than public or liturgical, quality of Donne's "Litany."

[91] Ibid., 341. [92] Ibid., 347. [93] Herbert, *Works*, 80.

by these non-rhymes is finally resolved in the last line of the poem, a prayer to God to fix the speaker's heart, his prayer, and his poem – and a prayer whose answer is marked by the final "ryme":

> O cheer and tune my heartlesse breast,
> Deferre no time;
> That so thy favours granting my request,
> They and my minde may chime,
> And mend my ryme.[94]

THE SACRIFICE OF THE HEART

> The sacrifice of God is a troubled sprete, a broken and a contrite hert (O God) shalt thou not despyse. (v. 17)[95]

The "broken and contrite heart" was a widely influential image from Psalm 51 in sixteenth- and especially seventeenth-century England. A complex literature and iconography of the heart was developed from Ps. 51:17 and a cluster of other biblical verses about hearts. Verses 16 and 17 proved particularly poignant for Christians, especially Protestants, since they seemed to prophesy Christ's fulfillment or supersession of the Law of Moses by the Gospel of Love in their emphasis on the superiority of inward contrition over outward sacrifices:[96] the "burnt offering" of verse 16, in which God "delightest not," could be interpreted as either the sacrifice of purification of the Jewish temple ceremony or, for Protestants, the ceremonialism of the Catholic Mass (also, of course, a "sacrifice"). Théodore de Bèze, in the translation of Anthony Gilby, explains the theological importance of Psalm 51:

> And there are joined in this Psalme also two principal pointes of true religion: the one, of original sinne: the other, of the abuse of sacrifices: as though the purgation of sinne consisted in that outward ceremonie, wheras on the contrarie part, the sacrifices that proceeded from unpure men, did not please God, and therefore forgiveness of sinnes must go before, which afterwards should be sealed in the hearts of the beleevers, by the sacrifices which are made and offered by faith.[97]

For Christians, the principal "sacrifice" was that of Christ on the cross, made out of love, for the redemption of mankind, and it was primarily this sacrifice which replaced those of the old Jewish rites. The "broken and

[94] Ibid., 79. [95] In Coverdale's Great Bible version (1539).

[96] See Ted A. Campbell, *The Religion of the Heart: A Study of European Religious Life in the Seventeenth and Eighteenth Centuries* (Columbia, SC, 1991), esp. chaps. 1 and 2.

[97] De Bèze, *Psalmes of David*, 113–14.

contrite heart" was the penitent's means of participating in the sacrifice of Christ and engaging the power of Christ's support in the petition for mercy, as Lock makes explicit in her sonnet on Ps. 51:16:

> Thy mercies praise, instede of sacrifice,
> With thankfull minde so shall I yeld to thee.
> For if it were delitefull in thine eyes,
> Or hereby mought thy wrath appeased be,
> Of cattell slayne and burnt with sacred flame
> Up to the heaven the vaprie smoke to send:
> Of gyltlesse beastes, to purge my gilt and blame,
> On altars broylde the savour shold ascend,
> To pease thy wrath. But thy swete sonne alone,
> With one sufficing sacrifice for all
> Appeaseth thee, and maketh thee at one
> With sinfull man, and hath repaird our fall.
> That sacred hoste is ever in thine eyes.
> The praise of that I yeld for sacrifice.[98]

Lock makes use here of the fact that "host" – meaning, among other things, "victim" or "sacrifice," from the Latin *hostia* – is also the designation of the bread in the Eucharist, the body of Christ who is the sacrificial victim offered up in the Mass. (A staunch Calvinist like Lock could hardly condone the Catholic view of the Mass, condemned by de Bèze, above, but even in Protestant terms the importance of Communion lay in the recognition of Christ's sacrifice.) As another English Protestant (William Hunnis) put it, the burnt offerings called for under the old dispensation "were but figures of that thing,/ which now to passe is come,/ That is, the lively sacrifice/ of Jesus Christ thy sonne."[99]

One interpretive dilemma for Christian or indeed any readers of Psalm 51 lies in the contradiction between verses 16–17 and 18–19. The former reject burnt offerings in favor of inner contrition; the latter assert that once Jerusalem is rebuilt, God will once again be happy with "burnt offerings and oblations" (Bishops' Bible). Scholars have long argued that these last two verses are a late addition to the psalm, inserted after the destruction of Jerusalem and the temple and reflecting the longing of the Jews in exile for the restoration of temple sacrifice.[100] Some metrical translators (Joye

[98] Lock, *Works*, 70. [99] Hunnis, *Seven Sobbes*, 54.

[100] See *The Interpreter's Bible*, 272 and *The Oxford Companion to the Bible*, ed. Bruce M. Metzger and Michael D. Coogan, 155. For a dissenting view, see Dahood's *Psalms II*, 9–10, where he argues that the last verses are original, the whole psalm dating from the period of exile, and the argument for later addition the result of the ascription to David, which is the real late addition. Few scholars would disagree that the heading connecting Psalm 51 to David and Bathsheba is a late addition, so

and Parker, for instance) ignored the problem and followed the Bible version, contradiction notwithstanding. Coverdale, in his metrical paraphrase, translated the final verse without change, but printed "Rom.xii" in the margin beside it.[101] Romans 12 begins, "I beseech you therefore, brethren, by the mercies of God, that ye present your bodies a living sacrifice, holy, acceptable unto God, which is your reasonable service," words repeated by the priest in the English Communion service.[102] This is a subtle way out of the problem, the marginal cross-reference implying that the final verses should be read allegorically. Other translators found bolder solutions. The boldest of all was Wyatt's paraphrase of Psalm 51, which also allegorizes the final verse but does so more explicitly than Coverdale's, within the text itself (punning, like Lock, on the various senses of "host"):

> The sacrifice that the Lord liketh most
> Is sprite contrite; low heart in humble wise
> Thou dost accept, O God, for pleasant host.
> Make Zion, Lord, according to thy will,
> Inward Zion, the Zion of the ghost.
> Of heart's Jerusalem strength the walls still.
> Then shalt thou take for good these outward deeds
> As sacrifice thy pleasure to fulfil.
> Of thee alone thus all our good proceeds.[103]

The rebuilding of Jerusalem is made metaphorical, and the temple is still (as in verses 16–17) the temple of the heart, whose sacrifice is "low heart in humble wise." The "outward deeds" are an expression of Protestant theology, the "works" which in contrast to "faith," as Luther stressed, do not justify, but which are still offered to God as a sign of his grace: "This sacrifice is not merit but a confession and testimony of the grace which your God has bestowed upon you out of sheer mercy."[104]

If the image of the heart was at the center of the cross-denominational "religion of the heart" which developed in the seventeenth century, it was also of major importance for seventeenth-century English poets. The image's popularity lay in the ease with which it could be visualized and in its flexibility as a metaphor. The heart represented an emphasis on internal

it is more likely that arguments for the late addition of the final verse, if they are indeed specious, derive from the Christian interpretation emphasizing the rejection of outward sacrifices. For the purposes of this study, the important point is that Christian readers in this period *perceived* a contradiction.

101 Coverdale, *Ghostly Psalms*, in *Remains*, 576.

102 "And here wee offre and present unto thee (O Lorde) oure selfe, oure soules, and bodies, to be a reasonable, holy, and lively sacrifice unto thee." *First and Second Prayer Books*, 223.

103 Wyatt, *Complete Poems*, 209.

104 *Luther's Works*, vol. 12, 409, commenting on Ps. 51:19.

devotion, which suited contemporary notions of piety, but it also symbolized strong emotion, which appealed to baroque aesthetics.[105] Representations of and meditations on the heart constitute a large category of emblem literature and, though not all contain specific references to Psalm 51, it is a text that influenced the whole heart-emblem tradition. George Wither includes an emblem based on Ps. 51:17 in Book 2 of *A collection of Emblemes* (1635). Beneath its motto, "*The* Sacrifice, *God loveth best,*/ *Are* Broken-hearts, *for* Sinne, *opprest,*" the picture shows a heart in flames on a stone or marble altar, with smoke rising up toward a sun in which are visible the Hebrew letters of the Tetragrammaton (see figure 5). Given his interpretation of hyssop as a symbol of martyrdom, Nicholas Cross might have approved of the emblem's engraving at least, since in the background, as a visual commentary on the burning sacrifice in the foreground, are two scenes of martyrdom: a figure being scourged on a cross on the right, and another being beheaded on the left. Wither's own verse for the emblem ignores the background – he borrowed the preexisting engravings from an earlier Dutch emblem book – but explains the central image, and expands on the motto from Psalm 51 in terms of the Protestant distinction between faith and works:

For, neither *gifts*, nor *workes*, nor *any thing*
(Which we can either *doe*, or *say*, or *bring*,)
Accepted is of *God*; untill he finde
A *Spirit-humbled*, and a *troubled-minde*.
A *contrite Heart*, is that, and, that alone,
Which *God* with love, and pitie, lookes upon.
    Such he affects; therefore (*Oh Lord*) to thee;
    Such, let my *Heart*, and, such, my *Spirit* bee.[106]

Wither's stress on what God "affects" (OED 2 "to fancy, like, or love") and on God's "love" and "pitie" draws out the emotional implications of the heart metaphor, which was, after all, a convention of secular love poetry as well.

A number of other emblem books were truly dominated by the heart motif.[107] Adapted from a continental source (Benedictus van Haeften's *Schola cordis*), Christopher Harvey's emblem book, *The School of the Heart*

[105] For the religious history, see Campbell, *Religion of the Heart*; for the literary history, see Lewalski, *Protestant Poetics*, esp. chap. 9, "George Herbert: Artful Psalms from the Temple of the Heart," as well as, focusing on emblem books, Mario Praz, *Studies in Seventeenth-Century Imagery*, 2nd ed., rev. (Rome, 1964).

[106] Wither, *Emblemes*, 77.

[107] Henry Hawkins's *The Devout Heart*, for instance. See Michael Bath, *Speaking Pictures: English Emblem Books and Renaissance Culture* (London, 1994), esp. 178–82.

56 *The School of the Heart.*

Embleme 14.

CORDIS CONTRITIO.

COR contritum et humiliatum

Deus, non deſpicies, Pſal. 50. 19

In partes quam mille velim contundere COR *hoc*

Quod fuit auctori ſponte rebelle ſuo.

14 *Michel van lochem excu.*

Figure 6. William Marshall, engraving, copied from Benedictus van Haeften, *Schola cordis* (Antwerp, 1629), for Christopher Harvey, *The School of the Heart* (London, 1647, rpr. 1664), no. 14, "The Contrition of the Heart."

(1647), features a heart in every emblem. Harvey has two emblems with mottoes from Ps. 51:17. The first, "The Contrition of the Heart," is based on the second half of the verse ("A broken and contrite Heart, O God, thou wilt not despise"), and features a figure holding a pestle pounding a heart in a mortar (see figure 6). The verse elaborates on the visual figure, the penitent complaining about his hard heart but then softening it with his tears of contrition:

But what I can do, Lord, I will, since what
        I would I cannot: I will try
        Whether mine heart, that's hard and dry,
Being calm'd, and tempered with that
        Liquor which falls
        From mine eye-balls
Will work more plainly, and yeeld to take
Such new impression as thy grace shall make,

In mine own conscience then, as in a mortar
        I'le place mine heart, and bray it there:
        If grief for what is past, and fear
Of what's to come be a sufficient torture,
        I'le break it all
        In pieces small:
Sin shall not find a sheard without a flaw,
Wherein to lodge one lust against thy Law.[108]

Blood and tears are then blended in "Seas of Blood" which the sinner is urged to weep. The mortar and pestle metaphor may derive from *An exposition after the maner of a contemplacyon upon the .li. psalme* by the Italian Franciscan Girolamo Savonarola (a popular book in sixteenth-century England, perhaps because its author was burned as a proto-reformer in 1498). In Savonarola's meditation, written in prison, the penitent prays, "whiles our sinnes are gathered together, into the mortar of the heart, beaten with the pestle of compunction, made into powder of repentaunce, & watered with teares: thereof is made an ointment and sacrifice most sweet, which redolent offering thou wilt not despise, namely, a contrite & humble hearte."[109] The ultimate source for both – certainly for Harvey, given the unusual verb, "bray" – may be Prov. 27:22, "Though thou shouldest bray a fool in a mortar among wheat with a pestle, yet will not his foolishness depart from him" (KJV). The introduction of the mortar is a logical response to the etymology of the word "contrite" (Coverdale's rendering of the Vulgate's *contritus*) from the Latin *conterere*, meaning to "grind" or "pound."

Harvey's second emblem based on Ps. 51:17 is "The Sacrifice of the Heart," which exhibits the motto "The sacrifices of God are a broken Heart." The emblem's picture is, like Wither's, a flaming heart on an altar, though the altar is both less monumental and more ornate, and the heart rests in an

108 Christopher Harvey, *The School of the Heart* (London, 1647, 3rd ed., 1676), 56.
109 Savonarola, *A Pithie Exposition*, sig. [Hv^{v}].

elaborate urn. The ubiquitous Anima figure (the woman representing the soul in religious emblems) kneels before the altar in prayer (see figure 7). Harvey's verse explains the substitution of grace for law, and then confesses an inability to offer anything worthy "to be presented in thy sight." "My self then I must sacrifice," he concludes in the conventional language of praise:

> Lord, be mine altar, sanctifie
> Mine heart thy sacrifice, and let thy Spirit
> Kindle thy fire of love, that I,
> Burning with zeal to magnifie thy merit,
> May both consume my sins, and raise
> Eternal trophies to thy praise.[110]

A third emblem by Harvey, "The Cleansing of the Heart," whose motto is Jer. 5:14 ("O Jerusalem, wash thine Heart from wickedness, that thou maist be Saved") may also echo the heart metaphor in Psalm 51, from its earlier occurence in verse 10 ("Create in mee a cleane heart, O God"); the reader would have the psalm in mind from Harvey's other emblems. This emblem's picture is of a fountain streaming from the hands, feet, and side of the winged Amor figure, cleansing the heart held up by Anima, and the poem explicates the visual metaphor of washing with Christ's blood (see figure 8). John Saltmarsh, an emblematist himself, included a meditation on Ps. 51:10 in his *Poemata Sacra*, though this book doesn't include actual pictures. Like Harvey, Saltmarsh closes with a prayer for God to wash his heart in Christ's blood, "the stream/ That runnes so freely from thee, bloudy scene."[111] He plays imaginatively on the traditional attribution of the psalm to David, but emphasizes David's share in the sin of Adam rather than the Bathsheba/Uriah affair:

> good David say,
> Where's that old heart of thine? for there I may
> Survey the picture of an aged sinne:
> The shadow of an apple blots that skinne.[112]

The typology thus looks forward as well as back, the sins of David, as a son of Adam, being washed clean by the blood of Jesus, the son of David.

The heart "broken and contrite" was as influential with poets as with the emblematists. Perhaps the most familiar example of such influence is

[110] Harvey, *School of the Heart*, 77.
[111] John Saltmarsh (c.1610–1647), *Poems upon some of the Holy Raptures of David*, printed with *Poemata Sacra* (Cambridge, 1636), 10.
[112] Ibid., 9.

76 *The School of the Heart.*

Embleme 19.

CORDIS SACRIFICIVM.

Sacrificium Deo, ſpiritus contribulatus. *Pſal. 50. 19.*

Non vituli cæſiue Deo placet hoſtia tauri:

COR mihi qui dedit hic COR ſibi poſcit amor.

Figure 7. William Marshall, engraving, copied from Benedictus van Haeften, *Schola cordis* (Antwerp, 1629), for Christopher Harvey, *The School of the Heart* (London, 1647, rpr. 1664), no. 19, "The Sacrifice of the Heart."

Figure 8. William Marshall, engraving, copied from Benedictus van Haeften, *Schola cordis* (Antwerp, 1629), for Christopher Harvey, *The School of the Heart* (London, 1647, rpr. 1664), no. 17, "The Cleansing of the Heart."

the first poem in George Herbert's *The Temple*, "The Altar" (which, as a shape-poem whose printed words form a visual image, is actually somewhat similar to an emblem itself). Herbert scholars have previously noted the relationship between this poem and Psalm 51.[113] Herbert's poem begins, "A

[113] On the allusion to Psalm 51, see Chana Bloch, *Spelling the Word: George Herbert and the Bible* (Berkeley, 1985), 63–64; Lewalski, *Protestant Poetics*, 302; and Richard Strier, *Love Known: Theology and Experience in George Herbert's Poetry* (Chicago and London, 1983), 191–95.

broken ALTAR, Lord, they servant reares,/ Made of a heart, and cemented with teares."[114] Herbert compresses most of the last four verses of Psalm 51 into this single complex image: the offered sacrifice is not a burnt-offering but a suitably "broken" heart. Of course, the heart is actually the altar on which the sacrifice is offered up as well as the sacrifice itself, and since the altar here is really Herbert's poem, it is thus the poem which is the offering, these carefully constructed words being the outward expression of the poet's contrite heart within. Herbert may have had in mind Calvin's comment on the last verse of Psalm 51, where he noted that Hosea 14:3 "calleth prayses wherin thanks are yeelded unto God [the calves of mens lippes]."[115] This is certainly one way of resolving the Psalm's apparently contradictory positions on animal sacrifice – not actual "yonge bullocks" but rather the "calves of mens lippes," or "praise."

Herbert's poem, shaped like the altar it describes, closes with the couplet that forms the altar's base, which alludes again to the sacrifice of Psalm 51:

> O let thy blessed SACRIFICE be mine,
> And sanctifie this ALTAR to be thine.[116]

The poem is thus based, in two senses, on Ps. 51:16–17. These verses provide, moreover, the dominating conceit of Herbert's entire volume. It becomes clear that *The Temple* of the title refers not to the old temple of Jerusalem, but to the temple of the heart described in the psalm. Herbert is also, no doubt, aware of New Testament references to this inner temple, as in Paul's question to the Corinthians (recalling, among other passages, Psalm 51), "know ye not that your body is the temple of the Holy Ghost which is in you . . .?" (1 Cor. 6:19). Barbara Kiefer Lewalski goes so far as to argue that Herbert presents *The Temple* "as a New Covenant psalter, the song-book of the new temple in the heart, with himself as a Christian David."[117] Once allusions to Psalm 51 in "The Altar" establish the psalm as one of the cornerstones of Herbert's volume (to adapt his architectural metaphor), the reader is predisposed to hear further allusions and echoes in subsequent poems. In "Love Unknown," for instance, the narrative depends on the explanation of sacrifice in Psalm 51. Herbert's allegory is complex, but essentially his speaker is trying to offer his Lord a sacrifice that will win his favor. His first attempts are misguided; he offers exactly those outward sacrifices in which God "delightest not," as the psalmist recounts:

114 Herbert, *Works*, 26. 115 Golding, *Calvin's Commentaries*, fol. [207v], brackets original.
116 Herbert, *Works*. 117 Lewalski, *Protestant Poetics*, 101, 246.

So I went
To fetch a sacrifice out of my fold,
Thinking with that, which I did thus present,
To warm his love, which I did fear grew cold.

The speaker is ignorant of the lesson of Ps. 51:16–17 (hence the title, "Love Unknown") and is shocked at the response to his offered lamb:

But as my heart did tender it, the man,
Who was to take it from me, slipt his hand,
And threw my heart into the scalding pan;
My heart, that brought it (do you understand?)
The offerers heart.[118]

Herbert's reader does not share the speaker's shock and puzzlement, presumably, because he is aware of the psalm that explains God's sacrificial preferences: "The sacrifice of God is a troubled spirit; a broken and contrite heart, O God, shalt thou not despise."

No seventeenth-century poet was quite so fascinated by Psalm 51 as Herbert, but many wrote poems alluding to the heart's sacrifice of verses 16–17. Indeed, there are allusions in sixteenth-century verse as well, as in the opening of Isabella Whitney's lament, "IS. W. to C. B. in bewylynge her mishappes":

If heavie hartes might serve to be a sacrifice for sinne:
Or else, if sorrowes might suffice, for what so ere hath byn:
Then mine Oblacion, it weare made,
Whiche longe have lived in Mourners trade.[119]

Robert Davenport's "A Sacrifice" seems derivative of Herbert, though since the precise dating of the poem is impossible, it is hard to be sure:

HARK!
Did you not hear the mournful cries
Of a new-slain sacrifice?
Would you know what felt the smart?
'Twas a broken, bleeding heart.[120]

Davenport goes on to describe the priest ("celestial love"), the altar (built of "Secret sighs, true tears, deep groans"), and the fire ("pure zeal"). These

[118] Herbert, *Works*, 129–30.
[119] In *Isabella Whitney, Mary Sidney and Aemelia Lanyer*, 15. Whitney's *A sweet Nosgay*, in which this verse epistle appeared, was published in 1573.
[120] Davenport, "A Sacrifice," in *The New Oxford Book of Seventeenth Century Verse*, ed. Alastair Fowler (Oxford and New York, 1992), 344.

allegorizations are conventional, as is the closing prayer; however, the shouting match between Christ's blood and Abel's (alluding to the blood which "crieth out of the ground," Gen. 4:10) is an original and powerful typological conceit:

> Hail, holy flame! My heart refine;
> Purge it from dross; make it divine;
> Bathe it in that high-languaged blood
> Which out-speaks Abel's; in that flood
> Refine, reform it; fix it far
> Above my sins, a shining star.
> Take from it folly, give it fear:
> Kill it here, and crown it there.[121]

Another poet who was drawn to Psalm 51 is Ben Jonson, not a poet usually associated in any way with Herbert, or indeed with religious poetry. Nevertheless, a set of "Poems of Devotion" appears at the beginning of his *Underwoods*, and two of these three poems allude to Ps. 51:16–17. The first, "The Sinner's Sacrifice," a hymn to the Trinity, is written in Sapphic stanzas, two of which paraphrase the psalm verses:

> 3\. All-gracious God, the sinner's sacrifice,
> A broken heart thou wert not wont despise,
> But 'bove the fat of rams, or bulls, to prize
> An offering meet,
> 4\. For thy acceptance. O behold me right,
> And take compassion on my grievous plight.
> What odour can be, than a heart contrite,
> To thee more sweet?[122]

Jonson's second devotional poem, "A Hymn to God the Father," begins with a briefer allusion to the same psalm verses:

> Hear me, O God!
> A broken heart,
> Is my best part:
> Use still thy rod,
> That I may prove
> Therein, thy love.[123]

The heart's sacrifice (and its brokenness and contrition) became so common a figure in seventeenth-century lyric that it spilled over into secular

[121] Ibid., 344–45.
[122] *Ben Jonson: The Complete Poems*, ed. George Parfitt (Harmondsworth, 1975, rpr. 1988), 123.
[123] Ibid., 124.

literature as well (perhaps eventually diffusing into the commonplace of the broken heart, though at this point it loses any demonstrable connection to Psalm 51). Not surprisingly, the poems in Lady Mary Wroth's *The Countess of Montgomery's Urania* are full of hearts of all sorts, but at least one of them takes a lesson from Psalm 51:

> Here all alone in silence might I mourne:
> But how can silence be where sorrowes flow?
> Sighs with complaints have poorer paines out-worne;
> But broken hearts can only true griefe show.[124]

Even in the sacrifices of romantic love, the true test is the heart that is "broken." Katherine Philips ("the matchless Orinda") is much clearer in her secular parody of Psalm 51 in "Friendship's Mysterys, to my dearest Lucasia," which begins with the bold statement that "There's a religion in our Love." This "religion" follows much the same doctrine, however, as seventeenth-century Protestantism:

> Our hearts are mutuall victims lay'd,
> While they (such power in friendship ly's)
> Are Altars, Priests, and offerings made,
> And each heart which thus kindly dy's,
> Grows deathless by the sacrifice.[125]

Philips obviously knew Herbert's "The Altar," and the wit of her poem depends upon its turning to secular purposes the familiar language of devotional poetry based on Psalm 51.

Shifting genres from lyric to epic, there is an important allusion to the "contrite heart" in Milton's *Paradise Lost* (which is, after all, perhaps the most lyrical of epics, and a poem steeped in the Psalms). At the end of book 10, as the first act of repentance in human history, Adam and Eve pray to God for forgiveness. The prayer is Adam's idea:

> What better can we do, than to the place
> Repairing where he judg'd us, prostrate fall
> Before him reverent, and there confess
> Humbly our faults, and pardon beg, with tears
> Watering the ground, and with our sighs the Air
> Frequenting, sent from hearts contrite, in sign
> Of sorrow unfeign'd, and humiliation meek.[126]

[124] Wroth, *Poems*, 146.
[125] Katherine Philips, *The Collected Works of Katherine Philips, The Matchless Orinda*, vol. 1, *The Poems*, ed. Patrick Thomas (Stump Cross, 1990), 90–91.
[126] *Paradise Lost*, 10.1086–92, in *Complete Poems*, 431.

David's prayer of repentance in Psalm 51 provided the precedent for countless subsequent prayers, public and private, some of which have been quoted above. Milton's allusion to the psalm in *Paradise Lost*'s description of man's first penitence actually implies a reversal in the order of the allusion: the phrase "hearts contrite" becomes Adam's invention, only later alluded to in David's psalm. (This is a familiar strategy in Milton's poetry, whereby he establishes his own authorial originality in describing the origins of all "subsequent" writing.) The lines spoken by "our Father penitent" are repeated five lines later, to close the book. This type of precise and immediate repetition occurs nowhere else in the poem and certainly underlines the importance of the passage. It somewhat resembles the pattern of the Book of Common Prayer in which one reads first the rubric describing what should be said, and then the text itself, though its more obvious source is in the formulaic use of repetition in Homeric epic, as when a messenger repeats in exactly the same words what he has just been told to say.[127] Whether or not this repetition is intended to invoke the ritual repetition of the church liturgy, there are other clear signs that this scene is depicting the first "service" of penitential worship.

Continuing into book 11, the scene of penitence is witnessed now from heaven. As Adam and Eve "in lowliest plight repentant stood/ Praying" the narrator describes how "Prevenient Grace descending had remov'd/ The stony from thir hearts and made new flesh/ Regenerate grow instead." The allusion is to the hearts of stone and flesh of Ezek. 11:19, but the "contrition in his heart" which the Son describes the Father having sown in Man, and which the Son claims to have brought before the Father, confirms the central place of Psalm 51 in this "original" scene of penitence:

> See Father, what first fruits on Earth are sprung
> From thy implanted Grace in Man, these Sighs
> And Prayers, which in this Golden Censer, mixt
> With Incense, I thy Priest before thee bring,
> Fruits of more pleasing savor from thy seed
> Sown with contrition in his heart, than those
> Which his own hand manuring all the Trees
> Of Paradise could have produc't, ere fall'n
> From innocence. Now therefore bend thine ear
> To supplication, hear his sighs though mute;

[127] Thomas B. Stroup also sees a resemblance between this passage and the format of a "rubric and description," though he doesn't explore the matter further; see *Religious Rite and Ceremony in Milton's Poetry* (Lexington, KY, 1968), 39–40.

> Unskilful with what words to pray, let mee
> Interpret for him, mee his Advocate.[128]

Given the hostility of Milton and seventeenth-century Puritans to the high-church, "popish" ceremonialism reinstituted in the English Church by Archbishop Laud, it is surprising to find just such a service celebrated in heaven, complete with incense swung from a "Golden Censer." It may be, however, that ceremonies that were idolatrous on earth were acceptable and pleasing in heaven. After all, the scene of angelic worship in Isaiah 6 is in a house "filled with smoke," and the similar scene in Revelation 8 includes an angel "having a golden censer" from which ascends "the smoke of incense" (Rev. 8:3–4). In any case, Psalm 51 continues to be at the center of Adam and Eve's penitential liturgy, as it is in the Prayer Book rite for Ash Wednesday. The Son's request to the Father to "bend thine ear," to hear the Son's interpretation of the prayer of man, "Unskilful with what words to pray," while perhaps alluding to Ps. 17:6 ("incline thine eare to me" in the Geneva Bible), is at least analogous to the response derived from verse 15, "O Lord, open thou my lips." Furthermore, as Lewalski notes, though the description of the penitential scene at the end of book 10 is repeated, the prayer itself is never quoted, which emphasizes, she argues, the Son's point that "of themselves Adam and Eve can produce only mute sighs and unskillful words, which he as their Priest and Advocate must interpret and perfect."[129] As discussed above, this is the argument derived from Ps. 51:15 which was so central for Donne and Herbert.

The source of prayer, as Donne recognized, had to be God, and genuine contrition was required before God would listen. God would not despise a "broken and contrite heart," but it was not enough to offer a sacrifice of outward show. In the famous "chapel" scene in act 3, scene 3 of Shakespeare's *Hamlet*, Claudius attempts to pray, but he is aware of precisely the problem that Donne and Herbert work out in knotty detail.[130] Like David, the repentant king who was supposed to have composed the psalm, Claudius has committed murder, and the motive in both cases involves the lust for a woman, David's for Bathsheba, and Claudius's for Gertrude. Furthermore, in both cases, the murder victim is the husband of the coveted woman,

[128] *Paradise Lost*, 11.22–23, in *Complete Poems*, 433.

[129] Paradise Lost *and Rhetoric*, 252–53.

[130] I am indebted to Ramie Targoff for drawing my attention to this scene in *Hamlet*, though her interest is in theology and performance rather than the Davidic model and Psalm 51. See "The Performance of Prayer: Sincerity and Theatricality in Early Modern England," *Representations* 60 (Fall, 1997), 49–69.

Bathsheba's husband Uriah and Gertrude's husband, the elder Hamlet. As he ponders his condition, Claudius feels guilt and fears damnation, but then considers the extent of God's mercy:

> What if this cursed hand
> Were thicker than itself with brother's blood,
> Is there not rain enough in the sweet heavens
> To wash it white as snow?[131]

The "snow" simile, though it seems more natural coming from the king of Denmark than the king of Israel, is borrowed from Ps. 51:7, "wash me, & I shalbe whiter then snowe" (in the Geneva Bible version). The principal difference between David's situation and Claudius's lies in Claudius's total lack of true contrition. As he puts it,

> My words fly up, my thoughts remain below.
> Words without thoughts never to heaven go.[132]

It is not enough to desire forgiveness, or even to ask for forgiveness, without a heart genuinely "broken and contrite," and, as Claudius recognizes, one can hardly be forgiven for a sin the fruits of which one still possesses ("May one be pardon'd and retain th'offence?" 3.3.56). Indeed, it is for this reason that he rejects as naïve his first tentative "form of prayer," which may itself echo Psalm 51, "Forgive me my foul murder" (3.3.52), (recall the Seagar/Surrey version of Ps. 51:14, "from murder make me free"). On the other hand, Claudius's doubt is understandable, since David did in fact receive forgiveness despite remaining married to Bathsheba.

Herbert's "Love Unknown" provides a relevant gloss on Claudius's situation, though Herbert's concern is only with inattentive prayer, not prayer more profoundly hypocritical:

> Indeed a slack and sleepie state of minde
> Did oft possesse me, so that when I pray'd,
> Though my lips went, my heart did stay behinde.[133]

The contrite heart is the essential requirement, and Claudius lacks it. Shakespeare's allusion to Ps. 51:7 establishes the context for the prayer scene by evoking the most familiar penitential text in the Bible, and the most famous penitent, David. There may have been inherent in this scene a further allusion to the iconography of the penitent David (see figures 2–3) in its visual arrangement, with Claudius on his knees, hands outstretched,

[131] William Shakespeare, *Hamlet*, 3.3.43–46, *The Riverside Shakespeare*, 2nd ed.
[132] Ibid., 3.3.97–98. [133] Herbert, *Works*, 130.

likely crowned, perhaps with suggestive chapel props (an altar, a Bible). As discussed earlier, the visual argument for the saintliness of Charles I in Marshall's engraving for the *Eikon basilike* depends on the reader's recognition of the penitential stance as that of David, another king who sinned, but who was restored to grace because of his "broken and contrite heart." The same sort of iconographic association seems to have been encouraged in the audience of Claudius's pentitential scene in *Hamlet.* Given the lack of evidence for what Shakespeare's audience actually saw, one can only surmise, but the scene is at least potentially visually allusive, especially considering the clear verbal allusion to Psalm 51. As the audience watches and listens to Claudius, it is encouraged to contrast him with David, a king similar in his sinfulness but strikingly different in the genuineness of his heart's contrition.

CHAPTER 7

Psalm 137: singing the Lord's song in a strange land

Psalm 137 is unique in the Psalter in being datable to a specific period in the history of Israel. The subject of the psalm is the exile of the Jews in Babylon, after the Babylonians under Nebuchadnezzar conquered Judah, sacked Jerusalem, and destroyed the first temple in 587 B.C.E. The composition of the psalm seems to have occurred some time shortly after the return of the exiles to Jerusalem following the surrender of Babylon to Cyrus of Persia in 539 B.C.E., since references to the Exile are in the past tense, and the psalmist's use of the first person plural ("there *we* sat down") suggests that he was himself one of the exiles.[1] Despite the historical specificity of Psalm 137, it has from the earliest times been interpreted as also prophesying the contemporary circumstances of its readers, both Jewish and Christian. James Kugel points out, for example, that first-century Jews focused on the parallel between the period after the destruction of the first temple and their own time after the destruction of the second temple in 70 C.E. All that was required was an allegorical reading of "Babylon" as Rome, since the emphasis on mourning, memory, captivity, and revenge was appropriate to both periods.[2] This reinterpretation of "Babylon" was continued by Christian readers – scholarly exegetes as well as lay people – and it was in

[1] This somewhat naïve reading has the authority of tradition. On the relationship of Psalm 137 to the history of the Exile, see "Babylon" in *The Oxford Companion to the Bible*, and also James Kugel, "Psalm 137," chap. 7 of *In Potiphar's House: The Interpretive Life of Biblical Texts* (Cambridge, MA, 1994). Such simple dating as I suggest here is not, of course, reflected in the history of interpretation of this psalm, as Kugel points out. Rather, scholars committed to the Davidic authorship of the entire Psalter have argued for the pre-exilic dating of Psalm 137 (which thus is read as prophecy), and others have argued that it was written (perhaps by Jeremiah) at the beginning of the Exile rather than after it (Kugel, *Potiphar's House*, 174–80). The fact remains that the dating of this psalm is less problematic than any other in the Bible. Psalm 114 also refers to a specific event in Israel's past, the Exodus from Egypt, but, unlike the Babylonian Exile, the Exodus is not part of the historical record. In any case, in the text of Psalm 137, the psalmist does not claim to have been involved himself, so the psalm might have been written at any time.

[2] Kugel, *Potiphar's House*, 173–74.

large part the ease with which this label could be applied to any temporal or spiritual oppressor which made the psalm so powerful a resource for those who felt alienated and oppressed.

Psalm 137 is also perhaps the quintessential psalm of the Renaissance and the Reformation. Both of these were movements of renewal and rebirth, but they were based on the rediscovery and reappropriation of past cultures which remained fragmentary and to some extent irredeemably lost. In several respects many of the men and women of the sixteenth and seventeenth centuries were exiles, and the Psalm of Exile had particular resonance for them.[3] The experience of exile was conceived of in various ways, in the alienation felt by members of a religious minority (Protestant or Catholic, high church or low, depending on time and place), or that of political exiles in foreign countries, or the more abstract exile of the Christian soul from its home in heaven, a notion derived from Augustine's commentary on this psalm.[4] Of course, intellectual, political, and spiritual matters were intertwined in this period, and any individual might have felt the pressures of exile in all of these ways at once. Furthermore, poets and musicians were particularly drawn to Psalm 137, since it figures the problem of exile primarily in terms of the interruption of song. How can one sing the Lord's song in a strange land (whatever that "land" might be)? This psalm expresses an essential dilemma for the religious poet-singer, which over the centuries has made Psalm 137 one of the most translated, paraphrased, and adapted of all the Psalms.[5]

[3] On the Renaissance humanists' sense of alienation from the classical culture to which they were drawn, see Greene, *Light in Troy*, chap. 2, "Historical Solitude." On the alienation of sixteenth-century Reformers from the early Christian Church and their attempt to overcome this alienation by writing a history of the true Church through the Middle Ages, see Euan Cameron, "Medieval Heretics as Protestant Martyrs," in *Martyrs and Martyrologies*, ed. Diana Wood (Oxford and Cambridge, MA, 1993), 185–207.

[4] Augustine, *Expositions*, vol. 6, 158–77. Augustine reads the psalm in terms of his concept of "two cities": Jerusalem, the soul's heavenly home, and Babylon, its earthly exile.

[5] The focus of this study is Psalm 137 in England, but similar studies could be done for other countries. See, for instance, Damon DiMauro, "An Imitation of Marot's Psalm 137 in Garnier's *Les Juifves*," *French Studies Bulletin* (Autumn, 1993), 5–7; Bryant Creel, "Reformist Dialectics and Poetic Adaptations of Psalm 137, 'Super flumina Babylonis,' in Portugal in the Sixteenth Century," in *Camoniana Californiana*, ed. M. de L. Belchior and E. Martinez-Lopez (Santa Barbara, 1985). For evidence of the popularity of Psalm 137 among French poets, see the 1606 Paris publication of French paraphrases of Psalm 137 by Clément Marot, Philippe Desportes, Jacques Davy Du Perron, Guillaume Du Vair, Antoine Nervèze, and others (cited in Terrence Cave, *Devotional Poetry in France c.1570–1613* [London, 1969], 97, n. 1). The psalm also continued to draw poets, among others, long after the seventeenth century. For a few examples among many: Lord Byron paraphrased it twice, Heinrich Heine's "Jehuda ben Halevy" is a powerful poetic response to its expression of exiled longing for revenge, the Finnish composer Jean Sibelius set to music a paraphrase by the poet Hjalmar Procopé, and John Hollander's poem "Kinneret" is an extended meditation on the psalm.

STREAMS/TEARS

By the waters of Babylon we sat downe and weapte. (v. 1)[6]

This opening verse marks Psalm 137 as a lament, expressing the grief of the Israelites over the fall of Jerusalem. The riverside setting of the psalm was felt to be appropriate to its subject, and Renaissance translators often exploited the close connection between the two streams of water, the river and the tears of the weeping Jews. The usual reading, explicit in the psalm itself, was that the tears were triggered by memory (we wept "when we remembred Zion" in the KJV), with the parallel between flowing tears and flowing streams an accidental, if fortuitous, one.[7] Sir Francis Bacon, for example, begins with the Jews sitting "sad and desolate" beside the river. At the end of his second stanza the "stream of tears" which bursts forth from the eyes of the exiles seems to match and respond to the stream on whose banks they sit.[8] Some versions of the psalm link the waters more closely, as does Francis Davison's, whose mourners "with their streames his [Euphrates'] streame augmented," or Thomas Carew's, in which the weepers "filde the tyde" with their tears.[9] The idea for this pouring of water into water might easily occur to various poets independently, but the countess of Pembroke seems to have been the first to exploit it. In her version, the river "watreth Babells thanckfull plaine" and the "teares in pearled rowes" augment the "water with their raine."[10] The thankfulness of the plain here is a curious addition, especially with the use of "raine," which suggests God's equable raining "on the just and on the unjust" (Matt. 5:45). We hardly expect the tears of the exiles to be figured as bounty nourishing the land of Babylon, but perhaps this is to be read bitterly as a form of exploitation.

More in keeping with the conventional conception of the antagonistic relationship between Israel and Babylon, though singular in its representation of it, is Sir John Oldham's greatly expanded paraphrase, where the "vast Store" of the tears "increast the neighb'ring Tide." In the poem's opening lines the "great Euphrates" is said with its "mighty current" to "confine"

6 In Coverdale's translation from the Great Bible (1539).

7 An unusual alternative reading is that of the midrash Kugel describes as "Killer Euphrates," the Jews weeping at the riverbank because so many of them were poisoned by drinking it (*Potiphar's House*, 183).

8 *The Works of Francis Bacon*, ed. James Spedding, et al., vol. 7 (new ed., London, 1872), 284–85. Published in 1625, Bacon's psalms were dedicated to George Herbert.

9 Francis Davison (attr.), in Donne, *Poems*, vol. 1, 424–26. *The Poems of Thomas Carew*, ed. Rhodes Dunlap (Oxford, 1949, rpr. 1957), 149.

10 Pembroke, *Works*, vol. 2, 231.

Babylon "in watry limits."[11] The implications here seem to fit better what we expect the feelings of the Jews to be toward Babylon, and the metaphor, in effect, inverts the captor–captive relationship of the two, the Jews' tears serving not to water the thirsty Babylonian ground but to increase the walls of its natural confines, to bind it in. In John Saltmarsh's "Meditation I," on Ps. 137:1, the relationship between the tears and the streams is one of open contest:

> oh how your *fountains* gently vies
> With *rivers*, teares with waves, as if these drops
> Meant to outrunne thine, Babylon![12]

Saltmarsh's interpretation, like Oldham's, seems to suit the feelings of the exiles better than Pembroke's, though he goes on to consider other possibilities, first, that the "tears" want to "mingle waves" with the river, using the figure of "drowning sorrows" either in the sense of grief seeking a sympathetic response in nature or in the more literal sense of the despairing Jews seeking release through suicide (presumably unaware, as non-Christians, that self-murder was a mortal sin):

> Why weep ye o'er these banks? Should we suppose
> These rivers ow their current to your woes?
> Or of your joyes were ye so long forsook
> Ye came to drown your sorrows in this brook?

Saltmarsh then reintroduces the tension between the weepers and the river, the former desiring the latter to stay and pity them, while the latter "murm'ring flies;/ And talking to her banks, neglects your [the weepers'] eyes." This seems puzzling until a rather clumsy allegorization is introduced at the end of the poem, the river and the tears being suddenly cast as, respectively, the rich and the poor.[13]

The notion of superfluity (perhaps suggested by a bilingual pun on the familiar opening of the psalm in the Vulgate, "*super flumina*") is highlighted in several versions, with both the river and the tears bursting their banks. This seems to be what George Wither has in mind when he has the mourners "overcharg'd with weepings," as does Richard Crashaw, when he writes that "Harpes and hearts were drown'd in Teares" (which matches and parallels

[11] *The Poems of John Oldham*, ed. Harold F. Brooks and Raman Selden (Oxford, 1987), 140.

[12] John Saltmarsh, *Poems Upon Some of the Holy Raptures of David*, printed with *Poemata Sacra*, 1.

[13] Clumsy as it seems, the allegory may derive from Augustine and his reading of the river as "all things which here are loved, and pass away," including wealth, so that if a man "trust in uncertain riches, he is carried away by a stream of Babylon" (*Expositions,* 159, 169).

"great Euphrates flood" in his first stanza).[14] John Norris's paraphrase is more sophisticated in its use of this figure of flooding, blending the tears and the river together so that one cannot quite tell whether the flood is literal or figurative:

> Beneath a reverend gloomy shade
> Where *Tigris* and *Euphrates* cut their way,
> With folded arms and head supinely laid
> We sate, and wept out all the tedious day,
> Within its Banks grief could not be
> Contain'd, when, *Sion*, we remember'd thee.[15]

The grief of the Jews is described as a river bursting its banks, like the one beside which they sit. Or perhaps the Babylonian river not only sympathizes with but, through an unusual emblematic metonymy, actually becomes the grief of the exiles. More complex still is Edmund Elys's freer treatment of the psalm in his *Dia Poemata* (1655), in which the river (or "rivets," as it is here) is put forward as an alternative source of music, and a music more appropriate to the Exile than the "light mirth" of actual songs:

> These rivets yield us the fitt'st musick: we
> Account their murmures our best *harmony*:
> In them the Embleme of our fate appears:
> Their murmures show our groans, their streams our tears.[16]

Once again the streams of the river are linked to those of the mourners' weeping eyes, the former representing the latter as an "Embleme." The "*harmony*" referred to is only in part the actual audible "music" of the murmuring stream. More importantly, it is the inaudible harmony of a sympathetic "agreement of feeling or sentiment" (OED 2) or even of a more profound correspondence between different elements in nature, the "harmony" between the river and the Israelites partaking in small measure of the "*musica mundana*," that "harmony" of mathematical proportion described by Boethius which knits all creation together.[17]

The tears of this lament suggested to several Renaissance poets another biblical scene of weeping, that of the personified Jerusalem in Lamentations, the widow who "weepeth sore in the night" (Lam. 1:2, KJV). The

14 Wither, *Psalmes*. Crashaw, *Poems*, 104–05.

15 John Norris, *A Collection of Miscellanies* (Oxford, 1687), rpr. (from the 5th ed., 1710) in *Miscellanies of the Fuller Worthies' Library*, ed. Alexander B. Grosart (1871; rpr. in 4 vols. New York, 1970), vol. 3, 325. Page numbers are those of the New York reprint.

16 Edmund Elys, *Dia Poemata* (London, 1655), sig. C4^r.

17 For an extended treatment of this "music," see Hollander, *Untuning*, 20–51, and Palisca, *Humanism*, 161–90.

connection between the two passages is obvious enough, apart from verbal parallels, since they are both laments on the Babylonian Exile. Psalm 137, in which the exiled Jews weep on remembering Jerusalem before its fall, relates powerfully to Lamentations, in which it is the fallen Jerusalem herself who weeps, mourning the loss of her exiled children. Moreover, in Lamentations, as in the psalm, the mourning is triggered by memory: "Jerusalem remembered in the days of her affliction and of her miseries all her pleasant things that she had in the days of old" (Lam. 1:7, KJV). For readers who hear the echo of Lam. 1:4,[18] this intertextual relationship is signaled in some translations by the striking use of the word "desolate," as in those of Bacon ("When as we sat all sad and desolate") and Davison, in whose version the Jews hang up their harps,

> When, poore Syons dolefull state,
> Desolate;
> Sacked, burned and inthrall'd,
> And the Temple spoil'd, which wee
> Ne'r should see,
> To our mirthlesse mindes wee call'd.[19]

The widow of Lamentations may also lie behind the figure of Mother Jerusalem in George Sandys's translation ("When I forget thee, my dear mother") and, by implication, in Crashaw's ("They, they that have snatcht us from our Countries brest").[20] She is realized visually in Francis Quarles's emblem of Ps. 137:4 with its image of a woman sitting beside a river (see figure 9). The woman is a version of the feminine Anima so familiar from religious emblems, but Quarles complicates the figure in his poem. First, he confirms that this "woman" represents the earth-bound soul, a "pilgrim and a pris'ner," an "unransomed stranger/ In this strange climate."[21] This notion seems to be derived from Augustine's allegorical reading of the psalm, which applies the "stranger in a strange land" topos to the heavenward-yearning of a soul in earthly exile.[22] Quarles then reconfigures the symbolism in terms of the classical myth of Orpheus and Eurydice:

[18] ". . . all her gates are desolate" in the KJV.

[19] Bacon, *Works*, vol. 7, 284. Davison (in Donne, *Poems*, vol. 1), 424. Davison's use is the more striking of the two, the sharp line-break effectively figuring the desolation of Sion by the isolation of the word itself.

[20] G. Sandys, *Psalmes*. Crashaw, *Poems*, 105.

[21] Francis Quarles, *Emblemes* (London, 1636), 242.

[22] See above, n. 4. A lengthy passage from Augustine is included in Quarles's emblem, after the poem, on the contrast between those who praise God from earthly exile and those fortunate enough to be able to praise him in heaven "face to face" (quoting 1 Cor. 13:12).

Figure 9. Francis Quarles, *Emblemes* (London, 1635), book 4, no. 15.

> Ah! If my voice could, Orpheus-like, unspel
> My poor Euridice, my soul, from hell
> Of earth's misconstrued Heav'n.[23]

The woman is thus Anima (the soul) and Euridice (in the sense that the soul is captive in "hell" on earth), but she is also the widow from Lamentations, transposed to the riverside scene of the psalm.[24] Quarles's "pilgrim and a pris'ner too" sings from "hell-black dungeons," just as the singer of

[23] Quarles, *Emblemes*, 242.

[24] As if the emblem were not dense enough, the woman is also a type of Job, faced by three venerable men in robes and turbans (standing for Eliphaz, Bildar, and Zophar), who seem to be offering consolation; she replies, in the poem's opening line, "Urge me no more."

Lamentations calls upon the Lord "out of the low dungeon" (Lam. 3:55, KJV), and the ravens, wolves, and owls of Quarles's "vast desert" match the desolate Zion roamed by foxes (Lam. 5:18) and the bears, lions, ostriches, and sea monsters mentioned elsewhere in the book (Lam. 3:10, 4:3).[25]

A bolder use of the weeping woman, linking Psalm 137 and Lamentations, is found in Edmund Spenser's *The Ruines of Time*, partly an elegy for Sir Philip Sidney, in which the subject of the first section is that condition of exile from the classical past (in this case, of Rome) which was so fundamental to the Renaissance.[26] Here, though, the woman is a demonic parody of her biblical original. The connection to Psalm 137 and Lamentations 1–2 is made clear by several allusions, but Verlame, the lamenting, personified woman-city of Spenser's poem, is not a version of Jerusalem or Jerusalem-in-exile but rather a version of what the psalmist looks forward to, that is, an eye-for-an-eye reduction of Babylon (and Edom) to the ruinous state in which it has left Jerusalem.[27] This is especially appropriate for Spenser, since for late sixteenth-century Protestants "Babylon," in Psalm 137 and Lamentations, as in Revelation, had come to stand for Catholic Rome, and, despite the initial allusive parallel to Jerusalem, it is Rome for which Verlame stands, as both the ancient classical city and the contemporary papal one.[28]

The poet, "beside the shore/ Of silver streaming *Thamesis*," thinks of Verlame, the ancient city of Roman Britain which once stood there, but "Of which there now remaines no memorie," the ultimate revenge in the context of Psalm 137 where the psalmist struggles to retain memory of

[25] Quarles, *Emblemes*, 242.

[26] The echoes of Psalm 137 are noted by Gordon Braden, "riverrun: An Epic Catalogue in *The Faerie Queene*," *English Literary Renaissance* 5 (1975), and Lawrence Manley, *Literature and Culture in Early Modern London* (Cambridge, 1995), 168–79. See also Deborah Cartmell, "'Beside the shore of siluer streaming *Thamesis*': Spenser's *Ruines of Time*," *Spenser Studies* 6 (1985), 77–82.

[27] As Cartmell notes ("'Beside the shore'"), the vision of the fall of Babylon in Rev. 18:2 is also important for this passage.

[28] Of course, as Kugel shows, even first-century Jews interpreted "Babylon" as Rome, reading the psalm as prefiguring the destruction of the second temple (*Potiphar's House*, 173–74). For one influential working out of the Rome/Babylon figure in Protestant terms, see Luther's anti-papal tract, *On the Babylonian Captivity of the Church*. Indeed, Luther quotes Psalm 137 in this context, followed by a puzzling curse – "May the Lord curse the barren willows of those streams!" – which may be explained as an allusion to Christ's cursing of the barren fig tree in Matthew 20, interpreted through one of Augustine's peculiar allegorizations from his commentary on Psalm 137 (Luther was, after all, an Augustinian friar). Augustine interprets the willows of Ps. 137:2 as men "thoroughly bad," so barren of "true faith and good works" that they are beyond hope. In the context of the crucial Reformation debate on faith versus works, Luther's reading of Augustine would obviously emphasize the former. See Luther, *On the Babylonian Captivity*, trans. A. T. W. Steinhauser, rev. Frederick C. Ahrens and Abdel Ross Wentz, in *Three Treatises* (Philadephia, 1970), 209, and Augustine, *Expositions*, vol. 6, 163.

Jerusalem.[29] Across the river, he sees the forgotten city personified, "A Woman sitting sorrowfullie wailing," her eyes weeping "streames of teares" as she proceeds to tell her story.[30] Here the figures of Psalm 137 and Lamentations 1–2 are combined and inverted. The poem has other ironies, such as the disappearance of the Thames from the vicinity of the town, which Verlame attributes to "great griefe."[31] In the tradition of translating and paraphrasing Psalm 137, however, the sympathetic grief of the river is consistently figured by images of flooding, mirroring the exiles' tears, not by drying up, which would suggest the absence of weeping and the river's abandonment of Verlame.

Perhaps because its riverside setting appealed to the Thames-fixated Spenser, echoes of Psalm 137 seem to haunt his poetry. No. 8 of the emblems in *A Theatre for Worldlings* shows "Hard by a rivers side, a wailing Nimphe," a personification of Rome much like Verlame.[32] Even Colin Clout's hanging up of his pipe at the end of *The Shepheardes Calendar* may be a transposition from biblical to pastoral elegy of the gesture of the Jewish harpers from Psalm 137.[33] Patricia Parker has suggested, furthermore, that the Israelites' harps (sometimes translated as "instruments") hanging on Babylonian trees may also lie behind the suspended, and impotent, weapons of the knight Verdant – "His warlike armes, the idle instruments/ Of sleeping praise, were hong upon a tree" – the victim of the enchantress Acrasia in book 2 of *The Faerie Queene*.[34] This psalm was obviously one with a singular resonance for Spenser.

HARPS/MUSIC

We hanged our harpes upon the willowes in the middes thereof. (v. 2)[35]

Perhaps the most memorable image in this psalm is the hanging of the harps on the trees near the river. However, despite the vividness of this figure in the collective memory of English poetry, there is some disagreement about what precisely these instruments were. The most common English

[29] Edmund Spenser, *The Ruines of Time*, lines 1–2, 4, in the *Yale Shorter Poems*. On memory, see below, 235–40.
[30] Ibid., lines 9, 12.
[31] Ibid., line 141. Some believed the Thames had at some point changed its course. See note to line 2.
[32] In the *Yale Shorter Poems*, 477.
[33] Ibid., 208 ("November," line 141, "Here will I hang my pype upon this tree").
[34] *Faerie Queene*, 2.12.80, cited in Patricia Parker, *Literary Fat Ladies: Rhetoric, Gender, Property* (London, 1987), 55–66.
[35] Geneva Bible (1560).

rendering of the Hebrew "*kinnor*" (an instrument something like a lyre)[36] is "harps," but confusion persists due to the Vulgate's use of "*organa*," a generic term for "instruments" that has even been rendered occasionally as English "organ" – a rather cumbersome thing to hang on a tree, even in its medieval portative form. Jerome himself decided against "*organa*" in his retranslation of the Psalter from the Hebrew, shifting to "*citharas*," and this was also the translation used in the Protestant Latin Bible of Junius and Tremellius.[37] Some of the English translators hedged their bets, like William Whittingham, who, for the "Sternhold and Hopkins" psalter, translated the word as the pair, "harps & instruments."[38] This pairing was also used by William Barton in his mid-seventeenth-century psalter, while Matthew Parker has the equally ambivalent, but more awkward, "Harpes and Organs."[39] The engraver of the frontispiece to Jeremy Taylor's 1644 *Psalter of David* offered an even wider range of instruments (figure 10). On either side of the penitential King David are the familiar harps hanging in the trees, signaling a visual allusion to Psalm 137, but the artist also includes lutes, a viol, a cornett, and a trumpet.[40]

Accuracy of translation was not, of course, the only factor in the selection of instruments. Other poets, notably the emblematists, envisioned the harps as various members of the string family. In a typically Renaissance syncretism, they often melded the biblical characters and narratives with apparently analogous ones in classical mythology. Two frequently linked figures were David, inspired by God, chanting psalms to the strains of his harp, and Orpheus, inspired by the muses, singing odes and hymns to the accompaniment of his lyre. In the Renaissance, especially after the late-sixteenth-century vogue for the lute song, English poets transformed Orpheus's lyre into a lute, and his songs into ayres.[41] Francis Quarles's

[36] See Curt Sachs, *The History of Musical Instruments* (New York, 1940), 106–08, and Eric Werner, "kinnor" in *New Grove Dictionary*, "Jewish Music 1.4 The Instruments of the Temple, (iv) *Chordophones*," vol. 9, 619–20.

[37] For Jerome's translations, see Lefèvre d'Etaples, *Quincuplex*. [Franciscus Junius and Immanuel Tremellius, trans.], *Bibliorum pars tertia, id est, quinque libri poetici, Latini recens ex Hebraeo facti* . . . (London, 1579). "Cithara" was, moreover, the term favored by the Greek translators of the Septuagint in their rendering of *kinnor*. Sachs concludes that the *kinnor* and *cithara* were similar, small rounded lyres with strings suspended from a horizontal crossbar. As he notes, the Egyptians used the related term, *k.nn.r*, for a lyre of this sort (107).

[38] *The Whole Booke of Psalmes*.

[39] Barton, *Book of Psalms in Metre*. [Parker], *Psalter*.

[40] For drawing my attention to this image (images of David and hanging harps are surprisingly scarce), I am indebted to Paula Loscocco. For a more detailed study of the image of hung-up Davidic harps from 1649–1660, see her forthcoming *Eikonoklastic Song: Milton and Royalist Poetics*.

[41] On the history of the lute song, see Spink, *English Song*, especially chaps. 1 and 2. For a detailed study of the use of the lute–harp–lyre cluster in representations of music in English poetry, 1500–1700, see Hollander, *Untuning*, 43–51, 128–45 and *passim*.

Figure 10. Unknown engraver, frontispiece to Jeremy Taylor, *Psalter of David* (London, 1644).

emblem of Psalm 137, as mentioned above, pictures a woman by a riverbank, holding a lute, which she appears to be putting away from herself. Confirming the metamorphosis from harp to lute, the poem begins:

> Urge me no more: this airy mirth belongs
> To better times: these times are not for songs.
> The sprightly twang of the melodious lute
> Agrees not with my voice.[42]

The lute and its songs are rejected, and the implication seems to be that the rejection is partly on generic grounds. Mirth is "airy" in its lightness, inappropriate for the poet's heavy mood, but it is also perhaps "ayrey," in that it belongs to the "ayre" or secular lute-song. In any case, the shift from harp to lute allows Quarles to include in his dismissal the musical recreations familiar to his Caroline readers.

In Edmund Arwaker's *Pia desideria*, on the other hand, there is a whole consort of instruments, all rejected. The first he mentions is the "warbling Lyre," which the poet's posited "Friends" (his interlocutors in this imaginary dialogue) suggest is most appropriate for dispelling grief.[43] Then follows an excursus on the power of music to lift the spirits, using the examples of sailors, shepherds, travelers, and soldiers, and the music of viols, the lute, the pipe, and the harp. The psalm is followed only loosely by Arwaker; he describes a more general condition of grief – a kind of psychological or emotional exile – at being "Fortune's wounded Captive." Once an accomplished musician who "Cou'd with *Israel's sweetest Singer* vie," his ability is now lost. The poet here notes that if he were to sing, in his reduced state, "'twou'd be/ Some doleful *Emblem* of my misery."[44] When, in exile, he thinks on his "lov'd Country," the result is that his "*Lute*," his "*Voice*," and his "*Mind*" all "lose their harmony."[45] Arwaker uses "harmony," as Elys did, in the sense of musical concord and also in the more abstract sense of concord between elements of the self, what for Boethius and subsequent theorists of *musica speculativa* was termed "*musica humana*," the smaller-scale human equivalent of "*musica mundana*."[46]

42 Quarles, *Emblemes*, 241.

43 Edmund Arwaker, trans., *Pia desideria, or Divine Addresses* (London, 1690), 151–52. Arwaker's verse is "Englished" from the Latin of Herman Hugo, whose Dutch emblem book is the source of Quarles's image (reproduced in turn in Arwaker).

44 The description of the scene as "emblem" may derive from Elys or it may simply have become a commonplace, especially after Quarles. Saltmarsh also calls the hanging of the harps an "embleme."

45 Arwaker, *Pia desideria*, 151–54.

46 The importance for medieval and Renaissance music theory of the tripartite division of music in Boethius's *De Institutione Musica* is discussed in Hollander, *Untuning*, 24–26. I use these terms throughout for convenience and consistency, recognizing that the concepts so designated may have been differently named by some sixteenth- and seventeenth-century writers.

If, to various interpretive ends, authors altered the instrument hung up by the Israelites, they also, for similar reasons, altered its condition. Nothing is said of the instruments in the Hebrew psalm (or the Vulgate or English Bibles) beyond their location in the trees, but the metrical translators and emblematists could not resist elaborating, usually to emphasize the sympathetic connection between the instruments and their owners. Most simply, the harps are "silent" (James I/Sir William Alexander, G. Sandys), "mute" (Davison), or "dumbe" (Carew), the figurative point of these adjectives being made explicit in the version of Sir John Denham:

> Our Harps, to which we lately sang,
> Mute as ourselves, on Willows hang.[47]

Oldham is similarly direct, with harps "as mute and dumb as we," and Norris's harps are "sad, as well as we."[48]

Many of the poets were then drawn to say something of the strings of the instrument. Davison's harps are "unstrung," as are George Sandys's, Carew's, and Henry King's.[49] The point of the unstringing may lie in an implicit and commonplace Latin pun on "*cor/chorda*," linking strings and hearts, the source of the English idiom "heartstrings." This buried pun is made explicit in Phineas Fletcher's paraphrase, when the Israelites respond to the Babylonian request to "Take down your harps, and string them":

> Were our harps well tun'd in every string,
> Our heart-strings broken,
> Throats drown'd and soken
> With tears and sighs, how can we praise and sing
> The King of heav'n under an heathen king?[50]

Once again, the point of the wordplay is to emphasize sympathy between the exiles and their harps (and also, of course, the river, in the "drown'd and soken" throats, which plays on the "streams/tears" motif). Oldham's paraphrase makes the point clear:

> Our Harps, as mute and dumb as we,
> Hung useless and neglected by,
> And now and then a broken String would lend a Sigh,
> As if with us they felt a Sympathy,
> And mourn'd their own and our Captivity.[51]

47 James I [William Alexander], *The Psalmes of King David translated by King James* (Oxford, 1631). G. Sandys, *Psalmes*. Davison (in Donne, *Poems*, vol. 1), 424. Carew, *Poems*, 149. Denham, *Psalms*.

48 Oldham, *Poems*, 140. Norris, *Collection*, 325.

49 Davison (in Donne, *Poems*, vol. 1), 424. G. Sandys, *Psalmes*. Carew, *Poems*, 149. King, *Psalmes*.

50 Fletcher, *Poetical Works*, vol. 2, 253.

51 Oldham, *Poems*, 140.

This passage also seems to invoke (as the others may in more veiled fashion) the Aeolian harp. This instrument, "played" by the wind as it blows across the strings, was, in its modern form, invented by Athanasius Kircher in the seventeenth century and popularized by poets from James Thomson to the Romantics (for whom it was a potent symbol), but its actual origins are much earlier.[52] In fact, a legend recorded in the Babylonian Talmud records that David used to hang his harp ("*kinnor*") over his bed, and was woken in the night to the sound of the wind blowing through its strings, whereupon, inspired by that music, he would compose psalms.[53] So the notion, if not the name, of the Aeolian harp is linked from antiquity with the instrument of the psalmist. The OED does not record a use of the word "sympathy" in the sense of "sympathetic vibration" until the nineteenth century, but that certainly seems to be one of the senses of the word in this passage from Oldham, used as a figure for the emotional sympathy of the familiar pathetic fallacy.[54]

Some poets were particularly drawn to the subject of music in Psalm 137, often playing with familiar musical puns, as in, for example, Saltmarsh's first meditation:

> No *stops*
> In this sad Musick? how these mourners seem,
> As though they wept *division* with thy stream![55]

These are relatively commonplace puns but interesting nevertheless.[56] The term "stops" can refer to the stopping of a lute string to produce a pitch, as well as a rank of organ pipes or a set of jacks on a harpsichord (the latter less likely without specific reference to keyboard instruments). It may also suggest, as well as non-musical cessation, a break or "rest" in the music. Musical and non-musical meanings also converge in "division," which refers to musical variation, usually above a ground bass, but also as a descant above a melody, as well as the less specialized sense of "separation" or

52 See Sachs, *History*, 402–03.

53 See *The Hebrew–English Edition of the Babylonian Talmud: Berakoth*, trans. Maurice Simon (London, 1984), chap. 1, 3b.

54 The phenomenon of sympathetic vibration would have been familiar to any string player, as evidenced by Jacob Cats's emblem of love as sympathetic vibration between two identically tuned lutes, reproduced in Hollander, *Untuning*, between 242 and 243. For an English example, see Izaak Walton's *Life of Dr. John Donne*, 41 ("And, though 'tis most certain, that two Lutes, being both strung and tun'd to an equal pitch, and then, one plaid upon, the other, that is not totcht, being laid upon a Table at a fit distance, will (like an Eccho to a trumpet) warble a faint audible harmony, in answer to the same tune").

55 Saltmarsh, *Poemata Sacra*, 1 (italics added).

56 See Hollander, *Untuning*, 134 and 139, for instance, quoting Sir John Davies's punning on "Stoppes" and Sidney's on "divisions," respectively.

even "disagreement" or "conflict" (in keeping with the "vying" between the "tears and waves" several lines further on). Interestingly, Saltmarsh's two puns work in opposite directions. In the first case, given the context – why are you weeping so much? – "stops" means primarily "cessation," and the musical senses are secondary. In the second, though it is used metaphorically, "division" means primarily "musical variation," the weeping of the mourners "played" to the accompaniment of the stream. This time the more familiar non-musical sense is secondary, perhaps occurring even only in retrospect after Saltmarsh later introduces the note of competition between the weepers and the river.

One version of Psalm 137 which offers a particularly elaborate development of the musical motif is the lute-song "As by the streames of *Babilon*" by England's only notable poet-composer, Thomas Campion. His translation of Psalm 137 appears in the first of his *Two Bookes of Ayres* (c.1612–13), the one containing "*Divine and Morall Songs*," which also included his version of Psalm 130 ("Out of my soules deapth to thee"). Campion's translation is highly compressed, but by using a pair of dense puns – one playing an English word against its Latin root and one playing general senses against specialized ones from musical theory and practice – he is able to achieve much in little space. The first pun occurs in the lines describing the harps:

> Aloft the trees that spring up there
> Our silent Harps wee pensive hung.[57]

The wordplay here depends upon the etymology for "pensive" in the Latin root, "*pendeo/pendere*" or "to hang" (Lewis and Short, *A Latin Dictionary*, s.v. *pendeo*, I.B.I).[58] The Latin word can also mean "to be suspended, interrupted, discontinued" (ibid., II.C) as well as "to be in suspense, to be uncertain, doubtful, irresolute, perplexed" (ibid., II.E), which corresponds to the principal English sense of "pensive" (OED 1, "full of thought; plunged in thought; thoughtful, meditative, musing; reflective: often with some tinge of seriousness or melancholy"). The immediate etymology is actually from the French *penser*, meaning simply "to think," but Campion's play against the ultimate Latin etymon allows him to combine the physical situation of the harps with the mental state of the captive Jews in a complex figure of sympathy or "harmony." The complexity lies partly in a rather Miltonic syntactic ambiguity (deriving from Latin syntax), which allows "pensive" to modify either, or both, of the two words which it follows, "Harps" and

57 Campion, *Works*, 74.

58 Hollander comments on this pun in his "The Case of Campion," chap. 4 of *Vision and Resonance*, 80.

"wee." Strictly speaking, the harps and the exiles are "pensive" in different ways, the former in the Latin sense of "hanging" and the latter in the English (and French) sense of "thoughtful," but the senses blend together and Campion's harps are also "pensive" in the same way that Norris's are "sad," sharing the mental state of their owners.[59]

Campion's second pun is more complex than his first, and, though it doesn't concern the harps directly, it does develop the theme of music in the psalm. The key is the final word of Campion's paraphrase of verse 6:

> Fast to the roofe cleave may my tongue,
> If mindelesse I of thee be found:
> Or if, when all my joyes are sung,
> *Jerusalem* be not the ground.[60]

"Ground" here means primarily the "basis" or even "subject" of the song, a song, that is, *about* Jerusalem. The word also has a musical sense, however, as Walter R. Davis notes in his edition of Campion. He defines "ground" in this sense as "the basic melody on which variations are built," which is essentially the musical sense given in the OED (6c).[61] As the *Harvard Dictionary of Music* defines it, however, "ground refers most particularly to English music of the late 16th and the 17th century, where it means either a repeating bass line or the entire composition in which that bass appears."[62] This does not quite contradict Davis, but his use of "melody," while it could be taken to refer to a bass line, is more likely to be understood by modern readers as the tune one hears usually in the "melody" line.[63] The distinction is more than a quibble, since it leads to further implications for Campion's pun. A passage from Campion's own *A New Way of Making Fowre Parts in Counter-point* describing the bass line in a composition may clarify this point:

59 It should be noted that Sir Edwin Sandys, George Sandys's brother, also uses "pensive" in his paraphrase of Psalm 137, but without the complexity of Campion's wordplay: "Ah, *Sions* wrongs to pensive minds appear." Since *Sacred Hymns* (no author, but generally attributed to E. Sandys) was published in 1615, however, he may have borrowed the word from Campion's earlier publication and had some sense of the bilingual pun.

60 Campion, *Works*, 74.

61 Ibid., n. 28.

62 "Ground, ground bass" in *New Harvard Dictionary of Music*, 355.

63 Davis's definition is accurate when "ground" is used in conjunction with "descant," as in sonnets by Daniel and Drayton (see Hollander, *Untuning*, 132–33) or Shakespeare's *Richard III*, 3.7.49. This is a specialized and perhaps literary usage. One can find examples in other poets of "ground" used in the more usual sense of "ground-bass" as in Campion. See Sidney, *Arcadia*, book 3 ("And though my mones be not in musicke bound,/ Of written greefes, yet be the silent ground," in *The Countess of Pembroke's Arcadia*, ed. Maurice Evans [Harmondsworth, 1977], 663), and Jonson, *Love's Welcome at Welbeck* ("Welcome is all our Song, is all our sound,/ The treble part, the Tenor, and the Ground," cited in OED, s.v. "ground" 6c).

These foure parts by the learned are said to resemble the foure Elements; the Base expresseth the true nature of the earth, who being the gravest and lowest of all the Elements, is as a foundation to the rest. The Tenor is likened to the water, the Meane to the Aire, and the Treble to the Fire. Moreover, by how much the water is more light than the earth, by so much is the Aire lighter then the water, and Fire then Aire. They have also in their native property every one place above the other, the lighter uppermost, the waightiest in the bottome. Having now demonstrated that there are in all but foure parts, and that the Base is the foundation of the other three, I assume that the true sight and judgement of the upper three must proceed from the lowest, which is the Base, and also I conclude that every part in nature doth affect his proper and naturall place as the elements doe.[64]

Campion stresses the point that, just as the earth is the "foundation" of the "composition" of nature, so is the bass the "foundation" of a musical composition. How more neatly to express this than in the twin senses of "ground," which can be both "earth" and "bass"? As it works in Campion's Psalm 137, the "ground" is still more complex, since the psalmist is insisting that "*Jerusalem*" must and will be the "ground" of his song. It will be, first, in the sense that it will the subject of the song, second, in the sense that it will be literally the earth on which he stands when he sings (he cannot sing the Lord's song in a strange land, so he will defer singing until his return to his native country – precisely what the original psalmist seems to have done), and thirdly, in the musical sense that "Jerusalem" will be the bass line of the composition upon which the other parts of the song are built.[65]

This last sense may seem forced, however appropriate it may be for a poet-composer, but it gains clarity and support from the traditional theoretical description of the musical bass to which Campion is indebted. As Davis notes (citing the musicologist Manfred Bukofzer), the passage in Campion's *New Way* just quoted may derive from Gioseffo Zarlino's *Istituti Harmonichi* in which he refers to the bass as "*fondamento dell' harmonia*."[66] Zarlino's analogy is somewhat more elaborate than Campion's:

As the earth is the foundation of the other elements, the bass has the function of sustaining and stabilizing, fortifying and giving growth to the other parts. It is the foundation of the harmony and for this reason is called bass, as if to say the base

[64] Thomas Campion, *A New Way of Making Fowre Parts in Counter-point*, in Campion, *Works*, 327.

[65] I fancy another sense too, though hard to prove, in which "Jerusalem" is the name for the tune on which the song is "grounded." I know no contemporary tune by this name, but it is easy to posit its existence, on the analogy with other tunes named after places, such as the Canterbury, the Cambridge, and the Winchester tunes (see the 1619 edition of *The Whole Booke of Psalmes*, STC 2566). More recent hymnals, of course, include Parry's "Jerusalem," usually sung to part of Blake's *Milton*, "And did those feet in ancient times." At the very least, the idea of a tune so named might well have occurred to Campion.

[66] Campion, *Works*, 327, n. 5. Zarlino's *Istituti* was published in Venice in 1558.

and sustenance of the other parts. If we could imagine the element of earth to be lacking, what ruin and waste would result in universal and human harmony! Similarly a composition without a bass would be full of confusion and dissonance and would fall to ruin.[67]

As noted above, other poets and translators of Psalm 137 worked with the many senses of "harmony" current in the Renaissance, from the "*musica instrumentalis*" with which Campion's treatise is mainly concerned, to the more abstract "*musica humana*," and "*musica mundana*." It may not be too much to say, then, that in Campion's poem the psalmist claims Jerusalem to be the "ground" in the sense that it is the foundation of the cosmic harmony, of Creation itself, as well as simply of the music of the psalm. Jerusalem, with its temple, was the center of the world for the psalmist, of course, but for Campion Jerusalem is also the "new Jerusalem," the heavenly city of Rev. 20:2, making it the center of both heaven and earth. Campion's dense pun suggests, then, that Jerusalem must be the subject of the psalmist's song, the actual place in which he stands to sing, the source (bass) of the music, and the foundation of the cosmic harmony which is the source of the song's inspiration as well as the ultimate subject of its praise.

REMEMBERING/FORGETTING

If I forget thee, O Ierusalem: let my right hand forget her cunning. If I doe not remember thee, let my tongue cleave to the roofe of my mouth; if I prefer not Ierusalem above my chiefe ioy. (vv. 5–6)[68]

Memory is at the heart of Psalm 137. The Jews struggle to keep alive their memory of Jerusalem in exile in Babylon, and to this end the psalmist vows that if he forgets Jerusalem his right hand should "forget her cunning." Furthermore, he prays to God to remember "the children of Edom" and their role in the destruction of Jerusalem. He doesn't elaborate, but it seems clear that this "remembering" is equivalent to vengeance and destruction: for God to "remember" the Edomites is for him to cast their actions back on their own heads. In the early English translations of this verse, there is an interesting confusion as to whether "hand" is the subject of the clause or the object in a passive construction. As so often, the Vulgate was the source of the confusion, since it renders the verse as "*oblivioni detur dextera mea*," which Miles Coverdale then translated as "let my right hand be

[67] Gioseffo Zarlino, *The Art of Counterpoint*, trans. Guy A. Marco and Claude V. Palisca (New Haven and London, 1968), 179.

[68] KJV (1611).

forgotten." This was corrected on the basis of the Hebrew by the Geneva Bible translators to "let my right hand forget to play." (Whittingham's version in "Sternhold and Hopkins" is "Then let my fingers quyte forget,/ the warbling harp to guyde.")[69] Whatever their variants, subsequent translations all have the hand forgetting rather than being forgotten. Coverdale's metrical paraphrase of the psalm, curiously, gives a version of this verse which is actually closer to the Geneva Bible than to his own prose Bible translation:

> Hierusalem, I say to the,
> Yf I remember the not truly,
> My honde playe on the harpe no more.[70]

The matter of "being forgotten" Coverdale saves for his final line, which is an addition entirely his own, but which depends on the sense of verse 5 in his prose translation with its emphasis on the horror of "being forgotten":

> Blessed shall he be that for the nones
> Shall throwe thy chyldren agaynst the stones,
> *To brynge the out of memorie.*[71]

Just as in his Bible, Coverdale called for his "hand" – a synecdoche for the songs which that hand composes and plays, both for the psalmist himself, and, by extension, for all the exiles – to be forgotten, so here he calls for the appropriate vengeance on Babylon: as the Babylonians' conquest of Jerusalem threatens the very memory of the city, so Babylon itself will be erased from human memory. (This figure doesn't quite work, since one result of the psalmist's hand/psalm not being forgotten is that the memory of Babylon lives on in the psalm's final verses.)

Apart from the question of the accuracy of translation, the rendering of this verse in the KJV (or the Geneva and Bishops' Bibles, all identical in this respect) was bound to appeal to poets, for the obvious reason that the "cunning" of the "right hand" – the psalmist's ability to play/sing/write – is of paramount importance to a writer. Some translators read the verse more narrowly, as did Matthew Parker (not, of course, primarily a poet), whose "I would my hand: went out of kinde:/ to play to pleasure them" calls for only a temporary lapse of skill to frustrate the Babylonians' desire for entertainment.[72] More characteristic is the general and total forgetting called for in Edwin Sandys's paraphrase:

69 *Whole Booke of Psalmes* (1562). 70 Coverdale, *Ghostly Psalms*, in *Remains*, 572.
71 Ibid. (italics added). 72 [Parker], *Psalter*.

Let parched tong to withering palat growe
And skilful hand no more his science knowe.[73]

The Latinate "science" here is also interesting, since it includes both specific technical mastery and knowledge in the broader sense (OED 2b or perhaps 3d and 1). Crashaw's paraphrase of this verse knits together music and memory so as to suggest, as Campion's does, that Jerusalem is the basis of the psalmist's music:

Ah thee Jerusalem! ah sooner may
This hand forget the mastery
Of Musicks dainty touch, then I
The Musicke of thy memory.[74]

The central concern of Psalm 137 with memory, and the essential connection between memory and poetry or song, may also lie behind Crashaw's choice, as well as Fletcher's and Oldham's, to translate the psalm into the form of a Pindaric ode.[75] The analogy between Hebrew and Greek literary forms, based always on an ignorance of the actual structure of Hebrew poetry, goes back at least to Jerome's question (cited previously), "What is more musical than the Psalter? which, in the manner of our Flaccus or of the Greek Pindar, now flows in iambs, now rings with Alcaics, swells to a Sapphic measure or moves along with a half-foot?"[76] Jerome's authority may lie behind Isaac Watts's remark accompanying his own translation of Psalm 137, that "Had *Horace* or *Pindar* written this Ode, it would have been the endless Admiration of the Critick, and the perpetual Labour of Rival Translators."[77] But the connection between psalms and odes may be more basic. Both words derive from Greek musical terms, "psalm" from *psalmos*, a song sung to a plucked instrument, and "ode" from *aeidein*, to sing or chant. More importantly, the origins of the English ode seem to lie in a sense of longing for the lost "presence of voice" – as it inhered in the Greek hymns and the Hebrew psalms – which Paul Fry describes: "By imitating hymnody . . . an ode reveals *its* conception of a hymn as a being-present to a transcendent, originary voice. The aim of the ode is to recover and usurp the voice to which hymns defer: not merely to participate in the presence

73 [Edwin Sandys], *Sacred Hymns* (London, 1615), 125.
74 Crashaw, *Poems*, 105.
75 The form of the English Pindaric is usually only loosely based on its original, consisting mainly of a series of stanzas of irregular line lengths. See Stephen F. Fogle and Paul H. Fry, "ode," in *New Princeton Encyclopedia*. On metrical psalms and the ode in the context of the sixteenth-century attempts to syncretize biblical and classical literature, see chap. 3.
76 From "Preface to Eusebius," cited in Kugel, *Idea of Biblical Poetry*, 152. See also above, chap. 3.
77 Watts, *Reliquiae Juveniles* (1734), cited in Davie, *Psalms in English*, 211.

but to *be* the voice."[78] He writes further that, "Like the hymn, the ode or 'hymn extempore' longs for participation in the divine, but it never participates communally, never willingly supplies a congregation with common prayer because it is bent on recovering a priestly role that is not pastoral but hermetic."[79] Fry is principally concerned with the Romantic ode and with a few of its precursors in the seventeenth century (by Ben Jonson, Michael Drayton, and John Milton), and the distance between hymn and ode, which the nineteenth-century poet longs to bridge, may be a common feature of these. For Renaissance poets translating Psalm 137, however, there was no such distance, since the psalm is hymn and ode simultaneously. This may be part of the reason so many seventeenth-century poets were drawn to the Psalms, and to Psalm 137 in particular, since it expresses the very problem which Fry argues is basic to the ode: how can I sing the Lord's song in exile (cut off from the "presence of voice" essential to any notion of inspired poetry)? By writing the psalm as an ode, or, conversely, casting their odes in the form of Psalm 137, the poets are able both to express the anxiety of loss and to recapture the "presence of voice." This presence derives from the psalm's status as Scripture, all of which is conceived of as, to some degree, divinely inspired. The psalm also enables the recapturing of the "communal participation" longed for (according to Fry) by later writers of odes, since there is a residual echo of common prayer in the psalmist's memory of temple worship, as well as a continuing connection between the Psalms and the liturgy due to their use in the Christian worship service.

The desire to reach back, to convert memory to presence so as to hear and even to join in with the primal heavenly song, is a frequent recurrence in Milton's poetry.[80] One such recurrence involves a brief but crucial allusion to Psalm 137. In book 3 of *Paradise Lost* the heavenly choir of angels sings a hymn of praise to the Father and the Son after the latter has offered to redeem the sin of Adam by sacrificing himself, "death for death."[81] As Diane McColley points out, the song is a broad paraphrase or extended allusion

[78] Fry, *The Poet's Calling*, 9. [79] Ibid., 7.

[80] Milton's ode "On the Morning of Christ's Nativity," for instance, given its own chapter in Fry's study, is concerned with memory and music. When the poet calls "Ring out ye Crystal spheres" so that "Time will run back, and fetch the age of gold," he has in mind a scene of singing, "when of old the sons of morning sung,/ While the Creator Great/ His constellations set." The poem attempts more than a simple recollection, however. Milton's call to the Muse to "prevent them [the "Star-led Wizards"] with thy humble ode," which is of course Milton's own far from humble one, uses "prevent" in a Latinate sense of *praevenire*, to come before. A more radical temporal displacement than mere remembering seems to be implied. See "Nativity Ode," lines 125, 135, 119–21, 24, in *Complete Poems*, 46, 43.

[81] *Paradise Lost*, 3.212, in *Complete Poems*, 263.

to the *Te Deum laudamus.*[82] Milton begins with "Thee Father," as the Latin hymn begins "*Te Deum*" ("We praise the, O God"), then moves to praise of the Son ("Thee next") in the second section of the angelic hymn, which corresponds to the *Te Deum*'s second section, "Thou art the kyng of glory, O Christe."[83] There are two explicit verbal allusions to the English *Te Deum* in the hymn: "Hee Heav'n of Heavens and all the Powers therein" (3.390), alluding to "To thee al Angels cry aloud, the heavens and all the powers therin," and "thy dear and only Son" (3.403), echoing "Thy honourable, true, and onely sonne."

The *Te Deum* itself incorporates several allusions to the Psalms in its final section, however, and it seems not to have been remarked that Milton's "*Te Deum*" follows suit.[84] Milton's hymn closes with an allusion to Ps. 137:5–6:

> thy Name
> Shall be the copious matter of my Song
> Henceforth, and never shall my Harp thy praise
> Forget, nor from thy Father's praise disjoin.[85]

Like the psalmist, Milton vows never to forget his proper subject, the praise of God (in this case figured by God's name rather than the name of Jerusalem as in Psalm 137). Milton is setting himself up as a psalmist, and his "hymn" as a psalm.[86]

The Psalms are after all primarily praise-songs, as indicated by their collective Hebrew title, *tehillim*, or "praises." The allusion to Psalm 137 involves more than simply a generic marking of Milton's inset poem. In both the *Te Deum* and Milton's "hymn" there is a shift in voice between first person plural and singular. The *Te Deum* begins with common prayer ("We") and ends with an individual petition, "O Lorde, in thee have I trusted: let me never be confounded."[87] Milton's shifting pronouns are more complicated, since they effectively blur the distinction between reported

[82] Diane McColley, "The Copious Matter of My Song," in *Literary Milton: Text, Pretext, Context*, ed. D. T. Benet and M. Lieb (Pittsburgh, 1994).

[83] *Paradise Lost*, 3.372, 383, in *Complete Poems*, 267. Quotations from the English *Te Deum* are Thomas Cranmer's from the 1549 Book of Common Prayer, in the Everyman edition of *The First and Second Prayer Books*, 22–23.

[84] The psalm verses alluded to in the *Te Deum* are 28:9, 114:2, 123:3, 33:22, 31:1, and 71:1. See *A Dictionary of Hymnology*, ed. John Julian (1908; rev. rpr. in 2 vols., 1957), 1120–21. Julian traces allusions to the Vulgate in the Latin version of the *Te Deum.*

[85] *Paradise Lost*, 3.412–15, in *Complete Poems*, 268.

[86] The *Te Deum* sets itself up in the same way – a patristic hymn posing as a psalm, both by means of its allusions to psalms in its final section and also in the myth of its spontaneous and inspired composition by Ambrose and Augustine at the latter's baptism by the former. See the article "Te Deum laudamus" in Julian's *Dictionary of Hymnology.*

[87] *First and Second Prayer Books*, 22, 23.

and direct speech. He begins with the former, signaled by "first they sung," but then shifts inexplicably to the latter, with "thy Name/ Shall be the copious matter of my song," only to snap back to third person at the end ("Thus they in Heav'n").[88] The point seems to be that Milton actually joins in the heavenly choir at this point, or at least would like to.[89] This marks the crucial difference between Milton's condition and that of the psalmist. While the latter is writing in exile, Milton has, at least through his bold conceit, come "home" in the most profound sense. The Augustinian reading of Psalm 137 is implicit in this maneuver – the "exile" which Milton has overcome in reaching back in time and up into heaven being that of the soul exiled from its home in the heavenly city. The other notable shift from the original psalm that Milton works in his allusion is one of genre: the psalmist sings an elegy, a lament for his state, and, anxious about the possibility of forgetting, vows to remember Jerusalem, calling on God to make him "forget his skill" if he forgets; Milton sings a hymn of praise in joy and confidence, without any hint of the danger of forgetting either his best subject or his poetic skill.

STRANGERS IN STRANGE LANDS

How shall we synge the Lordes songe in a straunge lande? (v. 4)[90]

The psalmist's anxiety about the loss of memory is at the heart of Psalm 137, and the source of this danger is the forced exile of the psalmist and his people from their true home. For those souls who, like Augustine, longed for their heavenly home, it mattered little where they were on earth. William Loe's 1620 *Songs of Sion*, for instance, a collection of metrical paraphrases and meditations on Psalms and other Scripture, was "set for the ioy of gods deere ones, who sitt here by the brookes of this worlds Babel, & weepe when they thinke on Hierusalem which is on highe."[91] Other writers felt a more earthly homesickness, however, for the obvious reason that many of them were actual exiles from their home countries. Coverdale, Whittingham, and Crashaw were all, for extended periods, living in exile on the continent,

88 *Paradise Lost*, 3.416, in *Complete Poems*, 268.

89 This is much the same strategy he uses in "At a Solemn Musick," at the end of which he looks forward "till God ere long/ To his celestial consort us unite,/ To live with him, and sing in endless morn of light." The first draft of this poem, rejected probably because of its extreme presumption, ended with "To live and sing with him" rather than "To live with him, and sing." Milton would like to be singing alongside God, but, at this stage of his career, this seems brash even to him.

90 Coverdale's Great Bible, 1539.

91 William Loe, *Songs of Sion* [Hamburg, 1620], sig. +4^{r}.

the first two as a result of their Protestant beliefs at times when England was officially Catholic, and the last, a Catholic among Protestants, for just the opposite reason. Indeed, even Loe's sense of exile may have been more worldly than his long-title suggests, since he was writing to those, like himself, "of the English nation residing at Hamborough [Hamburg]."[92] Even if not everyone experienced physical exile, the fear of being forced to live in a foreign country, away from family, friends, and, especially, one's native language, was a powerful one, powerfully expressed in the familiar psalm.

Alienation from the native language seems to have been a source of particular anxiety, as is implied in King's translation of Ps. 137:4:

> But how shall we sing the Lords Song,
> His Enemies among?
> Or tune His Notes in strangers Land,
> That cannot understand?[93]

The psalmist's problem here seems not one of singing temple songs before heathen Babylonians as it is, for instance, in Campion's ayre ("Is then the song of our God fit/ To be prophan'd in a forraine land?"), but rather of singing to an audience that doesn't know the language.[94] King's focus on language may derive from a traditional conflation of Babylon and Babel, based primarily on the fact that the latter is the Hebrew name for the former.[95] However, since the story of Babel in Genesis 11 concerns the fall from an original linguistic unity to a confusion of tongues, many interpreters of later biblical references to Babylon read into them the concern with language and confusion of the etiological Babel account. Once again, this tradition may originate with the typological reading habits of Augustine, who recounts the story of the fall of the tower as the early history of Babylon: "That is why the name 'Confusion' was given to the city; because it was here that the Lord confused the languages of all the earth."[96] The use of "Babel" rather than "Babylon" in several translations of Psalm 137 (Pembroke's quoted above, Edwin Sandys's, and Wither's, for example) may echo the early "history" of the city in Genesis 11, though the disyllabic name

[92] Ibid. [93] King, *Psalmes.*

[94] Campion, *Works*, 74. Of course, what the Babylonians cannot "understand" probably also includes the culture and the religious beliefs and practices which go along with the language, but the linguistic strangeness seems the primary sense here, to which the others are linked.

[95] See "Babylon," in *The Oxford Companion to the Bible.*

[96] Augustine, *The City of God*, trans. Henry Bettenson (Harmondsworth, 1972, rpr. 1986), 656. For the history of Babel's fall, see bk. 16, chaps. 4–5.

may sometimes also be a metrical convenience. Fletcher is more explicit in his paraphrase:

So shall thy towers
And all thy princely bowers,
Proud *Babel*, fall.[97]

He not only adds the towers to the psalm's Babylonian cityscape, but emphasizes pride as the sin which will bring about their fall, as it did in the traditional interpretation of the Babel story in Genesis.[98] Similar echoes of the fall of Babel occur in Davison ("And, thou Babel, when the tide/ Of thy pride") and Carew ("Sitting by the streames that Glide/ Downe Babells Towring wall").[99]

The Babel story's focus on language may also have been what suggested to Shakespeare the appropriateness of Psalm 137 as an expression of the Englishman's anxiety about living among those who don't know English. He incorporates an extended allusion to the psalm at a key point in *Richard II*. In act 1, scene 3, after Richard has banished him for life, Mowbray laments his sentence in what amounts to an inset paraphrase of Psalm 137:

The language I have learnt these forty years,
My native English, now I must forgo,
And now my tongue's use is to me no more
Than an unstringed viol or a harp,
Or like a cunning instrument cas'd up –
Or being open, put into his hands
That knows no touch to tune the harmony.
Within my mouth you have enjail'd my tongue,
Doubly portcullis'd with my teeth and lips,
And dull unfeeling barren ignorance
Is made my jailer to attend on me.
I am too old to fawn upon a nurse,
Too far in years to be a pupil now.
What is thy sentence [then] but speechless death,
Which robs my tongue from breathing native breath?[100]

97 Fletcher, *Poetical Works*, vol. 2, 253.

98 The language here is similar to that of the angel announcing the fall of Babylon in the section on the fall of Lucifer in Phineas Fletcher's *Purple Island* (1633): "*Babel*, proud *Babel's* fall'n, and lies as low as ground" (in *The Oxford Book of Seventeenth Century Verse*, ed. H. J. C. Grierson and G. Bullough (Oxford, 1934), 217. In this case, there is a further typological extension to the fall of Babylon in Revelation, which also recounts the defeat of the great dragon Satan (12:9).

99 Davison (in Donne, *Poems*, vol. 1), 426. Carew, *Poems*, 149.

100 Shakespeare, *King Richard II*, 1.3.159–73, *The Riverside Shakespeare*, 2nd ed. All further citations to this play will be from this edition. Act, scene, and line numbers will be included within the text.

The image of the unstringed harp to which Mowbray compares his "tongue" in foreign exile is familiar from many translations of Ps. 137:4 (compare George Sandys's "our silent harps, unstrung").[101] The "*cunning* instrument" and the ignorant "hands" of the player allude to verse 5 (the Bishops' Bible version, "let my right hande forget her cunning"). The imprisonment of the tongue behind "teeth and lips" derives from verse 6, "Let my tongue cleave to the roof of my mouth" (in the Geneva Bible version which Shakespeare most often used). Mowbray's lament is his own psalm of exile.

Psalm 137 seems to have been on Shakespeare's mind as he wrote *Richard II*, since he alludes to verse 6 again near the end of the play, when Aumerle seeks Bolingbroke's forgiveness for his involvement in treasonous plotting:

> For ever may my knees grow to the earth,
> My tongue cleave to my roof within my mouth,
> Unless a pardon ere I rise or speak.
> (5.3.29–31)[102]

Richard II begins with the double banishment of Mowbray and Bolingbroke, and these images of exile may have suggested the relevance of Psalm 137 to Shakespeare, but he may also have felt it appropriate to the play's larger concern with England as nation and homeland, the problems of good and bad rule, and the effect of a bad king on the health of the realm. Richard's reign is presented as a kind of fall from Paradise, most famously in John of Gaunt's prophecy of Richard's transformation of England's "blessed plot," the "other Eden, demi-paradise," into "a tenement or pelting farm" (2.1.50, 42, 60). (Interestingly, York's report of Gaunt's death shortly after this speech contains another echo of Psalm 137, when he reports, "His tongue is now a stringless instrument" [2.1.149].) This "fall" of England is also represented in terms of the fall of Jerusalem in act 1 scene 2, when Gloucester's widow mourns her fallen manor (Plashy, with its appropriately watery name), expressing her own bereavement, and, by extension, that of the realm – all due to Richard's sins:

> Alack, and what shall good old York there see
> But empty lodgings and unfurnish'd walls,
> Unpeopled offices, untrodden stones?
> And what hear there for welcome but my groans?
> Therefore commend me; let him not come there

[101] G. Sandys, *Psalmes*.

[102] Aumerle's allusion is noted, though without interpretive comment, by both Naseeb Shaheen in *Biblical References in Shakespeare's Plays* (Newark, 1999), 386 and Richmond Noble in *Shakespeare's Biblical Knowledge* (London, 1935; rpr. New York, 1970), 158.

To seek out sorrow that dwells everywhere.
Desolate, desolate, will I hence and die:
The last leave of thee takes my weeping eye.
(1.2.67–74)

The duchess is yet another version of the widow that "wepeth continually in the night" in Lamentations, the ruined Jerusalem personified. The allusion is here marked by the same key word from Lamentations (discussed above in relation to Bacon's and Davison's translations of Psalm 137): "Desolate, desolate."[103] As noted above, the linking of the laments for Jerusalem in Psalm 137 and Lamentations 1 was traditional. The England of *Richard II*, like the biblical Jerusalem, is in ruins because of the sins of her people and, especially, her king. There is, furthermore, a sense that this ruin is a kind of exile of England from its proper self, a condition of bondage imposed by the country's rightful king (Northumberland refers to Richard's misrule at 2.1.291 as a "slavish yoke," suggesting, with the psalm in mind, a "Babylonian" captivity). It is also intriguing, given the longing of the exiled psalmist for a return to Jerusalem, that the new king, Bolingbroke, believes the complete restoration of the kingdom requires a pilgrimage – to Jerusalem. He is ultimately unable to make the journey, and so passes the burden of atonement on to his son. Yet he does die, in ironic fulfillment of prophecy, in the "Jerusalem Chamber" of Westminster Abbey.

Like Shakespeare, many of his contemporaries read Psalm 137 in political terms, though in this period, as in that of the psalm's original Jewish readers, the "political" almost invariably included aspects of the religious. Whittingham's translation, written in exile in Geneva during Mary's reign, introduces a political note in verse 4 which was followed by many subsequent translators:

Alas (sayd we) who can once frame,
his sorrowfull hart to syng:
The prayses of our loving God,
thus under a straunge kyng?[104]

In this case, the psalmist's problem is not language or religion but the king, though for Whittingham the problem with the "king" (*Queen* Mary) was her religion. Similar terminology is used in the translation penned by William Barton during the Interregnum.[105] Barton's version is heavily

[103] See Lam. 1:1–4 (Geneva Bible). [104] *Whole Booke of Psalmes* (1562).
[105] Barton, *Psalms in Metre*.

indebted to the "Sternhold and Hopkins" psalter, but Whittingham's emphasis on the "straunge kyng" would have appealed to the Puritan Barton for obvious reasons, even though the two translators had different kings in mind. Bacon's translation also includes a "foreign king," but his point seems to be to contrast singing in exile on earth under an earthly, and therefore "foreign," king, with singing in Zion, the "seat and dwelling place" of the true king, Jehovah ("Hierusalem, where God his throne hath set").[106] Fletcher renders this contrast more explicit:

> With tears and sighs, how can we praise and sing
> The King of heav'n under an heathen king?[107]

Norris's refusal to sing "to those who're aliens to *our Heavenly* king" picks up on the same motif but shifts the emphasis back from the political to the religious.[108]

Another use of Psalm 137 as a song of primarily political exile is Edmund Waller's, in his poem "To Sir William Davenant upon his first two books of *Gondibert*, written in France." Waller, the translator of at least one psalm (104), converts the story of the exiled Israelites into one in which they are simply unable to sing in a foreign country. By reversing it he is able to give Davenant an original compliment:

> The drooping Hebrews banish'd harps unstrung
> At Babylon, upon the willows hung;
> Yours sounds aloud, and tell's us you excell
> No less in Courage, than in Singing well
> Whilst unconcern'd you let your *Country* know,
> They have impoverished themselves, not you.[109]

There is no suggestion in this thoroughly secular retelling of the psalm that the "Hebrews" were silent by choice, and for religious principles; they are represented as simply unable to sing abroad. Davenant is the more remarkable, since he can sing even in exile. Of course, the comparison cannot bear much scrutiny since, as Waller implies, Davenant was banished *by* his country not just *from* it. Waller's curse a few lines further along may also be derived from Psalm 137 (verses 7–9), with its call for mimetic revenge on Edom and Babylon, though once again Waller's point is secular rather than religious:

[106] Bacon, *Works*, 285. [107] Fletcher, *Poetical Works*, vol. 2, 253. [108] Norris, *Collection*, 326.

[109] Edmund Waller, *Poems &c. written upon several occasions, and to several persons* (London, 1664), 166. For a similar use of the inverted psalm figure as poetic compliment, see Dudley Digges's commendatory poem in G. Sandys's *Psalmes* (discussed above, chap. 2).

To banish those who with such art can sing,
Is a rude crime which its own Curse does bring.[110]

Davenant was in exile because he was, like Waller and many others in Paris at the time, a Royalist. Waller's use of Psalm 137 to praise his friend seems rather playful, but other Royalists turned to the psalm more seriously, and without emptying it of its religious connotations. The most powerful use of the psalm by the king's party is in the earl of Clarendon's *Contemplations and reflections upon the Psalms of David*, written, at least by the author's account, in 1647, while he was in exile on the isle of Jersey, just as Charles I was at that time in a state combining exile and captivity on the Isle of Wight.[111] Clarendon indicates in his title that he will apply the Psalms "to the Troubles of the Times," and in none of his contemplations is this application more poignant than the one on Psalm 137. He focuses on love of country as the basis for the pain of exile: "They who have not a very strong Affection of Heart for their Country, cannot love any other Thing, hardly God himself."[112] The aim of the piece is to emphasize the parallel conditions of the Israelites after the Babylonian conquest and of Englishmen loyal to King Charles I after his defeat by the Parliamentarians. To this end he quotes from Isaiah, who seems in this context a prophet of the English Civil War, "*Your Country is desolate, your Cities are burnt with Fire, and it is desolated as overthrown by Strangers.*"[113] Clarendon's reading of Psalm 137 is entirely in terms of his own condition:

To have escaped the present Slaughter, and fled from the Calamity, might have been looked upon as Safety, at least as a Reprieve, which always administers some Hope; but when there was to be no more returning, and that they who got away were never more to see their Native Country, they were looked upon in a better Condition, who lost their Lives at home, and it was thought a Preferment to be buried in their own Country. To ask of those who are carried away captive out of it, to be merry, is the Insolence of a proud Conqueror; and he who can comply

[110] Waller, *Poems &c.*, 167.

[111] The work was published long after this, so whether Clarendon's account of the circumstances of the composition of the *Contemplations* can be trusted is an open question. The dating of the work to December 26, rather appropriately the feast of St. Stephen, the first martyr, may be cause for further suspicion. It is also noteworthy that, though the title of the work reads "Jersey. Dec. 26. 1647," the preface to his children describes the work as having begun in Spain, "in the time of a former Banishment." Whatever the details, the important point, clearly, is that Clarendon wished the *Contemplations* to be associated with the Royalist exile, and that Psalm 137 was useful to him in making this association.

[112] Henry Hyde, first earl of Clarendon, *Contemplations and reflections upon the Psalms of David*, in *Miscellaneous Works of the Right Honourable Edward, Earl of Clarendon* (London, 1751), 745.

[113] Ibid. (italics original).

with it, are worthy to be Slaves, having a Mind prepared for it, by the Expiration of all his Affections for his Country, which ought to be dearer to him than his Life, or any thing his Life can be supplied with.[114]

The reader might well ask whether Clarendon is writing here about the Jews or the Royalists, and where in the psalm, moreover, or anywhere else in the Bible, there is mention of the exiles as those "who escaped the present Slaughter, and fled," rather than those who were forcibly led away captive.

Clarendon's appropriation of the psalm is bold but not unique, and is actually entirely in keeping with Charles I's own attempt, using allusions to the psalms, to recast himself as the suffering and penitent King David in the *Eikon basilike*, attacked so vehemently by Milton.[115] Some years after the Restoration, Edward Pelling, the chaplain to the duke of Somerset, gave a sermon on the anniversary of Charles I's "martyrdom" (January 30), taking as his text Ps. 137:1, in which he goes even further than Clarendon in reading the psalm as a comment on contemporary events:

> The *Story*, is of *Them*: the *Application* of it, is for *Us*; and at the very first view we may easily accommodate this sad Text to this sadder Day. For, do but Date the Captivity, *Stylo Novo*: instead of *By the Rivers of Babylon*, read, *In a Land of Confusion*, (a *Babel* in our own Countrey:) Shift you [*sic*] Pious Thoughts from the Monarch of *Jerusalem*, to the Memory of our Own Soveraign, a Greater, a Better than *Zedekiah*, (the Mirrour of Princes, the Noblest of Martyrs, the Wonder of Ages, and the Honour of Men:) . . . Remember those manifold Miseries that were *throughout*; some, the *Praeface*; others, the *Epilogue* to the dismal Tragoedy of this Day; and then tell me, Wherin Our Captivity differ'd from that in the text, unless it did in This, that 'twas more Infamous and Reproachful, because at Home; and 'twas not (God be Blessed) for Seventy years; 'twas not so Lasting as Our Sins; the Deliverance out of it was too Quick and Hasty for the Repentence of those Miscreants who made us Captives.[116]

This application of the exile in Psalm 137 to the exile of Englishmen "at Home" requires a considerable interpretive leap, and shows once again the flexibility of the conception of "exile," as demonstrated by its interpreters ever since the first-century rabbis read, in the Babylonian conquest of Jerusalem, its conquest in their own time by the Romans, and since Augustine explained the psalm as a lament for the "exile" of all human souls from heaven.

[114] Ibid., 746.

[115] For the engraved frontispiece, see fig. 2, and, on its connection to Psalm 51, chap. 6 above.

[116] Edward Pelling, *A Sermon Preached on The 30th of January, 1684. The Day of Martyrdom of King Charles I. Of Blessed Memory.* (London, 1685), 2–3.

KILLING CHILDREN

Blessed shal he be that taketh & dasheth thy children against the stones. (v. 9)[117]

Many readers of Psalm 137 are uncomfortable with the fact that it is a curse as well as a lament, an expression of what C. S. Lewis calls "the spirit of hatred which strikes us in the face . . . like the heat from a furnace mouth."[118] The final call for God to bless those who throw the Babylonian children against the stones has been an embarrassment to some Christians, but others have relished the promise of vengeance it seems to offer.[119] Translators have responded to this verse with considerable ingenuity, though few have been as bold as Christopher Smart, who felt the need for a complete revision in his translation of the psalm's ending:

> But he is greatest and the best,
> Who spares his enemies profest,
> And Christian mildness owns;
> Who gives his captives back their lives,
> Their helpless infants, weeping wives,
> And for his sin atones.[120]

Part of the impact of Smart's revision lies in his pointed substitution of "atones" for the "stones" one expects for this rhyme, familiar from the standard translations of the psalm (its final word in the Great Bible/Book of Common Prayer, the Geneva Bible, and the KJV).

Some writers retain the curse, but avoid the children, like Edwin Sandys, who substitutes the more inclusive metonymy "thy cursed seed," which then leaves him free to increase the bloodthirstiness of the final line: "With dasht-out brains the crying stones to feed."[121] Bacon's version inserts the children into verse 7 ("Remember thou, O Lord, the cruel cry/ Of Edom's children"), which lays the blame on their heads and turns them from literal children into all the "offspring" of Edom and Babylon, adults and children alike.[122] Other translations simply wallow in the gore:

> Thrice blest, that turns thy mirth to grones;
> That burns to ashes
> Thy towers, and dashes

[117] Geneva Bible (1560). [118] C. S. Lewis, *Reflections on the Psalms* (New York, 1958), 20.

[119] The 1962 Book of Common Prayer for the Anglican Church of Canada goes so far as to omit the verse (as well as other distressingly violent passages, including all of Psalm 58).

[120] Christopher Smart, *Selected Poems*, ed. Karina Williamson and Marcus Walsh (Harmondsworth, 1990), 247.

[121] [E. Sandys], *Sacred Hymns*, 125. [122] Bacon, *Works*, 285.

Thy brats 'gainst rocks, to wash thy bloudie stones
With thine own bloud, and pave thee with thy bones.
(Fletcher)[123]

Happy, who, thy tender barnes
From the armes
Of their wailing mothers tearing,
'Gainst the walls shall dash their bones,
Ruthless stones
With their braines and blood besmearing.
(Davison)[124]

Men shall bless the hand that teares
From the Mothers softe embraces
Sucking Infants, and besmeares
With their braynes, the Rugged faces
Of the Rockes and stony places.
(Carew)[125]

Blest, yea thrice-blessed be that barbarous Hand
(Oh Grief! that I such dire Revenge commend)
Who tears out Infants from their mother's Womb,
And hurls 'em yet unborn unto their Tomb.
Blest he, who plucks 'em from their Parents' Arms,
That Sanctuary from all common Harms;
Who with their Skulls and Bones shall pave thy Streets all o'er
And fill thy glutted Channels with their scatter'd Brains & Gore.
(Oldham)[126]

Oldham's parenthetical grief at having to utter such a curse hardly mitigates his obvious relish in the charnelhouse details of his paraphrase. Donald Davie, who calls Oldham's paraphrase "the most horrible of psalm-versions into English," also criticizes Wither for indulging in an unchristian relish for the psalm's final verse (which in his first version blesses him who "braines thy babes in stony places").[127] This is not quite fair, however, since in the prose prayer printed between his two translations of the psalm, Wither allegorizes the Edomites/Babylonians into "spiritual destroyers," which implies that the vengeance called for might be similarly "spiritual," and what the blessed man "brains" turn out to be not Babylonian infants at all, but "sin, & heresies in their first birth."[128] There is a long tradition of such

[123] Fletcher, *Poetical Works*, vol. 2, 254. [124] Davison (in Donne, *Poems*, vol. 1), 426.

[125] Carew, *Poems*, 150. [126] Oldham, *Poems*, 143.

[127] Davie, *Psalms in English*, 167, 112. Wither, *Psalmes*.

[128] Wither, *Psalmes*, 272. Wither's translation also reads, "he *will* prove a blessed one," which makes the phrase prophecy rather than a personal desire for vengeance. In his preface to the *Psalmes*,

allegorical escapes from this verse. Augustine, for instance, in answer to his own rhetorical question, "What are the little ones of Babylon?" answers "Evil desires at their birth."[129] Calvin allows himself and his readers no such easy escape, insisting on a literal reading:

And although it seeme a cruell thing, when hee wysheth theyr tender Babes, whiche as yet coulde doo no harme, too bee dashed and brayned agaynst the stones: yet notwithstanding forasmuche as he speaketh not of his own head, but fetcheth his words at Gods mouth, it is nothing else but a proclayming of Gods juste judgement: like as also when the Lorde avoucheth, that looke what measure eche man hath used toward others, the same shalbe measured againe unto himselfe. Math, 7.2.[130]

The punishment of those "which as yet coulde doo no harme" may have held particular interest for Calvin, so much concerned with election and predestination. It may also be that Calvin's harsh reading of Ps. 137:9, like his theology of life on earth as perpetual warfare, derived in part from his own experience of political and religious strife in mid-sixteenth-century France.[131] The French Civil Wars, like the English, may have inured their participants and victims to a level of violence otherwise unacceptable to Christian readers of the Psalms.

This verse calling for vengeance was in fact invoked during the English Civil War, by Stephen Marshall in his "fast sermon" to Parliament, *Meroz Cursed*. It takes as its text Judges 5:23, "Curse ye Meroz (said the Angell of the Lord) curse ye bitterly the inhabitants thereof, because they came not to the helpe of the Lord, to the helpe of the Lord against the mighty" (Geneva Bible). Not surprisingly in a sermon about cursing, Marshall comes to discuss Ps. 137:9. He admits that it seems harsh but affirms its justice in the context (and, by implication, in his own context, England in the 1640s):

What *Souldiers heart* would not start at this, not only when he is in *hot blood* to cut downe *armed* enemies in the *field*, but afterward *deliberately* to come into a subdued *City*, and take the *little ones* upon the *speares point*, to take them by the heeles and beat out their *braines against the walles*, what inhumanitie and barbarousnesse would this be thought? Yet if this work be to revenge Gods Church

Wither explains this strategy: "In regard some abuse the propheticall Imprecations, as if David had given exemplary warrant of Cursing their enimies, I have (to prevent that prophanation) otherwhile expressed that by the Future tense, which many do translate by the imparative mood; whereby, those passages, the more planely may appear, prophetically intended" (sigs. [A7^{v}–A8^{r}]).

129 Augustine, *Expositions*, 176.

130 Golding, *Calvin's Commentaries*, fol. 227^{r}.

131 On Calvin's notion of "perpetual warfare," see William J. Bouwsma, *John Calvin: A Sixteenth Century Portrait* (New York and Oxford, 1988), 182–88.

against *Babylon*, he is a *blessed man that takes and dashes the little ones against the stones*.[132]

In this sermon, whose subject is essentially "if you're not for us, you're against us," there is no allegorization. The vengeance called for is most literal, and this is, after all, in keeping with the spirit of the psalm. It is an interesting case of the broad influence of the Psalms that both sides in the Civil War turned to the same psalm for solace or support. Any condition of alienation or estrangement could be interpreted as exile, and "Babylon," as noted above, could be applied to any convenient enemy and oppressor. In his *Scripture Vindicated*, attacking Marshall's *Meroz Cursed*, Edward Symmons wrote with some exasperation, "Under the notion of Babylon [are comprehended] the King and his children, the nobility and the gentry, the ministers of the Gospel of Jesus Christ, and Christians of all sorts."[133]

Renaissance translators and paraphrasers of Psalm 137 clearly found in this psalm a source of consolation for a variety of conditions of exile, alienation, loss, and estrangement. Interpretations of the psalm ranged from the personal and occasional to the cosmic and existential.[134] On the personal level, Izaak Walton compared John Donne's retirement after the death of his wife to the mourning exile of the Israelites "by the rivers of *Babylon*, when they remembered *Sion*."[135] Anthony Gilby, on the other hand, translating Théodore de Bèze, explained the meaning of Psalm 137 in universal (if Christian) terms, in that it teaches us "that there is a time of silence under the crosse, when the powers of darknes hath his time, notwithstanding that we must retaine alwaies our constancie, not onlie in faith, but also in zeele, least we betraie the truth with our silence."[136] Despite their differing priorities, translators of Psalm 137 shared fundamental motivations: lament for exile, anxiety over loss, tension between the need to express grief and

132 Stephen Marshall, *Meroz Cursed, or, A Sermon preached to the Honourable House of Commons, At their late Solemn Fast, Febr. 23. 1641.* (London, 1641), 11–12.

133 Cited in Christopher Hill, *English Bible*, 112. I am indebted to Hill's discussion of the range of interpretation of biblical "Babylon" by Englishmen of "all sorts."

134 In the medieval scheme of four levels of scriptural meaning, this would have been called reading at the anagogic level. See Lewalski (*Protestant Poetics*, 8), citing Dante's reading of Psalm 114.

135 Walton, *Lives*, 51–52. Interestingly, he writes that during this time Donne spent his days and nights in "*Lamentations*." Like Spenser, Walton was a writer who had Psalm 137 much on his mind. In *The Compleat Angler*, he cites the psalm as evidence of his claim that "the very sitting by the river's side is not only the quietest and fittest place for contemplation, but will invite any angler to it" (Oxford edition, 1915, 42). I owe this citation to Annabel Patterson.

136 De Bèze, *Psalmes of David*, 331.

the inability to do so, and the desire for revenge. Though particular applications of Psalm 137 diverged according to religious and political views or the situations of the translators, the variety of its interpretations testifies to the way in which the Psalms were imaginatively transformed to harmonize with the particular concerns of their sixteenth- and seventeenth-century English readers.

Conclusion

Luther and Calvin understood how easy it is to memorize the Psalms when they are attached to powerful music. I can attest to this, having sung and chanted them from the age of nine, as a choirboy in the Anglican Church of Canada. Later, as a young professional musician, I sang psalm settings in churches of many denominations – including Roman Catholic (Latin rite) and Episcopal (both "low" and ultra-"high") – as well as, occasionally, synagogues, and then as a soloist and ensemble member in secular concert settings. Many psalms, in whole or in part, remain embedded in my memory, partly because of the beautiful chant settings by Thomas Tallis, William Byrd, and Henry Walford Davies, and the more elaborate compositions of composers like Monteverdi, Orlando Gibbons, Bach, Handel, and others. And although I have spent years reading dozens of different psalm translations in researching this book, none of them has managed to displace the Coverdale Psalter that lodged in my inner ear from early and repeated exposure to the liturgy, both spoken and sung, of the Anglican Book of Common Prayer.

My experience is far from unique. Poets Derek Walcott and Seamus Heaney, for instance, have both incorporated into their poetry early memories of Psalm 42, "Like as the hart desireth the waterbrooks." In his elegy for her, *The Bounty*, Walcott recalls learning this psalm from his mother while growing up in St. Lucia:

> when the cattle-bell of the chapel summoned our herd
> into the varnished stalls, in whose rustling hymnals I heard
> the fresh Jacobean springs, the murmur Clare heard
>
> of bounty abiding, the clear language she taught us,
> "as the hart panteth," at this, her keen ears pronged
> while her three fawns nibbled the soul-freshening waters,

"as the hart panteth for the water-brooks" that belonged
to the language in which I mourn her now.[1]

Similarly, in another hemisphere, but at roughly that period, Seamus Heaney was listening to the same psalm, as he recounts in "Clearances," which, like Walcott's poem, is an elegy dedicated to his mother:

Elbow to elbow, glad to be kneeling next
To each other up there near the front
Of the packed church, we would follow the text
And rubrics for the blessing of the font.
As the hind longs for the streams, so my soul.[2]

If these poems are honestly autobiographical, which seems likely given their subject, then the Psalms are part of Heaney's and Walcott's abiding childhood memories, just as they are of mine. Even misheard, the Psalms stick in the memory, as John Hollander reminds us, recounting the joke about the child who transforms the penultimate verse of Psalm 23 from the consoling "Surely goodness and mercy shall follow me all the days of my life" into the somewhat unnerving "Surely Good Mrs. Murphy shall follow me all the days of my life."[3] Hollander describes some of his own, less comical, "Mrs. Murphys," confessing that "coming to linguistic terms with the half-understood English text . . . marked the growth of my inner ear for poetry."[4] As the final chapters of this book have shown, early modern poets also cut their teeth on the Psalms, developing an English poetics in the process of wrestling with the apparent confusions and contradictions of the biblical texts.

For many, even today, when churchgoing is a far from universal experience, the Psalms remain part of our collective cultural memory. Without some recollection of Psalm 137, the titles of novels like Elizabeth Smart's *By Grand Central Station I Sat Down and Wept* or David Malouf's *Remembering Babylon* would make little sense. The same is true, even if only superficially, of best-sellers like Peter Tremayne's medieval mystery, *Valley of the Shadow*, or the western *Shadow Valley* by Barry Cord, which allude to Psalm 23. In sixteenth- and seventeenth-century England, when church attendance was a regular part of everyone's weekly calendar, required by law even for those not prompted by natural inclination, the Psalms were an even more

[1] Derek Walcott, from "The Bounty," in *The Bounty* (New York, 1997), 8.

[2] Seamus Heaney, from "Clearances" ("in memoriam M. K. H., 1911–1984"), in *Opened Ground: Selected Poems 1966–1996* (New York, 1998), 288. The poem was first published in *The Haw Lantern* (1987).

[3] John Hollander, "Hearing and Overhearing the Psalms," in *The Work of Poetry* (New York, 1997), 114.

[4] Ibid., 116.

essential part of common culture. In conditions of stress and suffering, the Psalms were a source of comfort when ordinary language failed. Hus (1415), Luther (1546), Melanchthon (1560), and Lady Jane Grey (1553/54) all uttered as their last words the words from Ps. 31:5 that Christ himself quoted just before his death, "Lord [Father], into thy hands I commend my spirit" (Luke 23:46).[5] Jane Grey drew more heavily on the Psalms in her final prayer, quoted in Foxe's *Actes and Monuments*:

> How long wilt thou be absent? for ever? O Lord, hast thou forgotten to be gracious, and hast thou shut up thy loving-kindness in displeasure? Wilt thou be no more entreated? Is thy mercy clean gone for ever, and thy promise come utterly to an end for evermore? Why dost thou make so long tarrying? Shall I despair of thy mercy, O God? Far be that from me.[6]

This prayer is a pastiche of psalm verses that Foxe's readers would have recognized: Ps. 13:1 ("How long wylt thou forget me O Lorde? for ever?"), Ps. 77:8 ("Is his mercy clean gone for ever? And is his promise come utterly to an ende for evermore?"), and Ps. 40:17 ("make no long tarrying [O my God]"). Today, when national leaders like Bill Clinton and Trent Lott quote Psalm 51 to lend credence to their "broken and contrite hearts," they are aiming at the comparatively narrow, specialized audience that can still recognize the appropriateness of such a quotation.[7] By contrast, when the same psalm was alluded to in the *Eikon basilike* with the intention of representing Charles I as a seventeenth-century David, the author and engraver could count on every reader being able to recognize and interpret the allusions, even if, like Milton, they rejected their implications.

It is difficult for us today to realize the full extent to which, as Christopher Hill has argued, the Bible "was . . . the foundation of all aspects of English culture."[8] And if this is true of the Bible as a whole, it is true *a fortiori*

[5] On these last words, see Prothero, *The Psalms in Human Life*, 116, 122.

[6] Foxe, *Actes and Monuments*, 919.

[7] In a 1998 breakfast speech addressed to representative religious leaders Bill Clinton apologized for not being "contrite enough" in an earlier apology for his affair with Monica Lewinsky. "If I can maintain both a broken spirit and a strong heart," he concluded optimistically, "then good can come of this for our country as well as for me and my family." See "Clinton's Prayer Breakfast Speech" (AP Friday, September 11, 1998), at Washingtonpost.com, <http://www.washingtonpost.com/wp-srv/politics/special/clinton/stories/clintontext091198.htm>. In a 2003 speech in his hometown of Pascagoula, Mississippi, Trent Lott apologized for remarks he made that appeared to condone segregation, concluding, "I now fully understand the Psalm that says: 'a broken spirit: a contrite and humbled heart.'" See "Lott: Apology No. 4" at Salon.com, <http://www.salon.com/politics/feature/2002/12/14/apology/print.html.> The fact that two men from opposite ends of the political spectrum cite the same psalm verse in their contrite apologies suggests either that they share a speech writer (which seems unlikely) or that the psalm still has some claim to universality, at least among Southern American Christians.

[8] Hill, *English Bible*, 7.

of the Psalms. Not only were they among the most memorable of biblical texts, but, as the personal utterances of David, that most fully human of Old Testament heroes, they spoke most directly to (and from) the human condition. The wide variety of the Psalms made them applicable to almost all Christians in almost any situation, which is one reason readers since St. Basil had described them as a kind of condensation of all of Scripture, a Bible in miniature. The primary purpose of this study has been to explore how this miniature Bible was interpreted and put to various uses by its early modern readers.

Although the scope of this book has been kept deliberately broad, there are still many avenues of psalm culture that it has not explored, due to the usual limitations of time, space, and competence. The range of psalters discussed in chapter 2, for instance, is a small sample of dozens produced during the seventeenth century, though the selection is intended to be representative. Even the psalters included here are represented by only a smattering of their individual psalms. More extensive scholarship and analysis could be pursued with the psalters of George Wither and George Sandys, for example, as well as with psalters produced during the Interregnum. The Coverdale Psalter, incorporated in the Book of Common Prayer, has had an enormous impact on the development of English language and literature, but has received little attention from literary critics. Whole monographs could be written about the place of the Psalms in the cultures of early modern Scotland and New England. Much critical work also remains to be done on the Psalms as (and in) English literature. Even the Sidney Psalter, though there is a developing critical interest in it, especially in the wake of the valuable Oxford edition of Pembroke's *Works*, is a major poetic achievement offering opportunities for further study.[9] A full list of potential areas for future research in psalm culture or the Psalms and English literature might be as long as this volume. It should include the history and influence of the Penitential Psalms, the relationship between English psalms and the continental or Hebrew exegetical traditions, the Psalms in music and the visual arts (and connections from or back to literature), not to mention the importance of the Psalms for individual authors (Wyatt, Spenser, Milton, Cowley).[10] One of the most active areas of research into early

[9] At the very least, a discerning publisher might recognize the need for a new edition of the complete Sidney Psalter, including the psalms of both Philip and Mary in a single, affordable volume. Rathmell's edition has been out of print for years.

[10] This selection of topics is based on papers, most representing scholarly work in progress, presented at the December 2002 Barnard College conference on David in the Middle Ages and Renaissance.

modern psalm culture currently is focused on the writing and devotional activities of early modern women. For a variety of reasons, including the social sanctions inhibiting women from writing in more "masculine" literary genres, early modern women often translated the Psalms.[11] Mary Sidney Herbert, the countess of Pembroke, is the preeminent example, but many women composed metrical translations that never found their way into print, and that still wait to be discovered in archives in Britain and the United States.[12] Like their male counterparts, female writers also paraphrased or alluded to the Psalms. Examples from Anne Vaughan Lock, Isabella Whitney, Lady Mary Wroth, and Katherine Philips have been discussed in this study, but the sample has necessarily been limited to poems paraphrasing or alluding to Psalms 23, 51, and 137.

Certainly, the kind of analysis practiced in the final chapters of this book can be extended to other psalms, and would also allow for an examination of the Psalms' influence on a huge range of works of literature, art, and music, and political, biblical, and theological commentary. A focus on Psalms 55, 58, or 109, for instance, might reveal much about the role of the Psalms as a model for invective or satire (touched on to some extent in chapter 7, concerning the last verses of Psalm 137, and, in reference to the translation of Psalm 55 by prisoners in the Tower, in chapter 4). Psalm 104 was a favorite of metrical translators (like Vaughan, and the eighteenth-century nature poet, James Thomson), who were drawn to its description of the details of the created world. This probably explains the echo of the psalm's eighteenth verse ("The hye hylles are a refuge for the wylde goates, and so are the stony rockes for the conyes," in Coverdale's Great Bible version) in Michael Drayton's chorographic poem, *Poly-Olbion*:

[11] On the Psalms and early modern women, see Margaret P. Hannay, "'So May I with the *Psalmist* Truly Say': Early Modern Women's Psalm Discourse," in *Write or Be Written: Early Modern Women Poets and Cultural Constraints*, ed. Barbara Smith and Ursula Appelt (Aldershot and Burlington, 2001), 105–34. For a somewhat different perspective on psalm translation and women writers, arguing that early modern attitudes to the work of translation were quite different from our own, see Suzanne Trill, "Sixteenth-Century Women's Writing: Mary Sidney's *Psalmes* and the 'Feminity' of Translation," in *Writing and the English Renaissance*, ed. William Zunder and Suzanne Trill (London, 1996), 140–58.

[12] One intriguing example is Osborn Manuscript b. 217 in Yale's Beinecke Rare Book and Manuscript Library. This anonymous translation appears to be part of a complete metrical psalter, and shows signs of having been prepared for publication (there are many corrections and emendations to the text, some pasted in on tiny slips of paper). A note in a different hand than that of the translator seems to ascribe these psalms to "the Ladie Amey Daughter of the E. of Castlehaven." The earl of Castlehaven was one of the most notorious libertines of the early seventeenth century, executed for "high crimes" in 1631. None of his three daughters was named "Amey," but the anonymous ascription offers at least the tantalizing possibility of a psalm translation connected to one of the great scandals of Jacobean England.

> When as those monstrous Hills so much that us despise
> (The Mountaine, which forsooth the lowly Valley mocks)
> Have nothing in the world upon their barren Rocks,
> But greedy clambring Goats, and Conies, banisht quite
> From every fertill place.[13]

Many poets seem to have enjoyed Psalm 104's "mining Coneys" that "shroud in rocky Cells" (in Sir Henry Wotton's paraphrase),[14] but others were drawn to the metaphor of majesty and honor as God's clothing. The hymn near the beginning of Aemelia Lanyer's *Salve Deus Rex Judaeorum* (a poem generally thick with biblical language), for instance, echoes Ps. 104:1–2 (compare Lanyer's "With Majestie and Honour is He clad,/ And deck'd with light, as with a garment faire" to the Psalm's "Prayse the Lord O my soule: O Lord my God, thou art become exceadyng gloryous, thou art clothed with maiesty and honoure").[15] The psalm's fourth verse that describes God making his "angels spirites" and his "ministers a flaming fire" (Bishops' Bible) is echoed in *Hamlet* 1.4.39 and *Othello* 5.2.8.[16]

The choice of a different psalm would lead to a whole new range of material. Psalm 42, for example, was widely paraphrased and alluded to. Anne Lake Prescott has already explored some of the ramifications of the psalm's thirsty deer relevant to Spenser's *Amoretti*.[17] Prescott sets Spenser's allusion in a wide contextual web that includes the poetry of Marguerite de Navarre, patristic commentary, the English liturgy, and hunting manuals. The wider influence of the psalm remains to be explored. Geoffrey Whitney's emblem for Psalm 42 is included in Prescott's essay, along with images of deer from Valerianus's *Hieroglyphica* (Lyons, 1615) and Thomas Churchyard's *Discourse* (1578), but there are many more English emblems based on this psalm.[18] Francis Quarles has one featuring two human figures, one standing in (as?) a fountain, with water streaming from hands, side,

[13] Michael Drayton, *Poly-Olbion*, in *The Works of Michael Drayton*, ed. J. William Hebel, vol. 4 (Oxford, 1961), 294.

[14] Sir Henry Wotton, "A Translation of the CIV. Psalm to the Original Sense," in *Poems by Sir Henry Wotton, Sir Walter Raleigh and Others*, ed. Rev. John Hannah (London, 1845), 38. First published in the *Reliquiae Wottonianae* (2nd expanded ed., 1654).

[15] Aemelia Lanyer, *Salve Deus Rex Judaeorum*, lines 73–74, in *The Poems of Aemelia Lanyer*, ed. Susanne Woods (New York and Oxford, 1993), 54. Ps. 104:1–2 in Coverdale's Great Bible (1539) translation. I am indebted for this point to Kari Boyd McBride, who very kindly shared with me with some of the exciting work ("Radical Conformity: Aemelia Lanyer and the Book of Common Prayer") that she and John C. Ulreich are doing on Lanyer, whose poetry is obviously steeped in the Psalms and other biblical literature.

[16] See Shaheen, *Biblical References*, 543, 597.

[17] Prescott, "The Thirsty Deer and the Lord of Life: Some Contexts for *Amoretti* 67–70," *Spenser Studies* 6 (1985): 33–76.

[18] Ibid., figs. 1–3.

and feet, and another on the back of a deer which is leaping toward the fountain. The accompanying poem allegorizes the image and Psalm 42, on which it is based:

> Not as the thirsty soyle desires soft showres,
>   To quicken and refresh her Embrion grain;
> Nor as the drooping Crests of fading flowres
>   Request the bounty of a morning Raine,
> Do I desire my GOD: These, in few houres,
>   Re-wish, what late their wishes did obtaine,
>   But as the swift-foote Hart does, wounded, flie
>   To th'much desired streames, ev'n so do I
> Pant after Thee, my GOD, whom I must find, or die.[19]

Quarles's engravings are taken from the 1624 *Pia desideria emblematis* of the Dutch emblematist Herman Hugo. In 1690, however, Hugo's book was "Englished" by Edmund Arwaker, who naturally uses the same engraving for Ps. 42:1 as Quarles (though reversed), and whose accompanying verses follow much the same allegorical interpretation. Christ is the fountain, the deer is the soul, which longs for the "Springs that in the heavenly Canaan flow" (or, elsewhere, "the pure Waters of the Well of Life") but which is pierced by "an Infernal Dart" and pursued by the "quick-nos'd Hounds" of "Hell's great Nimrod." (Quarles's hounds are more explicitly allegorized as "a Pack of deep-mouth'd Lusts.")[20] Both emblems blend the same classical and patristic sources (the Actaeon myth, Cyril, Augustine, and classical accounts of deer as perpetually thirsty and as the natural enemy of poisonous snakes) cited by Prescott. A later emblem, by John Hall, does not explicitly comment on Psalm 42, but alludes to it nevertheless to elaborate on the complicated thirst in Augustine's prayer, "Inebriate my heart, (Oh God! with the sober intemperance of thy love":

> Now love I all excess; now let me be
> An enemy to all sobriety!
> Can the faint hart, whose nimble footing stray
> Along the devious forrests all the day,
> Whilst that her foes as swift as lightning press
> Behind, yet not so swift as merciless,
> And scorching heat her parched intralls dry
> That in her self her greatest dangers lie;
> When she com's near cold streams, who as they pass
> Do with their silver footings clear the grass

19 Quarles, *Emblemes*, 285.
20 Arwaker, *Pia desideria*, 210–15 (some pages misnumbered in original). Quarles, *Emblemes*, 286.

Measure her thirst, but rather covets more
The naturall julip then she did before:
'Tis so with me (my God!) but I have been
Persued by enemies that to [i.e. do] lodg within.[21]

The allegorical reading of Christ as the fountain and the human soul as the thirsty deer is played out in non-emblematic poems too. The fountain streams more than water in Joseph Fletcher's passion poem, *Christes Bloodie Sweat*:

Gird on thy loines with veritie, and take
Salvation's helmet to secure thy head,
Bear up the shield of faith, and hourely shake
The Spirit's sword, and on thy watchfull bed
    Keepe centinell when all thy powers retreat,
    Then come and bath thee in His bloody sweat.

For as the Hart long hunted on the mountaines,
Breathlesse doth pant for life but all in vaine,
Untill revived in the lively fountaines,
He doth recover strength and breath againe:
    So we of breath, of life, are all depriv'd,
    Til in His bloody sweat we be reviv'd.[22]

Anne Bradstreet (to briefly extend the search across the Atlantic) adapts the traditional love allegory of Psalm 42 to a secular (albeit chastely conjugal) context, in a punning poem about her absent husband:

As loving Hind that (Hartless) wants her Deer,
Scuds through the woods and Fern with harkning ear,
Perplext, in every bush & nook doth pry,
Her dearest Deer, might answer ear or eye;
So doth my anxious soul, which now doth miss,
A dearer Dear (far dearer Heart) then this.

After ringing all the possible changes on hart/heart, and deer/dear, she concludes with the wish to

remain but one, till death divide
Thy loving Love and Dearest Dear,
At home, abroad, and everywhere.[23]

[21] John Hall, *Emblems with Elegant Figures 1658*, Scolar Press facsimile (Menston, 1970), 41.

[22] Joseph Fletcher, *Christes Bloodie Sweat, or the Sonne of God in his Agonie* (1613), in *The Poems of Joseph Fletcher, M.A.*, ed. Rev. Alexander Grosart (1869; rpr. New York, 1983), 164.

[23] "Another [Letter to her Husband, absent upon Publick employment]," in *The Complete Works of Anne Bradstreet*, ed. Joseph R. McElrath, Jr. and Allan P. Robb (Boston, 1981), 182–83.

Even this sampling demonstrates traces of only the first verse of Psalm 42; Quarles and Arwaker, for instance, both have emblems on verse 2 as well.

Despite the number of interesting possibilities for further studies in Renaissance psalm culture, this book will, I hope, have made its case: the Psalms were central to the literature and culture of early modern England to a degree that has not been widely appreciated. This book also argues, however, for a reassessment of the status of translation as a literary enterprise. George Steiner argues that it is by means of translation – broadly as well as narrowly conceived – that literatures and cultures are created, and this seems borne out by the development of the English Renaissance, since so many of the seminal literary achievements of the period were translations, from biblical and classical languages as well as foreign vernaculars. The peculiar combination of sacred and secular, Hebraic and Hellenic, that constituted early modern English culture depended upon the creative appropriation of the content of biblical and classical texts to serve the varied purposes of writers in sixteenth- and seventeenth-century England. This book explores the sometimes convoluted, often contested process by means of which the ancient foreign texts were transformed – translated – into early modern English. The Psalms, ancient Hebrew lyrics, were written for specific purposes that, by the sixteenth century, were largely forgotten. In the process of translation they became, however, a collection of peculiarly English lyrics that ministered "Instruction, and satisfaction, to every man, in every emergency and occasion."[24]

[24] Donne's second Prebend Sermon, describing the Psalms as the "Manna of the Church." See Introduction, n. 4.

Appendix

For convenient reference, the three psalms treated in depth in chapters 5, 6, and 7 are printed here in full, in the translation of Miles Coverdale for the Great Bible (1539). Since this was the translation that eventually came to be included in the Book of Common Prayer, it was among the best known, and it was also perhaps the only English version in wide currency throughout the entire period of this study.

PSALM 23

1 The Lorde is my shepherde, therfore can I lack nothing.
2 He shall fede me in a grene pasture, & leade me forth besyde the waters of comforte.
3 He shall converte my soule, & bring me forth in the pathes of righteousnes for hys names sake.
4 Yee though I walke thorow the valley of the shadow of death, I will feare no evell, for thou art with me: thy rodde & thy staffe comforte me.
5 Thou shalt prepare a table before me agaynst them that trouble me: thou hast annoynted my head with oyle, & my cuppe shalbe full.
6 But (thy) lovynge kyndnes and mercy shall folowe me all the dayes of my lyfe: & I will dwell in the house of the Lord for ever.

PSALM 51

1 Have mercy upon me (O God) after thy (greate) goodnes: according unto the multitude of thy mercyes, do away mine offences.
2 Wash me thorowly fro my wickednesse, & clense me fro my sinne.
3 For I knowleg my fautes, & my synne is ever before me.
4 Agaynst the onely have I sinned, and done this evell in thy syght: that thou myghtest be justifyed in thy sayinge, & cleare when thou art judged.

5 Beholde, I was shapen in wickednesse, & in synne hath my mother conceaved me.
6 But lo, thou requirest treuth in the inward partes, and shalt make me to understonde wisdome secretly.
7 Thou shalt pourge me with Isope, and I shal be cleane: thou shalt wash me, and I shalbe whiter then snowe:
8 Thou shalt make me hear of joye and gladnesse, that the bones which thou hast broken, maye rejoyse.
9 Turne thy face from my synnes, & put out all my misdedes.
10 Make me a cleane hert (O God) & renue a ryght sprete within me.
11 Cast me not awaye from thy presence, & take not thy holy sprete from me.
12 O geve me the comforte of thy helpe agayne, and stablish me with thy fre sprete.
13 Then shall I teach thy wayes unto the wicked, and synners shall be converted unto the.
14 Deliver me from bloud giltynesse (O God) thou that are the God of my health, and my tonge shall syng of thy righteousnesse.
15 Thou shalt open my lyppes (O Lord) my mouth shall shew thy prayse.
16 For thou desyrest no sacrifice, els wolde I geve it thee: but thou delytest not in burntofferynge.
17 The sacrifice of God is a troubled sprete, a broken and a contrite hert (O God) shalt thou not despyse.
18 O be favorable and gracious unto Sion, buylde thou the walles of Jerusalem.
19 Then shalt thou be pleased with the sacrifice of ryghteousnesse, with burntofferynges & oblacions: then shall they offre yonge bullockes upon thyne aultar.

PSALM 137

1 By the waters of Babylon we sat downe and weapte, when we remembred (the, O) Syon.
2 As for our harpes, we hanged them up upon the trees, that are therin.
3 For they that led us awaye captyve, required of us then a songe & melody in our hevynes: synge us one of the songes of Sion.
4 How shall we synge the Lordes songe in a straunge lande.
5 If I forget the, O Jerusalem, let my right hande be forgotten.
6 If I do not remembre the, let my tonge cleve to the rofe of my mouth: yee yf I preferre not Jerusalem in my myrth.

7 Remembre the chyldren of Edom, O Lorde, in the daye of Jerusalem,
how they sayd: downe with it, downe with it: even to the grounde.
8 O daughter of Babylon, thou shalt come to misery thy selfe: yee, happye
shall he be, that rewardeth the as thou hast served us.
9 Blessed shall he be, that taketh thy chyldren, and throweth them agaynst
the stones.

Bibliography

PRIMARY SOURCES

Ainsworth, Henry. *The Booke of Psalmes: Englished both in prose and metre.* Antwerp 1612.

Alison, Richard. *The psalmes of David in meter.* London, 1599.

Anon. Manuscript Commonplace Book. Osborn c.125. Beinecke Rare Book and Manscript Library. Yale University.

Old John Hopkins's and Thomas Sternhold's Petition to Parliament [etc]. London, 1699.

Arnold, Matthew. *Poetry and Criticism of Matthew Arnold.* Edited by A. Dwight Culler. Boston, 1961.

The Arundel Harington Manuscript of Tudor Poetry. Edited by Ruth Hughey. 2 vols. Columbus, OH, 1960.

Arwaker, Edmund. *Pia desideria: or, Divine addresses, in three books. . . . Written in Latine by Herm. Hugo, Englished by Edm. Arwaker, M.A.* London, 1690.

Aubrey, John. *Aubrey's Brief Lives.* Edited by O. L. Dick. Harmondsworth, 1949, rpr. 1982.

Augustine, St. *The City of God.* Translated by Henry Bettenson. Harmondsworth, 1972, rpr. 1986.

Expositions on the Book of Psalms. Vols. 5 and 6. Translated by H. M. Wilkins. Edited by John Henry Parker. Oxford, 1853, 1857.

Bacon, Sir Francis. *A Critical Edition of the Major Works.* Edited by Brian Vickers. Oxford and New York, 1996.

The Works of Francis Bacon. Vol. 7. Edited by James Spedding et al. New ed. London, 1872.

Barton, William. *The Book of Psalms in Metre.* London, 1644, rpr. 167?.

The Bay Psalm Book. A facsimile of the first edition of 1640. Chicago, n.d.

Bayly, Lewis. *The Practice of Pietie.* 7th ed. London, 1616.

Bèze, Théodore de. *The Psalmes of David, truely opened and explaned by Paraphrasis.* Translated by Anthony Gilby. London, 1581.

The Bible and Holy Scriptures [The Geneva Bible]. Geneva, 1560. Facsimile edition. Columbus, OH, 1998.

The Book of Common Praise (Revised 1938) being the Hymn Book of the Anglican Church of Canada. Toronto, n.d.

The Book of Common Prayer. Commonly called The First Prayer Book of Queen Elizabeth. Printed by Grafton 1559. Facsimile edition by William Pickering. London, 1844.

Boyle, Roger. *The Dramatic Works of Roger Boyle, Earl of Orrery.* Edited by William Clark Smith. 2 vols. Cambridge, MA, 1937.

Bradstreet, Anne. *The Complete Works of Anne Bradstreet.* Edited by Joseph R. McElrath and Allan P. Robbs. Boston, 1981.

Browne, Thomas. *The Works of Mr. Thomas Browne.* 4th ed. London, 1715.

Browne, Sir Thomas. *The Major Works.* Edited by C. A. Patrides. Harmondsworth, 1977.

Buchanan, George. *Paraphrasis Psalmorum Davidis Poetica.* London, 1583.

Bunyan, John. *The Pilgrim's Progress.* Edited by Roger Sharrock. Harmondsworth, 1965, rpr. 1987.

Calvin, John. *The Psalmes of David and others. With M. John Calvins Commentaries.* Translated by Arthur Golding. London, 1571.

Calvin's First Psalter [1559]. Edited by R. R. Terry. London, 1932.

Campion, Thomas. *The Works of Thomas Campion.* Edited by Walter R. Davis. New York, 1970.

Carew, Thomas. *The Poems of Thomas Carew.* Edited by Rhodes Dunlap. Oxford, 1949, corrected rpr., 1957.

Chapman, George. *The Poems of George Chapman.* Edited by Phyllis Brooks Bartlett. New York, 1962.

Chaucer, Geoffrey. *The Complete Poetry and Prose of Geoffrey Chaucer.* Edited by John H. Fisher. New York, 1977.

Clarendon, Edward Hyde, first earl of. *Contemplations and reflections upon the Psalms of David.* In *Miscellaneous Works of the Right Honourable Edward, Earl of Clarendon.* London, 1751.

Clarke, Danielle, ed. *Isabella Whitney, Mary Sidney and Aemelia Lanyer: Renaissance Women Poets.* Harmondsworth, 2000.

Coleridge, Samuel Taylor. *Poetical Works.* Edited by Ernest Hartley Coleridge. Oxford, 1969.

Cope, Sir Anthony. *Meditations on Twenty Select Psalms.* Reprinted from the edition of 1547. London, 1848.

Coverdale, Miles. *Remains of Myles Coverdale.* Edited for the Parker Society by George Pearson. Cambridge, 1846.

Cowley, Abraham. *A Critical Edition of Abraham Cowley's* DAVIDEIS. Edited by Gayle Shadduck. New York and London, 1987.

Cowper, William. *The Complete Poetical Works of William Cowper.* Edited by H. S. Milford. Oxford, 1913.

Crashaw, Richard. *The Poems English Latin and Greek of Richard Crashaw.* Edited by L. C. Martin. Oxford, 1927.

Cross, Nicholas. *The Cynosura, or, Saving Star that leads to Eternity. Discovered amidst the Celestial Orbs of Davids Psalms by way of Paraphrase upon the Miserere.* London, 1670.

Curzon, David, ed. *Modern Poems on the Bible: An Anthology.* Philadelphia and Jerusalem, 1994.

Dante. *The Divine Comedy 2: Purgatorio*. Edited and translated by John Sinclair. New York, 1939, rpr. 1980.

Letters of Dante. Translated by Paget Toynbee. 2nd ed. Oxford, 1967.

Davie, Donald, ed. *The Psalms in English*. Harmondsworth, 1996.

Davies, Sir John. *The Complete Poems of Sir John Davies.* Edited by Alexander B. Grosart. 2 vols. London, 1876.

Davies, John, of Hereford. *The Complete Works of John Davies of Hereford.* Chertsey Worthies' Library. Edited by Alexander B. Grosart. 2 vols. London, 1878.

Davison, Francis. *Davison's Poetical Rhapsody*. 2 vols. Edited by A. H. Bullen. London, 1890.

The Poetical Rhapsody. Edited by Sir Harris Nicolas. 2 vols. London, 1826.

Denham, Sir John. *A Version of the Psalms of David.* London, 1714.

Dod, Henry. *Al the Psalmes of David.* N.p., 1620.

Certaine Psalmes of David. London, 1603.

Donne, John. *The Poems of John Donne*. 2 vols. Edited by Herbert J. C. Grierson. Oxford, 1912.

"The second of my Prebend Sermons upon my five Psalmes. *Preached* at S. Pauls, *January* 29. 1625." In *Donne's Prebend Sermons*. Edited by Janel M. Mueller. Cambridge, MA, 1971. 91–111.

The Sermons of John Donne. Edited by George R. Potter and Evelyn M. Simpson. Vol. 5. Berkeley and London, 1959.

Drayton, Michael. *Poly-Olbion. The Works of Michael Drayton*. Vol. 4. Edited by J. William Hebel. Oxford, 1961.

Dryden, John. *Of Dramatic Poesy and Other Critical Essays*. 2 vols. Edited by George Watson. London and New York, 1962.

The Works of Virgil in English (1697). The Works of John Dryden. Vol. 5. Berkeley, Los Angeles, and London, 1987.

Duffett, Thomas. *Three Burlesque Plays of Thomas Duffett*. Edited by Ronald E. DiLorenzo. Iowa City, 1972.

Elys, Edmond. *Dia Poemata*. London, 1655.

England's Helicon. Reprinted from the edition of 1600 with additional poems from the edition of 1614. London, 1925.

The First and Second Prayer Books of King Edward VI. Everyman's Library. London and Toronto, 1968, rpr. 1977.

Fletcher, Joseph. *The Poems of Joseph Fletcher*. Edited by Alexander B. Grosart. 1869, rpr. New York, 1983.

Fletcher, Phineas. *Giles and Phineas Fletcher: Poetical Works*. 2 vols. Edited by Frederick S. Boas. Cambridge, 1909.

Foxe, John. *Actes and Monuments of these latter and perillous dayes*. London, 1563.

Fraunce, Abraham, *The Countesse of Pembrokes Emanuell.* 1591. Reprinted in *Miscellanies of the Fuller Worthies' Library*. Vol. 3. Edited by Alexander B. Grosart. 1872, rpr. New York, 1970.

Gascoigne, George. *The Complete Works of George Gascoigne*. 2 vols. Edited by John W. Cunliffe. Reprint edition. New York, 1969.

A Hundreth Sundrie Flowres. Edited by G. W. Pigman. Oxford, 2000.

Gauden, John. *Eikon basilike: The Portraiture of His Sacred Majesty in His Solitudes and Sufferings*. Edited by Philip A. Knachel. Ithaca, 1966.
Gay, John. *The Poetical Works of John Gay*. Edited by G. C. Faber. London, 1962.
Glemhan, Charles, trans. *Most Godly prayers compiled out of Davids Psalmes by D. Peter Martyr*. London, 1569.
Golding, Arthur. See Calvin, John.
The Greek Bucolic Poets. Edited and translated by J. M. Edmonds. Loeb Classics. Cambridge, MA, and London, 1912, rpr. 1996.
Habington, William. *The Poems of William Habington*. Edited by Kenneth Allott. London, 1948.
Hall, John. *Emblems with Elegant Figures 1658*. Scolar Press facsimile. Menston, 1970.
Hall, Joseph. *The Collected Poems of Joseph Hall*. Edited by A. Davenport. Liverpool, 1949.
Satires by Joseph Hall. Edited by Samuel Weller Singer. London, 1824.
Harvey, Christopher. *The School of the Heart*. London, 1647. 3rd edition, 1676.
Heaney, Seamus. *Opened Ground: Selected Poems 1966–1996*. New York, 1998.
Herbert, George. *The English Poems of George Herbert*. Edited by C. A. Patrides. London, 1974.
The Works of George Herbert. Edited by F. E. Hutchinson. Oxford, 1941, rpr. 1953.
Herbert, Mary Sidney, Countess of Pembroke. *The Collected Works of Mary Sidney Herbert Countess of Pembroke*. Vol. 2. *The Psalmes of David*. Edited by Margaret P. Hannay, Noel J. Kinnamon, and Michael G. Brennan. Oxford, 1998.
Herrick, Robert. *The Poems of Robert Herrick*. Edited by L. C. Martin. London, 1965.
The Hexaplar Psalter. Edited by William Aldis Wright. Cambridge, 1911.
The holie Bible [The Bishops' Bible]. London, 1568.
Holland, John. *The Psalmists of Britain: Records Biographical and Literary*. 2 vols. London, 1843.
The Holy Bible [The Authorized or King James Bible]. London, New York, and Toronto, n.d.
Hooker, Richard. *Of the Laws of Ecclesiastical Polity*. Book V. Vol. 2 of The Folger Library Edition of *The Works of Richard Hooker*. Edited by W. Speed Hill. Cambridge, MA, and London, 1977.
Horace. *Horace in English*. Edited by D. S. Carne-Ross and Kenneth Haynes. Harmondsworth, 1996.
The Odes of Horace. Edited and translated by David Ferry. New York, 1997.
Q. Horatii Flacci Carminum Libri IV. Edited by T. E. Page. London, 1883, rpr. 1970.
Hunnis, William. *Seven Sobbes of a Sorrowfull Soule for Sinne*. London, 1583.
The Hymnal 1982, according to the use of the Episcopal Church. New York, 1985.
The Interlineary Hebrew and English Psalter. Grand Rapids, 1970.
James I, [and William Alexander]. *The Psalmes of King David Translated by King James*. Oxford, 1631.

Jonson, Ben. *The Complete Poems*. Edited by George Parfitt. Harmondsworth, 1975, rpr. 1988.

Joye, George. *Davids Psalter*. [Antwerp], 1534.

Keats, John. *Complete Poems*. Edited by Jack Stillinger. Cambridge, MA, and London, 1978, 1982.

King, Henry. *The Poems of Henry King*. Edited by Margaret Crum. Oxford, 1965.

Poems and Psalms by Henry King DD. Edited by J. Hannah. Oxford and London, 1843.

The Psalmes of David from the New Translation of the Bible turned into Meter. London, 1651.

Langland, William. *Piers the Plowman*. Edited by W. W. Skeat. Oxford, 1924.

Lanyer, Aemelia. *The Poems of Aemilia Lanyer*. Edited by Susanne Woods. New York and Oxford, 1993.

Lawes, Henry. *Select Psalmes of A New Translation*. N.p., 1655.

Lefèvre d'Etaples, Jacques, ed. *Quincuplex Psalterium*. 1513. Facsimile reprint. Geneva, 1979.

Lock, Anne Vaughan. *The Complete Works of Anne Vaughan Lock*. Edited by Susan M. Felch. Tempe, AZ, 1999.

A Meditation of A Penitent Sinner. Edited by Kel Morin. Waterloo, 1997.

Loe, William. *Songs of Sion*. [Hamburg, 1620.]

Luther, Martin. *Luther's Works*. Edited by Jaroslav Pelikan. St. Louis, 1955–1986.

Three Treatises. Translated by A. T. W. Steinhauser. Revised by Frederick C. Ahrens and Abdel Ross Wentz. Philadelphia, 1970.

Marshall, Stephen. *Meroz Cursed, or, A Sermon preached to the Honourable House of Commons, At their late Solemn Fast, Febr. 23. 1641*. London, 1641.

Meads, Dorothy, ed. *The Diary of Lady Margaret Hoby 1599–1605*. London, 1930.

Milton, John. *Complete Poems and Major Prose*. Edited by Merritt Y. Hughes. New York, 1957.

Complete Shorter Poems. Edited by John Carey. 2nd ed. Harlow, Essex, and New York, 1977.

The New Oxford Book of Seventeenth Century Verse. Edited by Alastair Fowler. Oxford and New York, 1992.

Norris, John. *A Collection of Miscellanies*. 1687. Reprinted in *Miscellanies of the Fuller Worthies' Library*. Vol. 3. Edited by Alexander B. Grosart. 1872, rpr. New York, 1970.

Oldham, Sir John. *The Poems of John Oldham*. Edited by Harold F. Brooks and Raman Selden. Oxford, 1987.

The Oxford Book of Medieval Latin Verse. Edited by F. J. E. Raby. Oxford, 1959.

[Parker, Matthew], *The whole Psalter translated into English Metre. . . .* London, [1567].

Pelling, Edward. *A Sermon Preached on The 30th of January, 1684. The Day of Martyrdom of King Charles I. Of Blessed Memory.* London, 1685.

Pembroke, countless of. See Herbert, Mary Sidney.

The Penguin Book of Hymns. Edited by Ian Bradley. Harmondsworth, 1989.

Petrarca, Francesco. *Letters on Familiar Matters, Rerum familiarum libri XVII–XXIV*. Translated by Aldo S. Bernardo. Baltimore and London, 1985.
Philips, Katherine. *The Collected Works of Katherine Philips, The Matchless Orinda.* Vol. 1. *The Poems.* Edited by Patrick Thomas. Stump Cross, 1990.
The Phoenix Nest (1593). Edited by Hyder E. Rollins. Cambridge, MA, 1931, rpr. 1969.
Pope, Alexander. *The Poems of Alexander Pope*. Edited by John Butt. London, 1963, rpr. 1984.
The Portable Renaissance Reader. Edited by James Bruce Ross and Mary Martin McLaughlin. New York, 1961.
The Psalms in English. Edited by Donald Davie. Harmondsworth, 1996.
Puttenham, George. *The Arte of English Poesie*. 1589. Facsimile reprint. Kent, OH, 1970.
Quarles, Francis. *Emblemes.* London, 1635.
Hieroglyphikes of the Life of Man. Printed with *Emblemes.* London, 1639.
Raleigh, Sir Walter. *The Poems of Sir Walter Raleigh*. Edited by J. Hannah. London, 1875, 1892.
Ravenscroft, Thomas, ed. *The Whole Booke of Psalmes.* London, 1621.
Rochester, John Wilmot, earl of. *The Complete Poems of John Wilmot, Earl of Rochester*. Edited by David M. Vieth. New Haven, 1968.
Saltmarsh, John. *Poemata Sacra.* Cambridge, 1636.
[Sandys, Sir Edwin.] *Sacred Hymns: Consisting of fifti select psalms of David and others.* London, 1615.
Sandys, George. *A Paraphrase upon the Psalmes of David.* Printed with *A Paraphrase upon the Divine Poems*. London, 1648.
The Poetical Works of George Sandys. Edited by Richard Hooper. 2 vols. London, 1872.
Savonarola, Girolamo. *A Pithie Exposition upon the .51. Psalme.* Translated by Abraham Fleming. London, 1578.
The Scottish Metrical Psalter of 1635. Edited by Neil Livingston. Glasgow, 1864.
Seagar, Francis. *Certayne Psalmes select out of the Psalter of David.* London, 1553.
Sedgwick, Obadiah. *The Shepherd of Israel, or God's pastoral care over his people. Delivered in divers sermons on the whole twenty-third psalm*. London, 1658.
Shakespeare, William. *The Riverside Shakespeare*. 2nd edition. Edited by G. Blakemore Evans, with J. J. M Tobin. Boston and New York, 1997.
Sidney, Sir Philip. *Miscellaneous Prose of Sir Philip Sidney*. Edited by Katherine Duncan-Jones and Jan Van Dorsten. Oxford, 1973.
The Old Arcadia. Edited by Katherine Duncan Jones. Oxford, 1985.
The Poems of Sir Philip Sidney. Edited by William A. Ringler. Oxford, 1962.
Sidney, Sir Philip, and Mary, countess of Pembroke. *The Psalms of Sir Philip Sidney and the Countess of Pembroke*. Edited by J. C. A. Rathmell. Garden City, NY, 1963.
Simon, Maurice, trans. *The Hebrew–English Edition of the Babylonian Talmud: Berakoth*. London, 1984.
Smart, Christopher. *Selected Poems*. Edited by Karina Williamson and Marcus Walsh. Harmondsworth, 1990.

Smith, Gregory, ed. *Elizabethan Critical Essays*. Vol. 1. London, 1904.

Smith, Myles. *The Psalms of King David paraphrased*. London, 1668.

Smith, Samuel. *Davids Repentance. Or, A Plaine and Familiar Exposition of the Li. Psalme*. 7th ed. London, 1625.

Spenser, Edmund. *The Faerie Queene*. Edited by Thomas P. Roche, Jr. New Haven and London, 1981.

The Yale Edition of the Shorter Poems of Edmund Spenser. Edited by William Oram et al. New Haven and London, 1989.

Spingarn, J. E., ed. *Critical Essays in the Seventeenth Century*. 3 vols. Bloomington, IN, and London, 1957, rpr. 1968.

Stanyhurst, Richard. *Translation of the first Four Books of the Aeneis of P. Virgilius Maro: with other poetical Devices thereto annexed [June] 1582*. Edited by Edward Arbor. London, 1895.

Sternhold, Thomas. *Certayne Psalmes chosen out of the Psalter of David*. London, c.1549.

Strange, K. H., and R. G. E. Sandbach, eds. *Psalm 23: An Anthology*. Revised edition. Edinburgh, 1978.

Strigelius, Victorinus. *A Proceeding in the Harmonie of King Davids Harpe*. Translated by Richard Robinson. London, 1591.

Surrey, Henry Howard, earl of. *Henry Howard Earl of Surrey: Poems*. Edited by Emrys Jones. Oxford, 1964.

Tate, Nahum, and Nicholas Brady. *A New Version of the Psalms*. London, 1696.

Taylor, Jeremy. *Psalter of David*. London, 1644.

Theocritus. *Theocritus Idylls and Epigrams*. Translated by Daryl Hine. New York, 1982.

Tillotson, Geoffrey, Paul Fussell, Jr., and Marshall Waingrow, eds. *Eighteenth Century Literature*. New York, 1969.

Tomlinson, Gary, ed. *Source Readings in Music History: The Renaissance*. New York and London, 1998.

Vaughan, Henry. *Henry Vaughan: The Complete Poems*. Edited by Alan Rudrum. Revised edition. Harmondsworth, 1983.

Verstegan, Richard. *Odes in Imitation of the Seaven Penitential Psalmes*. [Antwerp], 1601.

Virgil. *Eclogues, Georgics, Aeneid*. Edited and translated by H. Rushton Fairclough. 2 vols. Cambridge, MA, and London, 1965.

The Georgics. Edited and translated by L. P. Wilkinson. Harmondsworth, 1982.

Walcott, Derek. *The Bounty*. New York, 1997.

Waller, Edmund. *Poems &c. written upon several occasions, and to several persons*. London, 1664.

Walton, Izaak. *The Compleat Angler*. Oxford, 1965.

The Lives of John Donne, Sir Henry Wotton, Richard Hooker, George Herbert, and Robert Sanderson. Oxford, 1927; rpr. 1973.

The Whole Booke of Psalmes, collected into Englysh metre by T. Starnhold, J. Hopkins & others. . . . London, 1562.

Wither, George. *A collection of Emblemes, Ancient and Modern*. London, 1635.

Exercises upon the First Psalme. 1620. Spenser Society reprint. New York, 1882, rpr. 1967.
A Preparation to the Psalter. 1619. Spenser Society reprint. New York, 1884, rpr. 1967.
The Psalms of David Translated into Lyrick-Verse. 1632. Spenser Society reprint. New York, 1881, rpr. 1967.
The Schollers Purgatory. London, 1624. Facsimile edition. Amsterdam, 1977.
Woodford, Samuel. *A Paraphrase of the Psalms of David.* London, 1667.
Wotton, Sir Henry. *Poems by Sir Henry Wotton, Sir Walter Raleigh and Others.* Edited by Rev. John Hannah. London, 1845.
Wroth, Lady Mary. *The Poems of Lady Mary Wroth.* Edited by Josephine A. Roberts. Baton Rouge and London, 1983.
Wyatt, Sir Thomas. *Sir Thomas Wyatt: The Complete Poems*. Edited by R. A. Rebholz. Harmondsworth, 1978.
Zarlino, Gioseffo. *The Art of Counterpoint*. Translated by Guy A. Marco and Claude V. Palisca. New Haven and London, 1968.

SECONDARY SOURCES

Alpers, Paul. *The Singer of the Eclogues: A Study of Virgilian Pastoral.* Berkeley, 1979.
What Is Pastoral? Chicago and London, 1996.
Alter, Robert. *The Art of Biblical Poetry*. New York, 1985.
Attridge, Derek. *Well-Weighed Syllables: Elizabethan Verse in Classical Metres.* Cambridge, 1974.
Bach, Inke, and Helmut Galle. *Deutsche Psalmdichtung vom 16. bis zum 20. Jahrhundert.* Berlin and New York, 1989.
Bainton, Roland. *Here I Stand: A Life of Martin Luther*. Nashville and New York, 1950.
Baroway, Israel. "The Accentual Theory of Hebrew Prosody." *ELH* 17 (1950): 115–35.
"The Bible as Poetry in the English Renaissance: An Introduction." *Journal of English and Germanic Philology* 32 (1933): 447–80.
"The Hebrew Hexameter: A Study in Renaissance Sources and Interpretation." *ELH* 2 (1935): 66–91.
"'The Lyre of David': A Further Study in Renaissance Interpretation of Biblical Form." *ELH* 8 (1941): 119–42.
"Tremellius, Sidney, and Biblical Verse." *Modern Language Notes* 49 (1934): 146–7.
Bartlett, Clifford. Notes to *Henry Lawes: Sitting by the Streams*. The Consort of Musicke. Directed by Anthony Rooley. Hyperion Records. London, 1984.
Bath, Michael. *Speaking Pictures: English Emblem Books and Renaissance Culture.* London, 1994.
Berman, Ronald. *Henry King and The Seventeenth Century*. London, 1964.
Blagden, Cyprian. *The Stationers' Company: A History, 1403–1959*. Cambridge, MA, 1960.

Bloch, Chana. *Spelling the Word: George Herbert and the Bible.* Berkeley, Los Angeles, and London, 1985.

Bloom, Harold. *The Anxiety of Influence*. London, Oxford, and New York, 1973.

Boddy, Margaret. "Milton's Translations of Psalms 80–88." *Modern Philology* 64 (1966): 1–19.

Bouwsma, William J. *John Calvin: A Sixteenth Century Portrait.* New York and Oxford, 1988.

Braden, Gordon. "riverrun: An Epic Catalogue in *The Faerie Queene*." *English Literary Renaissance* 5 (1975): 25–48.

Brennecke, Ernest, Jr. *John Milton the Elder and his Music*. New York, 1938.

Brook, V. J. K. *A Life of Archbishop Matthew Parker*. Oxford, 1962.

Brower, Reuben, ed. *On Translation*. New York, 1966.

Butterworth, Charles C. *The Literary Lineage of the King James Bible*. Philadelphia, 1941.

Cameron, Euan. "Medieval Heretics as Protestant Martyrs." In *Martyrs and Martyrologies*. Edited by Diana Wood. Oxford and Cambridge, MA, 1993.

Campbell, Ted A. *The Religion of the Heart: A Study of European Religious Life in the Seventeenth and Eighteenth Centuries*. Columbia, SC, 1991.

Cartmell, Deborah. "'Beside the shore of siluer streaming *Thamesis*': Spenser's *Ruines of Time*." *Spenser Studies* 6 (1985): 77–82.

Cave, Terrence. *Devotional Poetry in France c.1570–1613*. London, 1969.

Colie, Rosalie L. *The Resources of Kind: Genre-Theory in the Renaissance*. Berkeley, Los Angeles, and London, 1973.

Collinson, Patrick. *The Religion of Protestants: The Church in English Society 1559–1625*. Oxford, 1982.

Creel, Bryant. "Reformist Dialectics and Poetic Adaptations of Psalm 137, 'Super flumina Babylonis,' in Portugal in the Sixteenth Century." In *Camoniana Californiana*. Edited by M. De L. Belchior and E. Martinez-Lopez. Santa Barbara, 1985.

Cummings, Anthony M. "Toward an Interpretation of the Sixteenth-Century Motet." *Journal of the American Musicological Society* 34 (1981): 43–59.

Curtius, E. R. *European Literature and the Latin Middle Ages*. Translated by Willard R. Trask. Princeton, 1973.

Dahood, Mitchell, ed. *Psalms I, II, and III*. 3 vols. The Anchor Bible. New York, 1965, 1968, and 1970.

Danielson, Dennis, ed. *The Cambridge Companion to Milton*. Cambridge, 1989.

Davie, Donald. *The Eighteenth Century Hymn in England*. Cambridge, 1993.

Davis, Richard Beale. *George Sandys, Poet-Adventurer*. London and New York, 1955.

Dickens, A. G. *The English Reformation*. 2nd edition. University Park, PA, 1991.

Dictionary of National Biography (*DNB*). Edited by Sir Leslie Stephen and Sir Sidney Lee. 22 vols. Oxford, from 1882.

DiMauro, Damon. "An Imitation of Marot's Psalm 137 in Garnier's *Les Juifves*." *French Studies Bulletin* (Autumn, 1993): 5–7.

Doelman, James. "George Wither, the Stationers Company and the English Psalter." *Studies in Philology* 90:1 (Winter 1993): 74–82.

King James I and the Religious Culture of England. Cambridge, 2000.

Duffy, Eamon. *The Stripping of the Altars: Traditional Religion in England c.1400–1580*. New Haven and London, 1992.
Durr, R. A. *On the Mystical Poetry of Henry Vaughan*. Cambridge, 1962.
Earle, Alice Morse. *The Sabbath in Puritan New England*. New York, 1891.
Eco, Umberto. *Experiences in Translation*. Translated by Alastair McEwan. Toronto, 2001.
Elliott, Robert C. *The Power of Satire: Magic, Ritual, Art*. Princeton, 1960.
Elton, G. R. *The Parliament of England 1559–1581*. Cambridge, 1986.
Empson, William. *Some Versions of Pastoral*. London, 1986.
Ericksen, Roy T. "George Gascoigne's and Mary Sidney's Versions of Psalm 130." *Cahier-élisabéthains* 36 (1989): 1–9.
Fischlin, Daniel. *In Small Proportions: A Poetics of the English Ayre 1596–1622*. Detroit, 1998.
Fisken, Beth Wynne. "'The Art of Sacred Parody' in Mary Sidney's *Psalmes*." *Tulsa Studies in Women's Literature* 8:2 (Fall 1989): 223–39.
Fowler, Alastair. *Kinds of Literature: An Introduction to the Theory of Genres and Modes*. Cambridge, MA, 1982.
Freer, Coburn. *Music for a King: George Herbert's Style and the Metrical Psalms*. Baltimore and London, 1972.
"The Style of Sidney's Psalms." *Language and Style* 2:1 (1969).
Frost, Maurice. *English and Scottish Psalm & Hymn Tunes c.1543–1677*. Oxford, 1953.
Fry, Paul H. *The Poet's Calling in the English Ode*. New Haven and London, 1980.
Garrett, C. H. *The Marian Exiles*. Cambridge, 1938.
Glass, Henry A. *The Story of the Psalters*. London, 1888, rpr. 1972.
Grant, W. Leonard. *Neo-Latin Literature and the Pastoral*. Chapel Hill, 1965.
Greenblatt, Stephen. *Renaissance Self-Fashioning: From More to Shakespeare*. Chicago and London, 1980.
Greene, Roland. "Anne Lock's *Meditation*: Invention Versus Dilation and the Founding of Puritan Poetics." In *Form and Reform in Renaissance England: Essays in Honor of Barbara Kiefer Lewalski*. Edited by Amy Boesky and Mary Thomas Crane. Newark and London, 2000. 153–70.
"Sir Philip Sidney's Psalms, the Sixteenth Century Psalter, and the Nature of Lyric." *Studies in English Literature* 30:1 (1990): 19–40.
Greene, Thomas M. "Labyrinth Dances in the French and English Renaissance." *Renaissance Quarterly* 54 (Winter 2001): 1403–66.
The Light in Troy: Imitation and Discovery in Renaissance Poetry. New Haven and London, 1993.
Greer, David. "'. . . Thou court's delight': Biographical Notes on Henry Noel." *Lute Society Journal* 17 (1975): 49–59.
Grundy, Joan. *The Spenserian Poets*. London, 1969.
Gunkel, Hermann. *The Psalms: A Form-Critical Introduction*. Translated by T. M. Horner. Philadelphia, 1967; orig. 1951.
Guy, John. *Tudor England*. Oxford and New York, 1988.

Hale, John K. "Why Did Milton Translate Psalms 80–88 in April 1648?" *Literature and History* 3:2 (Autumn 1994): 55–62.

Hannay, Margaret P. *Philip's Phoenix: Mary Sidney, Countess of Pembroke.* New York and Oxford, 1990.

"'So May I With the *Psalmist* Truly Say': Early Modern English Women's Psalm Discourse." In *Write or Be Written: Early Modern Women Poets and Cultural Constraints.* Edited by Barbara Smith and Ursula Appelt. Aldershot and Burlington, 2001. 105–34.

Hardman, C. B. "Marvell's 'Bermudas' and Sandys' *Psalms.*" *Review of English Studies* 32:125 (1981): 64–67.

Harrison, Frank Ll. *Music in Medieval Britain.* London, 1958.

Hartman, Geoffrey H., and Sanford Budick, eds. *Midrash and Literature.* New Haven and London, 1986.

Heale, Elizabeth. "Lute and Harp in Wyatt's Poetry." In *Sacred and Profane: Secular and Devotional Interplay in Early Modern British Literature.* Edited by Helen Wilcox, Richard Todd, and Alasdair MacDonald. Amsterdam, 1996.

Helgerson, Richard. *The Elizabethan Prodigals.* Berkeley, Los Angeles, and London, 1976.

Hensley, Charles S. *The Later Career of George Wither.* The Hague and Paris, 1969.

Herron, Thomas. "Richard Stanyhurst's *Aeneis* (1582): Political Poetry?" Unpublished conference paper. Delivered at the Sixteenth Century Studies Conference. Cleveland, OH, November, 2000.

Hill, Christopher. *The English Bible and the Seventeenth-Century Revolution.* Harmondsworth, 1993.

"George Wither and John Milton." In *English Renaissance Studies Presented to Helen Gardner.* Edited by John Carey and Helen Peters. Oxford, 1980.

Hind, A. M. *Engraving in England.* 3 vols. Cambridge, 1952.

Hobbs, R. Gerald. "Hebraica Veritas *and* Traditio Apostolica: Saint Paul and the Interpretation of the Psalms in the Sixteenth Century." In *The Bible and the Sixteenth Century.* Edited by David C. Steinmetz. Durham, NC, and London, 1990.

Hollander, John. "Hearing and Overhearing the Psalms." In *The Work of Poetry.* New York, 1997. 113–28.

The Untuning of the Sky: Ideas of Music in English Poetry, 1500–1700. Princeton, 1961.

Vision and Resonance: Two Senses of Poetic Form. New York, 1975.

The Work of Poetry. New York, 1997.

Höltgen, Karl Josef. "New Verse by Francis Quarles: The Portland Manuscripts, Metrical Psalms, and the *Bay Psalm Book* (with text)." *English Literary Renaissance* 28:1 (Winter 1998): 118–41.

Hughes, Felicity A. "Gascoigne's Poses." *Studies in English Literature* 37 (1997): 1–19.

Hunter, William B. "Milton Translates the Psalms." *Philological Quarterly* 40 (1961): 484–94.

"The Sources of Milton's Prosody." *Philological Quarterly* 28 (1949): 125–44.

Huray, Peter le. *Music and the English Reformation, 1549–1660.* London, 1978.
Illing, Robert. *The English Metrical Psalter of 1562.* 3 vols. Adelaide, 1983.
Ravenscroft's Revision of Est's Psalter. 2 vols. Adelaide, 1985.
The Interpreter's Bible. Vol. 4. *Psalms; Proverbs.* New York and Nashville, 1955.
Jasper, David. "The Twenty-Third Psalm in English Literature." *Religion & Literature* 30:1 (Spring, 1993): 1–11.
Jeanneret, M. *Poésie et tradition biblique au XVIe siècle: Recherches stylistiques sur les paraphrases des psaulmes de Marot à Malherbe.* Paris, 1969.
Jeffrey, David Lyle, ed. *A Dictionary of Biblical Tradition in English Literature.* Grand Rapids, 1992.
Johnson, Ronald C. *George Gascoigne.* New York, 1972.
Jones, G. Lloyd. *The Discovery of Hebrew in Tudor England: A Third Language.* Manchester, 1983.
Julian, John, ed. *A Dictionary of Hymnology.* 1892. Revised reprint in 2 vols. London, 1957.
Kastor, Frank S. *Giles and Phineas Fletcher.* Boston, 1978.
King, John N. *English Reformation Literature: The Tudor Origins of the Protestant Tradition.* Princeton, 1982.
Spenser's Poetry and the Reformation Tradition. Princeton, 1990.
Krummel, D. W. *English Music Printing 1553–1700.* London, 1975.
Kuczynski, Michael P. *Prophetic Song: The Psalms as Moral Discourse in Later Medieval England.* Philadelphia, 1995.
Kugel, James. *The Idea of Biblical Poetry: Parallelism and its History.* New Haven and London, 1981.
In Potiphar's House: The Interpretive Life of Biblical Texts. 1st paperback ed. Cambridge, MA, 1994.
Lamb, Mary Ellen. "The Countess of Pembroke's Patronage." *English Literary Renaissance* 12 (1982): 162–79.
Gender and Authorship in the Sidney Circle. Madison, WI, 1990.
"The Myth of the countess of Pembroke." *Yearbook of English Studies* 11 (1981): 194–202.
Lange, Marjory E. *Telling Tears in the English Renaissance.* Leiden, New York, and Cologne, 1996.
Leaver, Robin. *Goostly Psalmes and Spiritual Songes: English and Dutch Metrical Psalms from Coverdale to Utenhove 1535–1566.* Oxford, 1991.
Lennon, Colm. *Richard Stanihurst the Dubliner 1547–1618.* Blackrock, 1981.
Lewalski, Barbara Kiefer. Paradise Lost *and the Rhetoric of Literary Forms.* Princeton, 1985.
Protestant Poetics and the Seventeenth-Century Religious Lyric. Princeton, 1979.
Lewis, C. S. *English Literature in the Sixteenth Century.* Oxford, 1954.
Reflections on the Psalms. New York, 1958.
McColley, Diane. "The Copious Matter of My Song." In *Literary Milton: Text, Pretext, Context.* Edited by Diana Treviño Benet and Michael Lieb. Pittsburgh, 1994.
McGrath, Alister E. *Iustitia Dei: A History of the Christian Doctrine of Justification.* 2 vols. Cambridge, 1986.

Manley, Lawrence. *Literature and Culture in Early Modern London.* Cambridge, 1995.
Marius, Richard. *Martin Luther: The Christian between God and Death.* Cambridge, MA, and London, 1999.
Marotti, Arthur F. *Manuscript, Print, and the Renaissance Lyric.* Ithaca and London, 1995.
Mason, H. A. *Humanism and Poetry in the Early Tudor Period.* London, 1959, rpr. 1980.
Matthews, W. H. *Mazes and Labyrinths: A General Account of their History and Development.* London, 1922.
Matthiessen, F. O. *Translation: An Elizabethan Art.* Cambridge, MA, 1931.
The New Grove Dictionary of Music and Musicians. Edited by Stanley Sadie. 20 vols. London and Washington, DC, 1980.
The New Harvard Dictionary of Music. Edited by Don Randel. Cambridge, MA, and London, 1986.
The New Princeton Encyclopedia of Poetry and Poetics. Edited by Alex Preminger and T. V. F. Brogan. Princeton, 1993.
Noble, Richmond. *Shakespeare's Biblical Knowledge.* London, 1935, rpr. New York, 1970.
Norbrook, David. "Levelling Poetry: George Wither and the English Revolution, 1642–1649." *English Literary Renaissance* 21:2 (Spring, 1991): 217–56.
Norton, David. *A History of the English Bible as Literature.* Cambridge, 2000.
Oesterley, W. O. E. *The Psalms.* 2 vols. London, 1939.
The Oxford Companion to the Bible. Edited by Bruce M. Metzger and Michael D. Coogan. New York and Oxford, 1993.
Palisca, Claude. *Humanism in Italian Renaissance Musical Thought.* New Haven, 1985.
Panofsky, Erwin. "*Et in Arcadia Ego*: Poussin and the Elegiac Tradition." In *Meaning and the Visual Arts.* Garden City, NY, 1955.
Patrick, Millar. *Four Centuries of Scottish Psalmody.* London, Glasgow, and New York, 1949.
Patterson, Annabel. *Pastoral and Ideology: Virgil to Valéry.* Berkeley and Los Angeles, 1987.
"Pastoral versus Georgic: The Politics of Virgilian Quotation." In *Renaissance Genres.* Edited by Barbara K. Lewalski. Cambridge, MA, and London, 1986.
Pidoux, Pierre, ed. *Le Psaultier huguenot du xvi*[e] *siècle. Mélodies et documents.* 2 vols. Basel, 1962.
Poggioli, Renato. *The Oaten Flute.* Cambridge, MA, 1975.
Post, Jonathan F. S. *Henry Vaughan: The Unfolding Vision.* Princeton, 1982.
Pound, Ezra. *ABC of Reading.* Norfolk, CT, n.d.
Praz, Mario. *Studies in Seventeenth Century Imagery.* 2nd rev. ed. Rome, 1962.
Prescott, Anne Lake. *French Poets and the English Renaisssance.* New Haven and London, 1978.
"King David as a 'Right Poet': Sidney and the Psalmist." *English Literary Renaissance* 19:3 (Spring 1989): 131–51.

"The Thirsty Deer and the Lord of Life: Some Contexts for *Amoretti* 67–70." *Spenser Studies* 6 (1985): 33–76.

Procter, Francis, and Walter Howard Frere. *A New History of the Book of Common Prayer with a Rationale of its Offices.* London, 1951.

Prothero, Rowland E. *The Psalms in Human Life*. London, 1907.

Prouty, C. T. *George Gascoigne: Elizabethan Courtier, Soldier, and Poet*. New York, 1942, rpr. 1946.

Radzinowicz, Mary Ann. *Milton's Epics and the Book of Psalms.* Princeton, 1989.

Toward "Samson Agonistes": The Growth of Milton's Mind. Princeton, 1978.

Revard, Stella P. *Milton and the Tangles of Neaera's Hair: The Making of the 1645 Poems.* Columbia and London, 1997.

Rohr-Sauer, P. von. *English Metrical Psalms from 1600 to 1660. A Study in the Religious and Aesthetic Tendencies of that Period.* Freiburg, 1938.

Rollinson, Philip. "The Renaissance of the Literary Hymn." *Renaissance Papers, 1968*. Durham, NC, 1969. 11–20.

Røstvig, Maren-Sophie. "Structure as Prophecy: The Influence of Biblical Exegesis upon Theories of Literary Structure." In *Silent Poetry: Essays in Numerological Analysis*. Edited by Alastair Fowler. London, 1970.

Sachs, Curt. *The History of Musical Instruments*. New York, 1940.

Schulte, Rainer, and John Biguenet, eds. *Theories of Translation: An Anthology of Essays from Dryden to Derrida*. Chicago and London, 1992.

Schwartz, Regina. *Remembering and Repeating: Biblical Creation in* Paradise Lost. Cambridge, 1988.

Scribner, R. W. *Popular Culture and Popular Movements in Reformation Germany*. London, 1987.

Seaver, Paul S. *Wallington's World: A Puritan Artisan in Seventeenth-Century London*. Stanford, 1985.

Sessions, Kyle C. "Song Pamphlets: Media Changeover in Sixteenth-Century Publication." In *Print Culture of the Renaissance*. Edited by Gerald P. Tyson and Sylvia S. Wagonheim. Newark, London, and Toronto, 1986.

Sessions, W. A. *Henry Howard the Poet Earl of Surrey*. Oxford, 1999.

"Surrey's Psalms in the Tower." In *Sacred and Profane: Secular and Devotional Interplay in Early Modern British Literature*. Edited by Helen Wilcox, Richard Todd, and Alasdair MacDonald. Amsterdam, 1996.

Shaheen, Naseeb. *Biblical References in Shakespeare's Plays*. Newark, 1999.

Sherwood, Terry G. *Herbert's Prayerful Art*. Toronto, 1989.

Smith, Eric R. "Herbert's 'The 23d Psalme' and William Barton's *The Book of Psalms in Metre*." *The George Herbert Journal* 8:2 (Spring, 1985): 33–43.

Smith, Hallett. "English Metrical Psalms in the Sixteenth Century and their Literary Significance." *Huntington Library Quarterly* 9 (1946): 249–71.

Smith, Nigel. *Perfection Proclaimed: Language and Literature in English Radical Religion*. Oxford, 1989.

Spink, Ian. *English Song: Dowland to Purcell*. London, 1974.

Steane, John. "Renaissance Gardens and Parks." In *The Cambridge Cultural History of Britain*. Vol. 3. *Sixteenth-Century Britain*. New York, 1992. 208–21.

Steele, R. *The Earliest English Music Printing*. London, 1965.

Steinberg, Theodore L. "The Sidneys and the Psalms." *Studies in Philology* 92:1 (Winter 1995): 1–17.

Steiner, George. *After Babel: Aspects of Language and Translation*. London, 1975.

Stevens, John. *Music and Poetry in the Early Tudor Court*. Cambridge, 1961.

Strier, Richard. *Love Known: Theology and Experience in George Herbert's Poetry*. Chicago and London, 1983.

Strong, Roy. *The Cult of Elizabeth*. Berkeley and Los Angeles, 1977.

Stroup, Thomas B. *Religious Rite and Ceremony in Milton's Poetry*. Lexington, KY, 1968.

Targoff, Ramie. *Common Prayer: The Language of Devotion in Early Modern England*. Chicago, 2001.

"The Performance of Prayer: Sincerity and Theatricality in Early Modern England." *Representations* 60 (Fall 1997): 49–69.

Temperley, Nicholas. *Music of the English Parish Church*. 2 vols. Cambridge, 1979.

Terry, R. R. *Calvin's First Psalter (1539)*. London, 1932.

Todd, Richard. "Humanist Prosodic Theory, Dutch Synods, and the Poetics of the Sidney–Pembroke Psalter." *Huntington Library Quarterly* 52:2 (Spring 1989): 273–93.

" 'So Well Attyr'd Abroad': A Background to the Sidney–Pembroke Psalter and Its implications for the Seventeenth-Century Religious Lyric." *Texas Studies in Literature and Language* 29 (Spring 1987): 74–93.

Trill, Suzanne. "Sixteenth-Century Women's Writing: Mary Sidney's *Psalmes* and the 'Femininity' of Translation." In *Writing and the English Renaissance*. Edited by William Zunder and Suzanne Trill. London, 1996. 140–58.

Twombly, Robert G. "Thomas Wyatt's Paraphrase of the Penitential Psalms of David." *Texas Studies of Literature and Language* 13:3 (Fall, 1970).

van Deusen, Nancy, ed. *The Place of the Psalms in the Intellectual Culture of the Middle Ages*. Albany, 1999.

von Rad, Gerhard. *Wisdom in Israel*. Translated by James D. Martin. London, 1972.

Watson, J. R. *The English Hymn: A Critical and Historical Study*. Oxford, 1997.

Weiner, Seth. "The Quantitative Poems and the Psalm Translations: The Place of Sidney's Experimental Verse in the Legend." In *Sir Philip Sidney: 1596 and the Creation of a Legend*. Edited by Jan van Dorsten et al. Leiden, 1986.

"Sidney and the Rabbis: A Note on the Psalms of David and Renaissance Hebraica." In *Sir Philip Sidney's Achievements*. Edited by M. J. B. Allen. New York, 1990.

Werman, Golda. *Milton and Midrash*. Washington, DC, 1995.

Westermann, Claus. *Praise and Lament in the Psalms*. Translated by Keith R. Crim and Richard N. Soulen. Atlanta, 1981; orig. 1961.

Whitehead, Lydia. "*A Poena et Culpa*: Penitence, Confidence and the *Miserere* in Foxe's *Actes and Monuments*." *Renaissance Studies* 4 (1990): 287–99.

Wilson, John. "Looking at Hymn Tunes: The Objective Factors." In *Duty and Delight: Routley Remembered*. Edited by Robin A. Leaver and James H. Litton. Norwich, 1985.

Woodhouse, A. S. P., and Douglas Bush, eds. *A Variorum Commentary on the Poems of John Milton.* Vol. 2. *The Minor English Poems.* New York, 1972.

Woods, Susanne. *Natural Emphasis: English Versification from Chaucer to Dryden.* San Marino, 1984.

Wrightson, Keith. *English Society 1580–1680.* New Brunswick, NJ, 1982, rpr. 1992.

Zim, Rivka. *English Metrical Psalms: Poetry as Praise and Prayer, 1535–1601.* Cambridge, 1987.

Index